John Henry Newman

The via Media of the Anglican Church

Illustrated in Lectures, Letters, and Tracts Written Between 1830 and 1841

John Henry Newman

The via Media of the Anglican Church
Illustrated in Lectures, Letters, and Tracts Written Between 1830 and 1841

ISBN/EAN: 9783337003029

Printed in Europe, USA, Canada, Australia, Japan

Cover: Foto ©ninafisch / pixelio.de

More available books at **www.hansebooks.com**

THE VIA MEDIA

OF

THE ANGLICAN CHURCH.

ILLUSTRATED IN LECTURES, LETTERS, AND TRACTS

WRITTEN BETWEEN 1830 AND 1841.

BY

JOHN HENRY CARDINAL NEWMAN.

IN TWO VOLUMES,

WITH A PREFACE AND NOTES.

VOL. II.

LONDON

LONGMANS, GREEN, AND CO.

AND NEW YORK: 15 EAST 16th STREET

1891

All rights reserved.

VOL. II.

OCCASIONAL

LETTERS AND TRACTS.

CONTENTS.

	PAGE
I.—SUGGESTIONS IN BEHALF OF THE CHURCH MISSIONARY SOCIETY, 1830.	1
II.—VIA MEDIA, 1834	19
III.—RESTORATION OF SUFFRAGAN BISHOPS. 1835	49
IV.—ON THE MODE OF CONDUCTING THE CONTROVERSY WITH ROME, 1836 (BEING NO. 71 OF TRACTS FOR THE TIMES)	93
V.—LETTER TO A MAGAZINE IN BEHALF OF DR. PUSEY'S TRACTS ON HOLY BAPTISM, 1837	143
VI.—LETTER TO THE MARGARET PROFESSOR OF DIVINITY ON MR. R. H. FROUDE'S STATEMENTS ON THE HOLY EUCHARIST, 1838	195
VII.—REMARKS ON CERTAIN PASSAGES IN THE THIRTY-NINE ARTICLES, 1841	259
VIII.—DOCUMENTARY MATTER CONSEQUENT UPON THE FOREGOING REMARKS ON THE THIRTY-NINE ARTICLES	357
IX.—LETTER TO DR. JELF IN EXPLANATION OF THE REMARKS, 1841	365
X.—LETTER TO THE BISHOP OF OXFORD ON THE SAME SUBJECT, 1841.	395
XI.—RETRACTATION OF ANTI-CATHOLIC STATEMENTS, 1843—1845	425

1.

SUGGESTIONS

RESPECTFULLY OFFERED TO

INDIVIDUAL RESIDENT CLERGYMEN OF THE UNIVERSITY,

IN BEHALF OF

THE CHURCH MISSIONARY SOCIETY,

BY

A MASTER OF ARTS.

1830.

(*Not published, but sent to a certain number of residents.*)

NOTICE.

I WROTE the following Letter and circulated it in the University in February, 1830, at a time when I was one of the secretaries of the Oxford Branch of the Church Missionary Society. At that time I was on the whole Protestant in doctrine, with a growing disposition towards what is called the High Church. I had for many years greatly esteemed the Church Missionary Society, but thought it ought to be under the Bishops. I had made inquiries with a view to the possibility of my becoming one of its missionaries.

My object then in this Letter was at once to enlarge the circle of subscribers to the Society, and to direct and strengthen the influence of the University and thereby of the Anglican hierarchy, upon it. And with this view I urged that the Society itself, by its rules, did actually pledge itself to welcome that influence which I thought so necessary for it, and I considered it a great mistake in the mass of the clergy not to accept a position so frankly offered to them.

My Letter, however, gave great offence to the leading members of its Oxford Branch, to which I belonged; and at the next Annual Meeting, consisting mainly of junior members of the University, Dr. Symons of Wadham in the chair, they unanimously voted another, I forget who, into the office I held.

I did not leave the Association till, I think, four years afterwards, having in the meantime preached and had a collection in St. Mary's Church for it. On that occasion I recollect mentioning the "good man," (as I called him with great sincerity,) Dr. Wilson of Queen's, afterwards Canon of Winchester, a Calvinist by reputation, who introduced the Society to Oxford.

July, 1883.—This incident has been the occasion of much misrepresentation, and to prevent permanent mistakes I am obliged to add as follows:—

Four years ago, on Mr. L., a friend of mine, saying of me in a periodical of name, that there were various false stories in circulation about the part I played towards certain evangelical bodies (for instance at the time when I was secretary to the Bible Society, an office which I never held), a correspondent of the editor wrote to him to say that what Mr. L. treated "as an amusing myth," was an affair in which he (the writer) "was a personal actor;" that "if I denied that I was ever a secretary to the Bible Society, the denial must have been barely that I was secretary in the year 1826," whereas he (the writer) spoke of 1829 and 1830; that "when" the secretary "presented his Report" I "moved 254 amendments" to it; that "the number of emendations" (he repeated) "was 254," though "Mr. L. made it 250;" that "they were designed to transform the evangelical style of the Report into one which was "perhaps better;" that "meanwhile I had written" and circulated "a most hostile tract" or letter; and that, at the Annual Meeting that followed, it was carried unanimously "that the Rev. J. H. Newman should be no longer secretary."

The two main points in this uncalled-for and unfounded contradiction to Mr. L.'s statement which I think it necessary to deny, are first, that the occurrence which my assailant writes about took place in the Bible Society, whereas it took place in the Church Missionary Society, as the pamphlet which follows sufficiently shows; and next, that I moved 254 amendments to the secretary's Annual Report.

1. As to the first charge, it does but involve a question of memory, and is important only so far as it bears upon the general trustworthiness whether of Mr. L.'s account, or of the one contradictory to it. Now I deny that

I ever was secretary to any Bible Society. I was indeed a member of the Oxford Branch, and spoke at two Annual Meetings, but I know I never was secretary to it, and never spoke or wrote against it. All that I recollect of my two speeches is, that Dr. Shuttleworth, afterwards Bishop of Chichester, said of one of them that it was the only good one delivered at the meeting. This my own denial would be enough, but in addition to it, it is pleasant to me to be able to say that Mr. L.'s opponent himself, on second thoughts had the candour in a subsequent letter to withdraw what he had so strongly asserted in his first. He writes, "If Cardinal Newman means that the Letter or Tract to which I referred was directed to the question, not of the Bible Society, but of the Church Missionary Society, *I am sure that his memory is likely to be better than mine;* he scores a line under the words which I have printed in italics. He proceeds, "In fact I never had a copy of the Tract; I only read it at the time."

2. Secondly, as to the question of "*amendments moved*" by me, which he says ran to the number of 254, his using elsewhere the word "emendations" instead of what he calls "amendments," seems to explain the difficulty of the wonderful number to which they ran. Not one "amendment" did I "move," as far as I remember or

believe; but it is very likely, from what he says, that at a preliminary meeting the intended Annual Report was read to the Committee, of whom I was one; and, though I recollect nothing about it now, perhaps or probably I objected to the conventional Evangelical phraseology in which it was drawn up, and the friends of its author on counting up my proposed "emendations" of style, found 254 *words* affected by my criticism. I am sure there was no moving, voting, and dividing upon them. If this explanation will not hold, I can give no other; anyhow, in the received meaning of the word, the notion of 254 *amendments* is absurd.

I am glad that in my lifetime so wholesale a charge has been made and refuted.

P.S.—The following letter to me from Mr. [Archdeacon] R. I. Wilberforce under the early date of Oct. 2, 1828, will illustrate my pamphlet. It shows that my criticism on the Church Missionary Society was that of others also, in the years during which I made it, and that I was doing nothing unreasonable or unfair in attempting to make the Society's obedience to Episcopal authority a fact as well as a profession. Mr. Woodruff, I believe, was one of the chief officials of the Society in 1828.

Oct. 2, 1828.—I have just seen Woodruff here, who tells me that the only objection to such a rule as [Provost] Hawkins seemed to desiderate in the Church Missionary Society was, that it would seem to imply that such a principle was not what they had acted on hitherto. But they had always acted upon the general rule of conforming to the laws of the Church, and have therefore conceived that their missionaries would, of course, be under Episcopal authority. Is there any law of the kind you mention in the Propagation Society?—R. I. W.

What Dr. Hawkins and I, not to say Mr. R. I. Wilberforce, felt in 1828 and 1830, Mr. Hope Scott independently of us felt in 1837. This appears from a passage in the (unpublished) memoir of him, on which the Editor observes, "It is remarkable that, in the year 1830 Mr. Newman, as the Secretary of the Oxford Association of the Church Missionary Society, had already printed and circulated a pamphlet in the University, in behalf of this very subordination which Mr. Hope in 1837 advocated," vol. i. p. 120.

SUGGESTIONS

IN BEHALF OF

THE CHURCH MISSIONARY SOCIETY.

Rev. Sir,

  Persons whose names carry weight with them ought not to consider the application of a stranger an intrusion. You are a sharer in that aggregate of influence which determines the movements of our Oxford community. I address you as such; and, unless I ask an audience of unreasonable length, find my apology in the very circumstance which induces me to seek it.

I am to speak a few words in behalf of the Church Missionary Society, which I would fain see generally countenanced by the clergy; yet so far am I from being blind to the existing defects of that institution, praiseworthy as are its aim and exertions, that it is a keen sense of them that has led me to the step I am now taking.

Perhaps the faults exhibited in its proceedings are felt by those who have closely examined them even more strongly than by yourself. I do not defend the circumstances of its origination, which must be ascribed indeed to motives worthy of all respect, but at the same time evinced little regard for the duty of Church order and canonical obedience. Nor has it yet cleared itself, except in part, from the dishonour of its first irregularities; which, though not seated in its constitution, still are mischievous attendants on its actual operations. And because I think they *are* great, yet accidental evils;— evils especially as regards the interests of that Church to which the Society is attached, distracting her present and still more endangering her future peace; and yet removable at the word of our ecclesiastical rulers, without any compromise of principle on their part: on these accounts it is that I anxiously and earnestly call upon those who have the power promptly and with one accord to put an end to them.

The facts of the case are these. A society for missionary purposes, supported mainly by members of the Church of England, professing her doctrines and discipline, and making use of her name, has extended its operations into every diocese of the kingdom; and (as far as its object is concerned) has laid out anew the Church's territory, dividing it into districts of its own appointing. It has moreover remodelled our ecclesiastical system, the functions of which are brought under the supreme direction of a committee of management in London; with which all its members are in immediate or ultimate correspondence, and which at various times has sent out its representatives through the country, preachers and (indirectly) lay-advocates, to detail its proceedings in large assemblies, and collect contributions for its great object.

Moreover, its practice of addressing itself to the multitude in public meetings,—besides offending against the peculiar sobriety of our Church's character,—has a direct tendency to disarrange her parochial system; to give a prominence to preaching over other religious ordinances, which neither her formularies nor the annals of her history sanction; and to make the people, not the Bishop, the basis and moving principle of her constitution.

And further, by sending out missionaries for the propagation of the Gospel, this Society has taken on itself a function which, not less than that of ordination, is to be considered the prerogative of the supreme rulers of the Christian Church.

To finish the summary of the evils existing in the proceedings of this Society, the doctrines held by some of its most active directors, though not acknowledged perhaps by the individuals themselves to be Calvinistic, still are more or less such practically, whatever dispute may be raised about the exact meaning of words and phrases.

The sum expended by the Society in the course of the last year exceeded 55,000*l*. It has two hundred and twenty-two Associations—It numbers, in all, nine Bishops among its members; and, as far as it is possible to form an estimate from the subscription list attached to the Report, above fourteen hundred clergy.

That a society thus availing itself of the name of our Church, yet actually conducted on principles so widely different from those which her doctrine and discipline imply, and advocated moreover with such zeal, and as yet with such singular success, is doing secret injury to her highest domestic objects—the pure, sober, and adequate religious training of her people,—can hardly be doubted.

On the probable increase of the mischief, some light is thrown by the circumstance, that, while there is a visible resemblance in *actual administration* between the system of this and other missionary societies of recent origin, there appears on the other hand an inclination in some persons who are favourable to these latter institutions to detach it still further from the Church, and to connect it in a more formal way with their own bodies:[1]—an object which, it is presumed, cannot be attained without the Church's losing many respectable members, lay, and even clerical, who support the Society; nor even prosecuted without weakening, to an indefinite extent, their attachment to her principles and interests.

—I have detailed plainly and openly the errors visible in the conduct of the Church Missionary Society; but do not suffer them to *engross* your attention. I have mentioned them not on their own account, but for the sake of exhibiting their unfavourable bearing on the well-being of the Church. Let me entreat you to go on, from considering these *mistakes*, to consider the EVIL. Contemplate this state of things, not as a fact merely exciting your disapprobation of the Society, but as a mischief of melancholy interest to a body of which you are a member. View it, not as if you were an indifferent spectator, but as feeling that it involves a grave *practical* question, which claims an answer from *you.*—*How should the clergy act in relation to this Society?*—This is a problem to be solved amid opposite difficulties; in considering which, provided no principle be compromised, we must be determined by the suggestions of an enlarged Christian expediency.

Now, in viewing this question, we must not dwell on the manner of its first establishment. The spirit which originated it gave no character to its *constitution*, and has in a great measure died away. We are considering the Society as it exists *at present*. Past faults may serve to confirm a condemnation, but cannot counteract a favour-

---

[1] Vid. New Model of Christian Missions, by the author of the Natural History of Enthusiasm; and Eclectic Review, January, 1830. On the other hand, it is a gratifying fact, that within the last few months, the Society has given up its connection with the Missionary Register.

able judgment formed on existing grounds; so we put them aside.

Taking the case then as it now stands, I beg you to observe, that all the existing evils are destroyed at once and for ever, directly the clergy throw themselves into the Society—which they may do without any sacrifice of principle on their part. In this respect there is a marked distinction between it and the Bible Society. To join the latter implies (as many think), a concession, that it is lawful for orthodox believers to co-operate with heretics, that the Bible directly supplies a complete rule of discipline as well as of doctrine, and that dissenters may be recognized as independent bodies on a footing with the Church. But in the case of this Society, the authority of our ecclesiastical rulers is acknowledged by its very name; which its regulations so well bear out, that you may search in vain through them all for any principle of a sectarian tendency. All clergymen who are subscribers are *ex officio* members of the managing committee;—the lay-members being limited to the number of twenty-four, six of whom vacate their seats at the end of every year. And for actual instances of their respect for our ecclesiastical system, when their foreign operations come in contact with it, I may refer to the uniform conduct of their Indian mission, witnessed as it is by the testimonies of Middleton and Heber, and illustrated by their munificent grant in aid of Bishop's College, Calcutta, first of 5000*l.*, then of 1000*l.* annually for several years.

So much on the question of *principle*.—And as to the *practicability* of legitimatizing this Society, its admission into the bosom of the Church is easy, *because* it may be done without compromise of principle. Not only has it placed itself in the hands of the Church by its rules, it has also (I believe) taken every opportunity, or rather used every solicitation, by which an approximation might be made towards a system of episcopal and archidiaconal superintendence. The conduct of its leading members has been on the whole marked by fairness, candour, a simple desire to do good, and an unaffected willingness to listen to advice offered from authority. Whatever is irregular in their proceedings may be attributed partly to their deficient insight into the duties implied in Church union, and into the genius of our ecclesiastical system; and partly to the mere absence of spiritual authorities, who alone can confirm the acts of a religious body. Its present irregularities spring from circumstances of a negative, not a positive character. Its directors are, it is plain, involved in a difficulty arising from the anomalous mode of the Society's first establishment—a difficulty from which the Church alone can extricate them, by supplying her sanction and guidance—and this, which they have no right to claim, I call upon her to do, not for their sake, but for her own. Why should we stand aloof, and allow our name to be used by a Society, without availing ourselves of that right of control over its movements which the assumption of that name gives us? Why should we not put an end at once to so distracting a state of things by the only way left us for remedying it, now that the time is gone by when we might hope to stop the progress of the Society by discountenancing it? And why should we not avail ourselves of its influence and its resources for those great missionary objects which it is our duty ever to keep in view; and in so doing, far from weakening our Church's exertions (according to the common objection) by diverting contributions from the Propagation Society, actually add ready-made, and at a small cost, and for an object which needs provision, a most efficient organ of Christian benevolence to the number of those through which the Church at present fulfils her peculiar duties? Why, because she has rid herself of the corruptions of the

Papal times, and the rashness of the age of Laud, should she not still retain some portion of the vigour and fearlessness which she possessed in both those periods of her history?

Things cannot remain as they are. This Society must approach to the Church, or recede from her. If with an unwise timidity we let things take their course, it will insensibly be familiarized to the principles and practices of schism, and be lost to us with its resources, actual success, prospects for the future, its piety and activity; in the process of its separation, perplexing and enfeebling that Church, which has already enemies enough without our providing others for her. As yet, however, our seats are kept for us in its ranks, and we may claim them. The clergy still may direct its movements and regulate its associations, and substitute the decencies of parochial order for the excitement of fortuitous and unauthorized speakers at a public meeting. In a word, they may annex it to the Christian Knowledge and Propagation Societies, as a sister-institution in the work of evangelical charity.

Even if the accomplishment of so great an object involved the temporary distraction of the Society, and the ultimate defection of a portion of its members, still it would be supremely desirable. But in fact, an important advantage is rarely attainable by so certain and unostentatious a proceeding as is here open to us. *It is only necessary for the clergy of each diocese and archdeaconry to take upon themselves the management of the Associations in their own neighbourhoods.* This would be a gradual mode of connecting the Society with the Church, should it be thought unwise for her higher authorities to take the lead, by giving their support to the Parent Institution. To existing irregularities in preaching and public meetings, a stop would be put at once; and the influence of the Associations would soon be felt reacting on the Committee in London. When a beginning is once fairly made, I have good hope the ultimate completion of the design is secured; and honoured will be his name—whoever that dignitary or man of station be—who is the first to give his countenance to it, recommending it by the weight of his influence to a number of sound and right-minded clergy, and then securing for it the direct patronage of our spiritual rulers.

I have addressed you, Rev. Sir, as having your share of influence in our Oxford circle;—and I address you at this time as believing that a crisis is at hand in the ecclesiastical history of the Society. It will be something to have succeeded merely in awakening your attention to an important subject, though I fail to guide your judgment to the conclusions I myself have adopted. I take my leave, acknowledging the favour you have done me in giving me this patient hearing.

I am, etc.
A MASTER OF ARTS.

OXFORD,
Feb. 1, 1830.

Extract from the Laws and Regulations of the Church Missionary Society.

1. THIS institution shall be conducted by Patrons, Vice-Patrons, a President, Vice-Presidents, a Committee, and such officers as may be deemed necessary, *all being members of the Established Church.*

3. Annual subscribers of one guinea and upwards, and if Clergymen, half-a-guinea, * * * * * * shall be members of this Society during the continuance of such subscriptions.

11. The Committee shall consist of twenty-four lay-members *of the Established Church,* and of *all such Clergymen* as are members of the Society. Eighteen members shall be annually appointed from the old Committee, and six from the general body.

17. The general Committee shall appoint the places where missions shall be attempted, shall direct the scale upon which they shall be

conducted, and shall superintend the affairs of the Society in general.

According to the Table prefixed to the last Report, the Society has 9 missions; viz. to West Africa, Mediterranean, North, South, and Western India, Ceylon, Australasia, West Indies, and North-west America—And in these 51 stations employs 28 Episcopal Clergy, 17 Lutheran ditto; 63 lay-teachers, men and women; and 205 native teachers; and supports 295 schools, for boys, girls, or adults, containing in all 12,419 scholars.

The Oxford Association includes 40 Clergymen, of which number about 30 are resident members of the University.

II.

VIA MEDIA.

(Being Nos. 38 and 40 of TRACTS FOR THE TIMES.)

1834.

VIA MEDIA.

No. I.

Laicus.—Will you listen to a few free questions from one who has not known you long enough to be familiar with you without apology? I am struck by many things I have heard you say, which show me that, somehow or other, my religious system is incomplete: yet at the same time the world accuses you of Popery, and there are seasons when I have misgivings whither you are carrying me.

Clericus.—I trust I am prepared, most willing I certainly am, to meet any objections you have to bring against doctrines which you have heard me maintain. Say more definitely what the charge against me is.

L. That your religious system, which I have heard some persons style the Apostolical, and which I so name by way of designation, is like that against which our forefathers protested at the Reformation.

C. I will admit it, *i.e.* if I may reverse your statement, and say, that the Popish system resembles the Apostolical. Indeed, how could it be otherwise, seeing that all corruptions of the truth must be like the truth which they corrupt, else they would not persuade mankind to take them instead of it?

L. A bold thing to say, surely; to make the earlier system an imitation of the later!

C. A bolder, surely, to assume that mine is the later, and the Popish the earlier. When think you that my system (so to call it) arose?—not with myself?

L. Of course not; but whatever individuals have held it in our Church since the Reformation, it must be acknowledged that they have been but few, though some of them doubtless eminent men.

C. Perhaps you would say (*i.e.* the persons whose views you are representing), that at the Reformation, the stain of the old theology was left among us, and has shown itself in its measure ever since, as in the poor, so again in the educated classes;—that the peasantry still use and transmit their Popish rhymes, and the minds of students still linger among the early Fathers; but that the genius and principles of our Church have ever been what is commonly called Protestant.

L. This is a fair general account of what would be maintained.

C. You would consider that the Protestant principles and doctrines of this day were those of our Reformers in the sixteenth century; and that what is called Popery now, is what was called Popery then.

L. On the whole: there are indeed extravagances now, as is obvious. I would not defend extremes; but I suppose our Reformers would agree with moderate Protestants of this day, in what they meant by Protestantism and by Popery.

C. This is an important question, of course; much depends on the correctness of the answer you have made to it. Do you make it as a matter of history, from knowing the opinions of our Reformers, or from what you consider probable?

L. I am no divine. I judge from a general knowledge

of history, and from the obvious probabilities of the case, which no one can gainsay.

C. Let us then go by *probabilities*, since you lead the way. Is it not according to *probabilities* that opinions and principles should *not* be the same now as they were three hundred years since? that though our professions are the same, yet we should not mean by them what the Reformers meant? Can you point to any period of Church history, during which doctrine remained for any time uncorrupted? Three hundred years is a long time. Are you quite sure we do not need a SECOND REFORMATION?

L. Are you really serious? Have we not Articles and a Liturgy, which keep us from deviating from the standard of truth set up in the sixteenth century?

C. Nay, I am maintaining no paradox. Surely there is a large religious party all around us who say the great body of the Clergy *has* departed from the doctrines of our Martyrs at the Reformation. I do not say I agree with the particular charges they prefer; but the very circumstance that they make them is a proof there is nothing extravagant in the notion of the Church having departed from the doctrine of the sixteenth century.

L. It is true; but the persons you refer to, bring forward, at least, an intelligible charge; they appeal to the Articles, and maintain that the Clergy have departed from the doctrine therein contained. They may be right or wrong; but at least they give us the means of judging for ourselves.

C. This surely is beside the point. We were speaking of *probabilities*. *What* change actually *has* been made, if any, is a further question, a question of *fact*. But before going on to examine the particular case, I observe that change of some sort was *probable;* probable in itself you can hardly deny, considering the history of the universal Church; not extravagantly improbable, moreover, in spite of Articles, as is sufficiently proved by the extensively prevailing opinion to which I referred, that the clergy *have* departed from them. Now consider the course of religion and politics, domestic and foreign, during the last three centuries, and tell me whether events have not occurred to increase this probability almost to a certainty; the probability, I mean, that the members of the English Church of the present day differ from the principles of the Church of Rome more than our forefathers differed. First, consider the history of the Puritans from first to last. Without pronouncing any opinion on the truth or unsoundness of their principles, were they not evidently further removed from Rome than were our Reformers? Was not their influence all on the side of leading the English Church further from Rome than our Reformers placed it? Think of the fall of the Scottish Episcopal Church. Reflect upon the separation and extinction of the Nonjurors, upon the rise of Methodism, upon our political alliances with foreign Protestant communities. Consider especially the history and the school of Hoadley. That man, whom a high authority of the present day does not hesitate to call a Socinian,[1] was for near fifty years a bishop in our Church.

L. You tell me to think on these facts. I wish I were versed enough in our ecclesiastical history to do so.

C. But you are as well versed in it as the generality of educated men; as those whose opinions you are now maintaining. And they surely ought to be well acquainted with our history, and the doctrines taught in our different schools and eras, considering they scruple not to charge such as me with a declension from the true Anti-popish doctrine of our Church. For what the doctrine of the Church is, what it has been for three centuries, is a matter of fact which without reading cannot be known.

---

[1] "It is true he was a Bishop, though a Socinian."—Bp. Blomfield's Letter to C. Butler, Esq., 1825.

L. Let us leave, if you please, this ground of *probability*, which, whatever you may say, cannot convince me while I am able to urge that strong objection to it which you would not let me mention just now. I repeat, we have Articles; we have a Liturgy; the dispute lies in a little compass, without need of historical reading :—do you mean to say we have departed from *them* ?

C. I am not unwilling to follow you a second time, and will be explicit. I reply, we *have* departed from them. Did you ever study the Rubrics of the Prayer Book ?

L. But surely they have long been obsolete ;—they are impracticable !

C. It is enough; you have answered your own question without trouble of mine. Not only do we not obey them, but it seems we style them impracticable. I take your admission. Now, I ask you, are not these Rubrics (I might also mention parts of the Services themselves which have fallen into disuse), such as in the present day incur the odium of being called Popish ? and, if so, is not this a proof that the spirit of the present day has departed (whether for good or evil) from the spirit of the Reformation ?—and is it wonderful that such as I should be called Popish, if the Church Services themselves are considered so ?

L. Will you give me some instances?

C. Is it quite in accordance with our present Protestant notions, that unbaptized persons should not be buried with the rites of the Church ?—that every Clergyman should read the Daily Service morning and evening at home, if he cannot get a congregation ?—that in college chapels the Holy Communion should be administered every week ? —that Saints' Days should be observed ?—that stated days of fasting should be set apart by the Church ? Ask even a sober-minded really serious man about the observance of these rules; will he not look grave, and say that he is afraid of formality and superstition if these rules were attended to?

L. And is there not the danger?

C. The simple question is, whether there is more danger now than three centuries since? was there not far more superstition in the sixteenth than in the nineteenth century? and does the spirit of the nineteeth move with the spirit of the sixteenth, if the sixteenth commands and the nineteenth draws back?

L. But you spoke of parts of the Services themselves as laid aside?

C. Alas! . . . .

What is the prevailing opinion or usage respecting the form of absolution in the office for Visiting the Sick? What is thought by a great body of men of the words in which the Priesthood is conveyed? Are there no objections to the Athanasian Creed? no murmurs against the Commination Service? Does no one stumble at the word "oblations," in the Prayer for the Church Militant? Is there no clamour against parts of the Burial Service? No secret or scarcely secret complaints against the word "regeneration" in the Baptismal? No bold protestations against reading the Apocrypha? Now do not all these objections rest upon one general ground: viz. That these parts of our Services savour of Popery? And again, are not these the popular objections of the day?

L. I cannot deny it.

C. I consider then that already I have said enough to show that the Churchman of this day has deviated from the opinions of our Reformers, and has become more opposed than they [the latter] were to the system they protested against. And therefore, I would observe, it is not fair to judge of me, or of such as me, in the off-hand way which many men take the liberty to adopt. Men seem to think that we are plainly and indisputably proved to be Popish, if we are proved to differ from the generality of Churchmen now-a-days. But what if it turn out that they are silently floating down the stream, and we are upon the shore?

L. All, however, will allow, I suppose, that our Reformation was never completed in its details. The final judgment was not passed upon parts of the Prayer Book. There were, you know, alterations in the second edition of it published in King Edward's time; and these tended to a more Protestant doctrine than that which had first been adopted. For instance, in King Edward's first book the dead in CHRIST were prayed for; in the second this commemoration was omitted. Again, in the first book the elements of the LORD's Supper were more distinctly offered up to GOD, and more formally consecrated than in the second edition, or at present. Had Queen Mary not succeeded, perhaps the men who effected this would have gone further.

C. I believe they would; nay indeed they did at a subsequent period. They took away the Liturgy altogether, and substituted a Directory.

L. They? the same men?

C. Yes, the foreign party: who afterwards went by the name of Puritans. Bucer, who altered in King Edward's time, and the Puritans, who destroyed in King Charles's, both came from the same religious quarter.

L. Ought you so to speak of the foreign Reformers? to them we owe the Protestant doctrine altogether.

C. I like foreign interference, as little from Geneva, as from Rome. Geneva at least never converted a part of England from heathenism, nor could lay claim to patriarchal authority over it. Why could we not be let alone and suffered to reform ourselves?

L. You separate then your creed and cause from that of the Reformed Churches of the Continent?

C. Not altogether; but I protest against being brought into that close alliance with them which the world now-a-days would force upon us. The glory of the English Church is, that it has taken the VIA MEDIA, as it has been called. It lies *between* the (so called) Reformers and the Romanists; whereas there are religious circles, and influential too, where it is thought enough to prove an English Clergyman unfaithful to his Church, if he preaches anything at variance with the opinions of the Diet of Augsburg, or the Confessions of the Waldenses. However, since we have been led to speak of the foreign Reformers, I will, if you will still listen to me, strengthen my argument by an appeal to them.

L. That argument being, that what is now cried up as Protestant doctrine, is not what was considered such by the Reformers.

C. Yes; and I am going to offer reasons for thinking that the present age has lapsed, not only from the opinions of the English Reformers, but from those of the foreign also. This is too extensive a subject to do justice to in a conversation, even had I the learning for it; but I may draw your attention to one or two obvious proofs of the fact.

L. You must mean from Calvin; for Luther is, in some points, reckoned nearer the Romish Church than ourselves.

C. I mean Calvin, about whose extreme distance from Rome there can be no doubt. What is the popular opinion now concerning the necessity of an Episcopal Regimen?

L. A late incident has shown what it is; that it is uncharitable to define the Catholic Church, as "the body of Christians in every country governed by Bishops, Priests, and deacons;" such a definition excluding pious Dissenters and others.

C. But what thought Calvin? " Calvin held those men worthy of anathema who would not submit themselves to truly Christian bishops, if such could be had."[2] What would he have said then to the Wesleyan Methodists, and that portion of the (so called) Orthodox Dissenters, which is friendly at present to the Church? These allow that we, or that numbers among us, are truly Christian, yet make no attempts to obtain Bishops from us. Thus the age is more Protestant now than Calvin himself.

L. Certainly in this respect; unless Calvin spoke rhetorically under circumstances.

C. Now for a second instance. The following is his statement concerning the LORD's Supper. "I understand what is to be understood by the words of CHRIST; that He doth not only offer us the benefits of His death and Resurrection, but His very body, wherein He died and rose again. I assert that the body of CHRIST is really (as the usual expression is); that it is truly given to us in the Sacrament, to be the saving food of our souls." . . . . . "The SON of GOD offers daily to us in the Holy Sacrament, the same body which He once offered in sacrifice to His Father, that it may be our spiritual food." . . . . . . "If any one ask me concerning the manner, I will not be ashamed to confess that it is a secret too high for my reason to comprehend, or my tongue to express."[3] Now, if I were of myself to use these words, (in spite of the qualification at the end, concerning the *manner* of His presence in the Sacrament,) would they not be sufficient to convict me of Popery in the judgment of this minute and unlearned generation?

L. You speak plausibly, I will grant; yet surely, after all, it is not unnatural that the Reformers of the sixteenth

[2] Vide Mr. Perceval's Churchman's Manual, p. 13.
[3] Vide Tracts for the Times, No. 27.

century should have fallen short of a full Reformation in matters of doctrine and discipline. Light breaks but gradually on the mind: one age begins a work, another finishes.

C. I am arguing about a matter of fact, not defending the opinions of the Reformers. As to this notion of their being but partially illuminated, I am not concerned to oppose such a view, being quite content if the persons whom you are undertaking to represent are willing to admit it. And then, in consistency, I shall beg them to reproach me not with *Popery* but with *Protestantism*, and to be impartial enough to assail not only me, but "the Blessed Reformation," as they often call it, using words they do not understand. It is hard, indeed, that when I share in the opinions of the Reformers, I should have no share in their praises of them.

L. You speak as if you really agreed with the Reformers. You may say so in an argument, but in sober earnest you cannot mean to say you really agree with the great body of them. Neither you nor I should hesitate to confess they were often inconsistent, saying, at one time, what they disowned at another.

C. That they should have said different things at different times, is not wonderful, considering they were searching into Scripture and Antiquity, and feeling their way to the Truth. Since, however, they did vary in their opinions, for this very reason it is obvious I should be saying nothing at all, in saying that I agreed with them, unless I stated explicitly at what period of their lives, or in which of their writings. This I do state clearly: I say I agree with them as they speak in the formularies of the Church; more cannot be required of me, nor indeed is it possible to say more.

L. What persons complain of is, that you are not satisfied with the formularies of the Church, but add to them doctrines not contained in them. You must allow there is little stress laid in the Articles on some points, which are quite cardinal in your system, to judge by your way of enforcing them.

C. This is not the first time you have spoken of this supposed system of ours. I will not stop to quarrel with you for calling it ours, as if it were not rather the Church's; but explain to me what you consider it to consist in.

L. The following are some of its doctrines: that the Church has an existence independent of the State; that the State may not religiously interfere with its internal concerns; that none may engage in ministerial works except such as are episcopally ordained; that the consecration of the Eucharist is especially entrusted to Bishops and Priests. Where do you find these doctrines in the formularies of the Church; that is, so prominently set forth, as to sanction you in urging them at all, or at least so strongly as you are used to urge them?

C. As to urging them at all, we might be free to urge them even though not mentioned in the Articles; unless indeed the Articles are our rule of faith. Were the Church first set up at the Reformation, then indeed it might be right so to exalt its Articles as to forbid to teach " whatsoever is not read therein, nor may be proved thereby." I cannot consent, (I am sure the Reformers did not wish me,) to deprive myself of the Church's dowry, the doctrines which the Apostles spoke in Scripture and impressed upon the early Church. I receive the Church as a messenger from CHRIST, rich in treasures old and new, rich with the accumulated wealth of ages.

L. Accumulated?

C. As you will yourself allow. Our Articles are one portion of that accumulation. Age after age, fresh battles have been fought with heresy, fresh monuments of truth set up. As I will not consent to be deprived of the records of the Reformation, so neither will I part with those of former times. I look upon our Articles as in one sense an addition to the Creeds ; and at the same time the Romanists added their Tridentine articles. Theirs I consider unsound; ours as true.

L. The Articles have surely an especial claim upon you ; who have subscribed them, and are therefore more bound to them, than to other truths, whatever or wherever they be.

C. There is a popular confusion on this subject. Our Articles are not a *body of divinity*, but in great measure only protests against certain errors of a certain period of the Church. Now I will preach the whole counsel of GOD, whether set down in the Articles or not. I am bound to the Articles by subscription ; but I am bound, more solemnly even than by subscription, by my baptism and by my ordination, to believe and maintain the *whole* Gospel of CHRIST. The grace given at those seasons comes through the Apostles, not through Luther or Calvin, Bucer or Cartwright. You will presently agree with me in this statement. Let me ask, do you not hold the inspiration of Holy Scripture ?

L. Undoubtedly.

C. Is it not a clergyman's duty to maintain and confess it ?

L. Certainly.

C. But this doctrine is nowhere found in the Articles ; and for this plain reason, that both Romanists and Reformers admitted it ; and the difference between the two parties was, not whether the Old and New Testament were inspired, but whether the Apocrypha was of canonical authority.

L. I must grant it.

C. And in the same way, I would say, there are many other doctrines unmentioned in the Articles, only because they were not then disputed by either party; and others again, for other reasons, short of disbelief in them. I cannot indeed make my neighbour preach them, for he will tell me he will believe only just so much as he has been obliged to subscribe; but it is hard if I am therefore to be defrauded of the full inheritance of faith myself. Look at the subject from another point of view, and see if we do not arrive at the same conclusion. A statesman of the last century is said to have remarked that we have Calvinistic Articles, and a Popish Liturgy. This of course is an idle calumny. But is there not certainly a distinction of doctrine and manner between the Liturgy and the Articles? And does not what I have just stated account for it, viz. that the Liturgy, as coming down from the Apostles, is the depository of their complete teaching; while the Articles are polemical, and except as they embody the creeds, are mainly protests against certain definite errors? Such are my views about the Articles; and if in my teaching, I lay especially stress upon doctrines only indirectly contained in them, and say less about those which are therein put forth most prominently, it is because times are changed. We are in danger of unbelief more than of superstition. The Christian minister should be a witness against the errors of his day.

L. I cannot tell whether on consideration I shall agree with you or not. However, after all, you have said not a word to explain what your real differences from Popery are; what those false doctrines were, which you conceive our Reformers withstood. You began by confessing that your opinions and the Popish opinions had a resemblance, and only disputed whether yours should be called like the Popish, or the Popish like yours. But in what are yours different from Rome?

C. Be assured of this—no party will be more opposed to our doctrine, if it ever prospers and makes noise, than the

Roman party. This has been proved before now. In the seventeenth century the theology of the divines of the English Church was substantially the same as ours is; and it experienced the full hostility of the Papacy. It was the true Via Media; Rome sought to block up that way as fiercely as the Puritans did. History tells us this. In a few words then, before we separate, I will state some of my irreconcilable differences with Rome.[4] . . . .

L. Thank you for this conversation; from which I hope to draw matter for reflection, though the subject seems to involve such deep historical research, I hardly know how to find my way through it.

The Feast of St. James.

[4] [Vid. *supr.* vol. i. Preface, p. xxxii; and *infra*, Article xi; Retractation.]

VIA MEDIA.

No. II.

Laicus. I am come for some further conversation with you; or rather, for another exposition of your views on Church matters. I am not well read enough to argue with you; nor, on the other hand, do I profess to admit all you say: but I want, if you will let me, to get at your opinions. So will you lecture, if I give the subjects?

Clericus. To lecture, as you call it, is quite beyond me, since at best I have but a smattering of reading in Church history. The more's the pity; though I have as much as a great many others: for ignorance of our historical position as Churchmen is one of the especial evils of the day. Yet even with a little knowledge, I am able to see certain facts which seem quite inconsistent with notions at present received. For my practice, I should be ashamed of myself if I guided it by any theories. Here the letter and spirit of the Liturgy[1] is my direction, as it is of all classes of Churchmen, high and low. Yet, though I do not lay a great stress on such views as I gather from history, it is to my mind a strong confirmation of them, that they just account for and illustrate the conclusions to which I am led by plain obedience to my ordination vows.

L. If you only wish to keep to the Liturgy, not to change, what did you mean the other day by those ominous words in which you suggested the need of a *second Reformation?*

[1] [In these Tracts "Liturgy" stands for the Book of Common Prayer and Administration, &c.]

C. Because I think the Church has in a measure *forgotten* its own principles, as declared in the sixteenth century; nay, under stranger circumstances, as far as I know, than have attended any of the errors and corruptions of the Papists. Grievous as are their declensions from primitive usage, I never heard in any case of their practice directly contradicting their services;—whereas we go on lamenting once a year the absence of discipline in our Church, yet do not even dream of taking any one step towards its restoration. Again, we confess in the Articles that excommunication is a solemn duty of the Church under certain circumstances, and that the excommunicated person must be openly reconciled by penance, before he is acknowledged by the faithful as a brother; yet excommunication, I am told, is now a civil process, which takes place as a matter of course, at a certain stage of certain law proceedings. Here a *reformation* is needed.

L. Only of discipline, not of doctrine.

C. Again, when the Church, with an unprecedented confidence, bound herself hand and foot, and made herself over to the civil power, in order to escape the Pope, she did not expect that infidels (as it has lately been hinted) would be suffered to have the absolute disposal of the crown patronage.

L. This, again, might be considered matter of discipline. Our Reformation in the sixteenth century was one in matters of *faith;* and therefore we do not need a second Reformation *in the same sense* in which we needed it first.

C. In what points would you say the Church's *faith* was reformed in the sixteenth century?

L. Take the then received belief in purgatory and pardons, which alone was a sufficient corruption to call for a reformation.

C. I conceive the presumption of the Popish doctrine

on these points to lie in adding to the means of salvation set forth in Scripture. ALMIGHTY GOD has said that His SON's merits shall wash away all sin, and that they shall be conveyed to believers through the two Sacraments; whereas, the Church of Rome has added other ways of gaining heaven.

L. Granted. The belief in purgatory and pardons disparages the sufficiency, first of CHRIST's merits; next of His appointed sacraments.

C. And by "received" belief, I suppose you mean that it was the popular belief, which clergy and laity acted on, not that it was necessarily contained in any particular doctrinal formulary.

L. Proceed.

C. Do you not suppose that there are multitudes both among clergy and laity at the present day, who disparage, not indeed CHRIST's merits, but the Sacraments He has appointed? and if so, is not their error so far the same in kind as that of the Romish Church—the preferring Abana and Pharpar to the waters of Jordan? Take the Sacrament of Baptism. Have not some denominations of schismatics invented a rite of dedication instead of Baptism? and do not Churchmen find themselves under the temptation of countenancing this Papist-like presumption?— Again, there is a well-known sect, which denies both Baptism and the LORD's Supper. A Churchman must believe its members to be altogether external to the fold of CHRIST. Whatever benevolent works they may be able to show, still, if we receive the Church's doctrine concerning the means "generally necessary to salvation,"

---

[1] [Purgatory as little "disparages the merits of Christ," as the "open penance and punishment of sinners, in this world, that their souls might be saved in the day of the Lord," spoken of in the Anglican Commination Service; nor do pardons "disparage His Sacraments," for sacraments take away the guilt, and pardons the punishment, of sin.]

we must consider such persons to be mere heathens, except in knowledge. Now would there not be an outcry raised, as if I were uncharitable, did I refuse the rites of burial to such an one?

L. This outcry would not proceed from the better informed, or from the rulers of the Church.

C. Happily, we are not as yet so far corrupted. Our Prelates are still sound, and know the difference between what is modern and what is ancient. Yet is not the mode of viewing the subject I refer to, a *growing* one? and how does it differ from the presumption of the Papists? In both cases, the power of CHRIST's sacraments is denied; in the one case by the unbelief of restlessness and fear, in the other by the unbelief of profaneness.

L. Well, supposing I grant that the Church of this day is in a measure faulty in faith and discipline; more or less, of course, according to the diocese and neighbourhood. Now, in the next place, what do you mean by your *Reformation?*

C. I would do what our reformers in the sixteenth century did: they did not touch the existing documents of doctrine [2]—there was no occasion—they kept the creeds as they were; but they added protests against the corruptions of faith, worship, and discipline, which had grown up round them. I would have the Church do the same thing now, if I could: she should not change the Articles, she should add to them: add protests against the erastianism and latitudinarianism which have incrusted them. I would have her append to the Catechism a section on the power of the Church.

L. You have not mentioned any corruptions at present in worship; do you consider that there are such, as well as errors of faith and discipline?

C. Our Liturgy keeps us right in the main, yet there are what may be considered such, though for the most

---

[2] [This was the point too broadly contended for in No. 90, *infr.*]

part occasional. To board over the altar of a Church, place an orchestra there of playhouse singers, and take money at the doors, seems to me as great an outrage, as to sprinkle the forehead with holy water, and to carry lighted tapers in a procession.

L. Do not speak so harshly of what has often been done piously. George the Third was a patron of concerts in one of our Cathedrals.

C. Far be it from my mind to dare to arraign the actions of that religious king! The same deed is of a different nature at different times and under different circumstances. Music in a Church may as reverentially subserve the feelings of devotion as pictures or architecture; but it may not.

L. You could not prevent such a desecration by adding a fortieth article to the thirty-nine.

C. Not directly: yet though there is no article directly condemning religious processions, they have nevertheless been discontinued. In like manner, were an article framed (to speak by way of illustration) declaratory of the sanctity of places set apart to the worship of GOD and the reception of the saints that sleep, doubtless Churchmen would be saved from many profane feelings and practices of the day, which they give into unawares, such as the holding vestries in Churches, the flocking to preachers rather than to sacraments (as if the servant were above the Master, who is LORD over His own house), the luxurious and fashionable fitting up of town Churches, the proposal to allow schismatics to hold their meetings in them, the off-hand project of pulling them down for the convenience of streets and roads, and the wanton preference (for it frequently is wanton) of unconsecrated places, whether for preaching to the poor, or for administering sacred rites to the rich.

L. It is visionary to talk of such a reformation: the people would not endure it.

C. It is; but I am not advocating it, I am but raising a protest. I say this ought to be, "because of the angels,"[3] but I do not hope to persuade others to think as I do.

L. I think I quite understand the ground you take. You consider that, as time goes on, fresh and fresh articles of faith are necessary to secure the Church's purity, according to the rise of successive heresies and errors. These articles were all hidden, as it were, in the Church's bosom from the first,[4] and brought out into form according to the occasion. Such was the Nicene explanation against Arius; the English articles against Popery: and such are those now called for in this Age of schism, to meet the new heresy, which denies the holy Catholic Church—the heresy of Hoadley, and others like him.

C. Yes—and let it never be forgotten, that, whatever were the errors of the Convocation of our Church in the beginning of the eighteenth century, it expired in an attempt to brand the doctrines of Hoadley. May the day be merely delayed!

L. I understand you further to say, that you hold to the Reformers as far as they have spoken out in our formularies, which at the same time you consider as incomplete; that the doctrines which may appear wanting in the Articles, such as the Apostolical Commission, are the doctrines of the Church Catholic; doctrines, which every member of it holds as being such, prior to subscription; that, moreover they are quite consistent with our Articles, sometimes are even implied in them, and sometimes clearly contained in the Liturgy, though not in the Articles, as the Apostolical Commission in the Ordination Service; lastly, that we are clearly bound to believe, and all of us

---

[3] 1 Cor. xi. 10.

[4] [Here, as above, the principle of doctrinal development is accepted as true and necessary for the Christian Church.]

do believe, as essential, doctrines which nevertheless are not contained in the Articles, as e. g. the inspiration of Holy Scripture.

C. Yes—and further I maintain, that, while I fully concur in the Articles, as far as they go, those who call me Papist, do not acquiesce in the doctrine of the Liturgy.

L. This is a subject I especially wish drawn out. You threw out some hints about it the other day, though I cannot say you convinced me. I have misgivings, after all, that our Reformers only *began* their own work. I do not say they saw the tendency and issue of their opinions; but surely, had they lived, and had they had the opportunity of doing more, they would have given into much more liberal notions (as they are called) than you are disposed to concede. It is not by producing a rubric, or an insulated passage from the services, that you can destroy this impression. Such instances only show they were inconsistent, which I will grant. Still, is not the genius of our formularies towards a more latitudinarian system than they reach?

C. I will cheerfully meet you on the grounds you propose. Let us carefully examine the Liturgy in its separate parts. I think it will decide the point which I contended for the other day, viz. that we now are more Protestant than our Reformers.

L. What do you mean by Protestant in your present use of the word?

C. A number of distinct doctrines are included in the notion of Protestantism: and as to all these, our Church has taken the Via Media between it and Popery. At present I will use it in the sense most apposite to the topics we have been discussing; viz. as the religion of so-called freedom and independence, as hating superstition, suspicious of forms, jealous of priestcraft, advocating heart-worship;

characteristics, which admit of a good or a bad interpretation, but which, understood as they are instanced in the majority of persons who are zealous for what is called Protestant doctrine, are (I maintain) very inconsistent with the Liturgy of our Church. Now let us begin with the Confirmation Service.

L. Will not the Baptismal be more to your purpose? In it regeneration is connected with the formal act of sprinkling a little water on the forehead of an infant.

C. It is true; but I would rather show the general spirit of the Services, than take those obvious instances which, it seems, you can find out for yourself. Is it not certain that a modern Protestant, even though he granted that children were regenerated in Baptism, would, in the Confirmation Service, have inserted some address to them about the necessity of spiritual renovation, of becoming new creatures, &c.? I do not say such warning has not its appropriateness; nor do I propose to account for our Church's not giving it; but is it not quite certain that the present prevailing temper in the Church would have given it, judging from the prayers and sermons of the day, and that the Liturgy does not? Were that former day like this, would it not have been deemed formal and cold, and to argue a want of spiritual-mindedness, to have proposed a declaration, such as has been actually adopted, that " to the end that Confirmation may be ministered to the more edifying of such as shall receive it . . . none hereafter shall be confirmed, but such as can *say* the Creed, the LORD's Prayer, and the Ten Commandments," &c.; nothing being said of a change of heart, or spiritual affections? And yet, upon this mere external profession, the children receive the imposition of the Bishop's hands, "to *certify* them by this sign, of GOD's favour and gracious goodness towards them."

L. From the line you are adopting, I see you will find

Services more Anti-Protestant (in the modern sense of Protestant,) than that for Confirmation.

C. Take, again, the Catechism. What can be more technical and formal (as the persons I speak of would say,) than the division of our duties into our duty towards GOD and our duty towards our neighbour? Indeed, would not the very word *duty* be objected to by them, as obscuring the evangelical character of Christianity? Why is there no mention of newness of heart, of appropriating the mercies of redemption, and such like phrases, which are now common among so-called Protestants? Why no mention of justifying faith?

L. Faith is mentioned in an earlier part of the Catechism.

C. Yes, and it affords a remarkable contrast to the modern use of the word. Now-a-days, the prominent notion conveyed by it regards its properties, whether spiritual or not, warm, heart-felt, vital. But in the Catechism, the prominent notion is that of its object, the believing "all the Articles of the Christian faith," according to the Apostle's declaration, that it is, "the substance of things hoped for, the evidence of things not seen."

L. I understand; and the Creed is also introduced into the service for Baptism.

C. And still more remarkably into the Order for Visiting the Sick: more remarkably, both because of the season when it is introduced, when a Christian is drawing near his end, and also as being a preparation for the Absolution. Most comfortable, truly, in his last hour, is such a distinct rehearsal of the great truths on which the Christian has fed by faith with thanksgiving all his life long; yet it surely would not have suggested itself to a modern Protestant. He would rather have instituted some more searching examination (as he would call it,) of the state of the sick man's heart; whereas the whole of the minister's exhortation is what the modern school calls cold and formal. It ends thus:—" I require you to examine yourself and your estate, both toward GOD and man; so that, accusing and condemning yourself for your own faults, you may find mercy at our heavenly FATHER's hand for CHRIST's sake, and not be accused and condemned in that fearful judgment. Therefore, I shall rehearse to you the Articles of our Faith, that you may know whether you believe as a Christian man should, or no."

L. You observe the Rubric which follows: it speaks of a further examination.

C. True; still it is what would now be called formal and external.

L. Yet it mentions a great number of topics for examination:—" Whether he repent him truly of his sins, and be in charity with all the world; exhorting him to forgive, from the bottom of his heart, all persons that have offended him; and if he hath offended any other, to ask them forgiveness; and where he hath done injury or wrong to any man, that he make amends to the uttermost of his power. And, if he hath not before disposed of his goods, let him then be admonished to make his will, and to declare his debts, what he oweth, and what is owing to him; for the better discharging of his conscience, and the quietness of his executors." Here is an exhortation to repentance, charity, forgiveness of injuries, humbleness of mind, honesty, and justice. What could be added?

C. You will be told that worldly and spiritual matters are mixed together; and, besides, not a word said of looking to CHRIST, resting on Him, and renovation of heart. Such are the expressions which modern Protestantism would have considered necessary, and would have inserted as being so. They are good words; still they are not those which our Church considers *the* words for a sick-bed examination. She does not give them the prominence which is now given them. She adopts a manner of address which savours of what is now called formality. That our Church was no stranger to the more solemn kind of language, which persons now use on every occasion, is evident from the prayer "for a sick person, when there appeareth small hope of recovery," and "the commendatory prayer;" still she adopts the other as her ordinary manner.

L. I can corroborate what you just now observed about the Creed, by what I lately read in some book or books, advocating a revision of the Liturgy. It was vehemently objected to the Apostles' Creed, that it contained no confession of the doctrine of the atonement, nor (I think) of original sin.

C. It is well to see persons consistent. When they go full lengths, they startle others, and, perhaps (please GOD) themselves. Indeed, I wish men would stop a while, and seriously reflect whether the mere verbal opposition which exists between their own language and the language of the Services (to say nothing of the difference of spirit), is not a sort of warning to them, if they would take it, against inconsiderately proceeding in their present course. But nothing is more rare at this day than quiet thought. Every one is in a bustle, being bent to do a great deal. We preach, and run from house to house; we do not pray or meditate. But to return. Next, consider the first exhortation to the Communion: would it not be called, if I said it in discourse of my own, "dark, cold, and formal"? "The way and means thereto [to receive worthily] is,—First, to examine your lives and conversations by the rule of GOD's *commandments*, &c. . . . . . Therefore, if any of you be a *blasphemer* of GOD, an *hinderer* or *slanderer* of His word, an *adulterer*, or be in *malice*, or *envy*, or any other grievous crime, repent you of your sins," &c. Now this is what is called, in some quarters, by a great abuse of terms, "mere morality."

L. If I understand you, the Liturgy, all along, speaks of the Gospel dispensation, under which it is our blessedness to live, as being, at the same time, a moral law; you mean that this is its prominent view; and that external observances and definite acts of duty are made the means and the tests of faith.

C. Yes; and that, in thus speaking, it runs quite counter to the innovating spirit of this day, which proceeds rashly forward on large and general views,—sweeps along, with one or two prominent doctrines, to the comparative neglect of the details of duty, and drops articles of faith and positive laws and ceremonial observances, as beneath the attention of a spiritual Christian, as monastic and superstitious, as forms, as minor points, as technical, lip-worship, narrow-minded, and bigoted.—Next, consider the wording of one part of the Commination Service:— "He was wounded for our offences, and smitten for our wickedness. Let us, therefore, return unto Him, who is the merciful receiver of all true penitent sinners; assuring ourselves that He is ready to receive us, and most willing to pardon us, if we come unto Him with faithful repentance; if we will submit ourselves unto Him, and from henceforth walk in His ways; if we will take His easy yoke and light burden upon us, to follow Him in lowliness, patience, and charity, and be *ordered* by the governance of His Holy Spirit; seeking *always His glory*, and *serving* Him duly in our vocation with thanksgiving: *This if we do*, CHRIST will deliver us from the curse of the law," &c. Did another say this, he would be accused by the Protestant of this day of interfering with the doctrine of justification by faith.

L. You have not spoken of the daily service of the Church or of the Litany.

C. I should have more remarks to make than I like to trouble you with. First, I should observe on the absence of what are now called, exclusively, the great Protestant doctrines, or, at least, of the modes of expression in which it is at present the fashion to convey them. For instance, the Collects are summaries of doctrine, yet I believe they do not once mention what has sometimes been called the "articulus stantis vel cadentis Ecclesiæ." This proves to me that, true and important as this doctrine may be in a controversial statement, its direct mention is not so apposite in devotional and practical subjects as modern Protestants of our Church would consider it. Next, consider the general Confession, which prays simply that GOD would grant us "hereafter to live a godly, righteous, and sober life." Righteous and sober! alas! this is the very sort of words which Protestants consider superficial; good, as far as they go, but nothing more. In like manner, the priest, in the Absolution, bids us pray GOD "that the rest of our life hereafter may be pure and holy." But I have given instances enough to explain my meaning about the Services generally : you can continue the examination for yourself. I will direct your notice to but one instance more,—the introduction of the Psalms into the Daily Service. Do you think a modern Protestant would have introduced them into it?

L. They are inspired.

C. Yes, but they are also what is called Jewish. I do certainly think, I cannot doubt, that had the Liturgy been compiled in a day like this, only a selection of them, at most, would have been inserted in it, though they were all used in the primitive worship from the very first. Do we not hear objections to using them in singing, and a wish to substitute hymns? Is not this a proof what judgment would have been passed on their introduction into the Service, by Reformers of the nineteenth century? First, the imprecatory Psalms, as they are called, would have been set aside, of course.

L. Yes; I cannot doubt it; though some of them, at least, are prophetic, and expressly ascribed in the New Testament to the inspiration of the Holy Ghost.

C. And surely numerous other passages would have been pronounced unsuitable to the spiritual faith of a Christian. I mean all such as speak of our being rewarded according to the cleanness of our hands, and of our walking innocently, and of the LORD's doing well to those that are good and true of heart. Indeed, this doctrine is so much the characteristic of that heavenly book, that I hardly see any part of it could have been retained by present reformers but what is clearly predictive of the Messiah.

L. I shall now take my leave, with many thanks, and will think over what you have said. However, have you not been labouring superfluously? We know all along that the Puritans of Hooker's time *did* object to the Prayer Book: there was no need of proving that.

C. I am not speaking of those who would admit they were Puritans; but of that arrogant Protestant spirit (so called) of the day, in and out of the Church (if it is possible to say what is in and what is out), which thinks it takes bold and large views, and would fain ride over the superstitions and formalities which it thinks it sees in those who (I maintain) hold to the old Catholic faith; and, as seeing that this spirit is coming on apace, I cry out betimes, whatever comes of it, that corruptions are pouring in, which, sooner or later, will need a SECOND REFORMATION.

The Feast of St. Bartholomew.

III.

THE RESTORATION

OF

SUFFRAGAN BISHOPS,

A MEANS OF EFFECTING

THE MORE EQUAL DISTRIBUTION OF EPISCOPAL DUTIES,

AS CONTEMPLATED BY HIS MAJESTY'S

RECENT ECCLESIASTICAL COMMISSION.

1835.

ADVERTISEMENT.

THE writer of the following remarks thinks it advisable to state at the outset, with reference to the recent Commission, that,—without pronouncing how far and in what cases the formal approval of the Church to the Report of such a Commission may be dispensed with, agreeably to ecclesiastical usage,—or how far a Commission is of authority, in which the Lay Members outnumber the Clerical,—or how far it is expedient or pious to alienate for the benefit of other places endowments left for the uses of particular sees or parishes,—he desires to view the Commission as the expression of the Church's wish for certain changes in her economy, sanctioned and furthered by the King, as her supreme governor, at the instance of the Bishops, his natural ecclesiastical advisers. If the appointment of it be considered in any sense as an arbitrary interference of the State with her temporalities, it would, of course, be inconsistent with Church principles in any degree to recognize it.

March 12, 1835.

THE
RESTORATION OF SUFFRAGAN BISHOPS.

It has been the misfortune of the Established Church during the last several years, when, in common with our other institutions, its framework and actual operations have been freely discussed, that the plans recommended for the increase of its efficiency have taken the shape of reforms, and not of restorations of its ancient system. Nothing but the prevailing ignorance concerning ecclesiastical matters can adequately account for this mistake. Authors, not indisposed (to say the least) to the doctrine and discipline of the Church, have indulged in projects for its better adaptation to present circumstances, which, from their novelty and boldness, could only be justified by the absence of historical precedent and experience. They have not even taken the pains to ascertain its actual position relatively to the State and to the Nation; as if it had now, for the first time, made its appearance among us, and suddenly lighted upon our soil, based on no definite principles or engagements to which regard must necessarily be paid in all measures of alteration, however beneficial. Or, if they have seemed to understand the necessity of moving on the line of former ecclesiastical arrangements, they have not done more than catch at such acts of the Tudor sovereigns as are distinguished above the rest for their anomalous and extraordinary character; without attempting to enter into the genius, or accurately to settle the principles, of our religious institutions. Writers, thus regardless of the constitutional relation of the past towards the present, could not be expected to recognize the philosophical bond which connects one age with another, the correspondence of certain periods in the recurring cycles of human affairs, and the instruction thence derivable for our political conduct. Accordingly, far from feeling reverence for an institution which has, in one shape or other, existed in the country for at least 1200 years, they have not allowed it to avail itself of its antiquity even as a guide, but have considered it as a mere subject for external interference and for ingenious experiment.

2.

But, in truth, to such as turn their minds ever so little to its history and antiquities, it is evident that the Church is "like a man that is a householder, which bringeth forth out of his treasure things new and old." It is no birth of a day, no creation of a political crisis, no tender and inexperienced offspring of kings' courts or domestic retreats. It has from the first been thrown upon the world; and it knows the world well in all its artifices and all its wants. It has a store of weapons for all times and circumstances, (if it be allowed and keep in memory the use of them,) a vigorous principle of life, and an inherent self-renovating power. It has gone through all the periods of human society; from the state of luxury and decay, in which it originally found the world, to the age of revolutions which followed, thence to the night of barbarism, the second dawn of science, the growth of political freedom, and of the commercial spirit, and the ascendency of the law, down to the present day, when the over-civilization of its first period seems to have returned. It grew up against a military tyranny; it fearlessly threw itself upon the intelligence, and ruled the lawlessness of great cities; it extended itself over the broad country, into mountain recesses, and over boisterous seas. It had its persuasives for the feudal sovereign, as well as for the multitudes which were its first capture. It has since attached itself, among ourselves, to limited monarchy, and has been found to be the best bond and medium of intercourse between King and People. And all this it has often proved itself to be, by the mere instinct of its natural character, and when it was itself partially ignorant of its previous history and its true position. How is it possible that any juncture of affairs can occur, which it has not already met and overcome? Doubtless it is fully adequate to the gracious purpose for which it was founded, that of coping with human nature in all its forms; and has nothing to fear at the present time but from our ignorance of its resources, and the panic terrors, and loss of self-command, and credulous trust in empirics, thence resulting.

The chief problem, for example, before the Church at present, is how to supply the local wants of an overgrown and disaffected population; but this, serious as it is, is no novel one. No city can threaten religious truth more fiercely than Constantinople in the fourth and fifth centuries; a city created for the very purposes of imperial luxury, hallowed by no local antiquities, the home of no religious remembrances, the abode (in the historian's words) of a "lazy and indolent populace,"[1] the port of commerce, and (by a fortune unparalleled perhaps in any other city) the very focus of a speculative misbelief, and of the almost fanatic party which upheld it. Yet even here Christianity triumphed; triumphed so far as to maintain itself in place and authority for ages, and to be able to extend the light

[1] Gibbon, Hist. ch. xvii.

of religion to such as would receive it. What need have we to do more now, than to master and apply that policy (to borrow a statesman's word) which enabled the Church to achieve its early victories?

3.

These reflections, admitting of a minute and various application at the present time, are however only made here by way of introducing to the reader the particular measure which is to be the subject in the following pages; the restoration, in the larger or more populous dioceses, of the primitive institution of Suffragans, that is, District Bishops, as assistants to the Diocesans of each. At the same time, this instance itself, which is to engage our attention, will incidentally tend to recommend the important general principle under which it falls; viz. that, to improve our system, we have need, not of innovation, but rather of such historical knowledge, insight into human nature and our own national character, statesmanlike sagacity, wisdom, and sound judgment, as may enable us to develop the latent powers of the Church into the form most suitable to arrest and control the existing fashion of the times.

However, it may be necessary to add, that in what has been, or is to be, said about Antiquity, nothing is assumed as to its intrinsic authority at the present day. For though such authority may, in the opinion of many men, suitably be claimed for it, yet the primitive practice of the Church is here adduced either as a medium of historical experience, or in mere illustration of general principles otherwise established.

4.

Of the three subjects which are to engage the attention of the Ecclesiastical Commission lately appointed by his

Majesty, the first includes in it a reference "to the more equal distribution of episcopal duties," in "the several dioceses of England and Wales." Thus, the Royal testimony is expressly borne to the existence of an inconvenience which has long been felt by all well-wishers of the Church, the excessive ecclesiastical duties which weigh upon certain of the sees, and the desirableness of relieving them, in some way or other, of a portion of them. It is not, however, generally considered, that another of the heads of inquiry set before the Commissioners opens a way to the attainment of this object. The proposed consideration of "the state of the several cathedral and collegiate churches within the same" portion of the kingdom, "with a view to the suggestion of such measures as may render them most conducive to the efficiency of the Established Church," may obviously be made subservient, without any great difficulty, to the improvement of the diocesan system. And this, indeed, seems to be contemplated in the Commission itself; for in projecting "the prevention of the necessity of attaching by *commendam* to bishoprics benefices with cure of souls," it does in fact naturally lead the mind to the consideration of the deaneries and chapters, as the means through which an addition of income may be effected, when such benefices are withdrawn. But if the cathedral and collegiate dignities may be made subservient to diocesan purposes in this way, why may they not in another? Why should they not be made the means of relieving the overburdened sees of a portion of their present duties, as well as of detaching parochial responsibilities from certain others? Why not employ them in the endowment of a certain number of suffragan or assistant bishops, to take the charge of districts in relief of certain sees? If the necessity of such an addition to the present episcopal body can be shown, one would think there could not be a more appropriate application of the chapter dignities (supposing any new application to be made of any of them), nor one which would more recommend itself to the laity; whose solicitude has hitherto been directed towards the well-being of the inferior clergy, not from any want of personal respect or attachment as regards the Bishops, but because the laborious exertions of parochial ministers, and the deficiencies in the parochial system, are more before their eyes. Yet a very little consideration will teach us, that additional Bishops are called for in various districts as fully and urgently as additional clergy;—called for quite independently of the coincidence of our possessing places of emolument, which may be used in the creation of them. It is necessary to insist upon this; lest persons, who happen to have made up their minds to the application of the chapter dignities to other purposes, should feel towards the measure I am recommending, as towards a theory or project which interferes with their own particular plans for strengthening the Church; whereas, let them assign these dignities as they will, still it will be true, that an addition to our existing Bishops is desirable, in whatever way that addition is to be provided.

5.

The obvious reason for increasing our number of Bishops is the increase in the population. In Elizabeth's reign (1588), the population of England amounted only to 4,400,000; two centuries before (1378), to 2,300,000;[2] now it reaches to 13,897,187.[3] At the present time, the diocese of Chester contains 1,883,958 souls; that is, more than three-fourths of the whole population of England in the reign of Richard II. London has 1,722,685; York, 1,496,538; and Lichfield, 1,045,481; these three together being nearly equal to the whole population 250 years since. But such overwhelming charges speak for them-

[2] Hallam, Const. Hist. ch. i.   [3] Population Returns, 1831.

selves, even though there were no contrast in numbers between the sixteenth century and the nineteenth.

This *primâ facie* case for an addition is confirmed by the fact, that even three centuries ago, and prior to the increase, such a measure was actually contemplated by our Reformers. Prior to those local accumulations of population, which present so distressing a problem to the Christian philanthropist, and prior to that spirit of unbelief, and systematized opposition to the vital and ancient doctrines of religion, which is the perplexity of the orthodox churchman now, Cranmer, in the first years of his primacy, projected a considerable extension of the episcopal office. On the confiscation of the abbey lands (1539), he advised Henry with the proceeds to endow from fifteen to twenty new sees, five of which were actually created, and four now remain.[4] Another plan for increasing the efficiency of the Church, which he succeeded, as far as Parliament was concerned, in executing to the extent of his wishes, was the measure to which I shall more directly call the reader's attention in the sequel, the addition of Suffragans to the existing sees, to the number of twenty-six. It appears, then, that finding the whole number of Bishops twenty-one, he designed to raise it at least to sixty, that is, nearly to treble it, with a view to meet the wants of the Church in that day; whereas, five only, scarcely more than an eighth part of the addition he contemplated, were created.

Ussher, whose authority in matters of ecclesiastical discipline has always been popular, went much farther than Cranmer; though he had in part a different object in view in the reformation he proposed. He was desirous

---

[4] Westminster did not survive its first bishop. Bingham (Antiq. ix. 8) says Cranmer proposed "near twenty" sees. Short (Church Hist.) mentions, from Strype, a plan for twenty. Burnet (Hist. Reform. iii.) enumerates fifteen.

perhaps of removing from the episcopate some part of that secular appearance which accidentally attaches to it in inconsiderate minds, when the sees are few, and richly endowed; yet undoubtedly he is a witness, and a most important one, of the desirableness of what may be called a *resident* episcopacy, and of an increase of the number of Bishops for that purpose. In a plan which he drew up in 1641, when the first committee on Church affairs was formed, he proposed that suffragan Bishops should be appointed equal to the number of rural deans in each diocese, with a jurisdiction extending over the respective deaneries. This project, indeed, did not deserve, nor did it meet with success; but the testimony which it bears to the need of increased episcopal superintendence is corroborated by the Declaration put forth by Charles II. in 1660, in which suffragan Bishops are promised to the larger dioceses, though this intention was never fulfilled.

6.

Such is the evidence of later times; if, on the other hand, we recur to the infancy of English Christianity, we find the first founders of our Church equally decisive in the policy of multiplying its Episcopal centres, and of doing so gradually. Augustine, the first Archbishop of Canterbury, had been empowered by Gregory to erect another metropolitan see at York, on the understanding, even in that missionary era, that each province was to contain twelve sees. The subsequent conduct of the English Bishops, following up this intention by their own acts, is an independent witness to its wisdom. Dorchester, the first see of the West Saxons, during the rule of its second bishop, gave birth to Winchester; which in turn has been relieved, at a later date, of Exeter, Bath and Wells, Salisbury, and Bristol. But before this, Lindisfarne, in the north, had become the mother see of York, and thence, again, of Hexham and Whithern.⁵ By gradual additions like these the dioceses amounted to seventeen even in the time of Bede, who expresses his desire of a still further increase.⁶ Such was the shoot made by the Church after the Saxon invasion. Far more numerous in point of sees was the original British Church, which had been introduced from Gaul. At the synod of Brevy, held in the seventh century by reason of the Pelagian troubles, there are said to have been present as many as 118 British Bishops; and this report, even though it be an exaggeration, is an argument, by its very existence, of the prevalence of notions concerning Episcopal superintendence very different from the present.

Again, in Ireland, at one time, there were from fifty to sixty sees.

The primitive dioceses of southern and eastern Christendom were still more numerous, as is well known. The Churches in Italy were but rural Deaneries in extent,

---

⁵ Inett, vol. i. pp. 48, 90, &c.

⁶ Bede, writing in 735 to Egbert, Bishop of York, " recommends in terms very passionate and full of concern, the increasing the number of Bishops and secular clergy, to preach God's holy word in country towns and villages. For, saith he, there are many villages in the woody and mountainous parts, which for many years never saw the face of a Bishop, and have none to instruct them in the common principles of religion or morality, and yet there is no place but what pays tribute to their Bishop.—But, to perfect this great work, he tells Egbert, that he thought nothing so likely as to *increase the number of Bishops*, and advises that for that end this prelate, with the advice of Ceolwulf, King of Northumberland, and his council, should *erect several* new Bishoprics, and in order thereto, they should take several of the monasteries, and in them erect new sees; and that, by this means, York, according to the ancient platform of Gregory the Great, might be erected into a metropolitan see; and, if need require, he recommends that they should take the lands belonging to other monasteries. Thus, saith he, ' those houses of which we all know there are many, unworthy the name of monasteries, from serving the ends of vanity and luxury, may be brought to assist and bear a part *in the burthen of the Episcopal office.*'"
—Inett, vol. i. p. 156.

being not above five or six miles from each other. The kingdom of Naples (unless the revolutions of the last thirty years have occasioned any change) contains 147 sees, of which twenty are archbishoprics; and the state of Asia Minor, Syria, and Africa, was quite conformable to this model.[7]

I am far from supposing that we, in our altered circumstances, must do everything which former times have done; or that the English Church, united as it is to the State, need be conformed to the usage of the kingdom of the Two Sicilies; but I take leave to claim for the first age of Christianity, sanctioned as it is by the almost universal consent of after times, that it had a reason for what it did, and that there is some natural advantage to the Church in the multiplication of Bishops, (which may be hindered indeed, or become a disadvantage, or otherwise attained, under certain political circumstances, but) which sanctions and confirms arguments for that multiplication drawn from other sources.

7.

Such arguments are to be found in the enormous size of some of our present dioceses, as is partly allowed, partly implied, in the words of the Royal Commission. Considering the peculiar nature of the duties of a Christian Pastor, surely a population rising from 900,000 to 1,800,000 was never intended to be the charge of one man. I would not willingly seem to intrude into the concerns of others; but surely the inferior clergy and the laity are bound in duty, not indeed to go before, or to act without their Rulers, but to concur in such sentiments and measures as those Rulers seem to approve. If, indeed, *they* wished things to remain as they are, private men would have no right to speak on the subject; but we are sanctioned by the King's Commis-

---

[7] Vide Bingham, Antiq. ix.

sion to enlarge upon an evil which, I will venture to say, every thinking man will admit, the over-populousness of the existing dioceses. Such vast charges must be distressing even to the most vigorous minds; oppressing them with a sense of responsibility, if not, rather, engrossing, dissipating, and exhausting their minds with the mere formal routine of business. If they are able to sustain such duties, they are greater than the inspired lawgiver of Israel, who said, " I am not able to bear all this people alone, because it is too heavy for me." Nothing is more necessary to the Rulers of the Church, than that they should have seasons of leisure. A whirl of business is always unfavourable to depth and accuracy of religious views. It is one chief end of the institution of the ministerial order itself, that there should be men in the world who have time to think apart from it, and live above it, in order to influence those whose duties call them more directly into the bustle of it.

So much was this felt in early times, that places of retreat were sometimes assigned to the Bishops at a distance from their city, whither they were expected to betake themselves, during certain seasons of the year, for the purpose of collecting their minds. Doubtless such leisure may be abused, as everything else; but so far is clear, that while leisure may become an evil, an incessant hurry of successive engagements must be an evil, a serious evil to the whole Church, hurtful to any one, and more than personally hurtful, dangerous to the common cause, in the case of those who are by office guides of conduct, arbiters in moral questions, patterns of holiness and wisdom, and not the mere executive of a system which is ordered by prescribed rules, and can go on without them. And when it is recollected that, in addition to their ecclesiastical duties, our Prelates have their place in the councils of the realm, most beneficially to the nation (which, indeed, as a Christian people, is bound to uphold them there), not to mention the necessity of their meeting together annually for various ecclesiastical purposes, it must be evident to every one that they, more than any other order in the Church, require assistance in their dioceses, during at least a part of the year; and that to them especially applies an appellation, in its right and honourable sense, which is given by our adversaries with a mixture of pity and disrespect to others. The Bishops are the true "working Clergy;" and most undoubtedly, the moment they give us a hint of their wishes (which they recently have done in the Royal Commission), we are absolutely bound, we cannot without undutifulness omit, to evidence our interest, and promise our co-operation, in whatever they shall determine for the better administration of their dioceses, and meanwhile to assist them by such suggestions as we have reason to hope may not be unpleasing to them.

8.

What I have said suggests another view of the subject. Much is said about the advantages of a resident Clergy, and these certainly cannot easily be overrated; but surely there are as great benefits resulting from a resident Episcopacy also. I own I cannot enter into the views of those who, measuring the duties of the Bishop's office by the number of his Clergy, contend that, because these, though far more numerous than formerly, have not increased of late years proportionally to the population, therefore the country needs no increase of the Episcopal order; or who set against the increase of routine business, the present improvement of the roads, the expeditiousness of posting, and the promptness and precision of communications of all sorts. Certainly, if the office and work of a Bishop lie chiefly in being a referee, or controlling power, in matters of business, without present or personal superintendence, without the influence of name and character, without real jurisdiction, without actual possession and use of his territory; then, indeed, a modern writer's assertion will be true, that all the Bishops of England may be swept away without the people knowing the change.[3] If he is mainly the functionary of statutes, the administrator of oaths, an agent in correspondence about the building of churches, the management of societies, and the "serving of tables," important as these objects are, still surely they would be much better accomplished by putting the Episcopate into commission. One general board would manage the routine ecclesiastical business of the kingdom far more promptly and uniformly than a number of persons chosen without special reference to such qualifications. But if a Bishop is intended to bear with him a moral influence, to have the custody of the Christian Faith in his own place and day, and by his life and conversation to impress it in all its saving fulness of doctrine and precept upon the face of society, if he is to be the centre and emblem of Christian unity, the bond of many minds, and the memento of Him that is unseen, he must live among his people. Let us not forget that great ecclesiastical principle, which is as fundamental in Christianity, as in its nature it is the offspring of a profound philosophy. One Bishop, one Church, is a maxim so momentous, that, if his presence can by no expedient be made to extend through it, there is sufficient reason for dividing it into two. He is in theory the one pastor of the whole fold; and though by name an overseer or superintendent, yet his office lies quite as much in being seen in his diocese, as in seeing. Human nature is so constituted as to require such resting-places for the eyes and hearts of the many. Some minds there may be of peculiar make, whether of unusual firmness or

[3] Hallam, Const. Hist. ch. xv.

insensibility, who can dispense with authorities to steady their opinions, and with objects for the exercise of their affections; but such is not the condition of the mass of mankind. They cry out clamorously for guides and leaders, and will choose for themselves if not supplied with them. Here, then, Christianity has met our want in the Episcopal system, and in extending the influence of that system we are co-operating with it.

9.

Few persons can have witnessed the coming of one of our Bishops to consecrate some country church, or to confirm in some remote district, without being struck with the persuasive power of his presence in eliciting from the rural population a kindly and respectful feeling towards the Church over which he presides. The hour and circumstances of his coming are only one part of the benefit resulting from it. Days and days before the Confirmation, it is looked forward to as a great event. From the Clergyman down to the little child just come to school, all is expectation. Catechist and catechumens are all coming before him who is the representative and delegate of the Chief Pastor, who one day will visit once for all. Lessons are learned, admonitions given, with reference to a direct and immediate religious object. Let it not be objected that the novelty is the cause of this. Sunday comes once a week, yet does not, by its frequency, lose its force as a memorial of the next world. And there is one portion of the community, the largest, and to the Christian teacher the most interesting, to whom the presence of the Chief Pastor must be ever new,—the fresh and fresh generations of children, who are advancing forward from infancy to youth. It is obviously most necessary to impress them with dutiful feelings towards the Church. In the opening of life they are brought before the Bishop to make their first solemn confession, and to receive from his hand the fulness of those blessings which were made over to them in baptism. This, indeed, may be done with a small number of functionaries, by congregating the children who are to be confirmed into towns from the villages round. But no one who knows anything of large assemblies of young persons but will deprecate a necessity which has so injurious an effect to say the least on the solemnity of the sacred ordinance;—no one, I suppose, on the other hand, has witnessed the decency, the tranquillity, and the sanctity of those more private Confirmations which our Bishops, at an expense of personal convenience, are so ready to hold, but must understand the benefit which would accrue if such an arrangement could be the custom of the Church; I mean, the benefit of imparting to a religious rite those associations of home scenery and home faces which will endear to them in after-life the memory of the Administrators;—and no one but will confess, that, unless some very grave difficulties interfere, such familiar meetings between Pastor and flock are the true means of strengthening the Establishment with the people at large.

Viewing the matter even in a political light, I should say to the parties competent to do it,—Increase the number of our Bishops. Give the people objects on which their holier and more generous feelings may rest. After all, in spite of the utilitarianism of the age, we have hearts. We like to meet with those whom we may admire and make much of. We like to be thrown out of ourselves. The low-minded maintenance of rights and privileges, the selfishness which entrenches itself in its own castle or counting-house, the coldness of stoicism, and the sourness of puritanism, are neither the characteristics of Englishmen, nor of human nature. Human nature is not republican. We know what an immediate popularity is given to the cause of monarchy, when the sovereign shows himself to his people, and demands their loyalty. And, in like manner, those who watch narrowly may see all the purer and nobler feelings of our nature brought out in spectators, in a less enthusiastic, only because in a more reverential way, by the sight of the heads of the Church; when in proportion to the knowledge and religious temper of each, that flame of devoted and triumphant affection is kindled among them, which has ever led to the highest and most glorious deeds, which, as it is loyalty in the subject, is gallant bearing in the soldier, and piety in the child;—and, witnessing it, they will understand that this is the one point in which the Church, as a visible system, has the advantage of all sects; that this is, in fact, our characteristic, our peculiar treasure.

10.

True it is, that the struggle of Christianity mainly lies with the towns in this day, and not in the country; but I conceive that in towns, too, a mass of latent generosity and affectionateness exists, if we knew how to elicit it. The question is not, whether the prominent character of a town population is not evil, whether it is possible to turn it as a body in favour of the Church, but whether we have any right to leave to themselves those scattered embers of a nobler temper, which, over and above their own preciousness, would, if concentrated, be a powerful antagonist to the waywardness and the selfishness of the many. But, putting aside this part of the subject, surely if the presence of a Bishop is more persuasive in the country, it is more necessary in the town. It is scarcely too much to say, that our great cities require even a missionary establishment. They require the formal appointment of an Evangelist, commissioned to enlighten and reclaim those outskirts of Christendom, which, in the heart of a Christian country, tread very closely upon heathenism.

If the vice, the ignorance, the wretchedness there existing are to be anyhow met, it is not by the labours of a few parochial Clergymen, however exemplary and self-denying, occupied (as they are) with the services of their churches, the management of their vestries, the visitation of their sick, the administration of alms, and their domestic duties and cares, but by one of disengaged mind, intent upon the signs and the exigencies of the times, and vested with authority to promote co-operation among his fellow-labourers, and to conduct the Christian warfare on a consistent plan. In such populous neighbourhoods, every denomination of Christianity is organized for action, except that which we consider the true form of it; which, instead of being able to address itself to the thousands of ignorant and depraved who are to be found there, with the view of benefiting them, has to battle for its own existence against the combination of restless and inveterate enemies. Or if any organization is to be found there on the part of the Church, it is of a very ambiguous character;—some religious society, for instance, which has been founded among semi-dissenters, and admits them to membership and even to rule, which thinks it a great merit to avow its intention of furthering the interests of the Establishment, or considers it has at once proved its churchmanship, if it has succeeded in obtaining the names of some ecclesiastical dignitaries among its well-wishers and patrons. Or at best, a number of zealous and well-intentioned laymen, very little informed in the principles of their own communion, have contrived, perhaps, to set in motion some system of parochial visiting, which, carrying away by the force of novelty first the Clergy of the place, whether the latter will or no, and next themselves, and going apace towards Methodism and Dissent, seems to claim of the Church the grant of a resident Overseer, free from the secular business which besets Diocesan, Archdeacon;

and Incumbent, and able to guide and regulate the Church's movements.

11.

Such is the state of things at the best; but it may be far worse. Perhaps we shall find the Clergy, whom accident has thrown together in one place, differing from one another by various shades of opinion (as men always will differ), and going on to differ in conduct (as men need not differ), cold and distant towards each other, split into parties with leaders on both sides; and all this mainly for want of a common superior. The most friendly-disposed minds often feel the need of an umpire in matters of duty, when neither likes to have the responsibility of abandoning his own view for that of the other, and both would rejoice to be allowed to defer to a third person. And if this occur in the case of friends, much more is it true, when there is a want of familiarity and sympathy between the parties, a difference of ages, tempers, habits, judgments, or connexions, or some mutual jealousies and suspicions; and when the warmth of affectionate allegiance to a common superior is the only means of drawing out, kindling, and fusing together discordant minds. In this state of things, it will perhaps happen that some intrusive layman, scarcely a member of the Church, self-confident and ready-tongued, will become the ordinary arbiter of all differences, and the virtual ecclesiastical head of the place; or some adjacent landed influence will exert itself in acts subversive of that Establishment, towards which at best it entertains cold, perhaps unfriendly feelings. It is a question, indeed, whether the present most lamentable differences of religious opinions among the Clergy would ever have existed, had we been allowed a larger supply of ecclesiastical heads. To provide for soundness and unity of doctrine has been one special object of the Episcopal

Form from the first. The schools of philosophy were many and discordant; but the "One Faith," put into the hands of every Bishop, forthwith becomes the rallying point and profession of his whole diocese. So necessary is this, that in Protestant Germany, where the episcopal order has been suspended since the Reformation, schools of doctrine are found to arise from time to time (as under Spener, Neander, and the like), to supply the absence of authoritative teachers, as if nature witnessed in favour of Episcopacy; and this state of things is acquiesced in and defended by pious men from the evident necessity of the case, in spite of St. Paul's warning against taking Masters and setting up one against another. Without such instrumentality, both by way of stimulus and instruction, religious truth will languish; schools will arise and fall, and waste themselves in mutual quarrels; while the enemy will not fail to turn all such scandals and failures to the injury of religion itself.

12.

If the control I speak of is ever to be exercised, it must be soon. The evil does not admit of delay. Already almost, fulfilling the description of the historian, *nec vitia nostra nec remedia pati possumus;* our sufferings do but make us shrink from the treatment necessary for a cure. Educated in irresponsible freedom of word and action, we resist any external authority; so much so, that the view above given of the episcopal office, perhaps may startle, to say the least, some persons, who would fain consider themselves Churchmen. But are we not, if the truth must be spoken, tending to this—to learn to dispense with the episcopal system altogether? Is not this the upshot (so to say) of our present ecclesiastical and civil policy? Could indeed, as Hallam implies, the bulk of the laity, could a large number of the Clergy, give any answer, satisfactory even to themselves, if asked plainly what was the *use* of having Bishops? This is not the place to enter into any theological discussion concerning it, though some hints on the subject have been incidentally thrown out in the foregoing pages. Only let us observe carefully the fact. Does the popular religionist of the day know the benefit of them, who enlarges on the "orthodoxy" of certain Dissenters, who lays a stress on certain sectaries agreeing with the Church in "doctrine," who would direct Missions by means of Boards, and dissuades from dissent on the mere ground of the Church being the State Religion? Or on the other hand, does the popular politician,—who keeps his eye fixed upon the parochial Clergy, who considers them the essence of the Establishment, who makes their residence [9] up and down the country (not merely a most important, but) the one object of his solicitude, who would multiply and establish them (which indeed he may most beneficially do, but) to an undue preponderance and dangerous influence over the Episcopate, while he so fully recognizes in them mere instruments and adjuncts of the State, that it would be but consistent in him, if he could, to put them once for all under a Minister of Public Instruction? Lastly, in spite of the acknowledged influence of the Bishops within the range of their personal friends, is there not, if it may be said, a painful and growing separation of feeling, on the whole, between the Episcopal Bench and the Clergy? Is there not going on a gradual organization of the Clergy into associations and meetings, which threatens, unless the Bishops become part of it, to eject their influence, as something foreign to our system? If these things be true in any good measure, even though

---

[9] [This was a reference to the stress laid, at the time, by some defenders of the Establishment in and out of Parliament, on its securing a "resident gentleman" in every parish.]

exaggerated, it will follow that there is a tendency in the age to dispense with Episcopacy. Let us then understand our position. To those, indeed, who regard the Episcopal Order as the bulk of Christians for eighteen hundred years have regarded it, who see in it the pledge and the channel of the blessings of Christianity, associate it with the various passages of history with which it is implicated, and consider it as the instrument of numberless civil benefits, the thought of such a loss gives too piercing a pain to allow of their enlarging on it. All, however, that I say here is, let us see where we stand; let us do what we do wittingly; lest, perhaps, we one day rise in the morning, and to our surprise find our treasure gone.

13.

It follows to inquire, how best the evil, which I have been dwelling on, may be remedied; and of three methods which with that object have found advocates, one, I conceive, has already been set aside by the foregoing remarks as not meeting the necessities of the case, viz. the proposition to change the sites of the existing sees, and to remove them from the less to the more populous districts of the country. Independently of the objections which lie against so violent a measure as a new distribution of the ecclesiastical territory, it may be said that even the smaller dioceses are larger than would be desirable, were that territory to be divided afresh; that, such as those dioceses are at present, they are in some sort witnesses and memorials of a better state of things; and that, in matter of fact, more Bishops are wanted, and that to transfer the sees is only to shift about, not to remove the evil. Nor is such an expedient consonant with ecclesiastical usage. Here we may take the authority of Bingham, whose name, on such subjects, as every one knows, stands very high; he devotes a portion of his elaborate work on Christian Antiquities, to the consideration of the dioceses of the first ages, and his witness is as follows:—"One great objection," he says, "against the present Diocesan Episcopacy, and that which to many may look the most plausible, is drawn from the vast extent and greatness of some of the northern dioceses of the world, which makes it so extremely difficult for one man to discharge all the offices of the episcopal function. . . . . The Church of England has usually followed the larger model, and had great and extensive dioceses; for at first she had but seven bishoprics in the whole nation, and those commensurate in a manner to the seven Saxon kingdoms. Since that time, she has thought it a point of wisdom to contract her dioceses, and multiply them into above twenty; and if she should think fit to add forty or a hundred more, she would not be without precedent in the practice of the Primitive Church."[1]

Bingham's leaning then was towards an addition of dioceses after the primitive model; and this is a second suggestion which may be made for the remedy of our ecclesiastical deficiencies. But, direct and natural as it is, I shall leave it to be advocated by others. Any subdivision of dioceses, even though unattended with a suppression of sees elsewhere, must be considered unadvisable, for several reasons. For, over and above the legal difficulties which may attach to it, it is an organic change, and so irretrievable. It is a measure taken without trial, the abrupt passing into law of what is only an experiment. Moreover, as multiplying centres of government, it tends to dissipate the energies of the Church, and admits the risk of dissension and discordance of operation.

There is a third expedient, the creation of Suffragans, which is an increase of Bishops without an increase of sees. This seems to me in all respects the safest as well as simplest mode of relieving such Diocesans as at present

[1] Bingham's Antiq. ix. 8, fin.

are oppressed by an excess of pastoral duties. To this system our attention shall be directed in what follows.

14.

Suffragans, or district Bishops, Chorepiscopi (as they were anciently called), are Bishops located in a diocese, assistant to the see, without jurisdiction of their own, and ecclesiastically subject in all matters to the Diocesan. They are altogether his representatives and instruments, enabling him, as it were, to be in different parts of his diocese at once, and to continue his pastoral labour unremittingly, as it is called for. Their history is as follows:—

In primitive times the first step towards evangelizing a heathen country seems to have been to seize upon some principal city in it, commonly the civil metropolis, as a centre of operation; to place a pastor, that is (generally) a Bishop there, to surround him with a sufficient number of associates and assistants, and then to wait till, under the blessing of Providence, this Missionary College was able to gather around it the scattered children of grace from the evil world, and to invest itself with the shape and influence of an organized Church. The converts would, in the first instance, be those in the immediate vicinity of the Missionary or Bishop, whose diocese nevertheless would extend over the heathen country on every side, either indefinitely, or to the utmost extent of the civil province; his mission being without restriction to all to whom the Christian faith had never been preached. As he prospered in the increase of his flock, and sent out his clergy to greater and greater distances from the city, so would the homestead (so to call it) of his Church enlarge. Other towns would be brought under his government, openings would occur for stations in isolated places; till at length, "the burden becoming too heavy for him," he would appoint others to supply his place in this or that part of the province. To these he would commit a greater or lesser share of his spiritual power, as might be necessary; sometimes he would make them fully his representatives, or ordain them Bishops; at other times he would employ Presbyters for his purpose. In process of time, it would seem expedient actually to divide the province into parts; and here again the civil arrangement was followed, the several lesser cities becoming the sees of so many dioceses, coextensive with the districts of which those cities were the political centres. Thus at length there were as many sees as there were cities of the empire, and all of them in their respective places subordinate to the Metropolitan as he was called, or Bishop of the civil metropolis, from whom, always in the theory, often in fact, they sprang; while at the same time each had an independent internal jurisdiction of his own. The Bishops of the subordinate cities included in a province were called Suffragans to the Metropolitan, because they had the right of voting with him in the provincial council. In this sense it is that the Bishops of London, Rochester, Winchester, and the rest are suffragans of the Archbishop of Canterbury; but this, though the first and most appropriate sense of the word "Suffragan," must not be confused with that to which I have already appropriated it.

15.

The same process by which the organization of the province was conducted, was at the same time carried within the limits of its several dioceses also. According to the necessities of each (whether from its populousness or its extent, being mountainous perhaps or desert, with a scattered people, or but partially Christian), the Bishop appointed about himself a number of assistant Bishops and Presbyters, distributing them here and there as he judged best.[2] These assistant Bishops so far resembled in position the diocesans of a province, that they were scattered through a district and connected with a centre; but they differed from them in having no independent jurisdiction and territory of their own. They were not, like parish priests, fixed to one spot and with rights in it, but diocesan officials subject altogether to the see to which they were assistants, as being but the representatives and delegates of the Bishop holding it. These, then, are the ecclesiastical functionaries whose restoration I am advocating; Chorepiscopi, or Country-bishops, as they were anciently called, and in more modern times (though the reason is scarcely known), Suffragans.

The office of these Chorepiscopi, or district Bishops, was to preside over the country clergy, inquire into their behaviour, and report to their principal; also to provide fit persons for the inferior administrations of the Church. They had the power of ordaining the lower ranks of Clergy, such as the readers and sub-deacons; they might ordain priests and deacons, with the leave of the city Bishop, and administer the right of confirmation; and, what was a still greater privilege, they were permitted to sit and vote in councils. Thus, on the whole, their office bore a considerable resemblance to that of our Archdeacons or to the ancient Visitors; except, of course, that Archdeacons are Presbyters, and that they were Bishops, had the power of ordination and confirmation, and the reverence due by right to that high spiritual office, whether or not united to civil dignities.

[2] The country-Presbyters in like manner were called $\dot{\epsilon}\pi\iota\chi\omega\rho\iota o\iota$ $\pi\rho\epsilon\sigma$-$\beta\upsilon\tau\epsilon\rho o\iota$. Vide Concil. Neocæsar. Can. 13. Dr. Routh's note upon the thirteenth Canon of the Council of Ancyra, in which he vindicates the prerogative of ordination to the episcopal order against the presbyterian objections drawn thence, is but one out of the many benefits which he has conferred upon apostolical Christianity.

These Chorepiscopi or Suffragan Bishops did not last into the middle ages. From the time that Christianity was recognized by the State, there was a growing disposition on the part of the Bishops principal, to dispense with a subsidiary order. As their sees grew in wealth and civil importance, they are said to have become impatient of a class of ecclesiastics who were their equals in spiritual dignity, and who hindered them, in some sense, from enjoying monarchical rule in their respective dioceses. As early as the middle of the fourth century, a Provincial Council of Laodicea decreed, that for the future no Bishops should be provided for the country villages, but only the Visitors already spoken of; and though this local decision did not necessarily affect the other parts of Christendom, yet it was a symptom of what was secretly going on in the religious temper of those times, and the presage of what was to follow in succeeding centuries, till in the ninth the Pope caused a primitive institution to be set aside altogether.

16.

As to our country, situated at the furthest extremity of the West, it but slowly received that complete ecclesiastical organization, which sprang up in Asia almost under the feet of those who first "preached the good tidings" there. The early British Church, indeed, may have more nearly resembled the Eastern dioceses than did the Saxon; but if we commence with the time of Augustine (A.D. 596), we shall find from thence down to these last centuries, a partial indeed, but a growing wish to conform to the fully furnished system of Antiquity. Indeed, up to the present date, when (to mention what is a sign of the times) Rural Deans have been revived in various dioceses, there has been a continual effort of the Church, in spite of events which have from time to time thrown it back, to complete the development of its polity. The dioceses were originally

of the larger class, from the circumstance that the sees
were of the nature of Missionary Stations in a heathen soil.
Large as they were, and intended for subdivision by
Gregory, yet they had but insufficient increase, and little
internal organization all through the Saxon period, according to the most probable opinion. Arch-presbyters
indeed, or Rural Deans, there were, and Archdeacons;
but to these the Bishops delegated no large jurisdiction,
employing them occasionally according to circumstances.
An improvement was made upon this imperfect state of
things at the Conquest, by the accident of civil changes.
William separated the ecclesiastical from the secular
Courts, and this in the event threw upon the Bishops a
multiplicity of business, in which hitherto they had had
no concern.[3] Their time being no longer free for the
service of their dioceses, some new arrangement became
necessary in the ecclesiastical system, in order to supply
the consequent deficiency in pastoral superintendence.
Lanfranc was the first to divide his diocese into Archdeaconries and Deaneries, and was followed by Thomas
of York and Remigius of Lincoln, the latter of whom
created in his own as many as seven fixed Archdeaconries.[3]
The like improvement followed in other dioceses, in consequence of the decree of a council held at Winchester.
Even these means were not sufficient to relieve the Bishops,
especially since, holding baronies under the feudal tenure,
they were often called upon for personal service as vassals
of the Crown. This led to the introduction of Vicarii or
Coadjutors, as they still exist in the Roman communion;
Bishops, that is, who, without having a fixed position in the
dioceses, were substitutes for the Bishops in possession, and
relieved them of those duties for which secular engagements or other reasons incapacitated them. These too are
called Suffragans, though not Chorepiscopi. Sometimes

[3] Vide Inett, vol. ii. pp. 63—65.

they were agents of more than one Diocesan at once; and they evaded the ecclesiastical irregularity of being bishops at large, i.e. without local station in the Church, by being made (what is familiarly called) Bishops *in partibus*, i e. *in partibus infidelium*, according to a well-known arrangement in the Roman Catholic Church, which making it a rule not to recede from territory which once has been Christian, keeps up the complement of Bishops in those countries which have relapsed into heathenism, and employs them for various purposes in other parts of the Catholic world. Such were the Suffragan Bishops of the middle ages. For instance, we read of one Petrus Corbariensis or Corabiensis (whatever foreign see is thus denoted) in 1332, suffragan or coadjutor of several sees in the province of Canterbury; in 1531, of a Bishop of Sidon, and again of a Bishop of Hippo assisting Cranmer in the administration of his diocese.[4]

17.

This system of Coadjutors, though advantageous in itself and of ancient authority, evidently became an abuse, and destroyed the object of its own institution, if ever one man was allowed to serve at once several Churches. Accordingly, at the Reformation, Cranmer (as I have already incidentally noticed) obtained from Henry VIII. the restoration of the primitive system of the Chorepiscopi, under the received name of Suffragans, by an Act of Parliament passed in the twenty-sixth year of his reign, which is still in force; with this only difference between them and their predecessors in early times (if there really was even this), that, though still district Bishops, they were fixed in towns, not in villages, as the necessities of the case plainly required. London, Winchester, Bath and

---

[4] Collier, Eccl. Hist. vol. i. p. 531. Vide also Strype's Memorials of Cranmer, i. 9, and Wharton's Observations.

Wells, Salisbury, Lincoln and York, were among the sees thus assisted. "These" [Suffragans], says Burnet, "were believed to be the same with the Chorepiscopi in the primitive Church; which, as they were begun before the first Council of Nice, so they continued in the Western Church till the ninth century, and then, a decretal of Damasus being forged that condemned them, they were put down everywhere by degrees, and now revived in England. The suffragan sees were as follows: Thetford, Ipswich, Colchester, Dover, Guildford, Southampton, Taunton, Shaftesbury, Molton, Marlborough, Bedford, Leicester, Gloucester, Shrewsbury, Bristol, Penrith, Bridgewater, Nottingham, Grantham, Hull, Huntingdon, Cambridge, Pereth [sic], Berwick, St. Germain's, and the Isle of Wight;[5] twenty-six in all, the Diocesan in each case having the power of nominating two persons, out of whom the King chose, the Archbishop consecrating. No temporal provision is made for them by the Act, which instead supposes them to be beneficed, and extends to them a licence of non-residence, and "for the better maintenance of their dignity," the privilege of "holding two benefices with cure." It would seem also that the revenues of the see were expected to be made in some measure subservient to this purpose; for the Act provides that they shall not "take any profits of the places or sees whereof they shall be named . . . but only such profits . . . as shall be licensed and limited to them," &c. Sometimes, as we learn from the subsequent history, they were preferred to dignities in the chapter attached to the see.

[5] Burnet, Hist. Reform. iii. The Bishop's form of presenting nominees to the King, and his letters of Commission to them, are given in Strype's Cranmer, Appendix, Nos. xxi. xxii. The Suffragans were not obliged, by the Act of 26 Henry, to take their title from a town in the diocese where they served. In 1537, Bird, Suffragan of Penrith, was located in Llandaff, and Thomas, Suffragan of Shrewsbury, in St. Asaph. Wharton, on Strype, says this arrangement was afterwards altered.

Little is known about the history of this experiment, made under very different political circumstances from the present; but it came to an end in the reign of James the First. Dr. Routh enumerates as many as ten who exercised the office in the reigns of Henry, Edward, and Elizabeth.[6] The only plausible objection to which the institution was exposed, lay in the apprehension that in troubled times they might be made the agents of schismatical proceedings against the Church. But it is obvious that oaths might easily be imposed, restraining them, according to the intention of the office, as fully as Archdeacons, from all independent power and jurisdiction in the Church.[7] As easy would it be to preserve so marked a separation between them and the possession of the civil dignities of the see, as would prevent their ever being looked upon as diocesans elect in their respective neighbourhoods. It only remains to add, what I have above had occasion to mention, that Charles the Second, in his Declaration concerning

---

[6] Reliqu. Sacr. vol. iii. p. 439.

[7] Burnet, in his life of Bishop Bedell, p. 2 (ed. 1685), thinks it probable that Suffragans were discontinued in consequence of their interfering in some instances with the jurisdiction of the Sees. "He was put in Holy Orders (1590—1600) by the Bishop Suffragan of Colchester. Till I met with this passage, I did not think these Suffragans had been continued so long in England. How they came to be put down, I do not know; it is probable they did ordain all that desired Orders so promiscuously, that the Bishops found it necessary to let them fall. For complaints were made of this Suffragan, upon which he was threatened with the taking his Commission from him; for though they could do nothing but by a delegation from the Bishop, yet the orders they gave were still valid, even when they transgressed in conferring them," &c. In the Act of 26 Henry VIII., no provision is made for imposing on them oaths of obedience to their respective sees; without which, irregularities of course might be expected. The Non-juring Bishops appointed Suffragans (of Thetford and Ipswich, vid. Kettlewell's Life, p. 134), but only by way of keeping up their Succession without interfering with the diocesans in possession.

Ecclesiastical affairs, upon his restoration, promised their re-establishment, " because the dioceses, especially some of them, are thought to be of too large extent;" but for some reason or other the intention was not executed. It may be added that, for the towns mentioned in the Act of 26 Henry VIII., they might now be appointed by the competent authority without going anew to Parliament.

19.

In thus setting before the reader the past history of Suffragans, and the ground on which a restoration of this primitive office seems to be desirable at the present time, I must be considered to have gone almost to the limits of that liberty which is allowable in ecclesiastics in private station. To notice the particular sees which might be thus strengthened,—or any specific plan by which the additional provision might be made,—in what cases Archdeacons, or Chancellors, should be chosen,—in what cases Canons or Prebendaries, as exempt from the semi-civil engagements which press upon Archdeacons,[s]—whether certain chapter dignities should be annexed to the see providing Suffragans, or immediately to the Suffragans themselves,—requires a practical acquaintance with our ecclesiastical state, and a knowledge of details, which those only possess upon whom the decision depends. However, if, according to the popular rumour, no difficulty is to be found, not only in annexing stalls to town livings, but even in reconstructing dioceses, surely no very delicate process will be involved in such arrangements as would be required by the measure here recommended; and under this feeling it was suggested in the opening of these remarks, that the Royal Commission, in contemplating changes in the appli-

---

[s] R. Barnes, Chancellor of York, was in 1566 consecrated Suffragan of Nottingham. R. Rogers, Prebendary of Canterbury, was in 1569 consecrated Suffragan of Dover. Strype's Life of Parker, iii. 15.

cation of chapter dignities, did itself open a way to the restoration of the Suffragan system.

Without interfering, then, with questions of detail, which, unless they involved some objection to the measure itself, lie beyond the province of these remarks, a brief reference shall be made in conclusion to the serious political reasons which exist for strengthening the Church beyond the mere temporary repairs and expedients of the day. I say political reasons, for we all know, that, over and above its sacred character, which ever must be paramount in our thoughts, the Church is a special political blessing. It is confessedly a powerful instrument of state, a minister of untold temporal good to our population, and one of the chief bulwarks of the Monarchy. No institution can be imagined so full of benefit to the poorer classes, nor of such prevailing influence on the side of loyalty and civil order. It is a standing army, insuring the obedience of the people to the Laws by the weapons of persuasion; by services secretly administered to individuals one by one in the most trying seasons of life, when the spirit is most depressed, the heart most open, and gratitude most ready to take root there. And as evident is its growing importance at this era in our history, when Democracy is let loose upon us. Either the Church is to be the providential instrument of re-adjusting Society, or none at all is vouchsafed to us. The Church alone is able to do, what it has often done before,—to wrestle with lawless minds, and bring them under. The Church alone can encourage and confirm the better feelings of our peasantry, conciliate the middle classes, and check the rabble of the towns. The only question, debated on all hands, is, *how* it may be best made subservient to these purposes; and here it is that there is a want of large and clear-sighted views in a number of excellent men, sincerely attached both to its interests and to those of the Monarchy.

20.

I would suggest, then, that, if the Crown wishes, at this perilous juncture, to strengthen the Church for the Crown's advantage, it must not limit itself to improvements in the mere working of the system; it must relax in some degree those restraints which press upon the constitution of the Church as an Establishment. At present, though more exactly organized than any other branch of our Institutions, possessed of various powers and privileges, and capable in its own nature of the most vigorous and effective action, the Church has virtually little political independence, and is scarcely more than an instrument, nay, in many of its functions, almost a mere department of the Government. That, in spite of this, it really has a will of its own, and exerts an elevated moral influence, no one can doubt; but the opportunity of its doing so, is owing to the mere liberality of the State hitherto, which has not kept so firm a hold of it as it might have done. Though exposed, it is not yet subjected to State tyranny; and there would be no reason why it should not continue in its present circumstances, had not grave changes lately taken place in our civil constitution. It is as clear as it is deplorable, that, in consequence of these, the enemies of the Crown may be its professed servants, and use its ecclesiastical influence and patronage against it. Were the Church in the King's own hand, we might rest content; assured that he, for religion sake, to say nothing of inferior motives, would treat his truest and most loyal servant with due honour. But the balance of the Constitution having been disturbed, the state of things on one side of the Throne being new, and that on the other old, the Democracy may any day step in between the King and the Church, and turn the influence of the latter against himself. Should indeed so miserable an event take place, and the Crown's high and varied Church patronage come into the hands of a deliberately and systematically irreligious party, it will be for the Church to consider what becomes it upon the emergency, and surely the providence of God will raise up instruments of our deliverance in that day of rebuke, as He has done of old time. This is altogether another matter; but are members of the Church, are friends of the Monarchy, justified in risking a crisis, in which the Church, prevented from her customary loyal service, will have no duty remaining but to save herself?

21.

This consideration, if there were no other, would suffice to show, that something more is requisite at this moment than a bare improvement of the working of the Church system. The late civil changes involve the necessity of ecclesiastical; the more simple, silent, and gradual, the better, still changes such as will secure the foundation as well as the superstructure of the Church, and guarantee her immunity from the attempts of any profligate faction which may force its way into power. The same State interests which, at some former eras of our history, called for her entire subjection, surely now suggest her partial emancipation. There have been times, we know, when the Civil Power, consulting for its own independence, could do nothing else but fetter down the Church. When she was entangled in an alliance with Rome, the instinct of self-preservation dictated those memorable acts, on the part of the State, violent, yet intelligible in their policy, which broke her spirit. Again, when she took part with an unfortunate family, nothing remained to the new Governors of the Nation, but to deprive her Bishops, silence her Convocation, and bestow her emoluments on the partisans of the Revolution. Those distressing times have passed away. We are no longer exposed to the perplexities of a divided allegiance, whether on spiritual or civil grounds. The Episcopal form, ever repressive of democratic tendencies, is at present in the hands of an emphatically loyal Church. Loyalty, indeed, has been her badge since King Charles's days; and the constancy with which she once clung to his descendants, is at this day an evidence of her prospective fidelity to the present reigning family. Whatever portion of independence was bestowed on her now, would all be exercised one way. Putting duty out of the question, she has ten thousand motives for a jealous maintenance of the prerogatives of the Crown. If then it is the policy of the latter to create for itself friends, especially in the present peculiar circumstances of the Succession, let not its counsellors be so insensible to its interests, as to overlook the ready-formed servant and champion which stands beside it; which, restored to a substantive form, would afford it an effective protection, but which, as a mere dependent, will but become a weapon in hostile hands. And, if they see the expedience of cutting her bonds, let them do so while they can.

22.

It should be observed, moreover, that the same act of grace which would secure the Church against the practices of the Democracy, would also give her popular consideration. One chief part of political power confessedly consists in the display of power. The multitude of men have no opinions, and join the side which seems strongest. While the Church acts through indirect and concealed channels, she will have little influence upon public opinion. A score of Anarchists assembled at a tavern will make a greater impression on the social fabric than she. On the other hand, in proportion as her moral power is concentrated, and brought out in particular persons or appointments, will it inspire courage into its friends, or gain over those who else would fall away to the other side. If any one says that a modest and retiring influence is the peculiar ornament of the Church, I answer that it is her privilege in peaceful, not her duty in stirring times. Here is one secret of the success of Dissent. Men do not like to attach themselves to an impalpable system, to a quality, rather than an embodied form of religion. But such the Established Church ever must be, while possessed of no inherent liberty of action, no judicial or legislative powers, no ample provision of rulers and functionaries,—in a word, till she is seen in some sufficient sense to be *one*.

23.

I am far from imagining that great changes could be made at once, or that the Clergy, long accustomed to their present position, could be persuaded, without reluctance, to undertake their own concerns, or could at once duly fulfil such a task ; or that it would be ever advisable to leave them altogether to themselves, or that power should be put into the hands of the Clergy to the exclusion of the Laity. Or, to take particular cases, I could not desire at this moment to see the Convocation possessed of the privilege of free discussion on Church matters; the probability being, that from the long suspension of such liberty, the present exorbitant influence of the presbyterate, and other causes too painful to mention, scandalous dissensions, perhaps a schism, would be the result. Much less would any alteration be endurable, which tended to give to the Laity the election of their Ministers ; a measure utterly destructive of the Church, in the present vagueness of the qualification of Church membership. But there are improvements upon our existing condition which might fairly be begun at once; some of which, being mentioned in the King's Speech, afford a pleasing anticipation that Government is not insensible to the considerations here ventured on.

Such, for instance, is the intention of strengthening the discipline of the Church in the case of unworthy Ministers; who are at present sheltered, if Incumbents, by the Law's extreme jealousy of the rights of property. Such again will be our riddance of the necessity of marrying Dissenters; and thereby of degrading a high Christian ordinance into a civil ceremony. Such again, to proceed by way of illustration, would be the protection of the Clergy from all liability of legal annoyance for refusing the Lord's Supper to scandalous persons. Such, moreover, would be the restoration to the Church of some means of expressing an opinion on the theology of the day; which, though a delicate function, is urgently called for, now that the State has seemingly abandoned the office of conducting religious prosecutions, and when individuals are in various ways usurping a power not exercised by the rightful authority. Such, again, would be the repeal of the Statute of Præmunire, which, though plainly barbarous and obsolete, yet, as far as it is known, degrades the Church in the eyes of the Nation, by seeming to intimidate her in the exercise of her most solemn and acknowledged prerogatives. Lastly, such, in its degree, is the measure, which it has been the object of these pages to advocate; the appointment of Suffragans being a visible display and concentration of ecclesiastical power, and the substitution of the definiteness and persuasiveness of personal agency for the blind movements of a system.

24.

I must not conclude without briefly expressing my earnest hope, that nothing here said may be understood to recommend any perversion of the Church to mere political purposes. Her highest and true office is doubtless far above any secular object; yet He who has " ordained the powers that be," as well as the Church, has also ordained that the Church, when in most honourable place and most healthy action, should be able to minister such momentous service to the Civil Magistrate, as constitutes an immediate recompense of his piety towards her.[1]

[1] [Whatever is exact and important in the facts brought together in this Pamphlet was supplied to the Author by the friendly aid of the Ven. B. Harrison, the present Archdeacon of Maidstone.]

APPENDIX.

POPULATION AND BENEFICES OF THE SEPARATE DIOCESES.

(From the Returns of 1831.)

	Population.	Benefices.
Chester	1,883,958	616
London	1,722,685	577
York	1,496,538	828
Lichfield	1,045,481	623
Lincoln	899,468	1,273
Exeter	795,416	607
Winchester	729,607	389
Norwich	690,138	1,076
Durham	469,933	175
Canterbury	405,272	343
Bath and Wells	403,795	440
Salisbury	384,683	408
St. David's	358,451	451
Gloucester	315,512	283
Worcester	271,687	222
Chichester	254,460	266
Bristol	232,026	255
Hereford	206,327	326
Peterborough	194,339	305
Rochester	191,875	93
St. Asaph	191,156	160
Llandaff	181,244	194
Bangor	163,712	131
Oxford	140,700	208
Carlisle	135,002	128
Ely	133,722	156

COLLEGIATE CHAPTERS.

1. Brecon . . . . . Dean and Prebendaries.
2. St. Katherine's . . Master and Brethren.
3. Manchester . . . Warden and Fellows.
4. Ripon . . . . . Dean and Prebendaries.
5. Southwell . . . . Prebendaries.
6. Westminster . . . Dean and Prebendaries.
7. Windsor . . . . Dean and Canons.
8. Wolverhampton . . Prebendaries.

SEVENTEEN DIOCESES IN BEDE'S TIME (A.D. 731).

Kent . . . . 1. Canterbury.
                     2. Rochester.
East Saxons . . . . 3. London.
East Angles . . . . 4. Dumnock.
                     5. Helmer.
West Saxons . . . . 6. Winchester.
                     7. Sherburn.
Mercia . . . . . . 8. Lichfield.
                     9. Leicester.
                     10. Lindsey.
                     11. Worcester.
                     12. Hereford.
South Saxon . . . . 13. Selsey.
Northumberland . . . 14. York.
                     15. Lindisfarne.
                     16. Hexham.
                     17. Whithern.

IV.

ON THE MODE OF CONDUCTING THE CONTROVERSY WITH ROME.

(*Being No. 71 of* Tracts for the Times.)

1836.

ON THE MODE OF CONDUCTING THE CONTROVERSY WITH ROME.

THE controversy with Roman Catholics has overtaken us "like a summer's cloud." We find ourselves in various parts of the country preparing for it, yet, when we look back, we cannot trace the steps by which we arrived at our present position. We do not recollect what our feelings were this time last year on the subject,—what was the state of our apprehensions and anticipations. All we know is, that here we are, from long security, ignorant why we are not Roman Catholics, and they, on the other hand, are said to be spreading and strengthening on all sides of us, vaunting of their success, real or apparent, and taunting us with our inability to argue with them.

The Gospel of CHRIST is not a matter of mere argument: it does not follow that we are wrong, and they are right, because we cannot defend ourselves. But we cannot claim to direct the faith of others, we cannot check the progress of what we account error, we cannot be secure (humanly speaking) against the weakness of our own hearts some future day, unless we have learned to analyze and to state formally our own reasons for believing what we do believe, and thus have fixed our creed in our memories and our judgments. This is the especial duty of Christian Ministers, who, as St. Paul in the Acts of the Apostles, must be ready to dispute, whether with Jews or Greeks. That we are at present very ill practised in this branch of our duty (a point it is scarcely necessary to prove), is owing in a very great measure to the protection and favour which has long been extended to the English clergy by the State. Statesmen have felt that it was their interest to maintain a Church, which absorbing into itself a great portion of the religious feeling of the country, sobers and chastens what it has so attracted, and suppresses by its weight the intractable elements which it cannot persuade; and, while preventing the political mischiefs resulting whether from fanaticism or self-will, is altogether free from those formidable qualities which distinguish the ecclesiastical genius of Rome. Thus the clergy have been in that peaceful condition in which the presence of the civil magistrate supersedes the necessity of the struggle for life and ascendency; and amid their privileges it is not wonderful that they should have grown secure, and have neglected to inform themselves on subjects on which they were not called to dispute. It must be added, too, that a feeling of the untenable nature of the Roman faith, a contempt for the arguments used in its support, and a notion that it could never prevail in an educated country, have not a little contributed to expose us to our present surprise.

In saying all this, the writer does not forget that there is still scattered about the Church much learning upon the subject of Romanism, and much intelligent opposition to it; nor, on the other hand, does the present undertaking, of which this Tract is the commencement, pretend to be more than an attempt towards a suitable consideration of it on the part of persons who feel in themselves, and see in others, a deficiency of information.

It will be the object, then, of these Tracts, should it be allowed the editor to fulfil his present intention, to consider variously, the *one* question, with which we are likely to be attacked—why, in matter of fact, we remain separate from Rome. Some general remarks on the line of argument hence resulting, will be the subject of this paper.

2.

Our position is this. We are seated at our own posts, engaged in our own work, secular or religious, interfering with no one, and anticipating no harm, when we hear of the encroachments of Romanism around us. We can but honour all good Roman Catholics for such aggression; it marks their earnestness, their confidence in their own cause, and their charity towards those whom they consider in error. We need not be bitter against them; moderation, and candour, are virtues under all circumstances. Yet, for all that, we may resist them manfully, when they assail us. This then, I say, is our position, a defensive one; we are assailed, and we defend ourselves and our flocks. There is no plea for calling on us in England to do more than this,—to defend ourselves. We are under no constraint to go out of our way spontaneously to prove charges against our opponents; but when asked about our faith, we give a reason why we are this way of thinking, and not that. This makes our task in the controversy incomparably easier, than if we were forced to exhibit an offensive front, or volunteer articles of impeachment against the rival communion. "Let every man abide in the same calling wherein he was called," is St. Paul's direction. We find ourselves under the Anglican regimen; let every one of us, cleric and layman, remain in it, till our opponents have shown cause why we should change, till we have reason to suspect we are wrong. The *onus probandi* plainly lies with them. This, I say, simplifies our argument, as allowing us to content ourselves with less of controversy than otherwise would be incumbent on us. We have the strength of possession and prescription. We are not obliged to prove them incurably corrupt and heretical; no, nor our own system unexceptionable. It is in our power, if we will, to take very low ground; it is quite enough to ascertain that reasons cannot be brought why we should go over from our side to theirs.

But besides this, there are the Apostle's injunctions against disorder. Did we go over to the Roman Catholics, we should be fomenting divisions among ourselves, which would be a *primâ facie* case against us. Of course there are cases where division is justifiable. Did we believe, for instance, the English Church to be absolutely heretical, and Romanism to be pure and Catholic, it would be a duty, as the lesser evil, to take part in a division which truth demanded. But otherwise it would be a sin. Those dissenters who consider union with the State to be apostasy, or the doctrine of baptismal regeneration a heresy, are wrong, not in that they separate from us, but in that they so think of baptismal regeneration or of religious establishments.

And further, a debt of gratitude to that particular branch of the Church Catholic through which God made us Christians, through which we were new born, instructed, and (if so be) ordained to the ministerial office; a debt of reverence and affection towards the saints of that Church; the tie of that invisible communion with the dead as well as the living, into which the Sacraments introduce us; the memory of our great teachers, champions, and confessors, now in Paradise, especially of those of the seventeenth century,—Hammond's name alone, were there no other, or Hooker's, or Ken's,—bind us to the English Church, by cords of love, except something very serious can be proved against it. But this surely is impossible. The only conceivable causes for leaving its communion are, I suppose, the two following; first, that it is involved in some damnable heresy; or secondly, that it is not in possession of the sacraments: and so far we join issue with the Romanist, for these are among the chief points which he attempts to prove against us.

3.

However, plain and satisfactory as is this account of our position, it is not sufficient, for various reasons, to meet the need of the multitude of men. The really pious and sober among our flocks will be contented with it. They will naturally express their suspicion and dislike of any doctrine new to them, and it will require some considerable body of proof to convince them that they ought even to open their ears to it. But it must be recollected, that there is a mass of persons, easily caught by novelty, who will be too impetuous to be restrained by such advice as has been suggested. Curiosity and feverishness of mind do not wait to decide on which side of a dispute the *onus probandi* lies. The same feelings which carry men now to dissent, will carry them to Romanism; novelty being an essential stimulant of popular devotion, and the Roman system, to say nothing of the intrinsic majesty and truth which remain in it amid its corruptions, abounding in this and other stimulants of a most potent and effective character. And further, there will ever be a number of refined and affectionate minds, who, disappointed in finding full matter for their devotional feelings in the English system, as at present conducted, betake themselves, through human frailty, to Rome. Besides, *ex parte* statements may easily suggest scruples even to the more sensible and sober portion of the community; and though they will not at all be moved ultimately from the principle above laid down, viz. not to change unless clear reason for change is assigned, yet they may fairly demand of their teachers and guides what they have to say in answer to these statements, which do seem to justify a change, not indeed at once, but in the event of their not being refuted.

Thus then we stand as regards Romanism. Strictly speaking, and in the eyes of soberly religious men, it ought not to be embraced, even could it be made appear in some points superior to (what is now practically) the Anglican system; St. Paul even advising a slave to remain a slave, though he had the option of liberty. If all men were rational, little indeed would be necessary in the way of argument, only so much as would be enough to set right the misconceptions which might arise on the subject in dispute. But the state of things being otherwise, we must consult for men as they are; and in order to meet their necessities, we are obliged to take a more energetic and striking line in the controversy than can in strict logic be required of us, to defend ourselves by an offensive warfare, and to expose our opponents' argument with a view of recommending our own.

4.

This being the state of the case, the arguments to be urged against our Roman opponents ought to be taken from such parts of the general controversy as bear most upon *practice*, and at the same time kept clear of what is more especially sacred, and painful to dispute about. Their assault on us will turn (it is to be presumed) on strictly practical considerations. They will admit that the English Church approaches in many points very near to themselves, and for that very reason was wrong in separating from them:—that it is in danger as being schismatical, even if not heretical:—that our LORD commanded and predicted that His Church should be one; therefore, that the Roman and the Anglican communions cannot both be His Church, but that one must be external to it;—that the question to be considered by us is, what our *chance* is of being the true Church; and, in consequence, of possessing the sacraments:—that we confess Rome to be a branch of CHRIST's Church, and admit her orders, but that Rome does not acknowledge us; hence that it is safer for us to unite to Rome:—that we are, in matter of fact, cut off from the great body of the Church Catholic, and stand by ourselves:—that we suffer all manner of schism and heresy to exist, and to propagate itself among us, which it is inconceivable that the true Church, guided by the HOLY SPIRIT, should ever do:—that this circumstance, if there were no other, being a patent fact, involves a *primâ facie* case against us, for the consideration of those who are not competent to decide in the matter of doctrine:—that if our creed were true, GOD would prosper us in maintaining it, according to the promise:—moreover, were there no other reason, that our forms of administering the sacraments are not such as to make us sure that we receive GOD's grace in them.

These and the like arguments, we may suppose, will be urged upon the attention of our members, being not of a technical and scholastic, but of a powerful practical character; and such must be ours to oppose them. Much might be said on this part of the subject. There are a number of arguments which are scarcely more than ingenious exhibitions, such as would be admired in any game where skill is everything, but which as arguments tell only with those of our own side, while an adversary thinks them unfair. Their use is not here denied in matter of fact, viz. in confirming those in an opinion, who already hold it, and wish reasons for it. When a man is (rightly or wrongly) of one particular way of thinking, he needs, and (it may be added) allowably needs, very little argument to support him in it to himself. Still it is right that that argument should be substantially sound; substantially, because for many reasons, certain accidental peculiarities in the form of it may be necessary for the peculiarities of his mind, which has been accustomed to move in some one line and not in another. If the argument is radically unreal, or (what may be called) rhetorical or sophistical, it may serve the purpose of encouraging those who are already convinced, though scarcely without doing mischief to them, but certainly it will offend and alienate the more acute and sensible; while those who are in doubt, and who desire some real and intelligible ground for their faith, will not bear to be put off with such shadows.

Thus, for instance, to meet the charge of scepticism, brought against us by Roman Catholics, because we do not believe this or that portion of their doctrine, an argument has been sustained by Protestants, in proof of the scepticism of the Roman system. Who does not see that, Romanism erring on the whole in superstition not in scepticism, this is an unreal argument, which will but offend doubting and distressed minds, as if they were played with; however plausibly and successfully it might be sustained in a trial of strength, and whatever justice there really may be in it? Nor is it becoming, over and above its inexpediency, to dispute for victory not for truth, and to be careless of the manner in which we urge conclusions, however sound and important.

Again, when it is said that the saints cannot hear our prayers, unless GOD reveal them to them; so that Almighty GOD, upon the Roman theory, conveys from us to them those requests which they are to ask back again of Him for us, we are certainly using an unreal, because an unscriptural argument, Moses on the Mount having the sin of his people first revealed to him by GOD, that he in turn might intercede with GOD for them. Indeed, it is through Him "in whom we live, and move, and have our being," that we are able even in this life to hear the requests of each other, and to present them to Him in prayer. Such an argument then, while shocking and profane to the feelings of a Roman Catholic, is shallow even in the judgment of a philosopher. Here again may be mentioned the unwarrantable application of texts, such as that of

John v. 39, "Search the Scriptures," in disproof of the Roman doctrine that the Apostles have handed down some necessary truths by Catholic Tradition; or again, Eccles. xi. 3, "If the tree fall towards the south, or towards the north, in the place where the tree falleth, there it shall be," as a palmary objection to Purgatory.

The arguments, then, which we use, must be such as are likely to convince serious and earnest minds, who are really seeking for the truth, not amusing themselves with intellectual combats, or desiring to support an existing opinion anyhow. However popular these latter methods may be, of however long standing, however easy both to find and to use, they are a scandal; and, while they lower our religious standard from the first, they are sure of hurting our cause in the end.

5.

But again, our arguments must not only be true and practical, but we must see that they are not abstract arguments and on abstract points. For instance, it will do us little good with the common run of men, in the question of the Pope's power, to draw the distinction, true though it is, between his primacy in honour and authority, and his sovereignty or his universal jurisdiction. The force of the distinction is not here questioned, but it will be unintelligible to minds unpractised in ecclesiastical history. Either the Bishop of Rome has really a claim upon our deference, or he has not; so it will be urged; and our safe argument in answer at the present day will lie in waiving the question altogether, and saying that, even if he has, according to the primitive rule, ever so much authority, (and that he has some, for instance the precedence of other bishops, need not be denied,) it is in matter of fact altogether suspended, and under abeyance, while he upholds a corrupt system, against which it is our duty to protest. At present all will see he ought to have no "jurisdiction, power, superiority, pre-eminence, or authority, within this realm." It will be time enough to settle his legitimate claims, and make distinctions, when he removes all existing impediments to our acknowledging him; it will be time enough to argue on this subject, after first deciding the other points of the controversy.

Again, the question of the Rule of Faith is an abstract one to men in general, till the progress of the controversy opens its bearings upon them. True, the intelligible argument of ultra-Protestantism may be taken, and we may say, "the Bible, and nothing but the Bible," but this is an unthankful rejection of another great gift, equally from GOD, such as no true Anglican can tolerate. If, on the other hand, we proceed to take the sounder view, that the Bible is the *record* of necessary truth, or of matters of faith, and the Church Catholic's tradition is the *interpreter* of it, then we are in danger of refined and intricate questions, which are uninteresting and uninfluential with the many. It is not till they are made to see that certain notable tenets of Romanism depend solely on the Apocrypha, or on Tradition, not on Scripture, that they will understand why the question of the Rule of Faith is an important one.

6.

It has been already said, that our arguments must also keep clear, as much as possible, of the subjects more especially sacred. This is our privilege in these latter days, if we duly understand it, that with all that is painful in our controversies, we are spared that distressing necessity which lay upon the early Church, of discussing questions relative to the Divine Nature. The doctrines of the Trinity and Incarnation form a most distressing subject of discussion for two reasons; first, as involving the direct contemplation of heavenly things, when one should wish to bow the head and be silent; next, as leading to arguments about things possible and impossible with GOD, that is (practically) to a rationalistic line of thought. How He is Three and yet One, how He could become man, what were the peculiarities of that union, how He could be everywhere as GOD, yet locally present as man, in what sense GOD could be said to suffer, die, and rise again,—all these questions were endured as a burden by the early Christians for our sake, who come after; and with the benefit of their victories over error, as if we had borne the burden and heat of the day, it were perverse indeed in us, to plunge into needless discussions of the same character.

This consideration will lead us to put into the background the controversy about the Holy Eucharist, which is almost certain to lead to profane and rationalistic thoughts in the minds of the many, and cannot well be discussed in words at all, without the sacrifice of " godly fear," while it is well-nigh anticipated by the ancient statements and the determinations of the Church concerning the Incarnation. It is true that learned men, such as Stillingfleet, have drawn lines of distinction between the doctrine of transubstantiation, and that high mystery; but the question is, whether they are so level to the intelligence of the many, as to secure the Anglican disputant from fostering irreverence, whether in himself or his hearers, if he ventures on such an argument. If transubstantiation must be opposed, it is in another way; by showing, as may well be done, and as Stillingfleet himself has done, that, in matter of fact, it was not the doctrine of the early Church, but an innovation at such or such a time; but this is a line of discussion which requires learning both to receive and to appreciate.

7.

In order to illustrate the above view, the following are selected by way of specimen of those *practical grievances*, to which Christians are subjected in the Roman Communion, and which should be put into the foreground in the controversy.

1. The denial of the cup to the laity. Considering the great importance of the Holy Eucharist to our salvation, this seems a very serious consideration for those who seek to be saved. Our LORD says, "Except ye eat the flesh of the SON of Man and drink His blood, ye have no life in you."[1] If it be recriminated, as it sometimes is, that we think it no risk to sprinkle instead of immersing in baptism, it is obvious to answer that we not only do not forbid, we enjoin immersion; that we only do not forbid sprinkling in the case of infants, and that the laity are defrauded, if defrauded, by their own fault, or the fault of the age, not the fault of the Church.

2. The necessity of the priest's intention to the validity of the Sacraments. The Church of Rome has determined, that a Sacrament does not confer grace unless the priest

---

[1] [Catholics believe that "totus Christus," our Lord in body and blood, in soul, in divinity, in all that is included in His Personality, is present at once whether in the consecrated Host or in the Chalice. Indeed, how else can His Presence be spiritual? He who partakes of either species receives Him in His whole human nature as well as in His Divine; but His whole humanity is not present, if His blood be absent. And in fact communion was received from the first in one species only; in Scripture, Acts ii. 42, xx. 7; it is recognized as a custom by St. Cyprian and St. Dionysius in the ante-Nicene era, as well as by St. Basil, St. Jerome, and others later. It is known to have been in use in Pontus, Egypt, Africa, and Lombardy during the same period; perhaps also in Spain and Syria afterwards. Again: communion of children was almost universal in primitive times; it is still the custom in the Greek, Russian, and Monophysite Churches: is it then a less innovation to deny infant communion, as Anglicans do, than to deny communion in both species?]

means it to do so; so that if he be an unbeliever, nay,[2] if he, from malice or other cause, withholds his intention, it is not a means of salvation. Now, considering what the Romanists themselves will admit, the great practical corruption of the Church at various times,—considering that infidels and profligates have been in the Papal Chair, and in other high stations,—who can answer, on the Church of Rome's own ground, that there is still preserved to it the Apostolical succession as conveyed in its sacrament of Orders? what individual can answer that he himself really receives, in the consecrated host, even that moiety of the great Christian blessing which alone remains to him in the Roman Communion?[3] *We* indeed believe, (and with comfort) that the administration of the Sacrament is effectual in those Churches, in spite of their undermining their own claim to the gift. Still let it be recollected, no one can become a Romanist without professing that the Church he has joined has no truer certainty of possessing it than that Communion has, which, probably on the very account of its uncertainty in this matter, he has deemed it right to abandon.

3. The necessity of Confession. By the Council of Trent, every member of the Church must confess himself to a

---

[2] [This is not so; an unbeliever can consecrate validly. St. Thomas says, " Non obstante infidelitate potest [minister] intendere facere id quod facit ecclesia, licet æstimet id nihil esse; et talis intentio sufficit ad sacramentum."]

[3] [This objection can be retorted on the Anglican doctrine of the Sacraments. A malicious Anglican minister might make a point of only wetting the child's cap with the baptismal water, or, from disbelief in baptismal regeneration, might use so little water that it was not even a sprinkling, or from a habit of hurry and carelessness might use the words only once over a circle of children, whom he sprinkled separately, or might drop or interpolate words in the form of ordination or consecration, from a conscientious scruple as to saying, "Receive the Holy Ghost. Whose sins ".&c. At least form and matter are necessary in the belief of Anglicans, though intention is not.]

priest once a year at least. This confession extends to all mortal sins, that is, to all sins which are done deliberately and are of any magnitude. Without this confession, (which of course must be accompanied by hearty sorrow for the things confessed), no one can be partaker of the Holy Communion. Here is a third obstacle[4] in the way of our receiving the grace of the Sacraments in the Roman Church, which surely requires our diligent examination, before it be passed over. That there is no such impediment sanctioned in Scripture, is plain, yet to believe in it is a point of faith with the Roman Catholic. The practice is grievous enough; but it is not enough to submit to it: you must believe that it is part of the Gospel doctrine, or you are committing one of those mortal sins which are to be confessed; and you must believe, moreover, that every one who does not believe it, is excluded from the hope of salvation. But, not to dwell on the belief in the necessity of confession itself, consider the number of points of faith which the Church of Rome has set up. You must believe every one of them; if you have allowed yourself to doubt any one of them, you must repent of it, and confess it to the priest. If you knowingly omit any one such doubts which you have entertained, and much more if you still cherish it, your confession is worse than useless; nay, such conduct is considered sacrilege, or the sin against the HOLY GHOST. Further, if under such circumstances you partake of the Communion, it is a partaking of it unworthily to your condemnation.

8.

4. The unwarranted anathemas of the Roman Church

---

[4] [Catholics would consider the want of confession to be the real "obstacle" to communion. As to "points of faith" they accept them all on the *ground* that the infallible Church proposes them. If we doubt some, why believe any? They all come on the same authority. Vide next note.]

is a subject to which the last head has led us. Here let us put aside, at present, the prejudice which has been excited in the minds of Protestants, against the principle itself of anathematizing, by the variety and comparative unimportance of the subjects upon which the Roman Church has applied it in practice. Let us consider merely the state of the case in that Church. Every Romanist is, by the creed of his Church, in mortal sin, unless he believes every one else excluded from Christian salvation, who, with means of knowing, declines any one of those points which have been ruled to be points of faith. If a man, for instance, who has had the means of instruction, doubts the Church's power of granting indulgences, he is exposed, according to the Romanists, to eternal ruin.[5] Now this consideration, one would think, ought to weigh with those of our own Church who may be half-converts to the Roman; not that our own salvation is not our first concern, but that such cruelty as this is, such narrowing the Scripture terms of salvation, (for no one can say this doctrine is found in Scripture,) is a presumption against the purity of that Church's teaching. But a further reflection may be added to the above. Such as have not had an opportunity of knowing the truth, are, it must be observed, *not* exposed to this condemnation. This at first sight would seem a comfort to those whose relatives and friends have died in Protestantism. But observe, the Church of Rome, we know, retains the practice of praying for the dead. It will be natural for a convert from Protestantism, first of all, to turn his thoughts towards

[5] [It is a fundamental doctrine of the Catholic Church that as to matters of Christian Faith she cannot err in her teaching. It follows at once that whoever denies anything she teaches, as her power to grant Indulgences, denies an article of faith, and necessarily falls under an anathema. Of course then no one can belong to the Church who rejects what the Church, the "pillar and ground of the Truth," professes to have received from heaven.]

those dearest relations, say his parents, who have lived and died in involuntary ignorance of Catholicism. He is not allowed to do so, he can only pray for the souls in *Purgatory;* none have the privilege of being in Purgatory but such as have died in the communion of the Roman Church, and his parents died in Protestantism.⁶

5. Purgatory may be mentioned as another grievous doctrine of Romanism.⁷ Here again, if Scripture, as interpreted by tradition, taught it, we should be bound to receive it; but, knowing as we do, that even St. Austin questioned the doctrine in the fifth century, we may well suspect the evidence for it. The doctrine is this; that a certain definite punishment is exacted by Almighty God for all sins committed after baptism; and that they who have not by sufferings in this life, whether trouble, penance, and the like, run through it, must complete it during the intermediate state in a place called Purgatory. Again, all who die in venial sin, that is in sins of infirmity, such as are short of mortal,

---

⁶ [This is not so. Those who die in invincible ignorance are not in the place of lost souls; those who are not lost, are either in purgatory or in heaven.]

⁷ [There is no doctrine of the Church which so practically and vividly brings home to the mind and engraves upon it the initial element of all true religion,—sense of sin original and actual, as an evil attaching to one and all,—as does Purgatory. As to the thought that friends departed have to endure suffering, our comfort is that we can pray them out of it; but that all, save specially perfect Christians, before they pass to heaven endure, with sensitiveness in proportion to their sins, the pain of fire, is testified by almost a *consensus* of the Fathers, as is shown in No. 79 of the *Tracts for the Times.* This certainly is the doctrine of Antiquity, whatever want of proof there may be for the exact Roman doctrine. Tertullian speaks of purification in a subterranean prison; Cyprian of a prison with fire; Origen, Basil, Gregory Nazianzen, Gregory Nyssen, Lactantius, Hilary, Ambrose, Paulinus, Jerome, Augustine, all speak of fire. These positive testimonies are not invalidated by other passages which speak generally of rest and peace following upon death to holy souls, which are expressions frequent also in the mouths of Catholics now, in spite of their offering masses for those very dead of whom they thus hopefully speak.]

go to Purgatory also. Now what a light does this throw upon the death of beloved and revered friends! Instead of their "resting from their labours," as Scripture says, there are (ordinarily speaking) none who have not to pass a time of trial and purification, and, as Romanists are authoritatively taught, in fire, or a torment analogous to fire. There is no one who can for himself look forward to death with hope and humble thankfulness. Tell the sufferer upon a sick-bed that his earthly pangs are to terminate in Purgatory, what comfort can he draw from religion? If it be said, that it is a comfort in the case of bad men, who have begun to repent on their death-bed; this is true, I do not deny it; still the doctrine, in accordance, be it observed, with the ultra-Protestantism of this age, evidently sacrifices the better part of the community to the less deserving. Should the foregoing reasoning seem to dwell too much on the question of comfortableness and uncomfortableness, not of truth, I reply, first, that I have already stated that Scripture, as interpreted by tradition, does not teach the doctrine; next, that I am arguing against the Romanists, who are accustomed to recommend their communion on the very ground of its being safer, more satisfactory, and more comfortable.[8]

6. The Invocation of Saints. Here again the *practice* should be considered, not the *theory*. Scripture speaks clearly and solemnly about CHRIST as the sole Mediator.[9]

[8] [Here comes in the consolation afforded by the doctrine of Indulgences. Catholics believe that, by their own prayers, works, &c., in their lifetime, as appointed by the Church, and by their friends' prayers for them after their death, their just measure of Purgatory may be shortened or superseded.]

[9] [Our Lord bore the sins of the world: in that work of power and mercy, which is distinct from and above any other, He is the sole mediator, and whatever intercessory power the Saints have is from and in Him. If through gross ignorance this is or has been here or there forgotten, it is not the fault of the Church, which has ever taught it, but of the perversity of human nature.]

When prayer to the Saints is recommended *at all times and places*, as ever-present guardians, and their good works pleaded in GOD's sight, is not this such an infringement upon the plain word of GOD, such a violation of our allegiance to our only SAVIOUR, as must needs be an insult to Him? His honour He will not give to another. Can we with a safe conscience do it? Should we act thus in a parallel case even with an earthly friend? Does not St. John's example warn us against falling down before angels?[1] Does not St. Paul warn us against a voluntary humility and worshipping of angels? And are not these texts *indications* of GOD's will, which ought to guide our conduct? Is it not *safest* not to pay them this extraordinary honour?

7. The Worship of Images might here be added to these instances of grievances which Christians endure in the Communion of Rome, were it not that in England its rulers seem, at present, to have suspended the practice out of policy, though it is expressly recommended by the Council of Trent, as if an edifying usage. In consequence of this decree of the Church, no one can become a Roman-

---

[1] [I do not deny that the passage in the Apocalypse, xix. 10, xxii. 8, presents a difficulty when compared with Catholic tradition and practice. I should explain it thus:—In the Old Testament, the angel sometimes appears by himself as a messenger from God and then receives homage as such; sometimes he is the manifestation of a Divine Presence and thus becomes relatively an object of worship. The angel in Judg. ii. 1, was a messenger, so was the angel in Dan. x. 5; but the angels in Exod. iii. 2, Acts vii. 30, Josh. v. 13, Judg. vi. 11 and xiii. 3, were the attendants upon God. In the last three passages the manifestation is first of the angel, then of the Lord of angels. First it was an angel that appeared to Gideon, then "the Lord *looked upon* him," on which, recognizing the Divine Presence, he offered sacrifice. So Joshua first addressed the angel, but the words " Loose thy shoes," &c., told him who was there, and were equivalent in doctrine to "See thou do it not. Worship God" in the Apocalypse. This is pretty much St. Augustine's explanation of the difficulty. St. John mistook a messenger or servant of God for a Theophany.]

ist, without implying his belief that the usage is edifying and right; and this itself is a grievance, even though the usage be in this or that place dispensed with.²

9.

Such and such-like are the subjects which, it is conceived, should be brought into controversy, in disputing with Roman Catholics at the present day. An equally important question remains to be discussed; viz. What the informants are, which are to determine our judgment of Popery? Here its partisans complain of their opponents, that, instead of referring to the authoritative documents of the Roman Church, they avail themselves of any errors or excesses of individuals in it, as if the Church were responsible for acts and opinions which it does not enjoin. Thus the legends of relics, superstitions about images, the cruelty of particular prelates or kings, or the accidental fury of a populace, are unfairly imputed to the Church itself. Again, the profligacy of the Popes, at various periods, is made an argument against their religious pretensions as successors to St. Peter; whereas, they argue, Caiaphas himself had the gift of prophecy, and it is, they say, a memorable and instructive circumstance, that in matter of fact, among their worst popes are found the instruments, in God's hand, of some of the most important and salutary acts of the Church. Accordingly they claim to be judged by their formal documents, especially by the decrees of the Council of Trent.³

Now here we shall find the truth to lie between the two contending parties. Candour will oblige us to grant that

---

² [Very large numbers of men, whom no one would accuse of superstitiously confusing the Divine Object with the Image, still testify of themselves, that they pray much better with a carved or painted representative before them than without one.]

³ [On this subject, vid. Preface to the first volume of this Edition.]

the mere acts of individuals should not be imputed to the body; certainly no member of the English Church can in common prudence, as well as propriety, do otherwise, since he is exposed to an immediate retort, in consequence of the errors and irregularities which have in Protestant times occurred among ourselves. King Henry the VIIIth, the first promoter of the Reformation, is surely no representative of our faith or feelings; nor Hoadley, in a later age, who was suffered to enjoy his episcopate for forty-six years; to say nothing of the various parties and schools which have existed, and do exist among us.

So much then must be granted to our opponents; yet not so much as they themselves desire. For though the acts of individuals are not the acts of the Church, yet they may be the results, and therefore illustrations of its principles.[4] We cannot consent then to confine ourselves to a mere reference to the text of the Tridentine decrees, as Romanists would have us, apart from the teaching of their doctors and the practice of the Church, which are surely the legitimate comment upon them. The case stands as follows. A certain system of teaching and practice has existed in the churches of the Roman communion for many centuries; this system was discriminated and fixed in all its outlines at the Council of Trent. It is therefore not unnatural, or rather it is the procedure we adopt in any historical research, to take the general opinions and conduct of the Church in elucidation of their Synodal decrees; just as we take the tradition of the Church Catholic and Apostolic as the legitimate interpreter of Scripture, or of the Apostles' Creed. On the other hand, it is as natural that these decrees, being necessarily concise and guarded, should be much less objectionable than

---

[4] [Yes, of its principles; but in the following sentences, the popular practices are made, not illustrations of its principles, but comments and interpretations of its doctrines, which is another matter.]

the actual system they represent. It is not wonderful, then, yet it is unreasonable, that Romanists should protest against our going beyond these decrees in adducing evidence of their Church's doctrine, on the ground that nothing more than an assent to them is requisite for communion with her. For instance, the Creed of Pope Pius, which is framed from the Tridentine decrees, and is the Roman Creed of Communion, only says " I firmly hold there is a Purgatory, and that souls therein detained are aided by the prayers of the faithful," nothing being said of its being a place of punishment, nothing, or all but nothing, which does not admit of being explained of merely an intermediate state. Now supposing we found ourselves in the Roman Communion, of course it would be a great relief to find that we were not bound to believe more than this vague statement, nor should we (I conceive) on account of the received interpretation about Purgatory superadded to it, be obliged to leave our Church. But it is another matter entirely, whether we who are external to that Church, are not bound to consider it as one whole system, written and unwritten, defined indeed and adjusted by general statements, but not limited to them or coincident with them.

10.

The conduct of the Catholics during the troubles of Arianism affords us a parallel case, and a direction in this question. The Arian Creeds were often quite unexceptionable, differing from the orthodox only in this, that they omitted the celebrated word *homoüsion*, and in consequence did not obviate the possibility of that perverse explanation of them, which in fact their framers adopted. Why then did the Catholics refuse to subscribe them? Why did they rather submit to banishment from one end of the Roman world to the other? Why did they become confessors and martyrs? The answer is ready. They interpreted the language of the creeds by the professed opinions of their framers. They would not allow error to be introduced into the Church by an artifice. On the other hand, when at Ariminum they were seduced into a subscription of one of these creeds, though unobjectionable in its wording, their opponents instantly triumphed, and circulated the news that the Catholic world had come over to their opinion. It may be added that, in consequence, ever since that era, phrases have been banished from the language of theology which heretofore had been innocently used by orthodox teachers.

Apply this to the case of Romanism. We are not indeed allowed to take at random the accidental doctrine or practice of this or that age, as an explanation of the decrees of the Latin Church; but when we see clearly that certain of these decrees have a natural tendency to produce certain evils, when we see those evils actually existing far and wide in that Church, in different nations and ages, existing especially where the system is allowed to act most freely, and only absent where external checks are present,* sanctioned moreover by its celebrated teachers and expositors, and advocated by its controversialists with the tacit consent of the whole body, under such circumstances surely it is not unfair to consider our case parallel to that of the Catholics during the ascendency of Arianism.

* [There are truths, which in the popular mind, taking men as they are, unavoidably pass into error, or what Protestants call corruption. It is not "that corrupt Church" (as they speak of us) that is in fault, but our corrupt nature. And the higher and more effective the truth, the greater is the chance of excess and perversion. So much so that faith is hardly real in a population, if it does not in fact involve a large percentage of superstition. In like manner, according to the teaching of Evangelical Protestants, a correct life may be expected as a matter of course to be attended by "self-righteousness." And so the exercise of reason incurs the risk of rationalism. Yet reason, correctness of life, and faith are gifts of God.]

Surely it is not unfair in such a case to interpret the formal document of belief by the realized form of it in the Church, and to apprehend that, did we express our assent to the creed of Pope Pius, we should find ourselves bound hand and foot, as the fathers at Ariminum, to the corruptions of those who profess it.

What seems to be a small deviation from correctness in the abstract system, becomes considerable and serious when it assumes a substantive form. This is especially the case with all doctrinal discussions, in which the undeveloped germs of many diversities of practice and moral character lie thick together and in small compass, and as if promiscuously and without essential differences. The highest truths differ from the most miserable delusions by what appears to be a few words or letters. The discriminating mark of orthodoxy, the *Homoüsion*, has before now been ridiculed, however irrationally, as being identical, all but the letter *i*, with the heretical symbol of the *Homœusion*. What is acknowledged in the Arian controversy, must be endured without surprise in the Roman, in whatever degree it occurs. We may be taunted as differing from the Romanists only in phrases and modes of expression; and we may be taunted, or despised, according to the fate of our Divines for three centuries past, as taking a middle, timid, unsatisfactory ground, neither quite agreeing nor quite disagreeing with our opponents. We may be charged with dwelling on trifles and niceties, in a way inconsistent with plain, manly good sense; but in truth it is not we who are the speculatists, and unpractical controversialists, but they who forget that " hæ nugæ seria ducunt in mala."

But again there is another reason, peculiar to the Roman controversy, which occasions a want of correspondence between the appearance presented by the Roman theology in theory, and its appearance in practice. The separate doctrines of Romanism are very different, in position, importance, and mutual relation, in the abstract, and when developed, applied, and practised. Anatomists tell us that the skeletons of the most various animals are formed on the same type; yet the animals are dissimilar and distinct, in consequence of the respective differences of their developed proportions. No one would confuse between a lion and a bear; yet many of us at first sight would be unable to discriminate between their respective skeletons. Romanism in the theory may differ little from our own creed; nay, in the abstract type, it might even be identical, and yet in the actual framework, and still further in the living and breathing form, it might differ essentially. For instance, the doctrine of Indulgences is in the theory entirely connected with the doctrine of Penance; that is, it has relation solely to this world, so much so that Roman apologists sometimes speak of it without even an allusion to its bearings elsewhere: but we know that in practice it is mainly, if not altogether, concerned with the next world,—with the alleviation of sufferings in Purgatory.

11.

Take again the instances of the Adoration of Images and the Invocation of Saints. The Tridentine Decree declares that it is good and useful suppliantly to invoke the Saints, and that the Images of CHRIST, and the Blessed Virgin, and the other Saints should "receive due honour and veneration;" words, which themselves go to the very verge of what could be received by the cautious Christian, though possibly admitting of a good interpretation. Now we know in matter of fact that in various parts of the Roman Church, a worship approaching to idolatrous is actually paid to Saints and Images, in countries very different from each other, as for instance, Italy and the Netherlands, and has been countenanced by eminent men and doctors, and that without any serious or successful protest from any quarter:⁶ further that, though there may be countries where no scandal of the kind exists, yet these are such as have, in their neighbourhood to Protestantism, a practical restraint upon the natural tendency of their system.

Moreover, the silence which has been observed, age after age, by the Roman Church, as regards these excesses, is a point deserving of serious attention;—for two reasons; first, because of the very solemn warnings pronounced by our Lord and His Apostle, against those who introduce scandals into the Church, warnings, which seem almost prophetic of such as exist in the Latin branches of it. Next, it must be considered that the Roman Church has had the power to denounce and extirpate them.⁷ Not to mention its use of its Apostolical powers in other matters, it has had the civil power at its command, as it has shown in the case of errors which less called for its interference; all of which is a proof that it has not felt sensitively on the subject of this particular evil.

12.

This may be suitably illustrated by an example. Wake, in his controversy on the subject of Bossuet's Exposition, observes that a Jesuit named Crasset had published an account of the worship due to the Virgin Mary, quite opposed to that which Bossuet had expounded as the doctrine of the Roman Church. Bossuet replies, " I have not read the book, but neither did I ever hear it mentioned there was anything in it contrary to mine, and that

⁶ [I reply *either* it is an exaggeration to say that the worship is idolatrous, *or* a misstatement to say that there has been no restraint or hindrance put upon it.]

⁷ [This charge is considered in the Preface to Volume I.]

Father would be much troubled if I should think there was." Wake, in answer, expresses his great surprise that Bossuet should not have heard any mention of a fact so notorious. Bossuet replies, "I still continue to say that I have never read Father Crasset's book which they bring against me." "I will only add here," he continues," that Father Crasset himself, troubled and offended that any one should report his doctrine to be different from mine, has made complaints to me; and in a preface to the second edition of his book, has declared, that he varied in nothing from me, unless perhaps in the manner of expression; which, whether it be so or no, I leave them to examine, who will please to give themselves the trouble."

Bossuet is known as the champion of a more moderate exposition of the doctrines of Romanism than that which has generally been put upon them. Now he either did agree with the Jesuit or he did not. If he did, not a word more need be said against the Roman doctrine, as will appear when I proceed to quote his words; if he did not, let the reader judge of the peculiar sensitiveness of a faith, (as illustrated in a prelate, who for his high qualities is a very fair representative of his church,) which can anathematize a denial of Purgatory, or a disapproval of the Invocation of Saints, yet can pass *sub silentio* a class of profanities, of which the following extracts are an instance.[8]

It must be first observed, that Father Crasset's book is an answer to a Cologne Tract entitled "Salutary Advertisements of the Blessed Virgin to her indiscreet Adorers;" which is said by Wáke, truly or not, (for this is nothing

[8] [There is a large private judgment allowed to individuals in the Church of Rome, and that very fact leads humble and charitable minds, while they profit by the toleration allowed to themselves, not to censure those who avail themselves of it for a different tone of religious sentiment. Much more would a great Prelate like Bossuet, whose words fall upon the world with great weight, be cautious of dealing side-blows on his friends and brethren.]

to the purpose,) to agree with Bossuet in its exposition of doctrine. This Tract was sent into the world with the approbation of the Suffragan Bishop of Cologne, of the Vicar-general, the Censure of Ghent, the Canons and Divines of Mechlin, the University of Louvain, and the Bishop of Tournay. Father Crasset's answer was printed at Paris, licensed by the Provincial, approved by three fathers of the Jesuit body appointed to examine it, and authorized by the King. I mention these circumstances to show that this controversy was not conducted in a corner; to which I may add that, according to Crasset, learned men of various nations had also written against the Tract, that the Holy See had condemned the author, and that Spain had prohibited him and his work from its dominions. We have nothing to do with the doctrine of this Tract, good or bad, but let us see what this Crasset's doctrine is on the other hand, thus put forth by the Jesuits in a notorious controversy, and accepted on hearsay by Bossuet with a studious abstinence from the perusal of it after the matter of it had been brought before him.

"Whether a Christian that is devout towards the blessed Virgin can be damned? *Answer.* The servants of the blessed Virgin have an assurance, morally infallible, that they shall be saved."[9]

---

[9] [It does not fall into my purpose to explain and thereby to defend these statements. In fact they could all be explained. E.g., when it was said that "the Blessed Virgin's servants have an assurance that they shall be saved," this was not meant to deny that her "servants" must love God and believe the Creed, live good lives and die holy deaths in order to deserve that title, or that "without holiness no one shall see God." Moreover, in order to belong to her confraternity, which Crasset speaks of, over and above the duties of a good Christian, it was necessary to recite every day the office of our Lady or that of the Church, or, if a man could not read, devotions instead of them, and to abstain on Wednesday, Friday, and Saturday. As to our Lady's "motherly authority," *vid. infr.* p. 128, &c.]

"Whether God ever refuses anything to the blessed Virgin? *Answer.* 1. The Prayers of a Mother so humble and respectful are esteemed a command by a Son so sweet and so obedient. 2. Being truly our Saviour's mother, as well in heaven as she was on earth, she still retains a kind of natural authority over His person, over His goods, and over His omnipotence; so that, as Albertus Magnus says, she can not only entreat Him for the salvation of her servants, but by her motherly authority can command Him; and as another expresses it, the power of the Mother and of the Son is all one, she being by her omnipotent Son made herself omnipotent.

"Whether the blessed Virgin has ever fetched any out of hell? *Answer.* 1. As to purgatory, it is certain that the Virgin has brought several souls from thence, as well as refreshed them whilst they were there. 2. It is certain she has fetched many out of hell: i. e. from a state of damnation before they were dead. 3. The Virgin can, and has fetched men that were dead in mortal sin out of hell, by restoring them to life again, that they might repent. . . .

"The practice of devotion towards her. 1. To wear her scapulary; which whoso does shall not be damned, but this habit shall be for them a mark of salvation, a safeguard in dangers, and a sign of peace and eternal alliance. They that wear this habit, shall be moreover delivered out of Purgatory the Saturday after their death. 2. To enter her congregation. And if any man be minded to save himself, it is impossible for him to find out any more advantageous means, than to enrol himself into these companies. 3. To devote oneself more immediately to her service," &c. &c.

"Woe unto the world because of offences! for it must needs be that offences come, but woe to that man by whom the offence cometh!"

13.

Bossuet's name has been mentioned in evidence of the really existing connection between the decrees of Trent and the popular opinions and practices in the Roman Church, as regards the matters they treat of. But the labours of that celebrated prelate in the cause of his Church introduce us to very varied and extensive illustrations of another remark which has been incidentally made in the course of this discussion.

It was observed, that the legitimate meaning of the Tridentine decrees might be fairly ascertained by comparing together those of the Latin Churches, where the system was allowed to operate freely, and those in which the presence of Protestantism acted as a check upon it. This has been remarkably exemplified in the history of the controversy during the last one hundred and fifty years, that is, since the time of Bossuet, who seems to have been nearly the first who put on the Tridentine decrees a meaning more consonant with Primitive Christianity, distinguishing between the doctrines of the Church, and of the Schools. This new interpretation has been widely adopted by the Romanists, and, as far as our own islands are concerned, may be considered to be the received version of their creed; and one should rejoice in any appearance of amelioration in their system, were not the present state of Italy and Spain, where no check exists, an evidence what that system still is, and what, in course of time, it would, in all probability, be among ourselves, did an universal reception of it put an end to the restraint which controversy at present imposes on them.[1]

Bossuet's Exposition, which contains the modified doctrine above spoken of, was looked at with great suspicion at Rome, on its first appearance, and was with difficulty acknowledged by the Pope. It is said to have been written originally with the purpose of satisfying Marshal Turenne, who became, in consequence, a convert to Romanism. It was circulated in manuscript several years, and was considered to be of so liberal a complexion,

---

[1] [According to what has been said above, I allow this, (*exceptis excipiendis,*) with the substitution for "where no check exists," of "where the Catholic Creed has got hold of the popular mind."]

according to the doctrine of that day, as to scandalize persons of the author's own communion, and to lead Protestants to doubt whether he dare ever own it. In the year 1671, it was, with considerable alterations, committed to the press with the formal approbation of the Archbishop of Rheims and nine other Bishops, but on objections being urged against it by the Sorbonne, the press was stopped, and not till after various alterations was it resumed, with the suppression of the copies which had already been struck off. It is affirmed by Wake, without contradiction (I believe) from his opponents, that even with these corrections it was of so novel an appearance to the Roman divines of that day, that an answer from one of them was written to it, before the Protestants began to move in the matter, though the publication was suppressed. The Roman See at last accorded its approbation, but not before the conversions which it effected had recommended it to its favour.[2]

14.

It may be instructive to specify some instances of this change of doctrine, or novel interpretation of doctrine (if it must be so called), which Bossuet is accused of introducing.

1. In the private impression of his Exposition, as the

[2] Nine years intervened between its publication and the Pope's approval of it. Clement X. refused it absolutely. Several priests were rigorously treated for preaching the doctrine contained in it; the university of Louvain formally condemned it in 1685. Vid. Mosheim, Hist. vol. v. p. 126, note. [This is from Maclaine, who in a matter of this kind is not always trustworthy. The Biographie Univ. says, " Bossuet l'imprima à peu d'exemplaires, le distribua aux évêques de France, en leur demandant leur observations, et après en avoir fait usage, l'ouvrage fut rendu public. C'est ce qui a donné lieu au bruit répandu par les Protestants, que Bossuet avait été obligé de retirer et de changer sa première édition. L'ouvrage fut hautement approuvé à Rome."]

suppressed portion of the edition may be called,[3] Bossuet says,—

"Furthermore, there is nothing so unjust as to accuse the Church of placing all her piety in these devotions to the Saints: *since on the contrary she lays no obligation at all on particular persons to join in this practice.* . . . . By which it appears clearly that the Church condemns only those who refuse it *out of contempt, or by a spirit of dissension and revolt.*"

In the second or published edition, the words printed in italics were omitted, the first clause altogether, and the second with the substitution of "*out of disrespect or error.*"

2. Again, in the private impression he had said,—

"So that it (the Mass) *may very reasonably be called a sacrifice.*"

He raised his doctrine in the second as follows:—

"So that *there is nothing wanting to make it a true sacrifice.*"

In giving these instances, I am far from insinuating that there is any unfairness in such alterations. Earnestly desiring the conversion of Protestants, Bossuet did but attempt to place the doctrines of his Church in the light most acceptable to them. But they seem to show thus much: first, that he was engaged in a novel experiment, which circumstances rendered necessary, and was trying how far he might safely go; secondly, that he did not carry with him the body of the Gallican divines. In other words, we have no security that this new form[4] of Romanism is more stable than one of the many forms of Protestantism

---

[3] [This is an unfair insinuation. The impression *was* private, and, as never intended for publication, was never "suppressed." What theologian, before publishing on an important subject, but would offer his writing to tohers for corrections?]

[4] [Not a new form, but a permanent aspect.]

which rise and fall around us in our own country, which are matters of opinion, and depend upon individuals.

15.

3. But again, after all the care bestowed on his work, Bossuet says, in his Exposition as ultimately published,—

"When the Church pays an honour to the Image of an Apostle or Martyr, the intention is not so much to honour the image, as to honour the apostle or martyr in the presence of the image. . . . . Nor do we attribute to them *any other virtue* but that of *exciting in us the remembrance* of those they represent," p. 8.[5]

To this the Vindicator of Bossuet adds,

"The use we make of images or pictures is purely as *representatives*, or memorative signs, which call the originals to our remembrance," p. 35.

Now with these passages contrast the words of Bellarmine, who, if any one, might be supposed a trustworthy interpreter of the Roman doctrine.

"The images of CHRIST and of the saints are to be venerated *not only by accident and improperly, but properly and by themselves*, so that *they themselves are the end of the veneration* [ut ipsæ terminent venerationem] as considered in themselves, and *not only as they are copies*." De Imagin. lib. ii. c. 21.

Again, in the Pontifical we are instructed that to the wood of the Cross "divine worship (*latria*) is due;"[6] and

---

[5] [The Tridentine definition says, "The images of Christ, the Virgin Mother of God, and of other saints are to be retained especially in churches, and due honour and veneration paid them, *not* because we believe that there is in them any divinity or virtue, on account of which they are to have observance, or because of them anything is to be asked, or because any trust is to be placed in images, as of old was the custom of the heathen, who in idols put their hope, but because the honour, which is shown to them, is referred to the prototypes, whom they represent."]

[6] [Vid. Pontif. Rom. p. 713, Mechl. 1845, Ord. ad recipiendum Imp. On the contrary, the Seventh General Council says distinctly that *latria*, divine

that saving virtues for soul and body proceed from it; which surely agrees with the doctrine of Bellarmine as contained in the above extract, not with that of Bossuet.

4. The Vindicator of Bossuet speaks of the Mass to the following effect:—

"The council tells us it was instituted *only to represent* that which was accomplished on the Cross, to perpetuate the memory of it to the end of the world, and apply to us the saving virtue of it, for those sins which we commit every day. . . . . When we say that CHRIST is offered in the Mass, we do not understand the word *offer* in the strictest sense, but *as we are said to offer to God what we present before Him*. And thus the Church does not doubt to say, that she offers up our Blessed JESUS to His FATHER in the Eucharist, in which He vouchsafes to render Himself present before Him."

But the Tridentine Fathers say in their Canons, that

"The Mass is a true and proper sacrifice; a sacrifice *not only commemoratory of that of the Cross*, but also truly and properly propitiatory for the dead and the living."[7]

And Bellarmine says,—

"A true and real sacrifice requires a true and real death or destruction of the thing sacrificed." De Missâ, lib. i. c. 27.

---

worship, is *not* to be paid to the Cross, and, as Bellarmine adds, the Eighth Council and Pope Hadrian say the same. It is true that Hales, St. Thomas, Caietan, and others, like the Pontificale, claim for the Cross, *latria;* but 1. Bellarmine considers they had never seen these authoritative decisions; and, 2. that they must have intended *latria* only *impropriè* and *per accidens*, that is, as in our House of Lords obeisance is made to the empty Throne, or the lectica or catafalk is incensed, though the corpse is not present.

Bellarmine's view is, that a real and direct veneration is to be paid to the Crucifix, as being blest and sacred, and also through it an indirect worship to our Lord; just as an alms, given to a poor man, is primarily given to the object of charity, but still for the honour and glory of Him who has identified Himself with His poorest members.]

[7] [Our Lord suffered once for all upon the Cross, yet still even now, when He is "on the throne of majesty in the heavens," He has "somewhat to offer, viz. that same precious Flesh and Blood, which once for all was offered on Calvary. Thus, as His present offering of His crucified body is one with His offering on Calvary, being its continuation, reiteration, presentation, or commemoration, so is it with the Mass.]

And then he proceeds to show how this condition of the notion of a sacrifice is variously fulfilled in the Mass.

16.

Leaving Bossuet, let us now turn to the history of the controversy in our own country, whether in former or recent times; and here I avail myself of an article of a late lamented Prelate[8] of our Church, in a periodical work ten years since.[9] As to the particular instances adduced, it must be recollected that they are not dwelt on as a sufficient evidence by themselves of that difference of view between members of the Roman Church at various times and places, which is under consideration, but as lively illustrations of what is presumed to be an historical fact.

The following extract is from Dr. Doyle's Evidence before the Committee of the House of Commons on the subject of the Roman Catholic doctrine:—

"The Committee find, in a treatise called 'A Vindication of the Roman Catholics,' the following curse: 'Cursed is every goddess worshipper, that believes the Virgin Mary to be any more than a creature, that honours her, worships her, or puts his trust in her more than in GOD; that honours her above her SON, or believes that she can in any way command Him.' Is that acknowledged? *Ans.* That is acknowledged; and every Roman Catholic in the world would say with Gother, Accursed be such person."

Such is the received Romanism of the English Papists at this day; and accordingly Dr. Challoner has translated the famous words in the office of the blessed Virgin,—

"Monstra te esse Matrem,
Sumat per te preces,"

---

[8] [Charles Lloyd, Bishop of Oxford, 1827—1829.]
[9] British Critic, Oct. 1825.

by

> " Exert the *Mother's* care,
> And us *thy children* own,
> To Him convey our prayer," &c.

On the other hand consider the following passage in the controversy between Jewell and Harding. Jewell accused the Roman Church with teaching that the blessed Virgin could command her SON. Harding replies as follows:—

> " If now any spiritual man, such as St. Bernard was, deeply considering the great honour and dignity of CHRIST's mother, do in excess of mind spiritually sport with her, bidding her to remember that she is a Mother, and that *thereby she has a certain right to command* her SON, and require, in a most sweet manner, that she use her right; is this either impiously or impudently spoken? Is not he, rather, most impious and impudent that findeth fault therewith?"[1]

Again, we find in Peter Damiani, a celebrated divine of the eleventh century, the following words:—

> " She approaches to that golden tribunal of divine Majesty, not asking, but commanding, not a handmaid, but a mistress."[2]

---

[1] [The words " Command thy Son " may bear a good sense, as being used in reference to Luke ii. 51; but a Decree of Inquisition of February 28, 1875, has animadverted on them. After reprehending the title " Queen of the Heart of Jesus," used by a certain pious Sodality, the Decree goes on to observe that the Sacred Congregation has before now " warned and reprehended " those who by such language " have not conformed to the right Catholic sense," but " ascribe power to her, as issuing from her divine maternity, beyond its due limits," and that " although she has the greatest influence with her Son, still it cannot be piously affirmed that she exercises command over Him."]

[2] [Prosa quam Dallæus allegat, ut invidiam faciat Catholicis, quasi B. Virginem Filio imperare putemus ad Patris dexteram sedenti, non est ab Ecclesiâ probata, et quibusdam tantum Missalibus olim inserta fuit; quamvis innoxius esset iste loquendi modus, " Jure Matris impera Redemptori," quemadmodum . . . Scriptura ait, " Deum obedisse voci hominis," quando orante Josue sol stet. . . . Hoc sensu B. Petrus Damianus, &c. Natal. Alex. Hist. Sæc. v. Diss. 25. Art. 2. Prop. 2.]

Albertus Magnus in like manner,—

"Mary prays as a daughter, requests as a sister, commands as a mother."

Another writer says,—

"The blessed Virgin, for the salvation of her supplicants, can, not only supplicate her Son, as other saints do, but also by her maternal authority command her Son. Therefore the Church prays, 'Monstra te esse Matrem;' as if saying to the Virgin, Supplicate for us after the manner of a command, and with a mother's authority."

After these instances, the article from which I cite asks, not unreasonably, "Upon whom does the anathema of Gother fall?"

17.

Enough, perhaps, has now been said on the mode in which it is expedient at the present day to carry on the controversy with Romanism,—which of its doctrines are to be selected for attack, what authorities are to be used in ascertaining them, and what arguments are to be employed against them. Some remarks shall be added before concluding, as to the best mode of conducting the defence of our own Church.

Let it be observed that, in our argument with the Romanists, we might, if needful, be very liberal in our confessions about ourselves, without at all embarrassing our position in consequence. While we are able to maintain the claim of our clergy to the ministration of the Sacraments, and our freedom from any deadly heresy, we have nothing to fear from any historical disclosures which the envy of adversaries might contrive against our Church, or from any external appearances which it may present at this day to the superficial observer. Whatever may be the past mistakes of individual members of it, or the tyranny of aliens over it, or its accidental connection with Protestant persuasions, still these hinder not its having "the ministration of the Word and Sacraments;" and having them, it has sufficient claims on our filial devotion and love. This being understood, then, the following remarks are made with a view of showing *how far*, if necessary, we may safely go in our admissions.

We may grant in the argument that the English Church has committed mistakes in the practical working of its system; nay, is *incomplete,* even in its formal doctrine and discipline. We require no enemy to show us the probability of this, seeing that her own Article expressly states that the primitive Churches of Antioch and Alexandria, as well as that of Rome, have erred, " not only in their living and manner of ceremonies, but also in matters of faith." Much more is a Church exposed to imperfection, which embraces but a narrow portion of the Catholic territory, has been at the distance of 1500 to 1800 years from the pure fountains of tradition, and is surrounded by political influences of a highly malignant character.

18.

Again, the remark may seem paradoxical at first sight, yet surely it is just, that the English Church is, for certain, deficient in particulars, because it does not profess itself infallible. I mean as follows. Every thoughtful mind must at times have been beset by the following doubt: "*How is it* that the particular Christian body to which I belong *happens* to be the right one? I hear every one about me saying *his own* society is alone right, and others wrong: is not each one of us as much justified in saying so as every one else? is not any one as much justified as I am? In other words, the truth is surely nowhere to be found pure, unadulterate and entire, but is shared through the world, each Christian body having a portion of it, none the whole of it." A certain liberalism is commonly the fruit of this perplexity. Men are led on to gratify the pride of human nature, by standing aloof from all systems, forming a truth for themselves, and countenancing this or that body of Christians according as each maintains portions of that which they themselves have already assumed to be the truth. Now the primitive Church answered this question, by appealing to the simple fact, that all the Apostolic Churches all over the world did agree together. True, there were sects in every country, but they bore their own refutation on their forehead, in that they were of recent origin; whereas all those societies in every country, which the Apostles had founded, did agree together in one, and no time short of the Apostles' could be assigned, with any show of argument, for the rise of their existing doctrine. This doctrine in which they agreed was accordingly called *Catholic* truth, and there was plainly no room at all for asking, "Why should my own Church be more true than another's?"—But at this day, it need not be said, such an evidence is lost, except as regards the articles of the Creed. It is a very great mercy that the Church Catholic all over the world, as descended from the Apostles, does at this day speak one and the same doctrine about the Trinity and Incarnation, as it has always spoken it, excepting in one single point, which rather *probat regulam* than interferes with it, viz. as to the procession of the HOLY GHOST from the SON. With this solitary exception, we have the certainty of possessing the entire truth as regards the high theological doctrines, by an argument which supersedes the necessity of arguing from Scripture against those who oppose them. It is quite impossible that all countries should have agreed to that which was not Apostolic. They are a number of concordant witnesses to certain definite truths, and while their testimony is one and the same from the very first moment they publicly utter it, so, on the other hand, if there be bodies which speak otherwise, we can show historically that they rose later than the Apostles.

This majestic evidence, however, only avails for the articles of the Creed, especially the Trinity and Incarnation. The primitive Church was never called upon, whether in Council or by its divines, to pronounce upon other points of faith, and the later Church has differed about them; especially about those on which the contest turns between Romanism and ourselves. Here neither Rome nor England can in the same sense appeal to Catholic testimony; and, this being the case, a member of the one or the other Church *might* fairly have the antecedent scruple rise in his mind, why his own communion should have the *whole* truth, why, on the contrary, the rival communion should not have a share of it, and the truth itself lie midway between them. This is the question of a philosophical mind, and the Church of Rome meets it with a theory, perfectly satisfactory, provided only it be established as a fact, viz. the theory of infallibility. The actual promise made, as they contend, to St. Peter's chair, as the centre of unity, would undoubtedly account for truth being wholly in the Roman Communion, not in the English, and solve the antecedent perplexity in question. But the English Church, taking no such high ground as this, certainly is open to the force, such as it is, of the objection, or (as it was just now expressed) on the *primâ facie* view of the case, is unlikely to have embraced the whole counsel of GOD, because she does not assume infallibility; and consequently, no surprise or distress should be felt by her dutiful sons, should that turn out to be the fact, which her own principles, rightly understood, would lead them to anticipate. At the same time it must carefully be remembered, that this admission involves no doubt or scepticism as regards the more sacred subjects of theology, of which the Creed is the summary; these having been witnessed from the first by the whole Church,—being witnessed too at this moment, in spite of later corruptions, both by the Latin and Greek Communions.

19.

A consideration has been suggested in the last paragraph, on which much might be said on a fitting occasion; it is (what may be called) a great Canon of the Gospel, that purity of faith depends on the *Sacramentum Unitatis*. Unity in the whole body of the Church, as it is the divinely blessed symbol and pledge of the true faith, so also it is the obvious means (even humanly speaking) of securing it. The *Sacramentum* was first infringed during the quarrels of the Greeks and Latins; it was shattered in that great schism of the sixteenth century which issued in some parts of Europe in the Reformation, in others in the Tridentine Decrees, our own Church keeping the nearest of any to the complete truth. Since that era at least, Truth has not dwelt simply and securely in any visible Tabernacle. This view of the subject will illustrate for us the last words of Bishop Ken as contained in his will:—"As for my religion, I die in the Holy Catholic and Apostolic faith, *professed by the whole Church before the disunion of East and West;* more particularly I die in the communion of the Church of England, *as it stands distinguished from* all Papal and Puritan innovations, and *as it adheres* to the doctrine of the Cross."

20.

A third antecedent ground for anticipating wants and imperfections in the English Church lies in the circumstances under which the reformation of its doctrine and worship was effected. It is now universally admitted as an axiom in ecclesiastical and political matters that sudden and violent changes must be injurious ; and though our own revolution of opinion and practice was happily slower and more carefully considered than those of our neighbours, yet it was too much influenced by secular interests, sudden external events, and the will of individuals, to carry with it any vouchers for the perfection and entireness of the religious system thence emerging. The proceedings, for instance, of 1536, remind us at once of the dangers to which the Church was exposed, and of its providential deliverance from the worst part of them: the articles then framed being, according to Burnet, "in several places corrected and tempered by the King's" (Henry's) "own hand." Again, the precise structure of our present Liturgy, so primitive and beautiful in its matter, is confessedly owing to the successive and counteracting influences exerted on it, among others, by Bucer and Queen Elizabeth. The Church did not make the circumstances under which it found itself, and therefore is free from the responsibility of imperfections to which these gave rise. These imperfections followed in two ways. First, the hurry and confusion of the times led, as has been said, to a settlement of religion incomplete and defective ; secondly, the people, not duly apprehending even what was soundly propounded, as being new to them, and unable to digest healthy food after long desuetude, gave a false meaning to it, went into opposite extremes, and fashioned into unseemly habits and practices those principles which in themselves conveyed a wholesome and edifying doctrine. These considerations cannot fairly be taken in disparagement of the celebrated men who were the instruments of Providence in the work, and who doubtless felt far more keenly than is here expressed the perplexities of their situation: but they will serve perhaps to reconcile our minds to our circumstances in these latter ages of the Church, and will cherish in us a sobriety of mind, salutary in itself, and calculated more than anything else to arm us against the arguments of Rome, and turn us in affection and sympathy towards the afflicted Church, which has been the "Mother of our new-birth." They will but lead us to confess that she is in a measure in that position which we fully ascribe to her Latin sister, *in captivity;* and they will make us understand and duly use the prayers of our wisest doctors and rulers, such as Bishop Andrewes, that God would please to "look down upon His holy Catholic and Apostolic Church, *in her captivity;* to visit her once more with His salvation, and to bring her out to serve Him in the beauty of holiness."

A fourth antecedent reason for anticipating practical imperfections in the Anglican system, (and to those mainly allusion is here made,) arises from the circumstance that our Articles, so far as distinct from the ancient creeds, are scarcely more than protests against specific existing errors of the 16th century, and neither are nor profess to be a system of doctrine. It is not unnatural then, however unfortunate, that they should have practically superseded that previous Catholic teaching altogether, which they were but modifying in parts, and though but corrections, should be mistaken for the system corrected.

21.

These reasonings prepare us to acquiesce in much of plausible objection being admissible against our Church, even in the judgment of those who love and defend it. When, however, we proceed to examine what its defects really are, we shall find them to differ from those of Rome in this all-important respect, which indeed has already been in part hinted, that they are but omissions. Rome maintains positive errors, and that under the sanction of an anathema; but nothing can be pointed out in the English Church which is not true, as far as it goes, and even when it opposes Rome, with a truly Apostolical toleration, it utters no ban or condemnation against her adherents. On the other hand, the omissions, such as they are, or rather obscurities of Anglican doctrine, may be supplied for the most part by each of us for himself, and thus do not interfere with the perfect development of the Christian temper in the hearts of individuals, which is the charge fairly adducible against Romanism. Such, for instance, is the phraseology used in speaking of the Holy Eucharist, which though protected safe through a dangerous time by the cautious Ridley, yet in one or two places was at least in intention defaced by the interpolations of Bucer, through an anxiety in some quarters to unite all the reformed Churches under episcopal government against Rome. And such is the omission of any direct safeguard in the Articles, against disbelief of the doctrine of the Apostolical Succession.

And again, for specimens of the perverse reception by the nation, as above alluded to, of what was piously intended, reference may be made to the popular sense put upon the eleventh article, which, though clearly and soundly explained in the Homily on Justification or Salvation, has been erroneously taken to countenance the wildest Antinomian doctrine, and is now so associated in the minds of many with this wrong interpretation, as to render almost hopeless the recovery of the true meaning.

22.

And such again is the mischievous error, in which the Church in her formal documents certainly has no share, that we are but one among many *Protestant* bodies, and that the differences between Protestants are of little consequence; whereas the English Church, as such, is not Protestant, only politically, that is, externally, or so far as it has been made an establishment, and subjected to national and foreign influences. It claims to be merely *Reformed*, not Protestant, and it repudiates any fellowship with the mixed multitude which crowd together, whether at home or abroad, under a mere political banner. That this is no novel doctrine, is plain from the emphatic omission of the word Protestant in all our Services, even in that for the fifth of November, as remodelled in the reign of King William; and again from the protest of the Lower House of Convocation at that date, on this very point, which would have had no force, except as proceeding upon recognized usages. The circumstance here referred to was as follows. In 1689 the Upper House of Convocation agreed on an address to King William, to thank him, "for the grace and goodness expressed in his message, and the zeal shown in it for the *Protestant Religion in general*, and the Church of England in particular." To this the Lower House objected, as importing, according to Birch in his Life of Tillotson, "*their owning common union with the foreign Protestants.*" A conference between the two Houses ensued, when the Bishops supported their wording of the address, on the ground that the Protestant Religion was the known denomination of the *common doctrine* of such parts of the West as had separated from Rome. The Lower House proposed, with other alterations of the passage, the words "Protestant Churches," for "Protestant Religion," being unwilling to acknowledge religion as separate from the Church. The Upper House in turn amended thus,—"the interest of the Protestant Religion in *this* and *all other* "Protestant Churches," but the Lower House, still jealous of any diminution of the English Church by this comparison with foreign Protestants, persisted in their opposition, and gained at length that the address, after thanking the King for his zeal for the Church of England, should proceed to anticipate, that thereby "the interest of the Protestant Religion in [not "this and "but] "all other Protestant Churches would be better secured." Birch adds, "The King well understood why this address omitted the thanks which the Bishops had recommended, for . . the zeal which he had shown for the Protestant Religion; and *why there was no expression of tenderness to the Dissenters, and but a cool regard to the Protestant Churches.*"

23.

Another great practical error of members of our Church has been their mode of defending its doctrines; and this has arisen, not from any direction of the Church itself, but, as it would appear, from mistaking, as already mentioned, the specific protests contained in its Articles for that Catholic system, which is the rightful inheritance of it as well as other branches of the Church. We have indeed too often fought Roman Catholics on wrong grounds, and given up to them the high principles maintained by the early Church. We have indirectly opposed the major premiss of our opponents' argument, when we should have denied the fact expressed in the minor. For instance; they have maintained that Transubstantiation was an Apostolical doctrine, as having been ever taught everywhere in the Church. We, instead of denying this fact as regards Transubstantiation, have acted as if it mattered very little whether it were true or not, (whereas the principle is most true and valuable,) and have proceeded to oppose Transubstantiation on supposed grounds of reason. Again, we have argued for the sole Canonicity of the Bible to the exclusion of tradition, not on the ground that the Fathers so held it, (which would be an irrefragable argument,) but on some supposed internal witness of Scripture to the fact, or some abstract and antecedent reasons against the Canonicity of unwritten teaching. Once more, we have argued the unscripturalness of image worship as its only condemnation; a mode of argument, which one would be very far indeed from pronouncing untenable, but which opens the door to a multitude of refined distinctions and pleas; whereas the way lay clear before us to appeal to *history*, to appeal to the usage of the early Church Catholic, to review the circumstances of the introduction of image worship, the Iconoclast controversy, the Council of Frankfort, and the late reception of the corruption in the West.

So much, then, on the objections which may be urged against the English Church, which relate either to mere omissions, not positive errors, or again to faults in the practical working of the system, and are in these respects dissimilar from those which lie against the Church of Rome, and which relate to clear and direct perversions and corruptions of divine truth. Should it, however, be asked, whence our knowledge of the truth should be derived, since there is so much of meagreness and mistake in our more popular expounders of it, it may be replied, first, that the writings of the Fathers contain abundant directions how to ascertain it; next, that their directions are distinctly propounded and supported by our Divines of the seventeenth century, though little comparatively at present is known concerning those great authors. Nor could a more acceptable or important service be done to our Church at this present moment, than the publication of some systematic introduction to theology, embodying and illustrating the great and concordant principles and doctrines set forth by Hammond, Taylor, and their brethren before and after them.

24.

Lastly, should it be inquired whether this admission of incompleteness in our own system does not lead to projects of change and reform, on the part of individuals; it must be answered plainly in the negative. Such an admission has but reference to the question of abstract perfection ; as a practical matter, it will be our wisdom, as individuals, to enjoy what God's good providence has left us, lest, striving to obtain more, we lose what we still possess.

OXFORD,
The Feast of the Circumcision, 1836.

V.

LETTER ADDRESSED TO A MAGAZINE

ON BEHALF OF

DR. PUSEY'S TRACTS ON HOLY BAPTISM

AND OF OTHER TRACTS FOR THE TIMES.

(Being No. 82 of the said Tracts.)

1837.

NOTICE.

I SHOULD hesitate for several reasons to include the following Letter among these republications, did it not serve to illustrate the state of the controversy at the time when it was written, and had it not been a step towards the 90th Tract.

In order to understand it aright, passages from publications of the day must first be given, out of which it grew.

1.

Dr. Pusey, in the second Volume of the Tracts for the Times (No. 69, *On Baptism, pp.* 134—137), writes as follows:—

"The term 'regeneration' came to be used for the visible change, or almost for sanctification; and its original sense, as denoting a privilege of the Christian Church, was wholly lost. . . . Undoubtedly, the pious men under the Old Dispensation were sanctified; and, in these days of ordinary attainment, how must we look back with shame and dejection upon the worthies of the elder Covenant, upon those 'three men, Noah, Daniel, and Job,' or upon Abraham, the Father of the faithful and the 'friend of God.' Greatly were they sanctified. . The Spirit of God . . purified the breast of the 'Preacher of righteousness' . . yet was not Noah therefore regenerate. . Regeneration is a privilege of the Church of Christ. . Sanctification on the contrary includes various degrees."

2.

And in the Advertisement to the same Volume occurred the following passage:—

"We have almost embraced the doctrine, that God conveys grace only through the instrumentality of the mental energies, that is, through faith, prayer, active spiritual contemplations, or (what is called) communion with God, in contradiction to the primitive view, according to which the Church and her Sacraments are the ordained and direct visible means of conveying to the soul what is in itself supernatural and unseen. For example, would not most men maintain, on the first view of the subject, that to administer the Lord's Supper to infants, or to the dying and insensible,[1] however consistently pious and believing in their past lives, was a superstition? and yet both practices have the sanction of primitive usage. And does not this account for the prevailing indisposition

[1] [Vid. Bingham, Antiq. xv. 4. § 9.]

to admit that Baptism conveys regeneration? Indeed, this may even be set down as the essence of Sectarian doctrine (however its mischief may be restrained or compensated, in the case of individuals), to consider faith, and not the Sacraments, as the instrument of justification and other Gospel gifts," &c.

3.

This was in 1835. Towards the end of the next year, a Protestant Magazine of established reputation was led to animadvert with great severity upon the above passages, and on the line of doctrine advocated in the Oxford Tracts, as follows :—

"In reply to the question which [a correspondent] puts to us, as to 'what authority' the doctrine which he quotes from the Oxford Tracts rests upon, we can only say, Upon the authority of the darkest ages of Popery, when men had debased Christianity from a spiritual system, a 'reasonable service,' to a system of forms, and ceremonial rites, and *opera operata* influences; in which, what Bishop Horsley emphatically calls 'the mysterious intercourse of the soul with its Creator,' was nearly superseded by an intervention of 'the Church'—not as a congregation of faithful men, in which the pure word of God is preached, and the sacraments are 'duly administered according to Christ's ordinance,' as the Church of England defines it—but as a sort of 'mediator between God and man,' through whom all things relating to spiritual life were to be conveyed. Those who could not understand that 'God is a Spirit, and they that worship Him, must worship Him in spirit and in truth,' and those who had neither the reality nor 'the appearance of spiritual life,' readily allied themselves to a religion of ceremonials, in which the Church stood in the place of God. And as the Popish priesthood found their gain in encouraging these ritual and non-spiritual views of Christianity, they eventually prevailed throughout Christendom, till the Reformation restored the pure light of Scripture, and taught men to look less to the priest and more to God; less to 'outward and visible signs,' and more to 'inward and spiritual graces;' and not to infer that, because their name stood upon the register of baptism, it was therefore enrolled in the Lamb's book of life, when there was no 'appearance' of spiritual vitality in their heart or conduct.

"This fatal reliance upon signs, to the forgetfulness of the things signified, was rendered more proclivious, from the circumstance that in the early Church persecution so purified its ranks, that there was little temptation for men to call themselves Christians who were not such in heart; and as adult converts were the first candidates for baptism, the outward and visible sign of regeneration was not resorted to till the inward and spiritual grace was already actually possessed; for there had been spiritually a 'death unto sin and a new birth unto righteousness,' before the party applied to make a public confession of his faith in Christ, at the risk of subjecting himself to all the secular perils which it involved.

"We have devoted so many scores, nay, hundreds of pages to the questions propounded in the extract from the Oxford Tracts (especially at the time of the Baptismal controversy, upon occasion of Bishop Mant's Tract, when not a few of our readers were thoroughly wearied with the discussion), that we are not anxious to obtrude a new litigation; but we have readily inserted the extract furnished by our correspondent, because nothing that we could say would so clearly show the unscriptural character of the whole system of the Oxford Tracts, as to let them speak for themselves. When the Christian reader learns that Noah, and Abraham, and Moses, and Job, and David, and Isaiah, and Daniel, were not regenerate persons, were not sons of God, were not born again, but that Voltaire was all this, because he had been baptized by a Popish priest, we may surely leave such an hypothesis to be crushed by its own weight. It is the very bathos of theology, an absurdity not worthy to be gravely replied to, that men were 'sanctified,' 'greatly sanctified;' were the friends of God, that 'the Spirit of God dwelt in their hearts, and wrought therein incorruption, self-denial, patience, and unhesitating, unwearied faith; who yet, having been 'by nature born in sin, and the children of wrath,' and never having been baptized, so as to be made 'the children of grace,' were still 'unregenerate,' and therefore, in Scripture language, 'children of the devil.' Sanctified, unregenerate friends of God! The Spirit of God dwelling in men, who, not being 'born again,' were of necessity, being still in their natural condition, 'children of the devil!' What next?

"We defy a score of Dr. Hampdens, even were they to give lectures in favour of pure Socinianism, to do so much mischief to the cause of religion, in a high academical station, as is done by setting forth such doctrine as that contained in the following passage from one of the Oxford Tracts;—for Socinianism makes no pretensions to be the doctrine of the Church of England, nor do any members of that Church profess to find it in Scripture; whereas the absurdity, the irrational fanaticism, the intellectual drivelling under the abused name of faith, which dictates such sentiments as the following, must disgust every intelligent man, and make him an infidel, if he is really led to believe that Christianity is a system so utterly opposed to common sense. The writer complains, that 'we have almost embraced the doctrine, that God conveys grace only through,' &c. [*as above*, p. 146.]

"Did ever any man, but the most ignorant Popish fanatic, till these our modern days, write thus? Administering the Lord's Supper (by which we feed upon Christ '*by faith with thanksgiving*'—that is, in a purely spiritual banquet) to infants, or to the dying or insensible, is not superstition, if it can be proved that there were in some former age some persons weak and ignorant enough to act or advocate such folly and impiety! Why not equally vindicate the Pope's sprinkling holy water upon the horses, or St. Anthony's preaching to the fishes? We will only say, Let those who adopt a portion of this scheme, and not the whole, mark well whither they are tending. Upon the showing of the Oxford Tracts themselves, the whole system hangs together. You are to adopt some irrational mystical system, by which grace is conveyed — not through 'faith, prayer, active spiritual contemplations, or (what is called) communion with God,' but—in the same manner that the Lord's Supper conveys grace when administered to an infant, or an insensible person. We have never been extreme in our views respecting the language used in our Liturgy concerning Baptism. We have thought that the words might be consistently used, either in reference to the undoubted privileges of Christian baptism; or in faith and charity, upon the principle stated in the Catechism, where it is said, 'Why then are infants baptized, when, by reason of their tender age, they cannot perform them? (faith and repentance.) Because they promise them both by their sureties; which promise, when they come to age, themselves are bound to perform.' Upon either of these principles we can cheerfully use our Baptismal Service. But if the use of it is to sanction the doctrine stated in this Tract; if we are to believe that baptism 'conveys to the soul what is in itself supernatural and unseen,' in the selfsame way that the Popish wafer is alleged to convey grace to infants and insensible persons— (why not to idiots?)—and if our Church Service is to be tortured to bear this meaning; then we confess, that the sooner such a stumbling-block is removed the better.

"The Oxford Tract writers will not allow us to connect the outward and visible sign of Baptism, or the Lord's Supper, with the inward and spiritual grace, through the medium of 'faith, prayer, active spiritual contemplations, or (what is called) communion with God,' but only through the selfsame channel by which 'primitive usage' supposed grace to flow to an infant or insensible person, when operated upon with the holy Eucharist. Nay, they sneer at and ridicule 'what is called' communion with God (poor Bishop Horsley's 'mysterious intercourse of the soul with its Creator'), as being something so 'called,' but without warrant; whereas true communion with God is through the intervention of 'the Church:' by which intervention there is this communion when the priest puts a consecrated wafer upon the lips of an infant or insensible person. The Church of England teaches, after Holy Scripture, that we are 'justified by faith;' Professor Pusey teaches that the Sacraments are the appointed instruments of justification. The learned Professor ought to lecture at Maynooth, or the Vatican, and not in the chair of Oxford, when he puts forth this Popish doctrine. It is afflicting beyond expression to see our Protestant Church—and in times like these—agitated by the revival of these figments of the darkest ages of Papal superstition. Well may Popery flourish! well may Dissent triumph! well may Unitarianism sneer! well may all Protestantism mourn, to see the spot where Cranmer and Latimer shed their blood for the pure Gospel of Christ, overrun (yet not overrun, for, blessed be God, the infection is not—at least so we trust—widely spread) with some of the most vain and baneful absurdities of Popery. We ask Professor Pusey how, as a conscientious man, he retains any office in a Church which requires him to subscribe to all the Thirty-nine Articles, and to acknowledge as Scriptural the doctrines set forth in the Homilies? Will any one of the writers, or approvers of the Oxford Tracts, venture to say that he does really believe all the doctrines of the Articles and Homilies of our Church? He may construe some of *the Offices* of the Church after his own manner; but what does he do with the Articles and Homilies? We have often asked this question in private, but could never get an answer. Will any approver of the Oxford Tracts answer it in print?"

The following letter was the consequence of this challenge.

LETTER TO THE EDITOR OF A MAGAZINE.

Part I.

Jan. 11, 1837.

Sir,—Through that courtesy, which is on the whole characteristic of your Magazine, in dealing with opponents, I am permitted to answer in its pages the challenge, made in a late number to Dr. Pusey and the writers of the Tracts for the Times, on certain points of their theology. The tone of that challenge, I must own, or rather the general conduct of your Magazine towards the Tracts, since their first appearance, has been an exception to its usual mildness and urbanity. However, I seize, as an ample amends, this opportunity of a reply, which, if satisfactory, will, as appearing in its pages, be rather a retractation on your part than an explanation on mine.

One would think that the Tracts had introduced some new articles of faith into English theology, such surprise at them has been excited in some quarters; yet, much as they have been censured, no attempt, that I know of, has been made to prove them guilty—I will not say, in any article of faith, but—even in any theological opinion, inconsistent with that religious system which has been received among us since the date of the "Ecclesiastical Polity." Indeed, nothing is more striking than the contrast exhibited in the controversy between the definiteness and precision of the attack upon them, and the vagueness of the reasons for making it. From the excitement on the subject for the last three years, one would think nothing was more obvious and tangible than the offence which they contained; yet nothing, not only to refute, but even to describe their errors definitely, has yet been attempted. Extracts have been made with notes of admiration; abuse has been lavished; invidious associations suggested; irony and sarcasm have lent their aid; their writers have been called Papists, and Non-jurors, and Lauds, and Sacheverells, and that not least of all in your own Magazine; yet I much doubt whether, for any light which you have thrown on the subject, its readers have, up to this hour, any more definite idea of the matter in dispute than they have of Sacheverell himself, or of the Non-jurors, or of any other vague name which is circulated in the world, meaning the less the oftener it is used. If your readers were examined, perhaps they would not get beyond this round of titles and epithets: or, at the utmost, we should but hear that the Tracts were corruptions of the Gospel, human inventions, systems of fallible men, and so forth. These are the fine words which you give your friends to feed upon, for bread.

Even now, Mr. Editor, when you make your formal challenge *apropos* of Dr. Pusey, you do not distinctly and pointedly say, as a man who was accusing, not declaiming, *what* you want answered. You ask, "Will any of the writers or approvers of the Oxford Tracts venture to say that he does really believe *all* the doctrines of the Articles and Homilies of our Church?" How unsuitable is this! Why do you not tell us *which* doctrine of the Articles you have in your mind, and then prove your point, instead of leaving us to guess it? One used to think it was the business of the accuser to bring proof, and not to throw upon the accused the *onus* of proving a negative. What! am I, as an approver of the Tracts, to go through the round of doctrines in Articles and Homilies, measuring Dr. Pusey first by one, then by the other, while the Editor sits still, as judge rather than accuser? What! are we not even to have the *charge* told us, let alone the proof? No; we are to find out both the dream and the interpretation.

2.

So much for the formal challenge which your Magazine puts forth; and I can find nothing, either in the remarks which precede it or in its acceptance of my offer, precisely coming to the point, and informing me *what* the charge against Dr. Pusey is. It is connected with the Sacraments, certainly: you wish him and his friends, according to your subsequent notice, " to reconcile *some* of the statements in them [the Tracts] respecting the Sacraments, with *some* of those in the Articles and Homilies!" In your remarks which precede the challenge, you do mention two opinions which you suppose him to hold, which I shall presently notice; but you are still silent as to the Article or Homily transgressed. This is not an English mode of proceeding: and I dwell on it, as one of the significant tokens in the controversy, as to what is the real state of the case and its probable issue. Here are two parties: one clamours loudly and unsparingly against the other, and does no more; that other is absorbed in his subject, appeals to Scripture, to the Fathers, to custom, to reason, in *its* defence, but answers not. Put the case before any sharp-sighted witness of human affairs, and he will give a good guess which is in the right. If, indeed, there is one thing more than another that brings home to me that the Tracts are mainly on the side of Truth—more than their reasonings, their matter, and their testimonies; more than argument from Scripture, or appeal to Antiquity, or sanction from our own divines; more than the beauty and grandeur, the thrilling and transporting influence, the fulness and sufficiency of the doctrines which they desire to maintain—it is this: the evidence which their writers bear about them, that they are the reviled party, not the revilers. I challenge the production of anything in the Tracts of an unkind, satirical, or abusive character; anything personal. One Tract only concerns individuals at all, No. 73; and that treats of them in a way which no one, I think, will find to be any exception to this remark. The writers nowhere attack your Magazine, or other similar publications, though they evidently as little admire its theology, as your Magazine approves of the theology of the Tracts. They have been content to go onward; to preach what is positive; to trust in what they did well, not in what others did ill; to leave Truth to fight its own battle, in a case where they had no office or commission to assist it coercively. They have spoken against principles, ages, or historical characters, but not against persons living. They have taken no eye for eye, or tooth for tooth. They have left their defence to time, or rather committed it to God. Once only have they hitherto accepted of defence, even from a friend,[2] a partner he indeed also, but not in those Tracts which he defended.

This, then, is the part that they have chosen; what your Magazine's choice has been, is plain even from the article which leads me to write this letter. We are there told of the Oxford writers "relying on the authority of the darkest ages of Popery;" of their advocating "the bathos in theology, an absurdity not worthy to be gravely replied to," of their "absurdity," "irrational fanaticism," "intellectual drivelling," of their writing like "the most ignorant Popish fanatic," of their "sneering and ridiculing," of their reviving the "figments of the darkest ages of Papal superstition," "some of the most vain and baneful

[2] Dr. Pusey's Earnest Remonstrance, in volume 3 of the "Tracts."

absurdities of Popery;" and all this with an avowal you do not wish to discuss the matter. Brave words surely! Well and good, take your fill of these, Mr. Editor, since you choose them for your portion. It does but make *our* spirits rise cheerily and hopefully thus to be encountered. Never were our words on one side, but *deeds* were on the other. We know our place, and our fortunes; to give a witness and to be condemned, to be ill-used and to *succeed*. Such is the law which God has annexed to the promulgation of the Truth; its preachers suffer, but its cause prevails. Be it so. Joyfully do we all consent to this compact; and the more you attack us personally, the more, for the very omen's sake, will we exult in it.

With these feelings, then, I have accepted your challenge, not for the sake of Dr. Pusey, much as I love and revere him; not for the sake of the writers of the Tracts; but for the sake of the secret ones of Christ, lest they be impeded in their progress towards Catholic truth by personal charges against those who are upholding it against the pressure of the age. As for Dr. Pusey himself, and the other writers, they are happy each in his own sphere, wherever God's providence has called them, in earth or heaven; and they literally do not know, and do not care, what the world says of them.

3.

Now, as I have already said, I cannot distinctly make out the precise charge brought against Dr. Pusey and his friends; that is, I cannot determine *what* tenet of his is supposed to be contrary to *which* of the Thirty-nine Articles. However, you condemn two of their statements,—the notion that the Sacraments may, for what we know, in certain cases be of benefit to persons unconscious during their administration; and next that Regeneration is a gift of the

New Covenant exclusively. I will take them in the order you place them in.

1. First, then, of Regeneration, as a gift peculiar to the Gospel.—You remark thus upon a passage from Dr. Pusey's work on Baptism, in which he contrasts regeneration and sanctification, and says, that the former is a gift of the Gospel exclusively, the latter is the possession of all good men : " We have devoted," you say, " so many scores, nay, hundreds of pages to the questions propounded in the extract from the Oxford Tracts (especially at the time of the Baptismal controversy, upon occasion of Bishop Mant's Tract, when not a few of our readers were wearied with the discussion), that we are not anxious to obtrude a new ligitation ; but we have readily inserted the extract furnished by our correspondent, because nothing that we could say would so clearly show the unscriptural character of the whole system of the Oxford Tracts, as to let them speak for themselves."—Now at first sight there might seem to be an inconsistency in your persisting for some years in speaking *instead of us,* then suddenly saying, it is best to let the Tracts *"speak for themselves,"* and then in the very next sentences, relapsing *in eandem cantilenam,* into the same declamatory tone of attack as before; but there is really none. In either case you avoid discussion, which, as you candidly confess, and very likely with good reason, you are tired of. I doubt not you are discouraged at finding that you have still to argue about what you have already settled once for all. Or rather, if you will let me speak plainly, and tell you my mind, perhaps there has been that in the religious aspect of the hour, which has flattered many who agree with you, and perhaps yourself, that the day of mere struggle was past, and the day of triumph was come ; that your principles were now professed by all the serious, all the active men in the Church, your old opponents drooping or dying off ; and that now,

by the force of character in your friends, or by influence in high places, your view of doctrine would be sure of making a permanent impression upon our religious system. And if so, you are not unnaturally surprised to find " uno avulso, non deficit alter ;" to find a sudden obstacle in your path, and that from a quarter whence you did not expect it ; and, in consequence, you feel stimulated to remove so inconvenient a phenomenon hastily rather than courteously. And hence, partly from weariness, partly from vexation, you would, if you could, carry your theological views by acclamation, not after discussion. If all this be so, you are quite consistent, whether you quote our words without comment, or substitute your own comment for them. In one point alone you are irretrievably inconsistent, to have inserted your challenge at the end of your article. You are safe while you eschew argument.

4.

But what is the very doctrine that has created this confusion ? It is Dr. Pusey's asserting, after primitive authorities, that the Old Fathers, though sanctified, were not regenerated. Is *this*, after all, the doctrine which contravenes the Articles, and is such that a divine who holds it should quit his Professorship ? In which of the Articles is a syllable to be found referring to the subject, one way or the other—except so far as they tend our way, as implying, from their doctrine of regeneration *in* baptism, that those who are not baptized, and therefore the Old Fathers, are not regenerate ? If then the plain truth must be spoken, what your Magazine wishes is to *add* to the Articles. Let this be clearly understood. This Magazine, which has ever, as many think, been over-liberal and lax in its explanations of our Services, and in its concessions to Dissenters, desires to forge for us a yoke of commandments, and, as I should hold, of commandments of men. Years ago, indeed, we heard of much from it in censure of Bishop Marsh's Eighty-seven Questions which put his private sense on our Church formularies; but it would seem that an Editor may do what a Bishop may not. In reviewing those arbitrary Questions, your Magazine pointedly spoke of the wisdom of the framers of the Royal Declaration prefixed to the Articles, which prescribes that they shall be taken in no new or peculiar sense; contrasting, to use its own words, " the spirit of peace, of moderation, of manly candour, and comprehensive liberality, which breathes throughout this Declaration, with the subtle, contentious, dogmatical, sectarian, and narrow-minded spirit which," it proceeded, " we grieve to say, pervades the Bishop of Peterborough's Eighty-seven Questions." (March, 1821.) But why is liberality to develope on one side only? Why must Regeneration by Baptism be an open question, but the Regeneration of the Patriarchs a close one? Why must Zuinglius be admitted, and the school of Gregory and Augustine excluded? Or do men by a sort of superstition so cleave to the word Protestant, that a Saint who had the misfortune to be born before 1517 is less of kin to them than heretics since? But such is your Magazine's rule: it is as zealous against Bishop Marsh for coercing one way, as against us for refusing to be coerced the other.

Will it be said that Dr. Pusey and others would do the same, if they could; that is, would limit the Articles to their own sense? No; the Articles are confessedly wide in their wording, though still their width is within bounds; they seem to include a number of shades of opinion. Your Magazine may rest satisfied that Dr. Pusey's friends will never assert that the Articles have any particular meaning at all. They aspire, and (by the divine blessing) intend, to have a successful fight; but not by narrowing the

Church's Creed to Lutheranism, Calvinism, or Zuinglianism after your pattern, but from a confidence that they are contending for the Truth, and as seeing that Providence is wonderfully raising up witnesses and champions of the Truth, not in one place only, but at once in many, as armed men from the ground.

But to return. It is hard to be put on our defence, as it appears we are, for opinions not against the Articles; but be it so. Let us hear the form of the accusation. You speak thus: " When the Christian reader learns that Noah, and Abraham, and Moses, and Job, and David, and Isaiah, and Daniel, were not regenerate persons, were not sons of God, were not born again, but that Voltaire was all this, because he had been baptized by a Popish priest, we may surely leave such an hypothesis to be crushed by its own weight." To be sure, the hypothesis *is* absurd, if your own sense is to be put upon the word " regenerate ;" but it will be observed, that it all depends upon this; and it is not evident that it will be absurd when Dr. Pusey's own sense is put upon his own words. If all who are sanctified are regenerate, then I say, it *is* absurd to say that Abraham was *not* regenerate, being sanctified. On the other hand, if *only* Christians are regenerate, then it is absurd to say that Abraham *was* regenerate, being not a Christian. What trifling upon words is this! what is the use of oscillating to and fro upon their different meanings? Surely, your business, Mr. Editor, was to prove his sense wrong, not to assume your own sense as undeniable, and to interpret his words by it; else, when *you* assert, "no one, unless regenerated on earth, shall enter heaven," he, in turn, might accuse you, quite as fairly, of denying the salvation of Abraham, because, in his view, Abraham was not regenerated on earth.

5.

I will now state briefly the view of Dr. Pusey, derived from the goodly fellowship of the Fathers, proved from Scripture, and called by your Magazine "the very bathos of theology." All of us, I suppose, grant that the Holy Spirit is given under the Gospel, in some sense, in which He was not given under the Law. The Homily (2nd of Faith) says so expressly: "Although they," the Old Testament saints mentioned Heb. xi., "were not named Christian men, yet was it a Christian faith that they had: God gave them then grace to be His children, as He doth us now. But now, by the coming of our Saviour Christ, we have received *more abundantly* the Spirit of God in our hearts, whereby we may conceive a greater faith, and a surer trust, than many of them had. But, in effect, they and we be all one: we have the same faith," &c. Though man's duties were the same, his gifts were greater after Christ came. Whatever might be the spiritual aid that was vouchsafed before, afterwards it was a Divine Presence in the soul, abiding, abundant, and efficacious. In a word, it was the Holy Ghost Himself: He influenced indeed the heart before, but is not revealed as residing in it. Now, when we consider the Scripture proof of this in the full, I think we shall see that this special gift, which Christians have, is really something extraordinary and distinguishing. And, whether it should be called Regeneration or no, so far is clear, that all persons who hold that there *is* a great gift since Christ came, which was not given before, do, in their degree, incur your censure, as holding a "very bathos of theology." You might say of them, just as you say of Dr. Pusey, "When the Christian reader learns that Abraham was sanctified, yet 'had not the Spirit, because that Jesus was not yet glorified,' we may leave the hypothesis to be crushed by its own weight."

ϵ.

Now for the Scripture proof. I contend, first, that there is a spiritual difference between Christians and Jews; and, next, that the accession of spiritual power, which Christians have, is called Regeneration. Let it be understood, however, that I am not adducing *proofs* of this, as if you had any claim on me for them; but showing your readers that, even at first sight, it is not so utterly irrational and unplausible a notion as to account for your saying, "What next?" in short, to show that the "absurdity" does not lie with Dr. Pusey.

The prophets had announced the *promise*. Ezek. xxxvi. 25—27: "I will sprinkle clean water upon you, and ye shall be clean . . . a *new heart* also will I give you, and *a new spirit* will I put *within* you . . . and I will put *My spirit within you.*" Again, xxxvii. 27: "My *tabernacle* also shall be with them." Vid. also Heb. viii. 10. In Isa. xliv. 3, the gift is expressly connected with the person of the Messiah: "I will pour water upon him that is thirsty, and floods upon the dry ground: I will pour *My Spirit* upon Thy seed, and My blessing upon Thine offspring."

Our Saviour refers to this gift as the *promise* of His Father, Luke xxiv. 49; Acts i. 4. He enlarges much upon it, John xiv.—xvi. It flows to us from Him: "Of His fulness have all we received." (John i. 16.)

St. John expressly tells us it was *not* given *before* Christ was glorified. (John vii. 39.) In like manner St. Paul says, that though the old fathers lived by faith, yet they received not the *promise.* (Heb. xi. 39.) And St. Peter, that even the prophets, though they *had* the prophetic Spirit—"the Spirit of Christ which was in them"—yet, after all, had not " the glory which should follow ;" which was " the Gospel *with the Holy Ghost sent down from heaven;*" that is, the Spirit, in the special Christian sense. Consider also St. Paul's use of the term "spirit," e. g. Rom. viii., as being the characteristic of the Gospel.

It is described in the New Testament under the same images as it is promised in the Old,—a tabernacle in us, and a fount of living water (1 Cor. iii. 17; vi. 19; 2 Cor. vi. 16—18; John iv. 14; vii. 38).

Nothing, I think, but the inveterate addiction to systematizing so prevalent can explain away texts which so expressly say that we have a Divine presence which the Jews had not.

Now, secondly, is this gift to be called Regeneration? I grant that there is a sense in which the terms applicable to Christian privileges are also applicable to Jewish. The Jews were "sons of God," were "begotten" of God, had "the Spirit," saw "the glory of God," and the like; but, in like manner, the Saints also in heaven, as their peculiar gift, will see "the glory of God," and Angels are "sons of God;" yet we know that nevertheless Angels and Saints are in a state different from the Jews. The question, then, still remains open, whether, in spite of the absence of discriminating terms, Christians also have not a gift which the Jews had not, and whether the word regeneration, in its proper sense, does not denote it.

Our proof then is simple. The word "regeneration" occurs twice only in Scripture; in neither can it be interpreted to include Judaism; in one of the two, most probably in both, it is limited to the Gospel; in Titus iii. 4, 5, certainly; and in Matt. xix. 28, according as it is stopped, it will mean the coming of Gospel grace, or the resurrection.[3]

---

[3] [This subject is also treated of in the author's Parochial Sermons, vol. vi. 13. Two opinions are here advanced, which require careful wording: that the Jews had not the gift of regeneration, and that they had not

7.

Such is some small portion of the Scripture notices on the general subject, which I bring to show that Scripture does not so speak as to make the view maintained by Dr. Pusey, with all Saints, guilty of absolute "absurdity" on the face of the matter, and a "bathos in theology." And the following consideration will increase this impression. In truth his view is simply *beyond*, not *against* your own opinion. It is a view which the present age cannot be said to deny, because it has not eyes for it. The Catholic Church has ever given to Noah, Abraham, and Moses, all that the present age of Protestantism gives to Christians. You cannot mention the grace, in kind or degree, which you ascribe to the Christian, which Dr. Pusey will not ascribe to Abraham; except, perhaps, the intimate knowledge of the details of Christian doctrine. But he con-

the indwelling of the Holy Ghost, both of these being the privilege of Christians.

I observe, in addition to what I have said in the text, that Nicodemus, "the master in Israel," knew nothing of gospel regeneration, and though a religious man, evidently had not received the gift; and that St. Thomas with the Schola holds generally that the Mosaic Sacraments did not cause grace *ex opere operato* and *physicè*, but only conferred legal sanctity, signifying, not anticipating, Gospel grace.

As to the second statement, though it is *de fide* that justification has never been bestowed by an external imputation, whether under the Old Law or now, but has always been consequent on an inward gift, still it must be observed that the author in the above passage expressly mentions sanctification as one of the Jewish privileges, though only a sanctification of a legal character, inward indeed but not that direct presence of the Holy Ghost which the Fathers predicate of Christian justification, nor a quality, habit, or permanent possession; while on the other hand theologians allow that a justification by imputation without inward sanctification might have been the rule in the revealed system, though it is not, and in fact in our own system venial sins are not necessarily wiped out by grace, and may be, and sometimes are, by extrinsic condonation.]

siders that Christians have a something beyond all this, even a portion of that heaven brought down to earth, which will be for ever in heaven the portion of Abraham and all saints in its fulness. It is not, then, that Dr. Pusey defrauds Abraham, but you defraud Christians. That special gift of grace, called "the glory of God,"[4] is as unknown to the so-called religious world in this country as to the "natural man." The Catholic Religion teaches, that, when grace takes up its abode in us, we have so superabounding and awful a grace tabernacled in us, that no other words describe it more nearly than to call it an Angel's nature. Now mark the meaning of this. Angels are holy; yet Angels before now have become devils. Keeping this analogy in view, you will perceive that it is as little an absurdity to say that Abraham was not regenerate, as to say that he was not an Angel; as little unmeaning to say that Voltaire had been regenerated, as it would be to say he became a devil, as Judas is actually called. Let me suit one or two of your sentences to this view of the subject, and then I will release you from the trouble of hearing more about it for a month. You will then speak thus: "When the Christian reader learns that Noah, Abraham, and Moses, were not Angels, yet that Judas became a devil, we may surely leave such an hypothesis to be crushed by its own weight. It is the very bathos of theology, an absurdity not worthy to be gravely replied to—that Jews were sanctified, the friends of God, had the grace of God in their hearts, and yet were not Angels. Sanctified, non-angelic friends of God! grace dwelling in any but Michael, Gabriel, the Cherubims and the Seraphims? What next?"

Alas! sir, that you should so speak of your own privieges! Perhaps it is my turn now to ask you, "What next?" and this I mean to do. Before proceeding to the

[4] [Viz. 2 Cor. iii. 18; 1 Pet. iv. 14; 2 Pet. i. 3.]

other opionion attributed by you to Dr. Pusey, I wish to learn what you will say to what is now offered you. Only I would remark, that the subjects which I have not yet touched upon *are* to come, when due attention shall be shown to your remarks about Justification, the Homilies, and kindred points.

Part II.

8.

March 3, 1837.

2. I now proceed to the second of the charges which you have brought against Dr. Pusey. After saying what is necessary upon it, I shall, as I promised, notice the subject of Justification, the Homilies, and the Articles; and shall intersperse the discussion with some remarks, as brief as is practicable, on the various matter which, as you happily express yourself, you have " ramblingly and cursorily set before your readers," in your animadversions on the portion of my Letter already published.

That portion occupies not so much as seven pages of your larger type, and that spread out into two numbers. It has elicited from you in answer about sixty pages of your closest. I think then I have a claim in courtesy, nay in justice, that you should put in the whole of this reply unbroken by a word of your own. I will not embrace the entire subject in it, but leave one portion for an after Number of your Magazine, that you may not say I burden you with too much at once. But what I send, I hope to see inserted without mutilation. Do grant me this act of fairness—you will have months upon months, nay, the whole prospective duration of your Magazine, for your reply: I, on the other hand, limit myself to *one* letter.

All I ask is the right of an Englishman, a fair and uninterrupted hearing.

9.

The second charge then which you bring against Dr. Pusey is this :—that he holds that the Sacraments may, for what we know, in certain cases, be of benefit to persons unconscious during their administration. You quarrel, however, with this mode of stating his supposed opinion : you say, " Mr. Newman misstates what we said. We were denying the utility of administering the Lord's Supper to infants or insensible persons, as the Papists employ extreme unction ; which Mr. Newman skilfully turns into a charge of our denying that there is any benefit in Infant Baptism" (p. 124). Now, I really think you leave the matter as you found it. You have said, the notion of the Holy Eucharist benefiting infants was "an absurdity," "intellectual drivelling," "irrational fanaticism," &c. I ask, then, *why* is not the doctrine that Holy Baptism benefits them, all these bad things also? Surely you are **speaking** of the very *notion* of infants being benefited by means of external rites, when you say it implies "a system utterly opposed to common sense." You must mean there is an *antecedent* absurdity in the notion ; antecedent to a consideration of the particular case. You speak, just as I have worded it, against the very notion that " the sacraments," one as well as the other, " may, for what we know, in certain cases, be of benefit to persons unconscious during their administration." What is an absurdity when supposed in one case, is an absurdity surely in the other. I cannot alter my wording of the argumentative ground which you take up against our doctrine.

Next let us consider the very passage which has led you to use these free epithets. It stands thus : " We have almost embraced the doctrine that God conveys grace only through the intrumentality of the mental energies, that is, through faith, prayer, active spiritual contemplation, or (what is called) communion with God, in contradiction to the primitive view, according to which the Church and her sacraments are the ordained and direct invisible means of conveying to the soul what is in itself supernatural and unseen. For example: would not most men maintain, on the first view of the subject, that to administer the Lord's Supper to infants, or to the dying and insensible, however consistently pious and believing in their past lives, was a superstition? and yet both practices have the sanction of primitive usage. And does not this account for the prevailing indisposition to admit that baptism conveys regeneration? Indeed, this may even be set down as the essence of sectarian doctrine (however its mischief may be restrained or compensated in the case of individuals), to consider faith, and not the sacraments, as the instrument of justification and other Gospel gifts."—These words you attribute to Dr. Pusey. You say, "Professor Pusey teaches that the sacraments are the appointed instruments of justification; the learned Professor ought to lecture at Maynooth, or the Vatican, and not in the chair of Oxford, when he puts forth this Popish doctrine." Again, in pp. 118, 119, you speak of Dr. Pusey's saying that the grace of the sacrament is unconnected " with the mental energies, that is, through faith, prayer, active spiritual contemplations, or what is called communion with God " (here you interpose of your own, " For shame, Dr. Pusey, to speak thus lightly of 'communion with God!'"); that "to administer the Lord's Supper to infants, or to the dying and insensible," is not " superstition," but "a practice having the sanction of primitive usage;" and "primitive usage," you add, " the Oxford Tracts " (Tracts for the Times) " teach is of Apostolical authority." It is quite clear you attribute the above sentences to Dr. Pusey.

Let me ask you then a question. Should any one accuse *you* of having written them, should you not be startled? Supposing I boldly attributed them to you, and retorted your interjection of indignation at them upon yourself, would you not consider it somewhat outrageous? Be judge then in your own case. Those sentences no more belong to Dr. Pusey than to you. They are not in his Tract. They are not his writing. No one man is chargeable with the work of another man. Not even were Dr. Pusey to profess he approved the general sentiment of the passage, would you have any right to charge him with the very wording of it. Every man has his own way of expressing himself; you have yours; Dr. Pusey might approve the sentiment, yet criticize the wording. All these strong sayings then against Dr. Pusey are misdirected. Mr. Editor, be sure of your man, before you attack him.

10.

However, let us examine the words, whosesoever they are. They occur in the Advertisement to the second volume of the Tracts. Now, in what they say about administering the Holy Eucharist to children or to the insensible, they do *not* enforce it, as you suppose, on "Apostolical authority." A usage may be primitive, yet not universal; may belong to the first ages, but only to some parts of the Church. Such a usage is either not Apostolical, else it would be everywhere observed; or at least not binding, as not being delivered by the Apostles *as* binding. For instance; the Church of Ephesus, on St. John's authority, celebrated the Easter-feast after the Jewish manner, yet such a custom is not binding on us. Now, supposing I said, "the great reverence in which the Jewish Dispensation was held in the best and purest ages, is shown in this, that the quartodeciman usage has primitive sanction;" must I necessarily mean that all Christendom, and all the Apostles,

observed Easter on the fourteenth day of Nisan? must I
mean that we are bound to keep it on that day? must I
mean to extol such a usage, and to advocate it? Yet
would it not in fact show in them who so observed it an
attachment to the usages which once had been divine?
Apply this instance to the sentence of this writer, who is
not Dr. Pusey, this Pseudo-Pusey, as I may call him; and
see whether it will not help your conception of his meaning. He does not say, he does not imply, that to
administer the second Sacrament to infants is Apostolic;
he does not consider it a duty binding on us. He does
but say, that *since* it has a sanction in early times, it is not
that "absurdity," "irrational fanaticism," and so forth,
which your Magazine says it is: and his meaning may be
thus worded: "Here is a usage existing up and down the
early Church, which, *right or wrong*, argues quite a different
temper and *feeling* from those of the present day. This
day, *on the first view of the subject*, calls it an absurdity;
that day did not." Surely it is fair to estimate inward
states of mind by such spontaneous indications. To warn
men against the religious complexion of certain persons at
present, I might say, "they belong to the Pastoral Aid
Society," though other men of the same religious sentiments
might not belong to it. To describe the temper of our
Bishops 130 years since, I should refer to the then attempt,
nearly successful, of formally recognizing the baptism of
Dissenters. Again, the character of Laud's religion may
be gathered even from the exaggerated account of his consecrating St. Catharine Cree's church, without sanctioning
that account.

When such indications occur in primitive times, though
they are not of authority more than in modern times, yet
they are tokens of what *is* of authority,—a certain religious temper, which *is* found everywhere, always, and in
all, though the particular exhibitions of it be not. In like

manner the spiritual interpretations of Scripture, which abound in the Fathers, may be considered as proving the Apostolicity of the principle of spiritualizing Scripture; though I may not, if it so happen, acquiesce in this or that particular application of it, in this or that Father. And so the administration of the Lord's Supper to infants in the church of Cyprian, Saint and Martyr, is a sanction of a principle, which you, on the other hand, call "an absurdity," "intellectual drivelling," and "irrational fanaticism." For my part, I am not ashamed to confess that I should consider Cyprian a better interpreter of the Scripture doctrine of the Sacraments, of "the minding of the Spirit" about them, than even the best divines of this day, did they take, as I am far from accusing them of doing, an opposite view. You, however, almost class the Saint among "ignorant fanatics," p. 119, and at least make him their associate and abettor.

Now, if this interpretation of the passage in question be correct, as I conscientiously and from my heart believe it to be, it will follow that you have not yet made good even the shadow of a shade of a charge of opposition to the Articles—not only against Dr. Pusey, but against the Tracts generally; for no one can say that any one of the Articles formally *forbids* us to consider that grace is conveyed *through* the outward symbols; while, on the other hand, one of them expressly speaks of "the body of Christ" as "given," as well as "taken, in the Supper;" words, moreover, which are known to have meant, in the language of that day, "given by the administrator;" and therefore, *through* the consecrated bread. At the same time, let it be observed I do not consider the writer of the Advertisement to say for *certain* that the outward elements benefit true Christians when insensible; only as much as this, that we cannot be sure they do not.

11.

Before closing this head of my subject, I shall remark on the words upon which you exclaim, "For shame, Dr. Pusey!" though he has no reason to be ashamed of what he did not write. They are these: "or what is called, communion with God." You often mistake, Mr. Editor, by not laying the emphasis on the right word in the sentence on which you happen to be commenting. This is a case in point. The stress is to be placed upon the word "*called*"—"what is *called* communion with God." The author meant, had he supplied his full meaning, "what is *improperly* called." There is nothing to show that he denies "the communion of saints" with God and with each other, and, in subordination to the mystical union, the conscious union of mind and affections. He only condemns that indulgence of mere excited feeling which has now-a-days engrossed that sacred title.

To show that this is no evasion or disingenuousness on my part (for you sometimes indulge in hints about me to this effect), I will give your readers one or two more instances of the same insensibility on your part to the emphatic word in a sentence, and the last of them a very painful instance.

1. I said, in the former part of my letter, that Dr. Pusey's friends insist on no *particular* or *peculiar* sense of the Articles,—a fault which I had just charged upon you. I had said you were virtually imposing additions: then I supposed the objection made, that *we* should do so, had we the power,—as is often alleged. To this I answer, "Your Magazine may rest satisfied that Dr. Pusey's friends will never assert that the Articles have any *particular* meaning at all." You have missed the point of this sentence: accordingly, you detach it from the context, and prefix it to the opening of the discussion, before it appears in its proper place in print; and when it does appear, you

print it in italics. This is taking a liberty with my text. However, to this subject I shall have occasion to recur.

2. Another instance occurs in your treatment of the Homilies and Mr. Keble. The Homily speaks of "the stinking puddles of *men's* traditions." You apply this as an answer to Mr. Keble's sermon, who speaks of *God's* traditions, even those which St. Paul bids us "hold;" and who considers, moreover, that no true traditions of doctrine exist but such as may be also proved from Scripture; whereas the Homily clearly means by men's traditions, that is, such as *cannot* be proved from Scripture. You would have escaped this mistake, had you borne in mind that traditions, "devised by men's imagination," are not Divine traditions, and that it as little follows that Catholic Traditions are to be rejected because Jewish and Roman are, as that the Christian Sabbath is abolished because the Jewish is abolished. But you saw that Mr. Keble said something or other about tradition, and you were carried away with the word.

3. The last mistake of this kind is a serious one. It is a charge brought against Dr. Pusey. He has said, "To those who have fallen, God holds out only a light in a dark place, sufficient for them to see their path, but not bright or cheering, as they would have it; and so, in different ways, man would forestall the sentence of his judge; the Romanist by the *sacrament* of penance, a modern class of divines by the *appropriation* of the merits and righteousness of our blessed Redeemer." You add three notes of admiration, and say, "We tremble as we transcribe these awful words," p. 123. I dare not trust myself to speak about such heedless language as it deserves. I will but say, in explanation of your misconception, that Dr. Pusey compares to Roman restlessness, not the *desiring* and *praying* to be clothed, or the doctrine that every one who

is saved must be clothed, in "the merits and righteousness of our blessed Redeemer," but the *appropriation* of them without warrant on the part of individuals. He denies that individuals who have fallen into sin have any right to *claim* them as their own already; he denies that they may "*forestall* the sentence of the Judge" at the last day; he maintains they can but flee to Christ, and adjure Him by His *general* promises, by His past mercies to themselves, by His present distinct mercies to them in the Church; but that they have no personal assurance, no right to appropriate again what was given them *plenarily* in baptism. This is his meaning; whereas you imply that he denies the duty of looking in faith to be saved *by* Christ's merits and righteousness; that he denies backsliders the *hope* of it. If you do not imply this, if you really mean that the *act of claiming* Christ's merits on the part of this or that individual (for of this Dr. P. speaks) is, as you express it, "a most Scriptural and consoling truth," and that it is "blasphemous," but for "the absence of wicked intention in the writer," to compare to the Roman penance the *confidence* which sinners are taught to feel that their past offences are *already* forgiven them,—if this be your meaning, I am wrong, but I am charitable, in saying you have mistaken Dr. Pusey.

Now I come to the consideration, which you especially press upon us, of (1) the Homilies, (2) the Articles, and (3) Justification.

12.

And first concerning the Homilies.

1. You ask, "How do these clergymen . . . . . *reconcile their* consciences to such declarations as those which abound, in the Homilies, affirming that the Church of Rome is 'Antichrist,' &c.?" And you say that you are considered "persecutors" or a persecutor, because you ask how I and others "reconcile such things in the Homilies with the

Oxford Tracts." Who considers you a persecutor? not I; nor should I ever so consider you for asking a simple question in argument. What I have censured you for, has been the use of vague epithets, calling names, and the like, which I really believe that you, Mr. Editor, in your sober reason disapprove as heartily as I do. For instance: I am sure you would think it wrong to proclaim to the world that such or such an one was an ultra-Protestant. It would be classing him with a party. There are ultra-Protestants in the world, we know; but we can know so little of individuals that we have seldom right to call them so, unless they themselves take the name. A man may hold certain ultra-Protestant *notions,* and we may say so; this is deciding about him just as far as we know, and no further. The case is the same in the more solemn matters of heaven and hell. We say, for instance, that they who hold anti-Trinitarian doctrines "will perish everlastingly;" but we dare not apply this anathema to this or that man; the utmost we say is, that he holds damnable errors, leaving his person to God. To say nothing of the religiousness of such a proceeding, you see how much of real kindness and considerateness it throws over controversy. Of course I do not wish to destroy what are facts; men *are* of different opinions, and they *do* act in sets. There is no harm in denoting this; many confess they so act. In conversation we never should get on, if we were ever using circumlocutions. But in controversy it does seem both Christian and gentlemanlike to subject oneself to rules; and, as one of these, to make a distinction between opinions and persons; to condemn opinions, to condemn them *in* persons, but not to give bad names to the persons themselves, till public authority sanctions it. If I think you have aught of the spirit of persecution in you—(and to be frank with you, and in observance of my own distinction, though you are not a "persecutor," you speak in somewhat of a persecuting *tone*,) it is not for perplexing me with questions, or overwhelming me with refutations, but because your style is "rough, rambling, and cursory." I think it *like* a persecutor to prefer mere general charges, to use unmeasured terms, to be oratorical and theatrical, and when challenged to speak definitely, to accuse the party challenging, of complaining, of being angry, and the like.

. 13.

Now to come to the Homilies. You ask how I reconcile my conscience to the Homilies calling Rome Antichrist, I holding, as I do, the doctrines of the Tracts. To this I answer by asking, if I may do so without offence, how *you* reconcile to your conscience the Homilies saying that "the Holy Ghost doth teach" in the book of Tobit? how you reconcile to your "subscription" that they five times call books of the Apocrypha "Scripture;" that Baruch is quoted as a "prophet" and as "holy Baruch," Tobit as "holy Father Tobit," the author of Wisdom and the Son of Sirach as "the Wise Man," and that the latter is said "certainly to assure us" of a heavenly truth; in a word, that the Apocrypha is referred to as many as fifty-three times? Here you see I have the advantage of you, Mr. Editor. For though I believe the Old and New Testament alone to be *plenarily* inspired, yet I do believe, according to the Homily, what you do not believe, that the Holy Ghost did speak by the mouth of Tobit. Here you see is the advantage of what you call my "scholastic distinctions," p. 193. When I said that the great gift of the Holy Ghost, called regeneration, was reserved for Christians, and yet that the Jews might be under His blessed guidance, you said I was drawing a scholastic distinction. This is one instance on your part of *calling names*. What do you mean by *scholastic*? Beware, lest, when you come to define it, you include unwittingly the most sacred truths under it. There are persons who think the Catholic doctrine of the Holy Trinity " scholastic ;" and so it is, but it is something more, it is Apostolic also. It is no proof that the distinction in question is not Scriptural, that it is, if it is, scholastic. However, anyhow, the " distinction " serves me in good stead as to this instance which you bring against me from the Homilies; it enables me to *understand* and to assent to their doctrine concerning the Apocrypha. I consider the gifts and operations of the Blessed Spirit to be manifold; some are outward, some inward, some sanctify, some are grants of power, some of knowledge, some of moral goodness. What He is towards Angels, towards glorified Saints as Moses and Elias, towards the faithful departed, towards Adam in Paradise, towards the Jews, towards the Heathen, towards Christians militant,—what He is in the Church, in the individual, in the Evangelist, in the Apostle, in the Prophet, in the Apocryphal writer, in the Doctor and Teacher,—is all holy, but admits of differences of kind and of degree. Life is the same in all living things; yet there is one flesh of men, another of fishes, another of birds: and so the spiritual gift in like manner may be the same, yet diverse; it may be applied to the heart or to the head, as an inward habit or an external impression; for one purpose, not for another; for a time, or for ever. Thus inspiration may be partial or plenary. This view of God's gracious influences you call scholastic. I, on the other hand, call the common division, into miraculous and moral or spiritual, jejune and unauthorized. However, whether I be right or you, I am at least able to do with mine, what you cannot with yours; —I can agree with the Homily. If you will not take my explanation, which I sincerely believe to be the right one you must " reconcile your conscience " to a better or to a worse; till you find one, you must reconcile it to a disagreement with the Homily.

14.

Now I will put another difficulty to you. The last Homily in the Volume is "against Disobedience and Wilful Rebellion." It is one of the most elaborate of them, consisting of no less than six parts. It advocates unreservedly the doctrine of passive obedience to the authorities under which we find ourselves by birth. *I hold this doctrine, you do not.*[5] Let me put before you some of the statements of this Homily,—the direct, explicit developments of its title. "If servants," it says, " ought to obey their masters, not only being gentle, but such as be froward, as well, and much more, ought subjects to be obedient, *not only to their good and courteous, but also to their sharp and rigorous princes,*" Part I. "A rebel is worse than the worse prince," ibid. "But what if the prince be undiscreet and evil indeed, and it is also evident to all men's eyes that he so is? I ask again, what if it belong of the wickedness of the subjects, that the prince is undiscreet and evil? shall the subjects both by their wickedness provoke God, for their deserved punishment, to give them an undiscreet or evil prince, and also rebel against him, and withal against God, *who for the punishment of their sins did give them such a prince?*" ibid. Now, considering the high Tory doctrine, as it is called, contained in such statements, I am led to ask you whether you approve of the Revolution, and the substitution of William III. for James II.; and, if you do, how you "reconcile your conscience" to give your adhesion to this Homily, and why you are not consistent enough to designate its writer and all "subscribers" to it "Lauds and Sacheverells."

[5] The charge against the Magazine was not of disloyalty, but of holding the *doctrine* that subjects may, under circumstances, rebel against their civil governors, e.g. as in the instance of the Revolution of 1688 in England, in Greece in 1821, in Spain in 1823, in France in 1830.

You are not the person, then, to take my conscience to task for not receiving every sentence of the Homilies as a formal enunciation of doctrine. I might, indeed, were it worth while, enlarge upon the venturousness of a writer, who seems, according to my apprehension, to hold that baptism is not a *means* of grace, but only "a sign, seal, and pledge," p. 167, and yet uses the Liturgy, being the man to make appeals to the conscience of others. But let this pass. Here, in the very instance of the Homilies which you urge, you do not come into court with clean hands. You shrink from certain portions of them; and yet you use strong language about the difficulty which you conceive others feel about other portions. Under these circumstances, were I merely writing for you, I should leave you to marvel either at my conscience, or at your own; but I write not for you alone; and in what I shall now say in explanation of my own bearing towards the Homilies, I may perhaps do something towards excusing yours.

15.

I say plainly, then, I have not *subscribed* the Homilies, though you say I have, pp. 151, 153; though you *add* to my subscription to the Articles this further subscription; nor was it ever intended that any member of the English Church should be subjected to what, if considered as an extended Confession, would indeed be a yoke of bondage. Romanism surely is innocent, compared with a system which would impose upon the "conscience" a thick octavo volume, written flowingly and freely by fallible men, to be received exactly sentence by sentence. I cannot conceive any grosser instance of a Pharisaical tradition than this would be. No: the Reformers would have shrunk from the thought of so unchristian a proceeding—a proceeding which would render it impossible (I will say) for any one member, lay or clerical, of the Church, who was subjected to such an ordeal, to remain in it. For instance: I do not suppose that any reader whatever would be satisfied with those political reasons for fasting, which, though indirectly introduced, are fully accepted and dwelt upon in the Homily on that subject. He would not like to subscribe the declaration that eating fish was a duty, not only as a bodily mortification, but as making provisions cheap, and encouraging the fisheries. He would not be able to approve of the association of religion with secular politics.

How, then, are we bound to the Homilies? By the Thirty-fifth Article, which speaks as follows: " The Second Book of Homilies . . . . doth *contain* a godly and wholesome *doctrine*, and necessary for these times, as doth the former Book of Homilies." Now, observe, this Article does not speak of every statement made in them, but of the "doctrine." It speaks of the view or cast or body of doctrine contained in them. In spite of ten thousand incidental propositions, as in any large book, there is, it is obvious, a certain line of doctrine which may be contemplated continuously in its shape and direction. For instance; if you say you disapprove the doctrine contained in the Tracts for the Times, no one supposes you to mean that every sentence and half-sentence is a lie. If this were so, then you are most inconsistent, after denouncing them, in considering, p. 167, that they "contain much that is godly and edifying, much that you are grateful for, and much that, if separated from its adjuncts, would be highly valuable in these days of liberalism and laxity." You even give logical reasons to show that there is no inconsistency in this, and you protest against the notion. And in like manner, I say, when the Article speaks of the *doctrine* of the Homilies, it does not measure the letter of them by the inch, it does not imply they contain no propositions which admit of two opinions;

but it speaks of a certain determinate teaching, and moreover adds, it is "*necessary* for *these times.*" Does not this, too, show the same thing? If a man said, The Tracts for the Times are *seasonable* at this moment, as their name assumes, would he not be considering them as taking a certain line, and bearing a certain way? Would he not be speaking, not of phrases or sentences, but of a "doctrine" in them, viewed as a whole? Would he be inconsistent, if after praising them as seasonable, he continued, "Yet I do not pledge myself to every view or sentiment in them; there are some things in them hard of digestion, or overstated, or doubtful, or subtle"?

Let us, then, have no more of superfluous appeals to our consciences in such a matter. Reserve them for graver cases, if you think you see such. If anything could add to the irrelevancy of the charge in question, it is the particular point in which you consider I dissent from the Homilies, even if I do, which will not be so easy to prove;—a question concerning the fulfilment of prophecy: viz. whether Papal Rome is Antichrist! An iron yoke indeed you would forge for the conscience, when you obliged us to assent, not only to all matters of doctrine which the Homilies contain, but even to their opinion concerning the fulfilment of prophecy. Why, *we* do not ascribe authority in such matters even to the unanimous consent of all the Fathers. But *you* allow us no private judgment whatever; your private judgment is all particular and peculiar.

16.

I might put what I have been saying in a second point of view. Take the table of contents prefixed to the Books of Homilies, and examine the headings; these surely, taken together, will give the substance of their teaching. Now I maintain that I hold fully and heartily the doctrine of the Homilies under every one of these headings: nor (excepting on Justification and Repentance) will you yourself be inclined to doubt it. The only point to which I should not accede, nor think myself called upon to accede, would be certain matters, subordinate to the doctrines to which the headings refer—matters not of doctrine, but of opinion, as that Rome is the Antichrist; or of historical fact, as that there was a Pope Joan, which, by-the-bye, I doubt whether you hold any more than I do. But now, on the other hand, can *you* subscribe the doctrine of the Homilies under every one of its formal headings? I believe you cannot. The Homily against Disobedience and Wilful Rebellion is in many of its elementary principles decidedly opposed to your sentiments. And yet it is you who tax another with not holding by the Homilies! Unless I had some experience that to be represented as "troublers of Israel" and "pestilent fellows" is the portion of those who fight against the Age, I should feel astonished at this.

I verily and in my conscience believe, that whether we take the text or the spirit of the Homilies, I do hold both the one and the other more exactly than those who question me. Do not, then, in future appeal to me, as if I for an instant granted that the Homilies were on your side;— but I propose to say more on this subject when I come to speak on Justification.

17.

2. It follows to speak of the Articles.

You imply that I put no sense at all upon them, but take them to mean anything; and subscription to be no test or measure of my opinions. Now is not this somewhat a strong charge to bring against a Clergyman? and particularly the member of a University which has, within the last two years, shown extraordinary, and almost unanimous, earnestness in maintaining the necessity of subscription, even in the case of undergraduates, against an external pressure? Why did not Dr. Pusey's friends quietly sit by, and leave others to set them free? Surely the facts of the case are strong enough to excuse a little charity, had certain persons any to give. They really do astonish me, after all—prepared as I am for such exhibitions—by the ease and vigour with which they fling about accusations; showing themselves perfect masters of their weapon. In one place you say that we hold that there is "not one baptized person, not one regenerated person, not one communicant, among all the Protestant churches, Lutheran or Reformed, except the Church of England, and its daughter churches," p. 122. Now, what would you say if we affirmed that you held that men could be saved by faith without works? You would think us very unscrupulous, and might use some strong words. Well, then, there is not a word, which you would apply to such a statement, that I might not with perfect sincerity and truth apply to yours. You have touched on a large subject, on which we have nowhere ventured any opinion whatever, and in which we do not hold what you have expressed—the subject of lay baptism—but on which an opinion is forthcoming when needed.

Another remarkable exhibition of the same controversial method is your asserting that one of the Tracts called the Dissenters "a mob of Tiptops, Gapes, and Yawns," pp. 172, 174, 177, 185, 186. Five times you say or imply it. Now it so happens that the Tract in question has nothing to do with Dissenters; but aims at those who wish alterations in the Liturgy on insufficient grounds, a circumstance which in itself excludes Dissenters. To those of your readers who do not know this excellent Tract (it is one of the parts of Richard Nelson), the following explanation will be acceptable. The subject of the Tract is the shortening of the Church Service. Tiptop is a "travelling man from Hull or Preston," who "quarters at" a public-house in Nelson's village, "sometimes for a fortnight at a time," and "dabbles in religion *as well as in politics;*" a man who is praised by his admirers as "talking beautifully, and expounding on *any* subject a person might choose to mention, politics, trade, agriculture, learning, religion, and what not." He "lectures about the Church Prayers" among other things; and among his hearers are Yawn, a farmer whose sons go to the Church school, and who himself "scarcely ever," as he boasts, "misses a Sunday," coming into the service "about the end of the First Lesson;" and Ned Gape, who also is a church-goer, though a late one. In what sense of the words, then, Mr. Editor, do you assert, that when Richard Nelson, in the end of the story, says that he "cannot stand by and see the noble old Prayer-book pulled to pieces, just to humour a mob of Tiptops, Gapes, and Yawns," that the writer calls Dissenters by those titles?

18.

Now for the meaning and authority of the Articles. You seem to me to confuse between two things very distinct; the holding a certain sense of a statement to be *true,* and imposing that sense upon others. Sometimes the two go together; at other times they do not. For instance, the meaning of the Creed (and again, of the Liturgy) is *known;* there is no opportunity for doubt here; it means but one thing, and he who does not hold that one meaning, does not hold it at all. But the case is different (to take an illustration), in the drawing up of a Political Declaration, or a Petition to Parliament. It is put together by persons, differing in matters of detail, though agreeing together to a certain point and for a certain end. Each narrowly watches that nothing is inserted to prejudice his own particular opinion, or stipulates for the insertion of what may rescue it. Hence general words are used, or particular words inserted, which by superficial inquirers afterwards are criticized as vague and indeterminate on the one hand, or inconsistent on the other; but, in fact, they all have a meaning and a history, could we ascertain it.[6] And, if the parties concerned in such a document are legislating and determining for posterity, they are respective representatives of corresponding parties in the generations after them. Now the Thirty-nine Articles lie between these two, between a Creed and a mere joint Declaration; to a certain point they have one meaning, beyond that they have no one meaning. They have one meaning, so far as they embody the doctrine of the Creed; they have different meanings, so far as they are drawn up by men influenced severally by the discordant opinions of the day. This is what I have expressed in the former part of my letter: "the Articles," I say, "are confessedly wide in their meaning, but still their width is within bounds: they seem to include a number of shades of opinion."

Next, as to those points (whatever they are) in which they cannot be said to have one meaning. Each subscriber indeed assigns that meaning which he at once holds himself and thinks to be the meaning; but this is his "particular" meaning, and he has no right to impose it on another. In saying, then, that I should put no "particular meaning" on portions of the Articles, I spoke not of *my own belief*, but of my enforcing that belief upon others. I do sincerely and heartily consider my sense of the Articles, on certain points to be presently mentioned, to be the true sense; but

---

[6] Hence *faith, justification, infection,* &c., are used, not defined in the Articles.

I do not feel sure that there were not represented at the drawing up of the Articles, parties and interests which led the framers, (not as doing so on a principle, but spontaneously, from the existing hindrances to perfect unanimity,) to abstain from perfect precision and uniformity of statement. What can be more truly liberal and forbearing than this view? yet for thus holding that Calvinists and others, whom I think mistaken, may sign the Articles as well as myself, I am said myself to sign them with "no meaning whatever." And you actually take my own sentiment out of my mouth, clothe it in the words of the Royal Declaration, and then gravely make a present of it to me back again, as if it were something wise and high of your own. "The Royal Declaration," you say, "prefixed to the Articles, congratulates the Church that all the clergy had 'most willingly subscribed' to them, 'all sorts taking them to be for them:' which shows that each conscientious individual had carefully examined into their meaning, and not that he signed them without attaching any 'particular meaning at all.'" p. 191. Of course;—these are just my sentiments.

Accordingly I go on to say, that I look forward to success, not by *compelling* others to take one view of the Articles, but by *convincing* them that mine is the right one. And this will explain what you call my "pugnacious terms." Were I fighting against individuals or a party in the Church, *this* would be party spirit: but then I should wish to coerce them or cast them out; whereas I am opposing principles and doctrines—so, I would fain persuade and convert, not triumph over those who hold them. I am not pugnacious; I am only "militant."

It will explain, too, what you consider my overweening and provoking language. For I consider I am but speaking what the Catholic Fathers witness to be Christ's Gospel. I am exercising no private judgment on Scripture; and while I will not enforce my own coercively, having no authority to do so, I will never put it forward hesitatingly, as if I did not think all other doctrines plainly wrong.

So much about myself. On the other hand, my charge against you is, and I repeat it, that you do wish to *add* to the Articles; that is in the same sense in which you accused Bishop Marsh of wishing to do so. You wish to impose upon me your particular or peculiar notion that the Patriarchs were regenerated; which is an invasion of private judgment, as permitted in our Church, as gross as if I strove to enforce on you my particular notion, in accordance with the Homily, that the Holy Ghost spoke " by the mouth of Tobit." Till you name the particular points of opinion for which you call on Dr. Pusey to resign his Professorship, and state the article or determination of the Church which he transgresses, I will never cease to say that (unwittingly, of course, not with bad intention) you do wish and aim to add to the Articles of subscription.

19.

To sum up what I have said, and to be at the same time more specific. I consider that the first five Articles have one definite, positive, dogmatic view, even that which has been from the beginning, the Catholic and Apostolic Truth on which the Church is built.

From the Sixth to the Eighteenth, I conceive to have one certain view also, brought out in its particular form at the Reformation; but, as in the Seventeenth, not clearly demonstrable to be such to the satisfaction of the world.

In the remaining Articles, taken *as a body*, I think there is less strictness, perspicuity, and completeness of meaning. Some, though clear and definite in their meaning, are but negative, or protestant, as being directed against the Romanists; others, which are positive, are derived from various schools; in others the view is left open or inchoate.

The first division I humbly receive as Divine, proveable from Scripture, but descending to us by Catholic tradition also. The next I admit and hold as deducible from Scripture by private judgment, tradition only witnessing here and there. The last division I receive only in the plain letter, according to the injunction of the Declaration, because I do believe in my conscience that they were not written upon any one view, and cannot be taken *except* in the letter; because I think they *never* had any one simple meaning; because I think I see in them the terms of various schools mixed together—terms known by their historical associations to be theologically discordant, though in the mere letter easy and intelligible.

20.

And now, lastly, I will say *why* I take these last Articles in that one particular meaning, in which I do take them, and not in another. This again is from no mere private liking or opinion; it is because I verily think the Church wishes me so to take them. We at this day receive the Articles, not on the authority of their framers, whoever they were, English or foreign, but on the authority, i.e. in the sense, of the Convocation imposing them, that is, the Convocation of 1571. That Convocation, which imposed them, also passed the following Canon about Preachers:—" In the first place, let them be careful never to teach anything in their sermons, as if to be religiously held and believed by the people, but what is agreeable to the doctrine of the Old and New Testament, *and collected from that very doctrine by the Catholic Fathers and ancient Bishops.*" This is but one out of the hundred appeals to Antiquity, which, in one way or other, our Church has put forth; but it is rendered special by its originating in the Convocation from which we receive the Articles. It is quite impossible that that Convocation wished us to receive and explain the doctrines contained in them in any other sense than that which " the catholic Fathers and ancient Bishops" drew from Scripture. Far from explaining away, I am faithfully maintaining them, when I catholicize them. It were well for themselves, had others as good a reason for Calvinizing or Zuinglizing them.

And all this shows how right I am in saying above that the Articles must not be viewed as in themselves a *perfect system* of doctrine. They are, on the face of them, but protests against existing errors, Socinianism and Romanism. For instance, how else do you account for the absence of any statement concerning the *Inspiration* of Scripture? On the other hand, the Canon of 1571, just cited, is a proof that the whole range of catholic doctrines is professed by our Church; not only so much as is contained in the Articles. Its reception of the primitive Creeds is another proof; for they reach to many points not contained in the Articles without them. To these documentary evidences may be added the 30th Canon of 1603. Speaking of the use of the Sign of the Cross, it says, " 'The abuse of a thing doth not take away the lawful use of it.' Nay, *so far was it from the purpose* of the Church of England to *forsake and reject* the churches of Italy, France, Spain, Germany, or any such like churches, in *all* things which they held and practised, that, as the Apology of the Church of England confesseth, it doth with reverence retain those ceremonies which do neither endamage the Church of God nor offend the minds of sober men; and *only* departed from them in those *particular* points wherein they were fallen, both from themselves *in their ancient integrity*, and from the Apostolical churches, which were their *first founders.*"

It is clear, then, that the English Church holds all that the primitive Church held, even in ceremonies, *except* there be some particular reasons assignable for not doing so in this or that instance ; and only does not hold the modern corruptions maintained by Romanism. In these corruptions it departs from Rome ; *therefore* these are the points in which it thinks it especially necessary to declare its opinion. To these were added the most sacred points of faith, in order to protest against those miserable heresies to which Protestantism had already given birth. Thus the Church stands in a *Via Media;* the first five Articles being directed against extreme Protestantism, the remaining ones against Rome. And hence, when the Royal Declaration says that they "contain the true doctrine of the Church of England, agreeable to God's word," which you quote, p. 169, as if it made against me, it speaks of the doctrine of the English church *so far* as distinguished from other churches. The Declaration does not say the doctrine of the Gospel, the doctrine of the Church Catholic, or the whole faith ; but it speaks of it in contrast with existing systems. This is evident from its wording ; for the clause "agreeable to God's word" evidently glances at Rome ; and the history of its promulgation throws abundant light on the fact that it was aimed against Calvinism and Arminianism. There is nothing, then, in these words to show that the Articles are a system of doctrine, or more than the English doctrine in those points in which it differs from Romanism and Socinianism, and embraces Arminianism and Calvinism.

No : our Apostolical communion inherits, as the promises, so the faith, enjoyed by the Saints in every age ; the faith which Ignatius, Cyprian, and Gregory received from the Apostles. We did not begin on a new foundation in King Edward's time ; we only reformed, or repaired, the superstructure. You must not defraud us, Mr. Editor, of our birthright, by turning what is a salutary protest into a system of divinity.

21.

Before proceeding to the subject of Justification, I will conclude what I have otherwise to say on your sixty pages, by adducing some further instances of what I consider misconceptions in them.[7] . . .

Here then I shall close for the present. One subject, and a most important one, remains; that of Justification. Before I commence it, I invite you to do, what you cannot decline. You have accused me frequently of "evasions," though not intentional ones, of course. I on the other hand accuse you, instead of coming to the point, of vague and illogical declamation, though not intentional either. Now, then, state definitely *what* Dr. Pusey's opinions are, for which he ought to give up his Professorship; and state also, *why*, that is, *what statements* of our Church his own oppose. *Till you do this,* I shall persist in saying you wish to add to the Articles of subscription. I challenge you to do this, and call your readers to attend to your answer; and then, in my next, I will do my best to meet it.

* * * * * *

N.B. November 1, 1837. The letter was not continued further, partly on account of the very unsatisfactory mode in which the above was printed in the pages of the Magazine, and partly because the challenge, repeated in its closing words, had not been met.[8]

[7] [As these were matters of detail and uninteresting, they are omitted here.]

[8] [The author did not let the subject of Justification drop; the next year (1838) he published a Volume of Lectures on it; and he completed what he had to say upon the Articles and Homilies, and on Justification with reference to them, four years later (1841) in Tract 90.]

VI.

A LETTER ADDRESSED TO THE REV. THE MARGARET PROFESSOR OF DIVINITY,

ON

MR. R. HURRELL FROUDE'S STATEMENTS CONCERNING THE HOLY EUCHARIST,

AND OTHER MATTERS THEOLOGICAL AND ECCLESIASTICAL.

1838.

A LETTER,[1]

&c.

Rev. Sir,

I MAKE no apology for troubling you with this Letter, for I cannot conceal from myself that I am one of those against whom your recent Publication is directed. My first impulse indeed, when I heard of the probability of its appearance, was to resolve not to answer it, and to recommend the same course to others. I have changed my mind at the suggestion of friends, who, I feel, have taken a sounder view of the matter; but my original feeling was, that we have differences and quarrels enough all around us, without my adding to them. Sure I am, that the more stir is made about those opinions which you censure, the wider they will spread. This has been proved abundantly in the course of the last few years. Whatever be the mistakes and faults of their advocates, they have that root of truth in them which, as I do firmly believe, has a blessing with it. I do not pretend to say they will ever become widely popular, that is another matter; Truth is never, or at least never long, popular;—nor do I say they will ever gain that powerful external influence over the Many, which Truth vested in the Few,

[1] [To this Letter, as originally published, applied the well-known paradox, "The author had not time to make it shorter." In consequence, he has now omitted or abridged some superfluous paragraphs which, as they stood, weakened its controversial force or were irrelevant to his purpose.]

cherished, throned, energizing in the Few, often has possessed;—nor that they are not destined, as Truth has often been destined, to be cast away and at length trodden under foot as an odious thing;—but of this I am sure, that at this juncture in proportion as these opinions are known, they will make their way through the community, picking out their own, seeking and obtaining refuge in the hearts of Christians, high and low, here and there, with this man and that, as the case may be; doing their work in their day, as raising a memorial and a witness to this fallen generation of what once has been, of what God would ever have, of what one day shall be in perfection; and that, not from what they are in themselves, because viewed in the concrete they are mingled, as everything human must be, with error and infirmity, but by reason of the spirit, the truth, the old Catholic life and power which is in them.

And, moreover, while that inward principle of truth will carry on their tide of success to those bounds wider or straiter, which, in God's inscrutable providence, they are to reach and not to pass, it is also a substitute for those artificial and sectarian bonds of co-operation between man and man, which constitute what is commonly called a party. I notice this, because though you do not use concerning their upholders the word *party*, you do speak of an existing "combination," "an indefinite and apparently numerous body of friends," nay you hint at a "formidable conspiracy;" words which mean more than that unity of action which unity of sentiment produces. Men who think deeply and strongly, will act upon their principles; and if they think alike, will act alike; and lookers on, seeing the acts, and not seeing the principles, impute that to concert which proceeds from unanimity, So much I would grant in the present case, and no more; unless the contingence of two persons thinking alike and acting on their thoughts be party spirit, it is impossible to help the appearance of party in cases where there is not the reality. Like actions inevitably follow; but their doers are not party men, till their own personal success becomes prior in their thoughts to that of their object.

2.

Such is the position in which the opinions and persons stand, whom you so heavily censure. And whatever be the consequence to those persons, I see nothing but advantage resulting to those opinions from such publicity and discussion as you are drawing upon them. As far as they are concerned, I should have no anxiety about addressing you; but a feeling of the miserable breach of peace and love which too commonly follows on such controversies, to say nothing of one's own private convenience, is enough to make any one pause before engaging in such a discussion. I cannot doubt you feel it also, and therefore I deeply regret that a sense of imperative duty should have obliged you to commence it. No one of course can deny that there may be cases when it is a duty to hazard such a result; the claims of truth must not be compromised for the sake of peace. No one has any cause to complain of those who, from a religious regard to purity of doctrine, denounce what others admire. But this I think may fairly be required of all persons, that they do not go so far as to denounce in another what they do not at the same time show to be inconsistent with the doctrine of our Church. Now this is the first thought which rises in my mind on the perusal of your Remarks. I do not find in them any proof of the contrariety of the opinions and practices, which you condemn, to our Church's doctrines. This seems to me an omission. You speak of an "increasing *aberration* from Protestant principles," "a disposition to *overvalue* the importance of Apostolical tradition;" "*exaggerated* and *unscriptural* statements," a "*tendency* to depreciate the principles of Protestantism," and to "palliate" the "errors of Popery," "gradual and near *approximation* towards" the "Roman superstitions" concerning "the Lord's Supper." Now this is all assertion, not proof; and no one person, not even a Bishop *ex cathedrâ*, may at his mere word determine what doctrine shall be received and what not. He is bound to appeal to the established faith. He is bound conscientiously to try opinions by the established faith, and in doing so appeals to an Unseen Power. He is bound to state in what respect they differ from it, if they do differ; and, in so doing, he appeals to his brethren. The decision, indeed, is in his own hands; he acts on his own responsibility; but before he acts he makes a solemn appeal before God and man. What is true of the highest authority in the Church, is true of others. We all have our private views; many persons have the same private views; but if ten thousand have the same, that does not make them less private; they are private till the Church's judgment makes them public. I am not entering into the question about what is the Church, and the difference between the whole Church and parts of the Church, or what are, what are not, subjects for Church decisions; I only say, looking at the English Church at this moment, and practically, that if there be two parties in it, the one denouncing, the other denounced, in a matter of doctrine, either the latter is promoting heresy, or the former is promoting schism. I do not see that there is any medium; and it does seem incumbent on the former to show he is not infringing peace, by showing that the latter is infringing truth.

3.

There is a floating body of opinions in every Church,

which varies with the age. They are held in one age, abandoned in the next. They are distinct from the Church's own doctrines; they may be held or abandoned, not without criticism indeed, because every man has a right to have his opinion about another's thoughts and deeds, and to tell him of it, but without denunciation. The English Church once considered persecution to be a duty; I am not here called on to give any opinion on the question; but certainly the affirmative side of it was not binding on every one of her members. The great body of English Churchmen have for three centuries past called the Lord's Table an Altar, though the word is not in our formularies: I think a man wrong who says it is not an Altar, but I will not denounce him; I will not write in a hostile tone against any person or any work which does not, as I think, contradict the Articles or the Prayer Book. And in like manner, there has ever been in our Church, and is allowed by our formularies, a very great latitude as regards the light in which the Church of Rome is to be viewed. Why must this right of private judgment be infringed? Why must those who exercise that right be spoken of in terms only applicable to heretical works, and which might with just as much and just as little propriety be retorted upon the quarter they came from? Mr. Froude's volumes are called in your Sermon an "*offensive* publication;" is this a term to be applied to writings which differ from us in essentials or non-essentials? they are spoken of not only as containing "startling and extravagant" passages, but "poison." What words do you reserve for heresy, for plain denials of the Creed, for statements counter to the Articles, for preachings and practices in disobedience to the Prayer Book? If at any time the danger from Romanism was imminent, it was at the time when the Articles were drawn up; what right has any one now of his own private authority to know better than their compilers, and to act as if those Articles were more stringent in their protest against it than they are? If the Church of the nineteenth century outruns the sixteenth in her condemnation of its errors, let her mould her formularies accordingly. When she has so done, she has a claim on her members to submit; but till then, she has a claim on them to respect that liberty of thought which she has allowed, nor to denounce without stating the formal grounds of their denunciation.

4.

I am speaking, on the one hand, of a public, severe, deliberate condemnation; and on the other of the omission of the grounds on which it is made. If grounds can be produced, of course I do not object; and in such case I leave it for those to decide, whether they be tenable, with whom the decision lies. Nor on the other hand can any fair objection be made to friendly expostulation, nay or to public remonstrance even without grounds stated, if put forward as resting on the personal authority of the individual making them. Men of wisdom need not for ever be stating their grounds for what they say: but then they speak not *ex cathedrá*, but as if "giving *their* judgment," their *own* judgment, "as those that have been faithful;" as "Paul the aged." The private judgment of one man is not the same as that of another; it may, if it so be, weigh indefinitely more than another's; it may outweigh that of a number, however able, learned, and well-intentioned. But then he gives it *as* private judgment; he does not come forward to denounce. And, again, to take the case of men in general, there will ever be difference of opinion among them about the truth, fairness, propriety or expedience of things said and done by each other. They have full right, as I have already said, or are even under a duty to speak their mind, though they speak it with pain ; and the parties spoken to must bear it, though they bear it with pain. All this need not infringe the bond of charity on the one side or the other. But to denounce publicly yet without stating grounds is a different procedure.

5.

And next, I am sorry, that, considering that you have used strong terms concerning Mr. Froude's Volumes, you have not judged it right to state that they contain as strong expressions against Popery as your pamphlet contains against those Volumes. Nay, you might without much trouble have even cited these, especially as you cite so many others which seem to you to countenance the errors of the Papal system ; but perhaps this was too much to expect. Yet at least you would have had no need to lose time in finding them, for some of the principal are brought together in the Preface, which you have evidently read. These strong disclaimers in the work in question tell the more from the unsuspicious way in which the Author made them; in private letters to friends, and in casual conversation, when nothing called for them but the genuine feeling of their truth on his part. They shall find here the place which you have denied them.

Speaking of Italy and Sicily, he says, "These Catholic countries seem in an especial manner to 'hold the Truth in unrighteousness.' And the Priesthood are themselves so sensible of the hollow basis upon which their power rests, that they dare not resist the most atrocious encroachments of the State upon their privileges. . . . I have seen priests laughing when at the Confessional; and indeed it is plain, that, unless they habitually made light of very gross immorality, three-fourths of the population [of Naples] would be excommunicated."[2] vol. i. pp. 293, 4.

Such a protest against the practical working of the existing Roman system abroad, is not much like a recommendation of it at home. I am sure your readers cannot be prepared for it. All you tell them is, from your title, that there is a "Revival of Popery," and, from your remarks, that Mr. Froude's Volumes help it forward. Certainly you do concede that the persons you speak of are not "*strictly* Papists ;" and that it would be "as uncharitable as it is untrue," to say, "that *within certain limits of their own devising* they are not actually opposed to the corruptions and the communion of Rome." p. 24. May I ask, *whose* "devising" the "limits" are, which enable *you* to assign to these persons their exact place in the scale of theology? Certainly not the devising of the Church; at least, you do not appeal to it. Such is the measure of consideration you show to them.

Again: on a friend's saying that the Romanists were schismatics in England and Catholics abroad, "No," he answered, "they are *wretched Tridentines* everywhere." p. 434.

In another place he speaks of "the atrocious Council" of Trent; and adds, "I own, it" (information concerning that Council) "has altogether changed my notions of the Roman Catholics; and *made me wish for the total overthrow of their system.*" vol. i. pp. 307, 8.[3]

---

[2] [Such language arises from a misconception of the rules and the action of the Catholic system. Immoral men are not publicly excommunicated in *foro externo*, but, being deprived of the sacraments, or at least of their grace, till they repent, they are but dead branches of the True Vine, and in a truer sense excommunicate than if they were cut off from the visible body.]

[3] [I cannot in fairness withdraw specimens such as these of the view taken by my very dear friend of Italy and its religion, though of course I leave them in the text with much pain. He was a man who did nothing by

Now from such passages I gather, that the author did consider the existing system of Rome, since the Council of Trent, to be a most serious corruption. Nay, he adds himself, that he wishes for its "*total overthrow.*" This is not like giving a helping hand towards "the Revival of Popery." However, the sole impression conveyed to your mind, by the passage, is, not the *direct* one that the Roman system *has been* hopelessly corrupt *since*, but, by *inference* that it was *not* hopelessly corrupt *before*. The latter point you enlarge upon; the former you let alone. Might I not put in a plea that you should not deduce *from* a premiss, without acknowledging that premiss *itself?*

6.

But now, as to this question concerning the Council of Trent, let us consider what it is Mr. Froude and others have said about it. Merely this,—not that the Church of Rome was not corrupt before the Council of Trent, but that its corruptions before that Council were for the most part *in* the Church but not *of* it; they were floating opinions and practices, far and wide received, as the Protestant opinions in our Church may be at this day, but, like these opinions in our own case, they were not, as a body, taken into the Church, and made the system of the Church till that Council.[4] And this is what Mr. Froude

halves. He had cherished an ideal of the Holy See and the Church of Rome partly erroneous, partly unreal, and was greatly disappointed when to his apprehension it was not fulfilled. He had expected to find a state of lofty sanctity in Italian Catholics, which he considered was not only not exemplified, but was even contradicted in what he saw and heard of them. As to the Tridentine definitions he simply looked at them in the light of obstacles to the union of Anglicans with the See of Rome, not having the theological knowledge necessary for a judgment on their worth.]

[4] Image worship had been sanctioned at the second Council of Nicæa; transubstantiation at the fourth Lateran.

means by his notions being "changed" about the Roman Catholics; he thought, till he was better informed, that the Church in Council might alter what the Church in Council had determined; but when he found that Romanists could not reduce to a matter of opinion what they had once exalted into a doctrine, that they could not unloose an anathema they had once tied, that, in his own words, "they were committed finally and irrevocably, and could not advance one step to meet us, even though the Church of England should again become what it was in Laud's time," then, while he called the Council "atrocious," he went on to "wish for the total overthrow" of the system, which is built upon it.

How different is this from approving of everything that took place in the Church before it! While bitterly mourning over the degradation and divisions of the Church Catholic, he is oppressed with the sudden sight of an apparently insuperable difficulty in the way of any future healing her wounds, the great and formal decision of the Roman Church at Trent, that points which had been before but matters of opinion, should be henceforth terms of communion. There was hope till this decision; there were the means of reformation. In the words of one of the Tracts you refer to, "If she (Rome) has apostatized, it was at the time of the Council of Trent. Then, indeed, it is to be feared, the whole Roman Communion bound itself, by a perpetual bond and covenant, to the cause of Antichrist.[5] But before that time, grievous as were the corruptions *in* the Church, no individual Bishop, Priest,

---

[5] [What the writer meant by these very strong words in 1833 "bound to the cause of Antichrist," except that he thought it right to follow the teaching of Field and Gilpin, presently quoted, it is difficult to say. That he did not in 1838 subscribe to the Protestant notion that "the Pope was Antichrist" is plain from what follows; it is also plain that he was ashamed of his language by the time he wrote this Letter.]

or Deacon, was bound by oath to the maintenance of them. Extensively as they were spread, no clergyman was shackled by obligations which prevented his resisting them ; he could but suffer persecution for so doing. He did not commit himself in one breath to two vows, to serve faithfully in the Ministry, and yet to receive all the superstitions and impieties which human perverseness had introduced into the most gracious and holiest of God's gifts." vol. i. No. 15.

I confess I wish this passage were not cast in so declamatory a form; but the substance of it expresses just what I mean. The Council of Trent did, as regards Roman errors, what, for all we know, (though God forbid !) some future synod of the English Church may do as regards Protestant errors,—take them into her system, make them terms of communion, bind upon her hitherto favoured sons their grievous chain ; and what that unhappy Council [6] actually did for Rome, that does every one in his place and according to his power, who, by declaiming against and denouncing those who dare to treat the Protestant errors as unestablished, gives a helping hand towards their establishment.

7.

I will quote two passages from very different persons in corroboration of what has been said, Dean Field and Bernard Gilpin. Dean Field says, that "none of those points of false doctrine and error which Romanists now maintain and we condemn were the doctrines of the Church *before the Reformation* constantly delivered, or generally

---

[6] [It is observable that at the commencement of the Oxford movement in 1833 the insuperable obstacle, felt by high Anglicans, to communion with Rome, was the doctrine of the Tridentine Council. By 1865 they seem to have got over it, and the Vatican decrees are the obstacle now. Will they be such in another forty years ?]

received, by all them that were of it, but doubtfully broached, and devised without all certain resolution, or factiously defended by some certain only, who, *as a dangerous faction, adulterated the sincerity of the Christian Verity, and brought the Church into miserable bondage."* *Of the Church, Append. to b.* iii. Elsewhere he speaks as follows :—" There is therefore a great difference to be made, *between the Church wherein our Fathers formerly lived and that faction* of the Pope's adherents, which at this day resist against the necessary reformation of the Churches of God, and make that their faith and religion, *which, in former times, was but the private and unresolved opinion of some certain only.* . . *Formerly, the Church of Rome was the true Church, but had in it an heretical faction : now the Church itself is heretical, and some certain only are found in it* in such degree of orthodoxy, as that we may well hope of their salvation." iii. 47.

Bernard Gilpin, whom I shall quote next, is the stronger evidence, inasmuch as he considered what I certainly cannot, that the Pope was the Antichrist; yet he implies that he only became so at Trent.[7] . . . " The Church of Rome kept the rule of faith entire, *until that rule was changed and altered by the Council of Trent; and from that time* it seemed to him a matter of necessity to come out of the Church of Rome, that so that Church which is true and called out from thence might follow the word of God."[8]

[7] [" As a boy of fifteen," I have said of myself,·" I had . . .fully imbibed [pure Protestantism] . . . The effect of this early persuasion remained a stain upon my imagination. . . I began in 1833 to form theories on the subject, which tended to obliterate it ; yet by 1838 I had got no farther than to consider Antichrist as, not the Church of Rome, but the spirit of the old Pagan city, the fourth monster of Daniel, which was still alive, and which had corrupted the Church which was planted there. . . I had a great and growing dislike, after the summer of 1839, to speak against the Roman Church herself or her formal doctrines." *Apolog.* pp. 120, 121.]

[8] Wordsworth, Eccles. Biogr. vol. iv. p. 94.

8.

Nothing surely is more intelligible than being in a Church, and not approving of the acts of its rulers or of large bodies in it. At this day there are many things said and done among us which you would as little approve as myself; and are we answerable for them? and though we should be silent when great and grievous errors were put forth, though we allowed books to go out to the world as if with our sanction when they had it not, though we gave persons out of doors the impression that we approved of them, though when controversy began we took no prominent share in it, though we sat still and let others bear the brunt and odium of it, ought we therefore to be identified with those errors whatever they are? Certainly not; though blameless in such a case we certainly should not be, nor without some sort of debt to them who worked for us. If Albigenses or Waldenses can be found who really did the office of witnesses in those strange times of mixed good and evil, let them have the praise of it; let the Church have the shame of it, for not doing the work herself and in a better way. But it is one thing to say the rulers of the Church were remiss or incapable; quite another that they agreed with their more stirring brethren, who acted instead of them, and usurped the Church's name, and abused her offices, and seemed to be more than they were. How then is it to the purpose to speak of the "systematic imposture of pretended miracles," "the portentous delusions of Purgatory and Transubstantiation," "the especial worship of the Virgin Mary," "the prohibition of Scripture," "the establishment of the Inquisition," &c. as existing before Trent? Who defends such things as these? who says the Church of Rome was free from them before Trent? Are not the Tracts, which you refer to, full of protestations against them, protestations quite as strong as those I read in your pamphlet? Why are the Tracts to be censured for stating a plain historical fact, that the Roman Church did not, till Trent, embody in her creed the mass of her present tenets, while they do not deny but expressly acknowledge her great corruptions before that era, while they give the history of Transubstantiation prior to Trent, (Nos. 27, 28,) of the Breviary worship of the Blessed Virgin prior to Trent, (No. 75,) of Purgatory prior to Trent, (No. 79,) while they formally draw up points in which they feel agreement with Romanists to be hopeless, (Nos. 38, 71,) and while they declare, (in large letters, to draw attention,) that, so long as Rome is what it is, "union" with it "is impossible"? (No. 20.) All that can be said against them is, that in discussing the Roman tenets, they use guarded language; and this I will say, that the more we have personal experience of the arduous controversy in question, the more shall we understand the absolute necessity, if we are to make any way, of weighing our words, and keeping from declamation.

9.

You speak as if the opinions held by the writers you censure were novel in our Church, and you connect them with the "*revival* of Popery." Does any one doubt that on all points of *doctrine* on which a question can occur, there is a large school in our Church, consisting of her far most learned men, mainly agreeing with those writers? Does any one doubt that their statements are borne out in the main by Hooker, Andrewes, Laud, Montague, Hammond, Bramhall, Taylor, Thorndike, Bull, Beveridge, Ken, and Wilson, not to mention others? how many are there of the doctrines you object to, which one or other or all of these great pastors and teachers do not maintain? I will confine myself to Bramhall, who flourished in the seventeenth century, and after holding the see of Derry in the reign of

Charles the First, and suffering in the great Rebellion, was made Archbishop of Armagh. And let it be observed that in thus drawing out one or two of the opinions of this great man, I am not making myself or any one else responsible for them; I am but showing how far divines may diverge from the views now popular, and yet be held in reverence both in their own day and since.

1. Of the Real Presence he thus speaks: "So grossly is he" (his Roman opponent) " mistaken on all sides, when he saith that '*Protestants*' (*he should say the English Church if he would speak to the purpose*) ' have a positive belief that the Sacrament is not the Body of Christ ;' which were to contradict the words of Christ, 'This is My Body.' He knows better that Protestants do not deny the *thing*, but their bold determination of the *manner* by Transubstantiation." *Works*, p. 226.—" Abate us Transubstantiation, and those things which are consequent of their determination of the *manner* of Presence, and we have no difference with them [the Romanists] to this particular. They who are ordained Priests ought to have power to consecrate the Sacrament of the Body and Blood of Christ, that is, *to make Them present* after such manner as they were present at the first institution, whether it be done by enunciation of the words of Christ, as it is observed in the Western Church, or by Prayer, as it is practised in the Eastern Church; or whether these two be both the same thing in effect, that is, that forms of the Sacraments be mystical prayers and implicit invocations." *Works*, p. 485. " Whether it be corporeally or spiritually, (I mean not only after the manner of a spirit, but in a spiritual sense,) whether it be in the soul only or in the Host also, whether by consubstantiation or transubstantiation, whether by production, or adduction, or conservation, or assumption, or by whatsoever other way bold and blind men here conjecture, we determine not." p. 21.

2. Concerning the Sacrifice of the Mass. "If his Sacrifice of the Mass have any other propitiatory power or virtue in it *than* to commemorate, represent, and apply the merit of the Sacrifice of the Cross, let him speak plainly what it is. *Bellarmine knew no more of this Sacrifice* than we." p. 172. "We acknowledge an Eucharistical Sacrifice of praise and thanksgiving; a commendative Sacrifice, or a memorial of the Sacrifice of the Cross; a representative Sacrifice, or, a representation of the Passion of Christ before the eyes of His heavenly Father; an impetrative Sacrifice, or an inpetration of the fruit and benefit of His passion, by way of real prayer; and, lastly, an applicative Sacrifice, or an application of His merits unto our souls. Let him that dare go one step farther than we do, and say that it is a suppletory Sacrifice to supply the defects of the Sacrifice of the Cross; or else let them hold their peace, and speak no more against us in this point of Sacrifice for ever." p. 255. "I have challenged them to go one step farther into it [the question of the Sacrifice of the Mass] than I do; and *they dare not*, or rather *they cannot*, without blasphemy." p. 418.

3. Concerning adoration *in* the Sacrament. "We ourselves adore Christ *in the Sacrament;* but we dare not adore the *species of Bread and Wine.*" p. 356.

4. Concerning Prayers for the Dead in Christ. "We condemn not all praying for the dead; not for their resurrection and the consummation of their happiness; but their prayers for their deliverance out of Purgatory." p. 356.

5. Concerning the Intercession of Saints. "For the 'intercession, prayers, merits of the Saints,' (taking the word 'merit' in the sense of the Primitive Church, that is, not for desert, but for acquisition,) I know no difference about them, among those men who understand themselves; but only about the last words, 'which they invocate in their Temples,' rather than Churches. A *comprecation* both

the Grecians and we do allow; an *ultimate* invocation both the Grecians and we detest; so do the Church of Rome in their doctrine, but they vary from it in their practice." p. 418.

6. Concerning Monasteries. "So as Monasteries were restrained in their number and in their revenues, so as the Monks were restrained from meddling between the Pastor and his flock; . . so as the abler sort, who are not taken up with higher studies and weightier employments, were insured to bestow their spare hours from their devotions in some profitable labour for the public good, that idleness might be stripped of the cloak of contemplative devotion; so as the vow of celibacy were reduced to the form of our English Universities, so long a fellow, so long unmarried; . . so as their blind obedience were more enlightened and secured by some certain rules and bounds; so as their mock poverty . . were changed into competent maintenance; and lastly so as all opinion of satisfaction and supererogation were removed; I do not see why Monasteries might not agree well enough with reformed devotion." p. 65.

7. Concerning the Pope. "He must either be meanly versed in the Primitive Fathers, or give little credit to them, who will deny the Pope to succeed St. Peter in the Roman Bishopric, or will envy him the dignity of a Patriarch within his just bounds." p. 299.

8. Concerning the relation of the English Church to Protestantism. "In setting forth the moderation of our English Reformers, I showed that we do not arrogate to ourselves either a new Church, or a new religion, or new holy orders. Upon this he falls heavily two ways. First he saith, 'It is false,' as he hath showed by innumerable testimonies of *Protestants*. . . . For what I said, I produced the *authority of our Church*, he letteth that alone, and sticketh the falsehood upon my sleeve. It seemeth

that he is not willing to engage against *the Church of England;* for still he declineth it, and *changeth* the subject of the question *from* the English Church to a *confused company of particular authors of different opinions,* of *dubious credit,* of *little knowledge* in our English affairs, tortured and wrested from their genuine sense." p. 225.

Certainly Bramhall was allowed more liberty of speech in matters of doctrine and opinion than is given to members of our Church now; yet his subscriptions were much the same as ours.

10.

I have been led to this subject from certain passages in Mr. Froude's Volumes, about the Council of Trent, which you have treated, not as evidence (which it is) that he shrinks from the Church of Rome, being what it is, but as a ground of complaint against him for not shrinking from it, when it was what it is not; passages, which are not fairly quoted, merely used for your purpose. One other protest on Mr. Froude's part against Romanism of a different character is still to come; I cannot find it in your publication.

He says, "Since I have been out here, I have got a worse notion of the Roman Catholics than I had. I really do think them idolaters, though I cannot be quite confident of my information as it affects the character of the priests. .... What I mean by calling these people idolaters is, that I believe they look upon the Saints and Virgin as good-natured people, that will try to get them let off easier than the Bible declares; and that, as they don't intend to comply with the conditions on which God promises to answer prayers, they pray to them as a come-off." * Pref. p. xiii.

[If by "good-natured people who will try to get them let off easier than the Bible declares,' is implied that we hold that the saints are willing

Now since you are properly diffuse on the subject of Idolatry, I wish this passage had occurred to you, as showing that, however much you found to censure in Mr. Froude's Volumes, he did concur in your view of Romanism on a point of no ordinary importance, viz. so far as "*really to think the Roman Catholics idolaters.*" And for a parallel reason I beg to offer my own avowal, which is pretty much the same. I would say then so much as this, that it is idolatry to bow down to any emblem or symbol as divine which God himself has not appointed;[1] and since He has not appointed the worship of images, such worship is idolatrous; though how far it is so, whether itself or in given individuals, we may be unable to determine. So far, then, I am happy to follow you; however you then say, "Will it then be credited by any one not already cognizant of the fact, that the Crucifix, the effective engine, the notorious emblem of Romish superstition, is once more becoming, with some professed Protestants, an object, not indeed of worship,—scarcely let us hope even of reverence, yet at least of religious interest." p. 30. Now that the crucifix, *if* possessed, ought not to be treated with reverence, is a sentiment into which I cannot enter. We treat the pictures of our friends with reverence. Statues of illustrious persons we treat with reverence; and we feel indignation, if they are damaged or insulted. Who among us would think better of a man, who, as being above preju-

to encourage us in living without faith, hope, and charity, without the practice of virtue, and without habitual self-rule, or are able to help us at the last after a bad life, except by gaining for us, what is so rare and so difficult on a death-bed, a true contrition, and a real detestation of our sins, and profound sorrow for our past bad life, our *cultus* of the saints certainly is idolatry. But we do not hold this; on the contrary we denounce it.]

[1] [*What* emblems or symbols did the author consider that "God Himself *had* appointed"? I suppose the Lamb and the Dove. Would he say then that we *might* bow down to these as divine yet not to a crucifix? But if to the crucifix, why not to an image or picture of the Blessed Virgin? or of St. Joseph? &c. We say God *has* (by His Church) sanctioned images.]

dice, used his Bible for a footstool? yet what is it but an English printed book? Again, would it not offend the run of religious men, to hear of persons making it a point to keep their hats on in Church? yet what is a Church but a building of brick or stone? Surely then it is impossible for any religious man, having a Crucifix, not to treat it with reverence; and perhaps there are few religious people in the ordinary walks of life, (such, I mean, as live by good principles and good feeling, without having their intellect specially exercised,) who would not treat it with due respect. But, while I grant this, I more than doubt whether a Crucifix, carved to represent life as such memorials commonly are, be not too true to be reverent, and too painful for familiar contemplation. I state this, however, as merely my own opinion; without knowing the opinion of others. So much I know, that the use of the Crucifix is in this place no badge of persons whose mode of thinking you would condemn. How many Crucifixes could be counted up in Oxford, I know not; but you will find them in the possession of those who are no special friends or followers of Mr. Froude, and perhaps cordial admirers, except of course on this one point, of the tenor of your publication.

11.

A few words are now necessary on another subject,— Mr. Froude's use of the word *Protestantism*, and his language concerning some of the Reformers. Your remarks here go to an encroachment on our liberty of thought and speech, such as I have before noticed. I will but ask by which of the Articles, by what part of the Prayer Book, is a member of our Church bound to acknowledge the Reformers, or to profess himself a Protestant? Nowhere. To force him then to do so, when he fain would not, is narrowing our terms of communion; it is in fact committing the same error which we urge against the Roman Catholics. The Church is not built upon, it is not bound up with, individuals. I do not see why Mr. Froude may not speak against Jewel, if he feels he has a reason, as strongly as many among us speak against Laud. Men are not denounced from high places for calling Laud a bigot or a tyrant, why then should not like terms be used against Jewel? One may dislike to hear Laud abused, and feel no drawings towards his abusers; yet may suffer it as a matter in which we must bear differences of opinion, however "offensive." This is the very distinction between our Church and (for instance) the Lutherans; that they *are* Lutherans, but we are not Cranmerites, nor Jewelists, but Catholics, members not of a sect or party, but of the Catholic and Apostolic Church. And while the name of Luther became the title, his dogmata were made the rule of faith, of his followers; his phrases were noted, almost his very words were got by rote. He was, strictly speaking, the *Master* of his school. Where has the English Church any such head? Whom does she acknowledge but Christ and His Apostles, and as their witness the consent of Fathers? What title has she, but as an old Father speaks, " Christian for her name and Catholic for her surname?" If there is one thing more than another which tends to make us a party, it is the setting up the names of men as our symbols and watchwords. Those who most deeply love their teachers, will not magisterially bring them forward, and will rather shun than denounce those who censure them.

At the same time if such expressions concerning Jewel and others, as occur in the Volumes under consideration, have been painful to any person, I wish to express my own deep concern at it. With the prospect of such a contingency, nothing but a plain sense of duty could justify their publication; and a duty it may have been with those who considered that an historical name was at this day made the sanction of serious religious errors. The least said here on such a subject, the better; let it only be recollected, that what is said about Jewel, is supported by passages quoted from his works. Shall we defend such passages, or deny his trustworthiness?

12.

And in like manner, if persons, aware that names are things, conscientiously think that the name of Protestantism is productive of serious mischief,—if it be the property of heresy and schism as much as of orthodoxy,—if it be but a negative word, such as almost forces on its professors the idea of a vague indefinite creed, bringing before them how much they may doubt, deny, ridicule, or resist, rather than what they must believe,—if the religion it generates mainly consists in a mere attack upon Rome, and tends to be a mere instrument of state purposes,—if it tends to swallow up devotion in politics, and the Church in the executive,—if it damps, discourages, stifles that ancient Catholic spirit, which, if true in the beginning, is true at all times,—and if on the other hand there be nothing in our formularies obliging us to profess it,—and if external circumstances have so changed, that what it was inexpedient or impossible to do formerly, is both possible and most expedient now,—these considerations, I conceive, may form a reason for abandoning the word. But here it will be sufficient to keep to the question of our obligation to profess it, and with this view I quote the following passage from one of the "Tracts for the Times."

"'The English Church," it says, "as such, is *not* Protestant, only politically; that is, externally or so far as it has been made an establishment, and subjected to national and foreign influences," &c.[2]

[2] [Vid. the passage supr. pp. 137—139.]

13.

Another question, already touched on, as to which we claim a liberty of opinion is, whether or not the Church of Rome is "the mother of harlots," and the Pope St. Paul's "man of sin." And as feeling it is fairly an open question, I see no need of entering at length into it, even did the limits of a Letter admit. How those divines who hold the Apostolical Succession can maintain the affirmative, passes my comprehension; for in holding the one and other point at once, they are in fact proclaiming to the world that they come from "the synagogue of Satan," and (if I may so speak) have the devil's orders. I know that highly revered persons have so thought; perhaps they considered that the fatal apostasy took place at Trent, that is, *since* the date of our derivation from Rome; yet if in "the seven hills," in certain doctrines "about the souls of men," in what you consider "blasphemous titles," and in "lying wonders," lies, as you maintain, the proper evidence that the Bishop of Rome is Antichrist, then the great Gregory, to whom we Saxons owe our conversion, was Antichrist, for in him and in his times were those tokens of apostasy fulfilled, and our Church and its Sees are in no small measure the very work of the "Man of Sin."

And the dissenting bodies among us seem to understand this well; for they respond to our attack upon Rome, by briskly returning it on ourselves. They know none of those subtle distinctions by which we distinguish in this matter between ourselves and our ancient Mother, but they apply at once to our actual state what we confess of our original descent. If Rome has "committed fornication with the kings of the earth," what must be said of the Church of England with her temporal power, her Bishops in the House of Lords, her dignified clergy, her prerogatives, her pluralities, her buying and selling of preferments, her patronage, her corruptions, and her abuses? If Rome's teaching be a deadly heresy, what is our Church's, which "destroys more souls than it saves"? If Rome be " Mystery " because it has mysterious doctrines, what are we with our doctrine of the Sacraments and those greater things which are in heaven? If "commanding to abstain from meats" be a mark of Antichrist's communion, why do we observe days of fasting and abstinence, and why have our most revered teachers of times past been men of mortified lives? If Rome has put a yoke on the neck of Christians, why have not we, with our prescribed form of prayer, our Saints' Days, our Ordinances, and our prohibition of irregular preaching? If Rome is accused of assuming divine titles and powers, is not our own Church vulnerable too, considering the Bishop ordains under the words, "Receive the Holy Ghost," and the priest has power given him "to remit and retain sins."

No; serious as are the corruptions of Rome, clear indeed as are the differences between her communion and ours, they do not lie in any prophetic criteria; we cannot prove her the enchantress of the Apocalyptic Vision, without incurring our share in its application; and our enemies see this and make use of it. I am not inventing a parallel; they see it, I say, and use it. They are now exulting, as they believe piously, in our Church's troubles, for they consider, that while she is established, she is " partaker of the sins" of Rome, and they see in those troubles the fulfilment of the prophecy, that the "ten horns" should "hate" the woman, and "make her desolate and naked, and eat her flesh, and burn her with fire." In the confiscations going on in Spain and Portugal, and in the acts against us of our own government at home, they recognize one and the same Retributive Dispensation. And they declare that we have not yet obeyed the exhortation which you address to your readers, "Come out of her, My people, that ye receive not of her plagues;" nor shall have, till we give up our stalls, our incumbencies, and our dignities, and are content to rest merely on our popularity, our powers of preaching, our acceptableness to our people, our efficiency, our industry, and our Christian perfection. Nor is this most odious, " offensive " view, as you will call it, a modern one, nor has it been used against us by orthodox dissenters only. It was carried out to its last consequences at the time of the Reformation. The followers of Socinus then proclaimed, as some of us do now, that Rome was Babylon, and then they went on to show that those who so thought could not consistently stop their reasoning till they were brought to the conclusion that Socinianism is the Gospel. According to the well-known lines they said,—

<blockquote>
Tota jacet Babylon ; destruxit tecta Lutherus,
Calvinus muros, sed fundamenta Socinus.
</blockquote>

14.

I will say no more on this subject than this ; that the 17th and 18th chapters of the Apocalypse, on which the supposed Scripture evidence against her principally rests, must either be taken literally, *or* figuratively ; now they do not apply to her unless they are taken partly in the one way, partly in the other. Take the chapters literally, and sure it is, Rome *is* spoken of; but then she must have literal merchants, ships, and sailors ; therefore is not Papal Rome but Pagan. Take them figuratively ; and then, sure it is, merchants and merchandize, *may* mean indulgences and traffickers in them ; but then the word Rome perhaps is figurative also, as well as her merchandize. Nay, I should almost say, it must be ; for the city is called not only Rome but Babylon ; and if Babylon is a figurative title, why should not Rome be? The interpretation then lies between Pagan Rome which is past, and some city, or power typified as a city, which is to come; and probably may be true both ways. But, if we insist on adapting the prophecy to Papal Rome, then we are reduced to take half of the one interpretation, half of the other; and by the same process, only taking in each case the *other* half, we may with equal success make it London, for London has *literally* ships and sailors, merchants and merchandize, and is a *figurative* Rome, as being an Imperial City.

And now I come to the main subject of discussion, which is so much more arduous than any of the others, that I fear it will occupy a long time; and that is the subject of the Holy Eucharist.

15.

Before entering upon it, I will notice three points in your publication connected with it, which call for remark.

You write as follows:—" The term Altar, as synonymous with the Lord's Table, *does not appear to have been adopted till about the end of the second century;* and then merely in a figurative sense, and *out of a spirit of accommodation,* as it should seem, to the *prejudices* of Jews and Pagans, who habitually reproached the Christians as having neither Altar nor Sacrifice," pp. 18, 19. You are of opinion that the word Altar was not used for the Lord's Table " till *about* the end of the second century." On the contrary I read it in as many as *four* out of the seven brief Epistles of St. Ignatius, at the end of the *first*. If you are right, even this glorious Saint and Martyr, the immediate companion of Apostles, acted in a " spirit of accommodation " to the " prejudices of Jews and Pagans." Do my eyes play me false in reading Ignatius, or in reading your " Revival of Popery " ?

First he uses it in his Epistle to the Ephesians:—" For if I in so short a season formed such an intimacy with your Bishop, not a human but a spiritual, how much more do I call you fortunate, who are so united to him, as the Church to Jesus Christ, and Jesus Christ to the Father, that all things may be concordant in unity? Let no one err; unless a man be *within the Altar* (ἐντὸς τοῦ θυσιαστηρίου) he comes short of the bread of God. For if the prayer of one and a second has such power, how much more that of the Bishop and all the Church?" §. 5.

Next, in that to the Magnesians:—" Let there be one prayer, one supplication, one mind, one hope, in love, in that joy which is irreprovable. There is one Jesus Christ to whom nought is preferable; all of you then run together as to one Temple, as *for one Altar* (ἐπὶ ἓν θυσιαστήριον). as for One Jesus Christ, who is come forth from One Father, and returned again to One." §. 7.

Thirdly, in that to the Trallians:—"Guard against such [sectarians,] and this will be if we are not puffed up, nor separated from Jesus Christ our God, and the Bishop, and the ordinances of the Apostles. He who is within *the Altar* (ἐντὸς θυσιαστηρίου) is clean; that is, he who does any thing without Bishop, and Presbytery, and Deacons, such a one is not clean in conscience." §. 7.

Lastly, in that to the Philadelphians:—" Be careful to use one Eucharist; for the Flesh of our Lord Jesus Christ is one, and one Cup for the uniting of His blood; *one Altar* (ἓν θυσιαστήριον), as one Bishop, together with the Presbytery, and Deacons my fellow-servants; that whatever ye do, ye may do after God." §. 4.

And while the list of ecclesiastical witnesses to the use of the word Altar for the Lord's Table begins as early as it can after the Apostles and Evangelists, (who use it also as I would contend, in Matt. v. 23. Heb. xiii. 10, but who are not at present under review,) it proceeds downwards, not only in an uninterrupted series, but with a sort of prerogative of usage; for it is very remarkable that, excepting one passage in a letter of St. Dionysius of

Alexandria, no ecclesiastical writer at all is found to use the word "Table" till St. Athanasius in the fourth century; and what is also remarkable, when St. Athanasius uses it, he does so with the explanation, "that is, the Holy Altar;" as if he were not using a word commonly adopted. On the contrary, the word Altar is used after St. Ignatius by St. Irenæus, Tertullian, St. Cyprian, Origen, Eusebius, St. Athanasius, St. Ambrose, St. Gregory Nazianzen, St. Optatus, St. Jerome, St. Chrysostom, and St. Austin.[3]

16.

The next point on which it is necessary to remark, is your saying, that the Tracts for the Times "appeal" on the subject of the Eucharist to the "half-converted German Reformers," that is, to Luther, and Melancthon, "and to the strong and unguarded expressions which their works supply;" and this you call an "alarming fact." I am very glad to find we are so well agreed in our judgments as to the authority of Luther and Melancthon in our Church; but I cannot allow that the Tracts do appeal to them, as you assert, or wish to shelter themselves behind them. Bp. Cosin, in the Tract you refer to, certainly does quote the Lutherans, but he also quotes Calvin, Bucer, and the French Protestants; and that, in order to show, that "*none* of the Protestant Churches doubt of the real (that is, true and not imaginary) presence of Christ's Body and Blood in the Sacrament;" and he "begins with the Church of England," quoting first our formularies, then the words of Bilson and Andrewes. In what sense then do you mean that the *writers* of the Tracts appeal to the *Lutherans*, when, *not* the writers, but only *Bp. Cosin* in the Tracts, appeals, *not* to the Lutherans, but to *the whole Protestant world?* Concerning the Real Presence itself something shall be said presently; meanwhile I do

[3] Vid. Johnson, Unbl. Sacr. vol. i. pp. 306-9.

not fear that any great number of readers will identify or connect with Luther's the doctrine held by Hooker, Andrewes, Bramhall, Cosin, Bull, Ken, and Leslie. It may be well to quote the words of the last-mentioned Divine concerning this work of Bp. Cosin, whose views you consider do not "fall much, if at all, short of what has been commonly termed Consubstantiation." "Bishop Cosin's History of Transubstantiation," he says to a Romanist, is "a little book, long printed both in English and Latin, not yet answered (that I hear), *and I believe unanswerable*, wherein you see a cloud of witnesses through the first ages of the Church, and so downwards, in perfect contradiction to this new article of your faith." (*Rome and England*, vol. iii. pp. 130, 1.) This is not the language of one who felt Cosin's book to be "an alarming fact."

17.

And thirdly, let me refer to two statements in Mr. Froude's Volumes, on which you dwell, to the effect that our present Communion Service is "a judgment on the Church," and that there would be advantage in "replacing it by a good translation of the Liturgy of St. Peter." The state of the case is this; the original Eucharistic form is with good reason assigned to the Apostles and Evangelists themselves. It exists to this day under four different rites, which seem to have come from four different Apostles and Evangelists. These rites differ in some points, agree in others; among the points in which they agree, are of course those in which the Essence of the Sacrament consists. At the time of the Reformation we in common with all the West possessed the rite of the Roman Church, or St. Peter's Liturgy. This formulary is called the Canon of the Mass, and except a very few words, appears, even as now used in the Roman Church, to be free from interpolation, and thus is distinguished from the Ordinary of the Mass, which is the additional and corrupt service prefixed to it, and peculiar to Rome.[4] This sacred and most precious monument, then, of the Apostles, our Reformers received whole and entire from their predecessors; and they mutilated the tradition of 1500 years. Well was it for us that they did not discard it, that they did not touch any vital part; for through God's good providence, though they broke it up and cut away portions, they did not touch life; and thus we have it at this day, a violently treated, but a holy and dear possession, more dear perhaps and precious than if it were in its full vigour and beauty, as sickness or infirmity endears to us our friends and relatives. Now the first feeling which comes upon an ardent mind, on mastering these facts, is one of indignation and impatient grief; the second, is the more becoming thought, that, as he deserves nothing at all at God's hand, and is blessed with Christian privileges only at His mere bounty, it is nothing strange that he does not enjoy every privilege which was given through the Apostles; and his third, that we are mysteriously bound up with our forefathers and bear their sin, or in other words, that our present condition is a judgment on us for what they did.

These, I conceive, to be the feelings which dictated to Mr. Froude the sentences on which you animadvert; the earlier is more ardent, the latter is more subdued. In the one he says of a friend, " I verily believe he would now gladly consent to see our Communion Service replaced by a good translation of the Liturgy of St. Peter, a name which I advise you to substitute in your notes to Hooker for the obnoxious phrase 'Mass Book.'" vol. i. p. 287. Lest any misconception of the author's meaning should arise from the use of the word " replaced," I would observe, that such "replacing" would not remove one prayer, one portion of our present Service; it would consist

[4] [What can this mean? The Ordinary consists of Gloria in excelsis, Collects, Epistle, Gospel, Creed, Offertory.]

but of addition and re-arrangement, of a return to the original Canon. The substance of this explanation is contained in the second volume of the Remains, (Essay on Liturgies,^s) and a reference to it would supersede it here. The other passage runs as follows : " By-the-bye, the more I think over that view of yours about regarding our present Communion Service, &c., as a judgment on the Church, and about taking it as crumbs from the Apostles' table, the more I am struck with its fitness to be dwelt upon as tending to check the intrusion of irreverent thoughts without in any way interfering with one's just indignation. If I were a Roman Catholic Priest, I should look on the administration of the Communion in one kind in the same light." vol. i. p. 410.

You see, from this last sentence, he thought nothing would be gained by going to Rome, unsatisfactory as might be our present case. Nay that he was not in favour even of changes in our own services, to meet the defects he felt in them, appears from the following passages in his Tract on the Daily Service, 1. "This, it will be said, is an argument, not so much for retaining the present form of the Prayer Book, as for reverting to what is older. In my own mind, it is an argument for something different from either, for *diffidence.* I very much doubt, whether in these days the spirit of true devotion is at all understood, and whether an attempt to go forward or backward may not lead our innovations to the same result. ' If the blind lead the blind, shall they not both fall into the ditch ? '" vol. ii. 382.

18.

And now at length let me proceed to the doctrine itself to which these remarks relate, the doctrine of the Holy Eucharist. Here I could have much wished that you had,

^s *Vid.* also the Introduction of Tract, No. 81.

at least in your Notes, drawn out that view of it which you consider to be Scriptural and Anglican. It would have been a great satisfaction to know where we both are standing, how far I can assent, how far I am obliged to dissent from your opinion. But, excepting from one or two half-sentences, I really can gather nothing to the purpose; I only see you do not hold, but rather condemn, a view which Bp. Cosin declares to be that of all "the Protestant" or "Reformed Churches." To this difficulty I must submit as I can; and instead of letting the course of my remarks run as a comment on your pages, shall be obliged against my will to answer you by a categorical view of my own.⁶

As regards then this most sacred subject, three questions offer themselves for consideration; first, whether there is a Real Presence of Christ in this Holy Sacrament, next what It is, and thirdly where. 1. On the Real Presence I shall not use many words of my own, because on the one hand it is expressly recognized by the Catechism and Homilies, (not to mention the language of the Service itself,) and on the other because you do not absolutely condemn such language, only you think it "highly ob-

⁶ [The Catholic doctrine is as follows; authorities for it shall be given lower down.

Our Lord is *in loco* in heaven, not (in the same sense) in the Sacrament. He is present in the Sacrament only in substance, *substantivè*, and substance does not require or imply the occupation of place. But if place is excluded from the idea of the Sacramental Presence, therefore division or distance from heaven is excluded also, for distance implies a measurable interval, and such there cannot be except between places. Moreover, if the idea of distance is excluded, therefore is the idea of motion. Our Lord then neither descends from heaven upon our altars, nor moves when carried in procession. The visible species change their position, but He does not move. He is in the Holy Eucharist after the manner of a spirit. We do not know how; we have no parallel to the "how" in our experience. We can only say that He is present, not according to the natural manner of bodies, but *sacramentally*. His Presence is substantial, spirit-wise, sacramental; an absolute mystery, not against reason, however, but against imagination, and must be received by faith.]

jectionable and dangerous" when "systematically and studiously adopted." I shall not therefore debate a point which the formularies of our Church decide, when they declare that "the Body and Blood of Christ" are "*verily and indeed* taken and received by the faithful *in* the Lord's Supper;" that "the Body of Christ is *given, taken,* and *eaten in* the Supper;" and that "thus much we must be sure to hold, that *in* the Supper of the Lord there is no vain ceremony, no bare sign, *no untrue figure of a thing absent,* but as the Scripture saith, . . . the communion of the Body and Blood of the Lord, in a marvellous incorporation, which by the operation of the Holy Ghost, the very bond of our conjunction with Christ, is through faith wrought in the souls of the faithful, whereby not only their souls live to eternal life, but they surely trust to win to their bodies a resurrection to immortality."[7] These passages seem to determine that the Body and Blood of Christ are not absent but present in the Lord's Supper; and if really, and in fact Christ's Body be there, His Soul is there, and His Divinity; for as the Article says, the two natures are "never to be divided;" therefore He is there, "One Christ," whole and entire. Nor does any one doubt of His Presence on our Altars as God, for He is everywhere; but the question is, whether His human nature also is present in the Sacrament.

In corroboration of the view here taken of the statements of our Church, I quote the following passage from Hooker, who, we all know, was not in this, any more than in other points, an extreme Divine. He argues that the three Schools of opinion in his day, the Romanists, the Lutherans, and the Sacramentaries, (the last, I need not say, being one which nowhere exists as a body at this day, but which originally was the school of Zuinglius and Œcolampadius,) might well waive the question among themselves, *how* Christ is present, upon the common con-

[7] Sermon of the Sacrament, Part I.

fession that He *is really* present. And he defends the Sacramentaries from the objection then urged against them, and since fulfilled in their descendants, that they admitted a Presence in words and explained it away; and, as believing they did not explain it away, he admits them into this compact of charity, as it may be called. He says, "*It is on all sides plainly confessed*, . . . that this Sacrament is a *true and real* participation of Christ, who thereby imparteth Himself, *even His whole entire Person*, as a mystical head unto every soul that receiveth Him, and that every such receiver doth thereby incorporate or unite himself unto Christ as a mystical member of Him, yea of them also whom He acknowledgeth to be His own. . . . . It seemeth therefore much amiss, that against them whom they term Sacramentaries so many invective discourses are made, all running upon two points, that the Eucharist is not a bare sign or figure only, and that the efficacy of His Body and Blood *is not all* we receive in this Sacrament. For no man, having read their books and writings which are thus traduced, can be ignorant that *both* these assertions *they plainly confess to be most true*. They *do not so interpret the words of Christ*, as if the name of His Body did import but *the figure of His Body;* and to *be* were only to *signify* His Blood. They *grant* that these Holy Mysteries, received in due manner, do instrumentally *both* make us partakers of the *grace* of that Body and Blood which were given for the life of the world, *and besides* also impart to us, even in *true and real, though mystical manner, the very Person of our Lord Himself, whole, perfect and entire,* as hath been showed."[8]

Elsewhere he says, "Doth any man doubt, but that *even from the flesh* of Christ our very bodies do receive that life which shall make them glorious at the latter day; and for which they are already accounted parts of His

[8] Eccl. Pol. v. 67, § 7, 8.

Blessed Body? Our corruptible bodies could never live the life they shall live, were it not that here they are joined with His Body which is incorruptible, and that *His is in ours* as a *cause* of immortality, a cause by removing through the death and merit of His own Flesh that which hindered the life of ours. Christ is therefore, both as God and as man, that true Vine whereof we both spiritually *and corporally* are branches. The mixture of His bodily *Substance* with ours is a thing which the Ancient Fathers disclaim. Yet the mixture of His Flesh with ours they speak of, to signify what *our very bodies*, through mystical conjunction, receive from *that vital* efficacy which we know to be in His; and from bodily mixtures they borrow diverse similitudes, rather to declare the *truth* than the *manner* of coherence between His Sacred, and the sanctified bodies of saints." [9]

19.

2. So much on the testimony of our Church and of her celebrated Divine to the doctrine of the Real Presence. But here it is objected that such a Presence is *impossible;* and this brings us to the question *how* Christ is present, which stands next for consideration. The objection takes this form,—if He is *really* here, He is *locally* here, but He is locally in heaven not here, therefore He cannot really be here, but is only said to be here. Now to take in hand this question.

In answer, Bellarmine maintains that our Lord can be locally here, though He is in heaven; for he lays it down as a certain truth that a body can be in two places at once.[1]

---

[9] Ibid. 56. § 9.

[1] [He does; however, St. Thomas says on the contrary that our Lord is *not* under the species *localiter*, but to show how much this difference is a mere matter of words, I will set down the chief points of the doctrine in statements of Bellarmine on the one hand, and of Billuart on the other, who

Accordingly he would say, that in the Sacrament that very Body, which died upon the Cross, and rose again and ascended, is locally present under the accidents of Bread.

Our Church, however, incidentally argues that a body cannot be in two places at once;[2] and that the Body of Christ is not *locally* present, in the sense in which we speak

---

professes to write as a Thomist. And I will begin with a passage from the Council of Trent, as a sort of text.

Concil. Trid. Sess. 13, c. 1.—Nec hæc inter se pugnant, ut ipse Salvator noster semper ad dexteram Patris in cœlis assideat juxta modum existendi *naturalem*, et in multis nihilominus aliis locis *sacramentaliter* præsens suâ *substantiâ* nobis adsit.

Billuart, pp. 356, 392, &c.—Corpus Christi est præsens in speciebus, non circumscriptivè, nec definitivè, sed sacramentaliter.

Ibid. p. 393, col. 1.—Corpus Christi est in Eucharistiâ ad modum substantiæ, seu sacramentaliter.

Bellarm. col. 349, 350.—Totus Christus existit in Sacramento ad modum substantiæ, non quantitatis.

Billuart, p. 357, col. 1.—Quantitas non est essentialis corpori, sed ejus proprietas.

Bellarm. col. 390 — Substantia cujuslibet rei non est per se divisibilis.

Ibid. col. 350.—Per substantiam non occupat locum.

Billuart, p. 393, col. 1.—Christus non est in hoc Sacramento ut in loco.

Bellarm. col. 350.—Substantia secundum se neque ordinem habet ad locum, neque ad corpora circumstantia.

Billuart, p. 357, col. 1.—[Ut] Corpus Christi in cœlo et altari [sit] à se divisum, requiritur ut medium [quoddam] sit contiguum extremis, seu illa secundum extremitates tangat, quod non fit respectu Corporis Christi.

Ibid. p. 393, col. 1.—Corpus Christi non se habet sub speciebus sicut qui movetur in navi.

Bellarm. col. 580.—Corpus Christi [dicitur] videri, tangi, frangi, et teri, mediantibus speciebus panis.

Billuart, p. 357, col. 1.—Non Corpus Christi propriè manducatur, sed species manducantur.

Bellarm. col. 351.—Christus in Eucharistiâ modum existendi corporum non habet, sed potius spirituum.

Billuart, p. 357, col. 1.—Hæc transcendunt imaginationem, quia imaginatio non transcendit continuum. . . . Imaginatio corrigenda est per fidem et rationem.]

[2] Vid. Notice at the end of the Communion Service.

of the Bread as being locally present. On the other hand she determines, as I have already said, that the Body of Christ is in some unknown way, though not *locally* yet *really* present, so that we after some ineffable manner partake of it. Whereas then the objection stands, Christ is not really here, because He is not locally here, she answers, He is really here, yet not locally.

20.

I will say directly what is meant by this; before doing so, however, let me briefly observe that there is nothing (as far as I am aware) in Mr. Froude's writings in countenance of the *local* presence on earth, as it is commonly understood, though he certainly did not sympathize with the Reformers at all in their mode of arguing on the subject. When he speaks of " making the Body and Blood of Christ," or indirectly adopts the phrase of " making the Bread and Wine the Body and Blood of Christ," he does not go beyond the doctrine of the Real Presence, which, as we shall see, need not be local; and in the use of the one phrase he is borne out by Hooker, who speaks of the Christian Ministry as having " power imparted " to it by Christ, " both over that mystical body which is the society of souls, *and* over that *Natural, which is Himself,* for the knitting of both in one, a work which Antiquity doth call the *making of Christ's Body;*" while he brings forward the other, not in his own words, but in the words of Bishop Bull, who says, " We are not ignorant that the ancient Fathers generally teach that the Bread and Wine in the Eucharist, by or upon the consecration of them, do become and *are made* the Body and Blood of Christ."

Mr. Froude's strong language, then, had the sanction of our Divines; how far, on the other hand, he was from agreeing with the Roman doctrine will be clearly seen from a passage of his writings, not yet published. In an unfinished Essay on Rationalism, speaking of the interpretation which supposes " This is My Body " to mean "This is a sign of My Body," he says, "This mode of speaking ... is true in one sense, and in every other gratuitous and improper. If it is intended simply to deny, that by the words 'This is My Body' our Lord meant, 'This is *that very* Body of Mine which you see before you sitting at the Table,' then indeed *the sentiment is true*, however awkward may be the expression of it.[3] But if the words 'Sign of My Body,' are understood to convey any idea *more definite and intelligible* than that which is conveyed in our Lord's own words, then most certainly that idea is unscriptural, it is a mere human invention fabricated to set the mind at rest, *where God has seen fit to leave it in uncertainty.*" Hence he says the very thing which I conceive our Church holds, that Christ's Body *is* present, but *how* it is present is a *mystery;* it being hidden from us how Christ can be really here, yet not locally. Both Protestant and Romanist attempt to explain how; Protestants by saying it is a mere figurative or nominal presence, and as to Romanists, I will quote Mr. Froude's own words about them which occur soon after: " Opposed to these errors, (the Protestant,) but *erroneous much for the same reason*, is the Roman Catholic dogma about Transubstantiation. Unlike the Protestant glosses, this does not attempt to explain away everything miraculous in the history of the Last Supper; but by explaining precisely *wherein* the miracle consists and *how* it is brought about, it aims like them at relieving us from a confession of ignorance,[4] and *so far must be*

[3] [I do not understand this. If it is beyond our power of conception that our Lord's body should be in two places at once, at least it is against the Christian faith that He should have two bodies.]

[4] [It is difficult for any one who really knows what the Catholic Church teaches on this subject, to understand how that teaching can be accused of "relieving our ignorance."]

regarded as a contrivance of human scepticism, to elude the claims of Faith, and to withdraw from the hidden Mysteries of religion the indistinctness in which God has thought fit to envelope them."[5]

21.

But now to return, what is the meaning of saying that Christ is really present, yet not locally? This was the second point I had to consider, and I will make two suggestions upon it, in both of which the Sacramental Presence shall be viewed as real, yet in neither local.

First, as to material things, what do we mean, when we speak of an object being present to us? How do we define and measure its presence? To a blind and deaf man that only is present which he touches. Give him hearing, and the range of things present to him enlarges; everything is present to him which he hears. Give him at length sight, and the sun may be said to be present to him in the daytime, and myriads of stars by night. Presence then is a relative word, depending on the channels of communication existing between the object and the person to whom it is present. It is almost a' correlative of the senses. A fly may be as near an edifice as a man: yet we do not call it present to the fly, because he cannot see it, and we do call it present to the man, because he can.

But we must add another element to the idea expressed by the word in the case of matter. A thing may be said to be present to us, which is so circumstanced as immediately to act upon us and to influence us, whether we are sensible of it or no. Perhaps then our Lord is present to us in the Sacrament in this sense, that, far as He is off us, He in it acts personally, bodily, and directly upon us,

---

[5] [He called the Roman view sceptical and rationalistic because, together with men of his day, he really did not know what the Roman view was, nor that he did not know it.]

though how He does so is as simply beyond us, as the results of eyesight are inconceivable to the blind. We know but of five senses,—we know not whether human nature is capable of more; we know not whether the soul possesses any instruments of knowledge and moral advantage analogous to them; but neither have we any reason to deny that the soul may be capable of having Christ present to it by the stimulus of dormant or the development of possible energies. As sight for certain purposes annihilates space, so other unknown conditions of our being, bodily or spiritual, may practically annihilate it for other purposes. Such may be the Sacramental Presence. We kneel before the Heavenly Throne, and distance vanishes; it is as if that Throne were the Altar close to us.

22.

This is my first suggestion; my second is as follows:— Our Lord, not only "did rise again from death," as the Article says, "and took again His Body with flesh, bones, and all things appertaining to the perfection of man's nature," but He rose with what St. Paul terms "a spiritual body;" so that now that He is in heaven, He is not subject to the laws of matter, and has no necessary relations to place, no dependence on its conditions; and, for what we know, His mode of making Himself present on earth, of coming and going, is as different from the mode natural to bodies by locomotion,—nearness being determined by intervals and absence being synonymous with distance,—as spirit is different from matter. He may be literally present in the Holy Eucharist, yet, not having become present by a movement and a transit, He may still be continuously on God's right hand: so that, though He be present with us in deed and in truth, it may be impossible, it may be untrue, to determine that He is in or about the elements, or in the soul of the communicant. These may be serviceable modes of speech according to the occasion; but the true result of all such inquiries is no more than the assertion with which we began, that He is present in the Holy Eucharist but not locally present. We, to whom the idea of space is a necessity, and who have no experience of spirits, are of course unequal to the conception of such an idea, and can only call a mystery what is as transporting and elevating to the religious sense, as it is difficult to the intellect.

Let it be observed that I am not proving or determining anything; I am only showing how it is that certain propositions which at first sight seem contradictions in terms, are not so; I am but pointing out ways of reconciling them. If even there is only one way assignable, the force of any antecedent objection against the possibility of reconciling them is removed, and there may be other ways supposable though not assignable.

23.

3. And now the way is clear to add a few words on the third point, viz. the relation of the consecrated elements to those Realities of which they are the outward signs.

The Roman Church, we know, considers that the elements of Bread and Wine depart or are taken away on Consecration, and that the Body and Blood of Christ take their place. This is the doctrine of Transubstantiation; and in consequence they hold that what is seen, felt, and tasted, is not Bread and Wine but Christ's Flesh and Blood, though the former look, feel, and taste remains.[6] This is what neither our Church, nor any of the late maintainers of her doctrine on the subject, even dreams of holding. Again, the Lutherans say that, though the Bread remains, the body of Christ is within [intra] the Bread; neither is this countenanced by any of the persons on whom you animadvert. These hold a Spiritual Presence to be

[6] [This is not accurate, vid. supr. note, p. 232.]

such as not to allow of being strictly co-extensive with place, in the way in which a bodily substance is, in the way in which the Bread is: therefore they cannot be said to countenance the Lutheran doctrine of Consubstantiation. What they do say is that Christ's Body *is* really and literally present, but they do not know *how;* it being a mystery, as I have said already, how, as being spiritual it can be really present, yet not locally or as bodies are.

It is true there is a passage in Mr. Froude's Letters in which he seems to assert that the Body of Christ is locally *in* the Bread; though this is, I apprehend, not really the case on a candid judgment of it. He finds fault with an expression in a Poem, which, speaking of the Lord's Supper, says, " There present in the heart, not in the hands, &c." He adds, " How can we possibly know that it is true to say, '*not* in the hands'?" p. 404; that is, he much disliked dogmatic decisions of any kind upon the subject. He does not rule that it *is* in the hands, but, with Hooker, he wishes the question left open; he disliked its being determined that it *was* in the heart in a sense in which it was *not* in the hands, seeing we know nothing of the matter. To say it was in *both* did not interfere with the doctrine of Christ's local presence in heaven; but to say that Christ *is* in the heart and *not* in the hands, *did* so fix His presence here as to make it local, and in consequence might be taken to interfere with that His one abiding presence at God's right hand. I am certain, from what I know of his opinions, that he did not mean, that the Body of Christ which is on God's right hand, was literally *in* the Bread.

But, without limiting our Lord's presence to the consecrated elements, it seems nothing but the truth to say that they are His immediate antecedents; so that whoever in faith receives them, at once and without assignable medium, is gifted with His Presence who is on God's right hand. As the breath is the immediate forerunner of the voice, as the face is the image of the soul, as a garment marks a bodily presence, so, I conceive, the elements are the antecedents of His Body and Blood, or what our Article calls, the "efficacious signs by the which He doth work invisibly in us," or, as Hooker calls them, His "instruments." And hence, whereas He is unseen, and His Presence ineffable, and known only by Its outward signs, we say that, when we receive them, we receive the awful Realities which follow on them; when we touch the one, with our spirit we touch the Other, when we eat the one, we eat the Other, when we drink the one, we drink the Other. And, whereas what is spiritual has no parts, and what is spiritual cannot receive in part, therefore when we speak of eating Christ's Body with our souls, the words cannot be grossly or absurdly taken to mean a partial or gradual communication of so Heavenly a Treasure, as happens in carnal eating; but in some unknown way the soul becomes possessed at once of Christ according to its nature, and as bodily contact is the mode in which Bread nourishes our bodies, so the soul, and the motions of the soul, and faith which is of the soul, as by an inward contact, is the mean and instrument of receiving Christ.

24.

Now let it be considered whether the following extracts from the Homilies and the Ecclesiastical Polity do not bear out the main points which have been insisted on. In consideration of the importance of the subject, I hope you will pardon their length.

"The true understanding," says the first part of the Sermon concerning the Sacrament, "of this fruition and union, which is betwixt the body and the Head, betwixt the true believers and Christ, and the Ancient Catholic Fathers both perceiving themselves and commending to their people, were not afraid to call this supper, some of them the Salve of immortality and sovereign preservative against death; other, a deifical communion; other, the sweet dainties of our Saviour, the pledge of eternal health, the defence of faith, the hope of the resurrection; other, the food of immortality, the healthful grace, and the conservatory to everlasting life. . . . It is well known that the meat we seek for in this supper is spiritual food, the nourishment of our soul, a heavenly refection, and not earthly; an *invisible* meal, and not bodily; a *ghostly substance*, and not *carnal*. . . . Take then this lesson, O thou that are desirous of this Table, of Emissenus, a godly father, that when thou goest up to the reverend Communion, to be satisfied with spiritual meats, thou *look up with faith* upon the Holy *Body and Blood of thy God*, thou marvel with reverence, thou *touch* It with thy *mind*, thou *receive* It with the hand of thy *heart*, and thou *take* It fully with thy *inward man.*"

Such is the language of the Homily, nor does Hooker come short of it. "The Bread and Cup," he says, "are His Body and Blood, because they are *causes instrumental*, upon the receipt whereof the participation of His Body and Blood ensueth. . . . Our souls and bodies quickened to eternal life are effects, the cause whereof is the *Person* of Christ: His Body and Blood are the true well-spring out of which this life floweth. So that His Body and Blood are in that very subject whereunto they minister life; not only by effect or operation, even as the influence of the heavens is in plants, beasts, men, and in everything which they quicken; but also by *a far more divine and mystical kind of union*, which maketh us one with Him, even as He and the Father are one. The Real Presence of Christ's most Blessed Body and Blood is not therefore to be sought for in the Sacrament, but in the worthy receiver of the Sacrament."[7]

[7] Eccles. Pol. v. 67. § 4, 5.

Soon after follows the well-known passage: "Such as love piety, will, as much as in them lieth, know all things that God commandeth, but especially the duties of service which they owe to God. As for His dark and hidden works, they prefer, as becometh them in such cases, simplicity of faith before that knowledge, which, curiously sifting what it should adore, and disputing too boldly of that which the wit of man cannot search, chilleth for the most part all warmth of zeal, and bringeth soundness of belief many times into great hazard. Let it therefore be sufficient for me, presenting myself at the Lord's Table, to know *what* there I receive from Him, without searching or inquiring of the *manner how* Christ performeth His promise. Let disputes and questions, enemies to piety, abatements of true devotion, and hitherto in this cause but overpatiently heard, let them take their rest. Let curious and sharp-witted men beat their heads about what questions themselves will; the very *letter* of the Word of Christ giveth plain security, that these Mysteries do, as nails, fasten us to His very Cross, that by them we draw out, (as touching efficacy, force, and virtue,) even the blood of His gored side; in the wounds of our Redeemer we there dip our tongues, we are dyed red both within and without; our hunger is so satisfied, and our thirst for ever quenched. They are things wonderful which he feeleth, great which he seeth, and unheard of which he uttereth, whose soul is possessed of this Pascha Lamb, and made joyful in the strength of this new wine. This bread hath in it more than the substance which our eyes behold; this Cup hallowed with solemn benediction availeth to the endless life and welfare both of soul and body; in that it serveth as well for a medicine to heal our infirmities and purge our sins, as for a sacrifice of thanksgiving. With touching it sanctifieth, it enlighteneth with belief; it truly comforteth us unto the Image of Jesus Christ. What these elements are in themselves, it skilleth not; it is enough, that to me which take them they are the Body and Blood of Christ. His promise in witness hereof sufficeth; His word He knoweth which way to accomplish. Why should any cogitation possess the mind of a faithful communicant but this, O my God, Thou art True—O my soul, thou art happy?"[8]

25.

What a contrast do glowing thoughts like these present to such teaching as has been too much in esteem among us of late years! For instance, to glean from your pages the few notices of your own opinion which are scattered there; what a difference there is between "visible symbols" of "His *absent* Body and Blood," and "Mysteries which, as nails, *fasten us to His very Cross;*"—between "the communion of the *benefits* of His sufferings and death," and "Holy Mysteries imparting not grace only, but *besides*, even in *true and real* though mystical manner, the *Very Person* of our Lord Himself, *whole, perfect, and entire;*"—between "signs *attended by the blessings* of Christ" and "*doth any man doubt* but that even from the *flesh* of Christ our *very bodies* do receive" everlasting "life;"—between "the body and blood of Christ" not "spiritually included in the elements" but "*spiritually received* by the faithful," and "Bread which hath in it *more than the substance* which our eyes behold," "a *ghostly substance*," "an *invisible meal!*" Alas! what a decrepiture has come on us since Hooker's day! "How has the fine gold become dim!" How has the promise of the spring played us false in the summer! How have the lean kine eaten up the fat kine, and the thin ears choked the full ones! What a spiritual famine, or rather what locusts and cankerworms are our portion! the olive-tree can be content with its own fatness, and the fig-tree with its

[8] Ibid. p. 67. § 5.

sweetness, and the vine reckons it much "to cheer god and man;" but the thin and empty ears of Zurich and Geneva think it scorn unless they devour and make a clean end of the pleasant and fair pastures of Catholic doctrine, which are our heritage :

> Interque nitentia culta
> Infelix lolium et steriles dominantur avenæ.

Indeed, the change, which the tone of our theology has undergone in the last two centuries, is almost too much for belief. Then, on the one hand, we find Hooker, earnest in vindicating even the Zuinglians from the charge of denying that Christ's Person as well as His grace, His Person whole and entire, is in the Lord's Supper, and Cosin confident in the agreement of *all* Protestants in the same doctrine; and now on the other hand we witness, not Zuinglians merely and Calvinists abjuring it, but even the Margaret Professor of Divinity in Oxford unable even in thought to distinguish it from Consubstantiation, considering it "highly objectionable and dangerous," and in spite of Hooker and Cosin, denying that individuals holding it, are "safe and consistent members of the Church of England." However, it is out of place to lament over these things, at a time when one trusts that they are (as it were) at low water mark and that the tide is turning. It is more to the purpose to remove every obstacle, however small, to its natural return ; and under this feeling I proceed to notice the only argument you use against the Real Presence, which has any plausibility.

26.

You state it thus : " The case of the profane Corinthians is a sufficient proof that they had never heard of Transubstantiation. Had St. Paul inculcated upon them that doctrine or *any other modification of the Real Presence* of Christ's Body and Blood in the elements of Bread and

Wine, their conduct would have been not simply incredible, but morally impossible." p. 18. Let us then consider the state of the case.

Whether it was possible for men, believing that in drinking of "the Cup of blessing" they communicated in Christ's blood, to drink of that Cup to intoxication, I need not determine, for I do not think the Corinthians were guilty of this crime. At the same time, if I must answer, it is enough to say, that, in truth, as no assignable limits can be put to the self-delusion and perverseness of the human heart, it would not surprise me if they were. The sins of the Israelites, such as the golden calf, murmuring at the manna, or looking into the ark; the dreadful history of Balaam, and the waywardness of Jonah; exhibit far stronger instances of inconsistency, than could have been anticipated beforehand as possible: and if human nature can go so far beyond our anticipations, I do not see why it should not go further. There is nothing to show that the intoxication in question had occurred before, or that it was intentional; and I think many persons will recollect particular occasions, when their own conduct before and after the Holy Communion has been such as to fill them with astonishment, as well as dismay, ever since. I do not then see any reason for deciding, that, had any very sacred idea been connected with the Eucharist in the minds of the Corinthians, they must of necessity have abstained from profaning it. A man must be very good and innocent to have a right to imagine, that such excess as theirs in spite of their knowledge was impossible; and since the majority of men are not such, I think that, plausible as the objection in question is at first sight, yet, even when made the most of, it will not weigh with that majority.

Have we never heard in our own times of the most shocking sins committed in prayer-meetings? Cannot persons possibly be betrayed, while the name of Christ is on their lips, into deeds of darkness?

Again, is there anything more terrible than instances of persons, while they lie, calling on God to strike them dead if they are lying? Yet are not instances recorded of the sin and the infliction? A monument is set up at Devizes in memory of such a dreadful occurrence. If we cannot help acknowledging that the one enormity has occurred, I see no reason for deciding that the other cannot occur. I do not say which is the greater sin; but it does seem as if one might more easily be seduced into fancying sensual indulgence to be a part of religion, and the excitement arising from excess to be devotional feeling, than into taking a false oath, and calling on Almighty God to curse and smite us for it.

The profession, then, that the Cup of blessing is really the communication of the Lord's Blood is no infallible safeguard against very heinous acts of sacrilege towards it; nor the circumstance of their profaning it, a proof that they did not believe in it. Indeed, does not the punishment inflicted on the offending Corinthians imply some dreadful profanation of something very sacred? Ananias and Sapphira were struck dead for lying to the Holy Ghost; the unworthy communicant is " weak and sickly," or " sleeps," that is, is visited by death. If we suppose that he does profane the Lord's Body and Blood, the punishment is intelligible; it is not intelligible, if it be but a want of self-restraint after a commemoration or an appropriation of Christ's merits. Death seems like the punishment of blasphemy; there is no blasphemy, whatever sin there be, in turning religious feasting into excess. Again, the phrases " eating and drinking judgment unto himself," as not " discerning the Lord's body," and being " guilty of the body and blood of the Lord," certainly do seem to imply some special act of blasphemy, of which the doctrine of the Real Presence does, and the doctrine of a mere appropriation does not, supply a sufficient explanation.

27.

So much taking the offence at the worst; but in matter of fact there does not seem any good reason for supposing that, strictly speaking, the excess in question was occasioned by the consecrated Cup; nor is such the interpretation given to the passage by St. Chrysostom, and other ancient commentators. In those early times it would appear, that the celebration of the Eucharist was often the first act of that social meal which Christians partook when they met together. Men under every dispensation, have, in their religious meetings, taken the firstfruits of their substance, and have solemnly offered them to God, in grateful acknowledgment of His bounty to them, and with prayer that they might be blessed to them, not only for bodily nourishment, but as a means of gaining His favour. Such were the sacrifices of thanksgiving among the Jews; and Christ retained the ordinance in His Church, only annexing to it a higher meaning, and more varied purposes, and more sacred benefits. The feast of God's visible good gifts was continued; but it was held chiefly for the poorer members of the Church, and furnished by the more wealthy, in accordance with the Divine command, "When thou makest a dinner or a supper, call not thy friends, nor thy brethren, neither thy kinsmen, nor thy rich neighbours, lest they also bid thee again, and a recompense be made thee. But when thou makest a feast, call the poor, the maimed, the lame, the blind; and thou shalt be blessed, for they cannot recompense thee, for thou shalt be recompensed at the resurrection of the just." And, whereas the choicest produce, whether of the earth, or of flocks or herds, had been selected for the sacred rite in the former sacrifices, the appointed materials of the Christian offering are Bread and Wine, the chief stays of bodily life; and whereas the old sacrifice had been both an acknowledgment to God, and a pledge of favour from Him, these holy elements were this and much more, at once a thankful remembrance, and also a symbolical pleading before Him of that all-sufficient Sacrifice which had once been offered on the Cross, and next, the actual means by which that Sacrifice is brought home in spirit and in truth to each believer.

28.

When then the Corinthians are said to have committed excess, there is no reason for supposing that the consecrated elements were the materials of it; rather the meal, which followed, which ought to have been a frugal repast, not to satisfy hunger so much as to be an opportunity of mutual friendliness, nor for the rich but for the poor, was made a mere animal refreshment or carnal indulgence, altogether out of character with a religious meeting. Hence he says, "What, have ye not houses to eat and drink in? or despise ye the Church of God, and shame them that have not," i.e. that are poor? Moreover, it is not certain that the word translated "is drunken" has strictly that meaning. It is the word in the Septuagint version in Gen. xliii. 34, which our Translation renders "they drank and were merry with him." Joseph's brethren ate and drank freely, indulged themselves as men who had met with unexpected good; which need not imply gross intemperance. And such seems to have been the sin of the Corinthians; they turned a religious meeting into a mere festivity, and thus evidenced a state of mind which could not have seriously and reverently taken part in the High Mystery with which it commenced. They who could end a religious rite by freely indulging in wine which had been offered up to God, and in part consecrated and given back to them as His blood, could not have really come in faith to that offering, consecration, and communion.

29.

The feast I have been describing seems to have been that which was called Agape, or the feast of charity, and is alluded to by St. Jude in a passage which corroborates what has been said. He mentions certain heretics who among their other sins committed in their love-feasts the same kind of fault as the Corinthians. "These are spots in your feasts of charity, when they feast with you *feeding themselves without* fear;" words which are parallel to St. Peter's, concerning those who " shall receive the reward of unrighteousness, as they that count it pleasure to riot in the day-time. Spots they are and blemishes, sporting themselves with their own deceivings, while they feast with you."

Such abuses as these, whether from the intrusion of heretics or the frailness of Christians, led to a speedy suppression of the Agape, as far as the Church could do so. But the practice lingered on in one shape or other for some centuries. The growth of the Christian body brought it into contact in various ways with heathenism; and those excesses, which had been in favour with a gross populace before their conversion were introduced into it by means of the Agape. Even at the end of the fourth century, St. Austin had to defend the Church against Faustus the Manichee, who maintained, on the ground of such irregularities, that the practice itself had had a heathen origin. In his reply he allows that the feast was abused, but he traces it to its original source, the Apostolic feast of charity, the real object of which was to provide a meal for the poor.[9] Shortly before, St. Ambrose had succeeded in suppressing it at Milan; but in Greece it continued even as late as the

[9] Vid. August. in Faust. xx. 21.

seventh century, as we learn from the Council in Trullo, which renewed against it a Canon passed at Laodicea in the fourth.

30.

However, though such was the perversion and consequent inexpedience of this primitive feast, and such the earnestness with which the Church even in the Apostles' days set herself against it, yet it must not be supposed that it was never anything but a scandal. In some of the descriptions left us of it by Antiquity, it appears as an innocent, or rather a beautiful and impressive ordinance. St. Chrysostom's account of it is very near the same as what I have been drawing out. He observes that the first Christians had all things in common; and that when the distinction of property came to be observed, which took place even in the Apostles' time, then this usage remained as a sort of shadow and symbol of it; that on certain days, after Sermon, Prayers, and Holy Communion, they did not break up at once, but took part rich and poor in a common feast, the rich supplying provisions, the poor feasting.' St. Chrysostom seems to speak of the earliest times; for shortly after or in other parts of the Church the feast seems to have been delayed till the evening. Pliny in his celebrated Letter to Trajan speaks of Christians as first "meeting on a certain stated day before it was light," and "addressing Christ in prayer as some God," and "binding themselves with a solemn oath" to keep the commandments, and next as "separating and then re-assembling and eating in common a harmless meal." Tertullian says the same thing in his Apology, and an extract from him will serve to show how suitable a sequel to the Eucharist the feast might be made.

[1] De Bapt. Christi, c. 4. (ii. 374. A.) vid. et in Nativ. c. 7. (364. E.) de S. Philogon. c. 4. (i. 449. E. et seqq.) in 1 Cor. H. 27. c. 3. (x. 245.) et c. 5. (247, 248.) in Rom. xvi. Hom. 30. (ix. 739. E.)

"Our feast," he says, "admits nothing indecorous, nothing indecent. We sit not down to eat, until prayer to God be made, as it were, the first morsel. We eat as much as will satisfy hunger, and drink as much as is useful for the temperate. We commit no excess, for we remember that even during the night we are to make our prayers to God. Our conversation is that of men who are conscious that the Lord hears them. After water is brought for the hands, and lights, we are invited to sing to God, according as each one can propose a subject from the Holy Scriptures, or of his own composing. This is the proof in what manner we have drunk. Prayer in like manner concludes the feast. Thence we depart, not to join a crowd of disturbers of the peace, nor to follow a troop of brawlers, nor to break out in any excess of wanton riot: but to maintain the same staid and modest demeanour, as if we were departing, not from a supper, but from a lecture."[2]

31.

And now enough has been said concerning the primitive Agape or Feast of Charity, a sacred rite yet a social meal,—so far a bodily refreshment as to become an occasion of excess, and so far under the shadow of the Sacramental feast as to make that excess sacrilege. Such an excess is spoken of by St. Jude and St. Peter and in both Apostles stands connected with divine judgments; why then should it not be the sin of the Corinthians? and if

---

[2] Apolog. 39. Mr. Chevallier's Translation has been borrowed, who adds the following beautiful passage from St. Cyprian. Et quoniam feriata jam quies, ac tempus est otiosum, quicquid inclinato jam sole in vesperam diei superest, ducamus hanc diem laeti; nec sit vel hora convivii gratiæ cœlestis immunis. Sonet psalmos convivium sobrium; et ut tibi tenax memoria est, vox canora, aggredere hoc munus ex more. Magis carrissimos pasces, si sit nobis spiritalis auditio; prolectat aures religiosa mulcedo. Ad Don. fin.

so, what is there more heinous, than unhappily we witness in other times and places, in persons first partaking the Lord's Supper, and afterwards proceeding to excess, and thus showing that they had partaken in a light and thoughtless spirit *because* they proceed to excess?

32.

I regret I cannot close this Letter without something like a protest respecting one matter. There is nothing unbecoming in any one, who has means of judging, interposing when he sees an ordinance of the Church disparaged, and I think your tone as regards mortification and penance, is such as to discourage persons from obeying certain rules of the Church respecting them. I much regret that, while censuring "rigid mortifications and painful penances," you have not given us to understand whether you mean "*rigid* mortifications and *painful* penances" or "mortifications and penances," as such; whether you object to them in toto, or only in excess. I wish, when speaking of "self-abasement" as Papistical, and of "*gloomy* views of sin after Baptism," you had said what views of it are at once appropriate to backsliders and yet not gloomy; whether you consider repentance itself cheerful or gloomy; whether every feeling must be called gloomy which is mixed with fear; whether every purpose is gloomy which leads to self-chastisement; whether every self-abasement savours of Popery, or what those are which do not so savour; whether any self-abasements are pleasant; whether the "indignation, fear, and revenge," of the Corinthians was pleasant or "gloomy;" or whether St. Paul's "bruising his body" was a mortification; whether (to come to our Church's words and rules) to confess an "*intolerable* burden of sins" is "gloomy;" whether it is pleasant to be "*tied and bound* with the chain of our sins," or to be "*grieved* and *wearied* with their burden;" whether "to *bewail* our own sinfulness" is a cheerful exercise; whether absolution does not imply a previous bond; whether "days of fasting or abstinence" are pleasant or "painful;" whether the "godly discipline," the restoration of which, as we yearly protest, is much to be wished, would not be "rigid" and "painful," and likely to "call us back at once to the darkest period of Roman superstition;" whether "turning to God with weeping, fasting, and praying," and "subduing by abstinence the flesh to the Spirit," is or is not likely "hopelessly to alarm and repel those abettors of low and rationalistic views of the Sacramental Ordinances, whom it is our especial object to win and persuade to a saving faith in their genuine and inestimable importance."

33.

Nor is this all; what the Church has enjoined, her most distinguished sons, of whatever school of thought, have practised. Let me then lay out some additional matter, besides her authorized documents, the details of which I wish duly adjusted with those vague and frightful words, "rigour," and "gloom," and "pain," and "Popery," to which otherwise the untaught may improperly refer them.

(1.) I begin with Jewel, because you have a zeal for him:—"being forewarned to leave the hold of his body . . . he did not after the custom of most men seek by all means violently to keep possession . . . to surfeit the senses, and stop all the passages of the soul. No; but by *fasting*, labour, and *watching*, he openeth them wider." *Life*, c. 32 fin.

(2.) B. Gilpin says to a friend, "As for the arguments touching *fasting*, God forbid that either I or any one should deny, yea *rather we exhort all persons* to the practice of it, only we desire to have the superstition and wicked opinions removed." *Wordsworth's Eccl. Biog.* iv. 148.

(3.) Hooker. "There might be many more and just occasions taken to speak of his books, which none ever did or can commend too much; but I decline them, and hasten to an account of his Christian behaviour and death at Borne; in which place he continued his customary rules of *mortification* and *self-denial;* was much in *fasting*, frequent in meditation and prayers, enjoying those blessed returns, which only men of *strict* lives feel and know, and of which men of loose and godless lives cannot be made sensible; for spiritual things are spiritually discerned." *Life,* ed. Keble, vol. i. p. 94.

(4.) Herbert. "Mr. Herbert took occasion to say, 'One cure for these distempers would be, for the Clergy themselves *to keep the Ember-weeks strictly,* and beg of their parishioners to join with them in *fasting* and prayers for a more religious Clergy.'" *Wordsw. E. B.* vol. iv. p. 538.

Again: "This Lent I am forbid utterly to eat any fish, so that I am fain to diet in my chamber at my own cost; *for in our public halls, you know, is nothing but fish and whitmeats: out of Lent also, twice a week, on Fridays and Saturdays, I must do so,* which yet sometimes I fast." *Ibid.* p. 560.

(5.) Hammond. "He both admitted and solemnly invited all sober persons to his familiarity and converse; and beside that, received them to *his weekly office of Fasting and Humiliation."* Life by Fell, p. 50.

"And now, though his physicians had earnestly forbidden his *accustomed Fastings,* and his own weaknesses gave forcible suffrages to their advice; yet he resumed his *rigours,* esteeming this calamity such a one as admitted *no exception*, which should not be outlived, but that it became men to be *martyrs* too, and deprecate even in death." *Ibid.* p. 73.

(6.) Bull. "Now Mr. Bull did not satisfy himself only with giving notice to his parishioners, which he could not well omit without neglecting his duty, but he led them to the observation of such holy institutions by his own example. For he had so far a regard to these holydays, as to cause all his family to repair to the church at such times; and on *the days of fasting and abstinence, the necessary refreshments of life were adjourned from the usual hours till towards the evening.* He was too well acquainted with the practice of the primitive Christians, to neglect such observances as they made instrumental to piety and devotion, and *had too great a value for the injunctions of his mother the Church of England*, to disobey where she required a compliance; but above all, he was too intent upon making advances in the Christian life, to omit a duty *all along observed by devout men* and *acceptable to God* under the Old and New Testament, both as it was helpful to their devotion, and became a part of it." *Life by Nelson*, ed. Burton, p. 54.

(7.) Leighton. "*He had no regard to his person, unless it was to mortify it* by a constant *low diet*, that was *like a perpetual fast.*" Burnet's Lives, p. 282. ed. Jebb.

(8.) Kettlewell too "observed likewise the *days of fasting and humiliation*, both those appointed by the Church, and those which were enjoined by the civil authorities. Wednesdays and Fridays in Lent he *abstained from flesh and drank small beer,* according to the Canon." *Life*, part ii. p. 24.

(9.) Lastly, Ken, in his Sermon on Daniel, thus speaks: "I do not exhort you to follow them [the ancients] any further than either our climate or our constitutions will bear; but we may easily follow Daniel, in *abstaining from wine,* and from the more *pleasurable* meats, and such an abstinence as this, *with such a mourning* for our own sins, and the sins of others, and the proper exercise of a primitive spirit *during all the weeks of Lent.* For what is Lent, in its original institution, but a spiritual conflict, to subdue the flesh to the Spirit, to beat down our bodies and to bring them into subjection? What is it, but a *penitential martyrdom* for so many weeks together which we suffer for our own and others' sins! A devout soul, that is able duly to observe it, fastens himself to the Cross on Ash Wednesday, and hangs crucified by contrition all the Lent long; that having felt in his closet the *burthen and the anguish,* the *nails and the thorns,* and tasted the *full of his own sins,* he may by his own crucifixion be better disposed to be crucified with Christ on Good Friday, and most tenderly sympathize with all the dolours, and pressures, and anguish, and torments, and desertion, infinite, unknown, and unspeakable, which God incarnate endured, when He bled upon the Cross for the sins of the world; that being purified by repentance, and made conformable to Christ crucified, he may offer up a pure oblation at Easter, and feel the power, and the joys, and the triumph of his Saviour's resurrection." Sermon on Daniel.

34.

I think then, if I may say so with due respect, that those who wish to obey their Church in the matter of fasting and abstinence, yet fear that "revival of Popish error" to which these practices tend, have a claim on you to draw some broad lines of distinction, or, in your own phrase, to *"devise* some *limits,"* which may enable them safely to do the one yet not encourage the other; lest they be saved from the "na'ural consequence" of such practices only by what you call elsewhere "a happy inconsistency," and "*for the present;*" and lest "their credulous flocks" at length fall under "the yoke of spiritual bondage," from which we have been set free by the Reformation.

35.

O that we knew our own strength as a Church! O that instead of keeping on the defensive, and thinking it much not to lose our niggardly portion of Christian light and holiness, which is getting less and less, the less we use it, instead of being timid, and cowardly, and suspicious, and jealous, and panic-struck, and grudging, and unbelieving, we had the heart to rise, as a Church, in the attitude of the Spouse of Christ and the Treasure-House of His grace; to throw ourselves into that system of truth which our fathers have handed down even through the worst times, and to use it like a great and understanding people! O that we had the courage and the generous faith to aim at perfection, to demand the attention, to claim the submission of the world! Thousands of hungry souls in all classes of life stand around us; we do not give them what they want, the image of a true Christian people, living in that Apostolic awe and strictness which carries with it an evidence that they are the Church of Christ. This is the way to withstand and repel Roman Catholics; not by cries of alarm, and rumours of plots, and dispute, and denunciation, but by living up to the creeds, the services, the ordinances, the usages of our own Church without fear of consequences, withour fear of being called Papists; to let matters take their course freely, and to trust to God's good Providence for the issue.

36.

And now to conclude. I am quite aware that some of

the subjects I have treated might be treated more fully and clearly. But neither the limits of a pamphlet, nor the time allotted me, admitted it. Yours did not appear till yesterday, and the Term ends in a very few days.

I am, Reverend Sir,

Your faithful Servant,

JOHN H. NEWMAN.

Oriel College, June 22, 1838.

VII.

REMARKS ON CERTAIN PASSAGES OF THE THIRTY-NINE ARTICLES.

(Being No. 90 of the Tracts for the Times.)

1841.

NOTICE.

1. This Tract was written under the conviction that the Anglican Thirty-nine Articles of Religion, of which it treated, were, when taken in their letter, so loosely worded, so incomplete in statement, and so ambiguous in their meaning, as to need an authoritative interpretation; and that neither those who drew them up, nor those who imposed them were sufficiently agreed among themselves, or clear and consistent in their theological views individually to be able to supply it.

2. There was but one authority to whom recourse could be had for such interpretation—the Church Catholic. She had been taught the revealed truth by Christ and His Apostles in the beginning, and had in turn taught it in every age to her faithful children, and would teach it on to the end. And what she taught, all her branches taught; and this the Anglican Church *did* teach, *must* teach, if it was a branch of the Church Catholic, otherwise it was not a branch; but a branch it certainly was, for, if it was not a branch, what had we to do with it? and

it being a branch, it was the duty of all its members, priests and people, ever to profess what the Universal Church had from the beginning professed, and nothing else, and nothing short of it, that is, what had been held *semper et ubique et ab omnibus*. Accordingly, it was their plain duty to interpret the Thirty-nine Articles in this one distinct Catholic sense, the sense of the Holy Fathers, of Athanasius, Ambrose, Augustine, and of all Doctors and Saints; it being impossible that in any important matters those Articles should diverge from that sense, or resist the interpretation which that sense required, inasmuch as the Divine Lord of the Church watched over all her portions, and would not suffer the Anglican or any portion to commit itself to statements which could not fairly and honestly be made to give forth a Catholic meaning.

3. And the circumstances under which the Thirty-nine Articles came into existence, favoured this view. Its compilers were not likely knowingly to exclude the possibility of a Catholic interpretation of them. Doubtless they wished to introduce the new doctrine, but it did not follow from that that they wished to exclude those who still held the old. The ambiguity above spoken of, in the instance of men so acute and learned as they were, could only be accounted for by great differences of opinions among themselves, and a wish by means of compromise to include

among the subscriptions to their formulary a great variety of the then circulating opinions, of which a moderate quasi-Catholicity was one. This would lead them to the use of words, which in the long-run, as they would consider, would tell in favour of Protestantism, while in the letter and in their first effect they did not enforce it.

4. It must be added, in corroboration, that, as is well known, the very Convocation which received and passed the Thirty-nine Articles, also enjoined that "preachers should be careful, that they should never teach aught in a sermon, to be religiously held and believed by the people, except that which is agreeable to the doctrine of the Old and New Testaments, and which the Catholic Fathers and ancient Bishops have collected from that very doctrine." Could they mean their Thirty-nine Articles to be inconsistent with that patristical literature, which at the same time they made the rule even for the interpretation of inspired Scripture?

5. This *primâ facie* view of the Thirty-nine Articles as not excluding a moderate Catholicism (that is, Roman doctrine, as far as it was Catholic) became more cogent, when it was considered that one of these Articles recognized, approved, and appealed to the two Books of "Homilies," as "containing a godly and wholesome doctrine," and by this appeal determined the *animus* and

drift of the Articles to be Catholic. It was evidence of this in two ways, positively and negatively:—positively, inasmuch as the Homilies, though hitherto claimed by the Evangelical party as one of their special weapons against the High Church (for instance, in their controversy with Bishop Marsh, and *supr.* pp. 153,4 by one of their Magazines) were found on a closer inspection to take a view more or less favourable to Rome as regards the number of the Sacraments, the Canon of Scripture, the efficacy of penance, and other points; and negatively, because the Homilies for the most part struck, not at certain Roman doctrines and practices, but at their abuse, and therefore, when, once these Homilies were taken as a legitimate comment on the Articles, they suggested that the repudiations of Roman teaching in the Articles were repudiations of it so far as it was abused, not as it was in itself.

6. Indeed, it may be further asked, if the Articles were not aimed at the abuses, doctrinal and practical, as drawn out in the Homilies, the abuses of times and places, of particular dioceses, schools, preachers, and people, against what could they be directed? Certainly not against any formal doctrines of Rome, call them Catholic or not, for the Tridentine Decrees were not promulgated till 1564, and the Thirty-nine Articles were agreed on in Convocation in 1562.

For these reasons it appeared likely, that when the

Articles were carefully handled, little in them would interfere with the liberty of teaching in the Church of England the *semper, ubique, et ab omnibus* of the Catholic Religion, the unanimous teaching of the Holy Fathers, the present teaching, as far as concordant, of the East and West.

The all-important question followed, whether the Articles, when examined, actually fulfilled this expectation for which there were several good reasons; whether, one by one, they were (as was said at the time) "patient, though not ambitious, of a Catholic interpretation." The Tract which follows made that experiment.

I ought to add, that, in this edition (1877), I have not thought it necessary to insert at full length the passages of the Homilies, as they were inserted originally in the Tract. This omission weakens indeed the Author's argument, but it is better than the alternative of their lavish exhibition. It is penance enough to reprint one's own bad language, without burdening it with the blatterant abuse of the Homilies.

Oct. 11*th*, 1883.—In Sir W. Palmer's "Narrative," just published, it is asserted that I was unwilling to submit my Tracts to revision before publication. Certainly, if he is speaking of revision on his part. But No. 90 was seen by Mr. Keble before publication, though not by Mr. Palmer; so, I believe, were the earlier ones; and when Mr. Palmer was strongly for the series being stopped, Mr. Keble was strong for its continuing.

CONTENTS.

		PAGE
	Introduction	269
§ 1.	Articles vi. & xx.—*Holy Scripture, and the Authority of the Church*	273
§ 2.	Article xi.—*Justification by Faith only*	281
§ 3.	Articles xii. and xiii.—*Works before and after Justification*	284
§ 4.	Article xix.—*The Visible Church*	288
§ 5.	Article xxi.—*General Councils*	291
§ 6.	Article xxii.—*Purgatory, Pardons, Images, Relics, Invocation of Saints*	294
§ 7.	Article xxv.—*The Sacraments*	310
§ 8.	Article xxviii.—*Transubstantiation*	315
§ 9.	Article xxxi.—*Masses*	323
§ 10.	Article xxxii.—*Marriage of Clergy*	327
§ 11.	Article xxxv.—*The Homilies*	330
§ 12.	Article xxxvii.—*The Bishop of Rome*	340
	Conclusion	344

Introduction.

It is often urged, and sometimes felt and granted, that there are in the Articles propositions or terms inconsistent with the Catholic faith; or, at least, when persons do not go so far as to feel the objection as of force, they are perplexed how best to reply to it, or how most simply to explain the passages on which it is made to rest. The following Tract is drawn up with the view of showing how groundless the objection is, and further of approximating towards the argumentative answer to it, of which most men have an implicit apprehension, though they may have nothing more. That there are real difficulties to a Catholic Christian in the Ecclesiastical position of our Church at this day, no one can deny; but the statements of the Articles are not in the number; and it may be right at the present moment to insist upon this. If in any quarter it is supposed that persons who profess to be disciples of the early Church will silently concur with those of very opposite sentiments in furthering a relaxation of subscriptions, which, it is imagined, are galling to both parties, though for different reasons, and that they will do this against the wish of the great body of the Church, the writer of the following pages would raise one voice, at least, in protest against any such anticipation. Even in such points as he may think the English Church deficient, never can he be party without a great alteration of sentiment to forcing the opinion or project of one school upon another. Religious changes, to be beneficial, should be the act of the whole body; they are worth little if they are the mere act of a majority.[1] No good can come of any change which is not heartfelt, a development of feelings springing up freely and calmly within the bosom of the whole body itself. Moreover, a change in theological teaching involves either the commission or the confession of sin; it is either the profession or the renunciation of erroneous doctrine, and if it does not succeed in proving the fact of past guilt, it, *ipso facto*, implies present. In other words, every change in religion carries with it its own condemnation, which is not attended by deep repentance. Even supposing then that any changes in contemplation, whatever they were, were good in themselves, they would cease to be good to a Church, in which they were the fruits not of the quiet conviction of all, but of the agitation, or tyranny, or intrigue of a few; nurtured not in mutual love, but in strife and envying; perfected not in humiliation and grief, but in pride, elation, and triumph. Moreover it is a very serious truth, that persons and bodies, who put themselves into a disadvantageous state, cannot at their pleasure extricate themselves from it. They are unworthy of release; they are in prison, and CHRIST is its keeper. There is but one way for them towards a real reformation—a return to Him in heart and spirit, whose sacred truth they have betrayed; all other methods, however fair they may promise, will prove to be but shadows and failures.

On these grounds, were there no others, the present writer, for one, will be no party to the ordinary political methods by which professed reforms are carried or compassed in this day. We can do nothing well till we act " with one accord;" we can have no accord in action till

[1] This is not meant to hinder acts of Catholic consent, such as occurred anciently, when the Catholic body aids one portion of a particular Church against another portion.

we agree together in heart; we cannot agree without a supernatural influence; we cannot have a supernatural influence unless we pray for it; we cannot pray acceptably without repentance and confession. Our Church's strength would be irresistible, humanly speaking, were it but at unity with itself: if it remains divided, part against part, we shall see the energy which was meant to subdue the world preying upon itself, according to our SAVIOUR's express assurance that such a house " cannot stand." Till we feel this, till we seek one another as brethren, not lightly throwing aside our private opinions, which we seem to feel we have received from above, from an ill-regulated, untrue desire of unity, but returning to each other in heart, and coming together to GOD to do for us what we cannot do for ourselves, no change can be for the better. Till we, her children, are stirred up to this religious course, let the Church, our Mother, sit still; let her children be content to be in bondage; let us work in chains; let us submit to our imperfections as a punishment; let us go on teaching with the stammering lips of ambiguous formularies, and inconsistent precedents, and principles but partially developed. We are not better than our fathers; let us bear to be what Hammond was, or Andrewes, or Hooker; let us not faint under that body of death, which they bore about in patience; nor shrink from the penalty of sins, which they inherited from the age before them.[2]

But these remarks are beyond our present scope, which is merely to show that, while our Prayer Book is acknowledged on all hands to be of Catholic origin, our Articles also, the offspring of an uncatholic age, are, through GOD's

[2] "We, thy sinful creatures," says the Service for King Charles the Martyr, "here assembled before Thee, do, in behalf of all the people of this land, humbly confess, that they were the *crying sins* of this nation, which brought down this judgment upon us," i.e. King Charles's murder.

good providence, to say the least, not uncatholic, and may be subscribed by those who aim at being catholic in heart and doctrine. In entering upon the proposed examination, it is only necessary to add, that in several places the writer has found it convenient to express himself in language recently used,[3] which he is willing altogether to make his own. He has distinguished the passages thus introduced by quotation marks.

[3] [That is, by himself, in former Tracts, Lectures, &c.]

§ 1.—*Holy Scripture and the Authority of the Church.*

Articles vi. & xx.—" Holy Scripture containeth all things necessary to salvation; so that whatsoever is not read therein, nor may be proved thereby, is not to be required of any man, that it should be believed as an article of the Faith, or be thought requisite or necessary to salvation. . . . . . . The Church hath [power to decree (statuendi) rites and ceremonies, and] authority in controversies of faith; and yet it is not lawful for the Church to [ordain (instituere) anything that is contrary to God's word written, neither may it] so expound one place of Scripture, that it be repugnant to another. Wherefore, although the Church be a witness and a keeper of Holy Writ, yet [as it ought not to decree (decernere) anything against the same, so] besides the same, ought it not to enforce (obtrudere) anything to be believed for necessity of salvation."[1]

Two instruments of Christian teaching are spoken of in these Articles, Holy Scripture and the Church.

Here then we have to inquire, first, what is meant by Holy Scripture; next, what is meant by the Church; and then, what their respective offices are in teaching revealed truth, and how these are adjusted with one another in their actual exercise.

1. Now what the Church is, will be considered below in Section 4.

2. And the Books of Holy Scripture are enumerated in the latter part of the 6th Article, so as to preclude question. Still, two points deserve notice here.

First, the Scriptures or Canonical Books are said to be those " of whose authority was never any doubt in the Church." Here it is not meant that there never was any

---

[1] These passages in brackets relate to rites and ceremonies which are not here in question.

doubt in *portions* of the Church or *particular* Churches concerning certain books, which the Article includes in the Canon; for some of them,—as, for instance, the Epistle to the Hebrews and the Apocalypse—have been the subject of much doubt in the West or East, as the case may be. But the Article asserts that there has been no doubt about them in the Church Catholic; that is, at the very first time that the Catholic or whole Church had the opportunity of forming a judgment on the subject, it pronounced in favour of the Canonical Books. The Epistle to the Hebrews was doubted by the West, and the Apocalypse by the East, only while those portions of the Church investigated the matter separately from each other, only till they compared notes, interchanged sentiments, and formed a united judgment. The phrase must mean this, because, from the nature of the case, it can mean nothing else.

And next, be it observed, that the books which are commonly called Apocrypha, are not asserted in this Article to be destitute of inspiration or to be simply human, but to be not canonical; in other words, to differ from Canonical Scripture, specially in this respect, viz. that they are not adducible in proof of doctrine. "The other books (as Hierome saith) the Church doth read for example of life and instruction of manners, but yet doth not apply them to *establish any doctrine.*" That this is the limit to which our disparagement of them extends, is plain, not only because the Article mentions nothing beyond it, but also from the reverential manner in which the Homilies speak of them, as shall be incidentally shown in Section 11. The compatibility of such reverence with such disparagement is also shown from the feeling towards them of St. Jerome, who is quoted in the Article, who implies more or less their inferiority to Canonical Scripture, yet uses them freely and continually, as if Scripture. He distinctly names many of the books which he considers not canonical, and virtually names them all by naming what *are* canonical. For instance, he says, speaking of Wisdom and Ecclesiasticus, " As the Church reads Judith, Tobit, and the Maccabees, without receiving them among the Canonical Scriptures, so she reads these two books for the edification of the people, not for the confirmation of the authority of ecclesiastical doctrines." (*Præf. in Libr. Salom.*) Again, " The Wisdom, as it is commonly styled, of Solomon, and the book of Jesus, son of Sirach, and Judith, and Tobias, and the Shepherd, are not in the Canon." (*Præf. ad Reges.*) Such is the language of a writer who nevertheless is, to say the least, not wanting in reverence towards the books he thus disparages.

A further question may be asked, concerning our received version of the Scriptures, whether it is in any sense imposed on us as a true comment on the original text; as the Vulgate is upon the Roman Catholics. It would appear not. It was made and authorized by royal command, which cannot be supposed to have any claim upon our interior assent. At the same time every one who reads it in the Services of the Church, does, of course, thereby imply that he considers that it contains no deadly heresy or dangerous mistake. And about its simplicity, majesty, gravity, harmony, and venerableness, there can be but one opinion.

3. Next we come to the main point, the adjustment which this Article effects between the respective offices of Scripture and the Church; which seems to be as follows.

It is laid down that, 1. Scripture contains all necessary articles of the faith; 2. either in its text, or by inference; 3. The Church is the keeper of Scripture; 4. and a witness of it; 5. and has authority in controversies of faith; 6. but may not expound one passage of Scripture to contradict another; 7. nor enforce as an article of faith any point not contained in Scripture.

From this it appears, first, that the Church *expounds and enforces the faith;* for it is forbidden to expound in a particular way, or so to enforce as to obtrude; next, that it derives the faith *wholly from Scripture;* thirdly, that its office is to educe an *harmonious interpretation* of Scripture. Thus much the Article settles.

Two important questions, however, it does not settle, viz. whether the Church judges, first, at her *sole discretion*, next, on her *sole responsibility;* i.e. first, what the *media* are by which the Church interprets Scripture, whether by a direct divine gift, or by catholic tradition, or by critical exegesis of the text, or in any other way; and next, who is to decide whether it interprets Scripture rightly or not;—first, what is her method, if any; and next, who is her judge, if any. In other words, not a word is said, on the one hand, in favour of there being no *external* rule or method to fix the interpretation of Scripture by, or, as it is commonly expressed, of Scripture *being the sole rule of faith;* nor on the other, of the *private judgment of the individual* being the ultimate standard of interpretation. So much has been said lately on both these points, and indeed on the whole subject of these two Articles, that it is unnecessary to enlarge upon them; but since it is often supposed to be almost a first principle of our Church, that Scripture is "the rule of faith," it may be well, before passing on, to make an extract [2] from a paper, published some years since, which shows, by instances from our divines, that the application of the phrase to Scripture is but of recent adoption. The other question, about the ultimate judge of the interpretation of Scripture, shall not be entered upon.

"We may dispense with the phrase 'Rule of Faith,' as applied to Scripture, on the ground of its being ambiguous; and, again, because it is then used in a novel sense;

[2] [British Critic, Oct. 1836, pp. 386—388.]

for the ancient Church made the Apostolic Tradition, as summed up in the Creed, and not the Bible, the *Regula Fidei*, or Rule. Moreover its use as a technical phrase seems to be of late introduction in the Church, that is, since the days of King William the Third. Our great divines use it without any fixed sense, sometimes for Scripture, sometimes for the whole and perfectly adjusted Christian doctrine, sometimes for the Creed; and, at the risk of being tedious, we will prove this, by quotations, that the point may be put beyond dispute.

"Ussher, after St. Austin, identifies it with the Creed;—when speaking of the Article of our LORD's Descent to Hell, he says,—

"'It having here likewise been further manifested, what different opinions have been entertained by the ancient Doctors of the Church concerning the determinate place wherein our Saviour's soul did remain during the time of the separation of it from the body, I leave it to be considered by the learned, whether any such controverted matter may be fitly brought in to *expound the Rule of Faith*, which, being common both to the great and small ones of the Church, must contain such varieties only as are generally agreed upon by the common consent of all true Christians.'—*Answer to a Jesuit*, p. 362.

"Taylor speaks to the same purpose: 'Let us see with what constancy that and the following ages of the Church did adhere to the Apostles' Creed, as the sufficient and perfect *Rule of Faith*.'—*Dissuasive*, part 2, i. 4, p. 470. Elsewhere he calls Scripture the Rule: 'That the Scripture is a full and sufficient *Rule* to Christians in faith and manners, a full and perfect declaration of the Will of GOD, is therefore certain, because we have no other.'—*Ibid.* part 2, i. 2, p. 384. Elsewhere, Scripture and the Creed : 'He hath, by His wise Providence, preserved the plain places of Scripture and the Apostles' Creed, in all Churches, to be the *Rule* and Measure of Faith, by which all Churches are saved.'—*Ibid.* part 2, i. 1, p. 346. Elsewhere he identifies it with Scripture, the Creeds, and the first four Councils: 'We also [after Scripture] do believe the Apostles' Creed, the Nicene, with the additions of Constantinople, and that which is commonly called the symbol of St. Athanasius; and the four first General Councils are so entirely admitted by us, that they, together with the plain words of Scripture, are made the *Rule* and Measure of judging heresies among us.'—*Ibid.* part 1, i. p. 131.

"Laud calls the Creed, or rather the Creed with Scripture, the Rule: "Since the Fathers make the Creed the *Rule of Faith;* since the agreeing sense of Scripture with those Articles are the *Two Regular Precepts,* by which a divine is governed about his faith,' &c.—*Conference with Fisher*, p. 42.

"Bramhall also: 'The Scriptures and the Creed are not two different Rules of Faith, but *one and the same Rule, dilated in Scripture, contracted in the Creed.*'—*Works*, p. 402. Stillingfleet says the same (*Grounds*, i. 4. 3.); as does Thorndike (*De Rat. fin. Controv.* p. 144, &c.). Elsewhere, Stillingfleet calls Scripture the Rule (*Ibid.* i. 6. 2.); as does Jackson (vol. i. p. 226). But the most complete and decisive statement on the subject is contained in Field's work on the Church, from which shall follow a long extract.

"'It remaineth to show,' he says, 'what is the Rule of that judgment whereby the Church discerneth between truth and falsehood, the faith and heresy, and to whom it properly pertaineth to interpret those things which, touching this Rule, are doubtful. The Rule of our Faith in general, whereby we know it to be true, is the infinite excellency of God.... It being pre-supposed in the generality that the doctrine of the Christian Faith is of GOD, and containeth nothing but heavenly truth, in the next place, we are to inquire by what Rule we are to judge of particular things contained within the compass of it.

"'This *Rule* is, 1. The summary comprehension of such principal articles of this divine knowledge, as are the principles whence all other things are concluded and inferred. These are contained in the *Creed of the Apostles*.

"'2. All such things as every Christian is bound expressly to believe, by the light and direction whereof he judgeth of other things, which are not absolutely necessary so particularly to be known. These are rightly said to be the Rule of our Faith, because the principles of every science are the Rule whereby we judge of the truth of all things, as being better and more generally known than any other thing, and the cause of knowing them.

"'3. The analogy, due proportion, and correspondence, that one thing in this divine knowledge hath with another, so that men cannot err in one of them without erring in another; nor rightly understand one, but they must likewise rightly conceive the rest.

"'4. Whatsoever *Books* were delivered unto us, as written by them, to whom the first and immediate revelation of the divine truth was made.

"'5. Whatsoever hath been delivered by all the saints with one consent, which have left their judgment and opinion in writing.

"'6. Whatsoever the most famous have constantly and uniformly delivered, as a matter of faith, no one contradicting, though many other ecclesiastical writers be silent, and say nothing of it.

"'7. That which the most, and most famous in every age, constantly delivered as a matter of faith, and as received of them that went before them, in such sort that the contradictors and gainsayers were in their beginnings noted for singularity, novelty and division, and afterwards, in process of time, if they persisted in such contradiction, charged with heresy.

"'These three latter Rules of our Faith we admit, not because they are equal with the former, and originally in themselves contain the direction of our Faith, but because nothing can be delivered, with such and so full consent of the people of GOD, as in them is expressed, but it must need be from those first authors and founders of our Christian profession. The Romanists add unto these the decrees of Councils and determinations of Popes, making these also to be the Rules of Faith; but because we have no proof of *their* infallibility, we number them not with the rest.

"'Thus we see how many things, in several degrees and sort, are said to be Rules of our Faith. The infinite excellency of GOD, as that whereby the truth of the heavenly doctrine is proved. The Articles of Faith and other verities ever expressly known in the Church as the first principles, are the Canon by which we judge of conclusions from thence inferred. The Scripture, as containing in it all that doctrine of Faith which CHRIST the SON of GOD delivered. The uniform practice and consenting judgment of them that went before us, as a certain and undoubted explication of the things contained in the Scripture. . . . So, then, *we do not make Scripture the Rule of our Faith, but that other things in their kind are Rules likewise;* in such sort that *it is not safe, without respect had unto them, to judge things by the Scripture alone,*' &c.—iv. 14. pp. 364, 365.

"These extracts show not only what the Anglican doctrine is, but, in particular, that the phrase 'Rule of Faith' is no symbolical expression with us, appropriated to some one sense; certainly not as a definition or attribute of Holy Scripture. And it is important to insist upon this, from the very great misconceptions to which the phrase gives rise. Perhaps its use had better be avoided altogether. In the sense in which it is commonly understood at this day, Scripture, it is plain, is *not*, on Anglican principles, the Rule of Faith."

§ 2.—*Justification by Faith only.*

Article xi —" That we are justified by Faith only, is a most wholesome doctrine."

The Homilies add that Faith is the sole *means*, the sole *instrument* of justification. Now, to show briefly what such statements imply, and what they do not.

1. They do *not* imply a denial of *Baptism* as a means and an instrument of justification; which the Homilies elsewhere affirm, as will be shown incidentally in a later Section.

" The instrumental power of Faith cannot interfere with the instrumental power of Baptism; because Faith is the sole justifier, not in contrast to *all* means and agencies whatever, (for it is not surely in contrast to our LORD's merits, or GOD's mercy,) but to all other *graces*. When, then, Faith is called the sole instrument, this means the sole *internal* instrument, not the sole instrument of any kind.

" There is nothing inconsistent, then, in Faith being the sole instrument of justification, and yet Baptism also the sole instrument, and that at the same time, because in distinct senses; an inward instrument in no way interfering with an outward instrument, Baptism may be the hand of the giver, and Faith the hand of the receiver."

Nor does the sole instrumentality of Faith interfere with the doctrine of *Works* being a mean also. And that it is a mean, the Homily of Alms-deeds declares in the strongest language, as will also be quoted in Section 11.

" An assent to the doctrine that Faith alone justifies, does not at all preclude the doctrine of Works justifying also. If, indeed, it were said that Works justify in *the same sense* as Faith only justifies, this would be a contradiction in terms; but Faith only may justify in one sense —Good Works in another:—and this is all that is here maintained. After all, does not CHRIST only justify? How is it that the doctrine of Faith justifying does not interfere with our LORD's being the sole justifier? It will, of course, be replied, that our LORD is the *meritorious cause*, and Faith the *means;* that Faith justifies in a different and subordinate sense. As then, CHRIST only justifies *in the sense* in which He justifies, yet Faith also justifies in its own sense; so Works, whether moral or ritual, may justify us in their own respective senses, though in the sense in which Faith justifies, it alone justifies. The only question is, *What* is that sense in which Works justify, so as not to interfere with Faith only justifying? It may, indeed, turn out on inquiry, that the sense alleged will not hold, either as being unscriptural, or for any other reason; but, whether so or not, at any rate the apparent inconsistency of language should not startle men; nor should they so promptly condemn those who, though they do not use *their* language, at least use St. James's. Indeed, is not this argument the very weapon of the Arians, in their warfare against the SON of GOD? They said, CHRIST is not GOD, because the FATHER is called the '*Only* GOD.'"[1]

2. Next we have to inquire *in what sense* Faith only does justify. In a number of ways, of which here two only shall be mentioned.

First, it is the pleading or impetrating principle, or constitutes our *title* to justification; being analogous among the graces to Moses' lifting up his hands on the Mount, or the Israelites eyeing the Brazen Serpent,—actions which did not merit GOD's mercy, but *asked* for it. A number of means go to effect our justification. We are justified by

---

[1] [Lectures on Justification, x., xii., pp. 226, 276, ed. 1874.]

CHRIST alone, in that He has purchased the gift ; by Faith alone, in that Faith asks for it; by Baptism alone, for Baptism conveys it; and by newness of heart alone, for newness of heart is the *sine qua non* life of it.

And secondly, Faith, as being the beginning of perfect or justifying righteousness, is taken for what it tends towards, or ultimately will be. It is said by anticipation to be that which it promises ; just as one might pay a labourer his hire before he began his work. Faith working by love is the seed of divine graces, which in due time will be brought forth and flourish—partly in this world, fully in the next.

§ 3.—*Works before and after Justification.*

Articles xii. & xiii.—" Works done before the grace of CHRIST, and the inspiration of His SPIRIT, ['before justification,' *title of the Article*,] are not pleasant to GOD (minimè Deo grata sunt); forasmuch as they spring not of Faith in JESUS CHRIST, neither do they make man meet to receive grace, or (as the school authors say) deserve grace of congruity (merentur gratiam de congruo); yea, rather for that they are not done as GOD hath willed and commanded them to be done, we doubt not but they have the nature of sin. Albeit good works, which are the fruits of faith, and follow after justification (justificatos sequuntur), cannot put away (expiare) our sins, and endure the severity of GOD's judgment, yet are they pleasing and acceptable (grata et accepta) to GOD in CHRIST, and do spring out necessarily of a true and lively Faith."

Two sorts of works are here mentioned—works before justification, and works after; and they are most strongly contrasted with each other.

1. Works before justification, are done " before the grace of CHRIST, and the inspiration of His SPIRIT."
2. Works before, "do not spring of Faith in JESUS CHRIST;" works after are " the fruits of Faith."
3. Works before " have the nature of sin;" works after are " good works."
4. Works before "are not pleasant (grata) to GOD;" works after "are pleasing and acceptable (grata et accepta) to GOD."

Two propositions, mentioned in these Articles, remain, and deserve consideration: First, that works *before* justification do not make or dispose men to receive grace, or, as the school writers say, deserve grace of congruity; secondly, that works *after*" cannot put away our sins, and endure the severity of GOD's judgment."

1. As to the former statement, to deserve *de congruo*, or of congruity, is to move the Divine regard, not from any claim upon it, but from a certain fitness or suitableness: as, for instance, it might be said that dry wood had a certain disposition or fitness towards heat which green wood had not. Now, the Article denies that works done before the grace of CHRIST, or in a mere state of nature, in this way dispose towards grace, or move GOD to grant grace. And it asserts, with or without reason, (for it is a question of *historical fact*, which need not specially concern us,) that certain schoolmen maintained the affirmative.

Now, that this is what it means, is plain from the following passages of the Homilies, which in no respect have greater claims upon us than as comments upon the Articles :—

"Therefore they that teach repentance *without a lively faith* in our SAVIOUR JESUS CHRIST, do teach none other but Judas's repentance, as all the schoolmen do which do *only* allow these three parts of repentance,—the contrition of the heart, the confession of the mouth, and the satisfaction of the work. But all these things we find in Judas's repentance, which, in outward appearance, did far exceed and pass the repentance of Peter. . . . This was commonly the penance which CHRIST enjoined sinners, 'Go thy way, and sin no more;' which penance we shall never be able to fulfil, *without the special grace* of Him that doth say, 'Without Me, ye can do nothing.'"—*On Repentance*, p. 460.

To take a passage which is still more clear :—

"As these examples are not brought in to the end that we should thereby take a boldness to sin, presuming on the mercy and goodness of GOD, but to the end that, if, through the frailness of our own flesh, and the temptation of the devil, we fall into the like sins, we should in no wise despair of the mercy and goodness of GOD : even so must we beware and take heed, that we do in no wise think in our hearts, imagine, or believe *that we are able to repent aright, or to turn effectually unto the* LORD *by our own might and strength*."—*Ibid.*, part i. fin.

The Article contemplates these two states,—one of justifying grace, and one of the utter destitution of grace; and it says, that those who are in utter destitution cannot do anything to gain justification; and, indeed, to assert the contrary would be Pelagianism. However, there is an intermediate state, of which the Article says nothing, but which must not be forgotten, as being an actually existing one. Men are not always either in light or in darkness, but are sometimes between the two; they are sometimes not in a state of Christian justification, yet not utterly deserted by God, but in a state something like that of Jews or of Heathen, turning to the thought of religion. They are not gifted with *habitual* grace, but they still are visited by Divine influences, or by *actual* grace, or rather *aid*; and these influences are the first-fruits of the grace of justification going before it, and are intended to lead on to it, and to be perfected in it, as twilight leads to day. And since it is a Scripture maxim, that "he that is faithful in that which is least, is faithful also in much;" and "to whomsoever hath, to him shall be given;" therefore it is quite true that works done *with* divine aid, and in faith *before* justification, *do* dispose men to receive the grace of justification;—such were Cornelius's alms, fastings, and prayers, which led to his baptism. At the same time it must be borne in mind that, even in such cases, it is not the works themselves which make them meet, as some schoolmen seem to have said, but the secret aid of God, vouchsafed, equally with the "grace and Spirit," which is the portion of the baptized, for the merits of Christ's sacrifice.

But it may be objected, that the silence observed in the Article as to there being an incomplete state between that of both justification and divine grace together, and that of neither, (viz. a state in which a soul has the influences of grace, but is not yet justified,) is a proof that there is no such half state. This argument, however, would prove too much; for in like manner there is a silence in the Sixth Article about a *judge* of the scripturalness of doctrine, yet a judge there must be. And again, few, it is supposed, would deny that Cornelius, before the Angel came to him, was in a more hopeful state, than Simon Magus or Felix. The difficulty then, if there be one, is common to persons of whatever school of opinion.

2. If works even *before* justification, when done by the influence of divine aid, gain grace, as we see in the instance of Cornelius, much more do works *after* justification. They are, according to the Article, " grata," " pleasing to GOD ;" and they are accepted, " accepta ;" which means that GOD rewards them, and that of course according to their degree of excellence. At the same time, as works before justification may nevertheless be done under a divine influence, so works after justification are still liable to the infection of original sin; and, as not being perfect, " cannot expiate our sins," or " endure the severity of GOD's judgment."

§ 4.—*The Visible Church.*

Art. xix.—" The visible Church of CHRIST is a congregation of faithful men (cœtus fidelium), in the which the pure Word of GOD is preached, and the Sacraments be duly ministered, according to CHRIST's ordinance, in all those things that of necessity are requisite to the same."

This is not an abstract definition of *a* Church, but a description of *the* actually existing One Holy Catholic Church diffused throughout the world; as if it were read, " The Church is a certain existing society of the faithful," &c. This is evident from the mode of describing the Catholic Church familiar to all writers from the first ages down to the age of this Article. For instance, St. Clement of Alexandria says, " I mean by the Church, not a place, but the *congregation of the elect.*" Origen: " The Church, the *assembly of all the faithful.*" St. Ambrose: " *One congregation,* one Church." St. Isidore: " The Church is a *congregation of saints,* collected on a certain faith, and the best conduct of life." St. Augustin: " The Church is *the people of God* through all ages." Again: " The Church is *the multitude* which is spread over the whole earth." St. Cyril: " When we speak of the Church, we denote the most holy *multitude of the pious.*" Theodoret: " The Apostle calls the Church the *assembly of the faithful.*" Pope Gregory: " The Church, a *multitude of the faithful* collected of both sexes." Bede: "The Church is the *congregation of all saints.*" Alcuin: " The Holy Catholic Church,—in Latin, the *congregation of the faithful.*" Amalarius: " The Church is *the people* called together by the Church's ministers." Pope Nicholas I.: " The Church, that is, the *congregation of Catholics.*" St. Bernard: " What is the Spouse, but *the congregation of the just?* " Peter the Venerable: " The Church is called *a congregation*, but not of all things, not of cattle, but *of men, faithful*, good, just. Though bad among these good, and just among the unjust, are revealed or concealed, yet it is called a Church." Hugo Victorinus : " The Holy Church, that is, *the university of the faithful.*" Arnulphus : "The Church is called *the congregation of the faithful.*" Albertus Magnus: " The Greek word Church means in Latin convocation ; and whereas works and callings belong to rational animals, and reason in man is inward faith, therefore it is called *the congregation of the faithful.*" Durandus : " The Church is in one sense material, in which divers offices are celebrated; in another spiritual, which is the *collection of the faithful.*" Alvarus : " The Church is the *multitude of the faithful*, or the university of Christians." Pope Pius II.: " The Church is the *multitude of the faithful* dispersed through all nations." Estius, Chancellor of Douay : " There is a controversy between Catholics and heretics as to what the word 'Church' means. John Huss and the heretics of our day who follow him, define the Church to be the university of the predestinate; Catholics define it to be the *Society of those who are joined to each other by a right faith and the Sacraments.*" [1]

These illustrations of the phraseology of the Article may be multiplied in any number. And they plainly show that it is not laying down any logical definition *what* a Church is, but is describing, and, as it were, pointing to the Catholic Church diffused throughout the world ; which, being but one, cannot possibly be mistaken, and requires no other account of it beyond this single and majestic one. The ministration of the Word and Sacraments is mentioned as a further note of it. As to the question of its limits, whether Episcopal Succession or whether intercommunion with the whole be necessary to each part of it,—these are

[1] These instances are from Launoy.

questions, most important indeed, but of detail, and are not expressly treated of in the Articles.

This view is further illustrated by the following passage from the Homily for Whitsunday :—

"Our Saviour CHRIST departing out of the world unto His FATHER, promised His Disciples to send down another COMFORTER, that should continue with them for ever, and direct them into all truth. Which thing, to be faithfully and truly performed, the Scriptures do sufficiently bear witness. Neither must we think that this COMFORTER was either promised, or else given, only to the Apostles, but also to *the universal Church of* CHRIST, *dispersed through the whole world.* . . . The true Church is *an universal congregation or fellowship of* GOD's *faithful and elect people*, built upon the foundation of the Apostles and Prophets, JESUS CHRIST Himself being the head corner-stone. And it hath always three notes or marks, whereby it is known: pure and sound doctrine, the Sacraments ministered according to CHRIST's holy institution, and the right use of ecclesiastical discipline," &c.

This passage is quoted in that respect in which it claims attention, viz. as far as it is an illustration of the Article. It is speaking of the one Catholic Church, not of an abstract Church which may have concrete fulfilments many or few; and it uses the same terms of it which the Article does of "the visible Church." It says that "the true Church is an *universal* congregation or fellowship of GOD's faithful and elect people," &c., which as closely corresponds to the *cœtus fidelium*, or " congregation of faithful men " of the Article, as the above descriptions from Fathers or Divines do. Therefore, the *cœtus fidelium* spoken of in the Article is not a definition, which kirk, or connexion, or other communion may, successfully or not, be made to fall under, but the enunciation and pointing out of a fact.

§ 5.—*General Councils.*

Article xxi.—" General councils may not be gathered together without the commandment and will of princes. And when they be gathered together, forasmuch as they be an assembly of men, whereof all be not governed with the SPIRIT and Word of GOD, they may err, and sometimes have erred, in things pertaining to GOD. Wherefore things ordained by them as necessary to salvation have neither strength nor authority, unless it may be declared that they are taken out of Holy Scripture."

That great bodies of men, of different countries, may not meet together without the sanction of their rulers, is plain from the principles of civil obedience and from primitive practice. That, when met together, though Christians, they will not be all ruled by the SPIRIT or Word of GOD, is plain from our LORD's parable of the net, and from melancholy experience. That bodies of men, deficient in this respect, may err, is a self-evident truth,— *unless*, indeed, they be favoured with some divine superintendence, which has to be proved, before it can be admitted.

General Councils then may err, *as such ;*—may err, *unless* in any case it is promised, as a matter of express supernatural privilege, that they shall *not* err; a case which lies beyond the scope of this Article, or at any rate beside its determination.

Such a promise, however, *does* exist, in cases when general councils are not only gathered together according to "the commandment and will of princes," but *in the Name of* CHRIST, according to our LORD's promise. The Article merely contemplates the human prince, not the King of Saints. While Councils are a thing of earth, their infallibility of course is not guaranteed; when they are a thing of heaven, their deliberations are overruled, and their decrees authoritative. In such cases they are *Catholic* councils; and it would seem, from passages which will be quoted in Section 11, that the Homilies recognize four, or even six, as bearing this character. Thus Catholic or Ecumenical Councils are General Councils, and something more. Some general councils are Catholic, and others are not.[1] Nay, as even Romanists grant, the same councils may be partly Catholic, partly not.

If Catholicity be thus a *quality*, found at times in general councils, rather than the *differentia* belonging to a certain class of them, it is still less surprising that the Article should be silent on the subject.

What those *conditions* are, which fulfil the notion of a gathering "in the Name of CHRIST," in the case of a particular council, it is not necessary here to determine. Some have included among these conditions, the subsequent reception of its decrees by the universal Church; others a ratification by the Pope.

Another of these conditions, however, the Article goes on to mention, viz. that in points necessary to salvation, a Council should prove its decrees by Scripture.

St. Gregory Nazianzen well illustrates the consistency of this Article with a belief in the infallibility of Ecumenical Councils, by his own language on the subject on different occasions.

[1] [Bellarmine makes this distinction between "General" and "Ecumenical," and, as being a contemporary of the compilers of the Articles, he may be fairly taken to interpret their word "General." This reference to Bellarmine's language is no after-thought of the writer of the Tract to shelter a distinction which was, at the time of publication accused of being subtle and sophistical, for he had Bellarmine in mind when he made it. Bellarmine says, "Concilia *generalia* approbata numerantur hucusque decem et octo." Then he speaks of "Concilia generalia *reprobata*," &c., &c. *De Concil.* l. 5. 6.]

In the following passage he anticipates the Article:—

"My mind is, if I must write the truth, to keep clear of every conference of bishops, for of conference never saw I good come, or a remedy so much as an increase of evils. For there is strife and ambition, and these have the upper hand of reason."—Ep. 55.

Yet, on the other hand, he speaks elsewhere of "the Holy Council in Nicæa, and that band of chosen men whom the HOLY GHOST brought together."—Orat. 21.

§ 6.—*Purgatory, Pardons, Images, Relics, Invocation of Saints.*[1]

Article xxii.—" The Romish doctrine concerning purgatory, pardons (de indulgentiis), worshipping (de veneratione) and adoration, as well of images as of relics, and also invocation of saints, is a fond thing (res est futilis) vainly (inaniter) invented, and grounded upon no warranty of Scripture, but rather repugnant (contradicit) to the Word of GOD."

Now the first remark that occurs on perusing this Article is, that the doctrine objected to is "the *Romish* doctrine." For instance, no one would suppose that the *Calvinistic* doctrine concerning purgatory, pardons, and image-worship, is spoken against. Not every doctrine on these matters is a fond thing, but the *Romish* doctrine. Accordingly, the *Primitive* doctrine is not condemned in it, unless, indeed, the Primitive doctrine be the Romish, which must not be supposed. Now there *was* a primitive doctrine on all these points,—how far Catholic or universal, is a further question,—but still so widely received and so respectably supported, that it may well be entertained as a matter of opinion by a theologian now; this, then, whatever be its merits, is not condemned by this Article.

This is clear without proof on the face of the matter, at least as regards Pardons. Of course, the Article never meant to make light of *every* doctrine about pardons, but a certain doctrine, the Romish doctrine, as indeed the plural form itself shows.

And such an understanding of the Article is supported by some sentences in the Homily on Peril of Idolatry, in which, as far as regards Relics, a *certain* " veneration " is

---

[1] [Vid. *infr.* Note 1, p. 349, at the end of this Tract.]

sanctioned by its tone in speaking of them, though not of course the Romish veneration.

The sentences referred to run as follows :—

"In the Tripartite Ecclesiastical History, the Ninth Book, and Forty-eighth Chapter, is testified, that 'Epiphanius, being yet alive, did work miracles: and that after his death, devils, *being expelled at his grave or tomb*, did roar.' Thus you see what authority St. Jerome (who has just been mentioned) and that most ancient history give unto the holy and learned Bishop Epiphanius."

Again :—

"St. Ambrose, in his Treatise of the Death of Theodosius the Emperor, saith, 'Helena found the Cross, and the title on it. She worshipped the King, and not the wood, surely (for that is an heathenish error and the vanity of the wicked), but she worshipped Him that hanged on the Cross, and whose Name was written on the title,' and so forth. See both the godly empress's fact, and St. Ambrose's judgment at once; they thought it had been an heathenish error, and vanity of the wicked, *to have worshipped the Cross itself, which was embrued* with our SAVIOUR CHRIST'S own precious blood."—*Peril of Idolatry, part* 2, *circ. init.*

In these passages the writer does not positively commit himself to the miracles at Epiphanius's tomb, or the discovery of the true Cross, but he evidently wishes the hearer to think he believes in both. This he would not do, if he thought all honour paid to relics wrong.

If, then, in the judgment of the Homilies, not all doctrine concerning veneration of Relics is condemned in the Article before us, but a certain toleration of them is compatible with its wording; neither is all doctrine concerning purgatory, pardons, images, and saints, condemned by the Article, but only "the Romish."

And further by "the Romish doctrine," is not meant the Tridentine doctrine, because this Article was drawn up before the decree of the Council of Trent. What is opposed is the *received doctrine* of that day, and unhappily of this day too, or the doctrine of the *Roman Catholic schools;* a conclusion which is still more clear, by considering that there are portions in the Tridentine doctrine on these subjects, which the Article, far from condemning, does by anticipation approve, as far as they go. For instance, the Decree of Trent enjoins concerning Purgatory thus:—"Among the uneducated vulgar let *difficult and subtle questions,* which make not for edification, and seldom contribute aught towards piety, be kept back from popular discourses. Neither let them suffer the public mention and treatment of *uncertain points,* or such as *look like falsehood.*" Session 25. Again, about Images : "*Due* honour and veneration is to be paid unto them, *not that we believe that any divinity or virtue is in them,* for which they should be worshipped (colendæ), or that *we should ask anything* of them, or that trust should be reposed in images, as formerly was done by the Gentiles, which used to place their hope on idols."—*Ibid.*

If, then, the doctrine condemned in this Article concerning Purgatory, Pardons, Images, Relics, and Saints, be not the Primitive doctrine, nor the Catholic doctrine, nor the Tridentine doctrine, but the Romish, *doctrina Romanensium,* let us next consider *what* in matter of fact this Romish doctrine is. And

1. As to the doctrine of the Romanists concerning Purgatory.

Now here there *was* a primitive doctrine, whatever its merits, concerning the fire of judgment, which is a possible or a probable opinion, and is *not* condemned. That doctrine is this: that the conflagration of the world, or the flames which attend the Judge, will be an ordeal through which all men will pass; that great saints, such as St. Mary, will pass it unharmed; that others will suffer loss; but none will fail under it who are built upon the right foundation. Here is one purgatorian doctrine not "Romish."

Another doctrine, purgatorian, but not Romish, is that said to be maintained by the Greeks at Florence, in which the cleansing, though a punishment, was but a *pœna damni*, not a *pœna sensûs;* not a positive sensible infliction, much less the torment of fire, but the absence of GOD's presence. And another purgatory is that in which the cleansing is but a progressive sanctification, and has no pain at all.

None of these doctrines does the Article condemn; any of them may be held by the Anglo-Catholic as a matter of private belief; not that they are here advocated, one or other, but they are adduced as an illustration of what the Article does *not* mean, and to vindicate our Christian liberty in a matter where the Church has not confined it.

On the other hand, what the doctrine is which is reprobated, is plain from the following passage of the Homilies.

"Now doth St. Augustine say, that those men which are cast into prison after this life, on that condition, may in no wise be holpen, though we would help them never so much. And why? Because the *sentence* of GOD is *unchangeable*, and cannot be *revoked again*. Therefore let us not deceive ourselves, thinking that either we may help others, or others may help us, by their good and charitable prayers in time to come. For, as the preacher saith, ' When the tree falleth, whether it be toward the south, or toward the north, in what place soever the tree falleth, there it lieth;' meaning thereby, that every mortal man *dieth either in the state of salvation or damnation*, . . . where is then the third place, which they call purgatory? Or where shall our prayers help and profit the dead? . . . Chrysostom likewise is of this mind, that, unless we wash away our sins in this present world, we shall find no comfort afterward. And St. Cyprian saith, that, after death, repentance and sorrow of pain shall be without fruit, weeping also shall be in vain, and prayer shall be to no purpose. Therefore he counselleth all men to make provision for themselves while they may, because, when they are once departed out of this life, there is no place for *repentance*, nor yet for satisfaction."—*Homily concerning Prayer*, pp. 282, 283.

Now it is plain from this passage, that the Purgatory contemplated by the Homily, was one for which no one will for an instant pretend to adduce even those Fathers who most favour Rome, *viz.* one *in which our state would be changed*, in which GOD'S sentence could be reversed. "The *sentence* of GOD," says the writer, " is *unchangeable, and cannot be revoked again; there is no place for repentance.*" On the other hand, the Decrees of the Council of Trent, after Augustine and Cyprian, (so far as those Fathers express or imply any opinion approximating to that of the Council,) teach that Purgatory is a place for *believers,* not unbelievers, not where men who have lived and *died in sin*, may gain pardon, but where those who have *already* been pardoned in this life, may be cleansed and purified for beholding the face of GOD. The Homily, then, and therefore the Article, does not speak of the Tridentine Purgatory.

The mention of Prayers for the dead in the above passage, affords an additional illustration of the limited and conditional sense of the terms of the Article now under consideration. For such prayers are obviously not condemned in it in the abstract, or in every shape, but *as offered with a view to rescue the lost from eternal fire.*

Hooker, in his Sermon on Pride, gives us a second view of the "Romish doctrine of Purgatory," from the schoolmen. After speaking of the *pœna damni*, he says,—

"The other punishment, which hath in it not only loss of joy, but also sense of grief, vexation, and woe, is that whereunto they give the name of purgatory pains, *in nothing different from those very infernal torments which the souls of castaways, together with damned spirits do endure*, save only in this, there is an appointed term to the one, to the other none; but for the time they last they are *equal*."—Vol. iii. p. 798.

Such doctrine, too, as the following may well be included in that which the Article condemns under the name of " Romish :"—

"In the 'Speculum Exemplorum' it is said, that a certain priest, in an ecstasy, saw the soul of Constantius Turritanus in the eaves of his house, tormented with frosts and cold rains, and afterwards climbing up to heaven upon a shining pillar. And a certain monk saw some souls roasted upon spits like pigs, and some devils basting them with scalding lard; but a while after, they were carried to a cool place, and so proved purgatory. But Bishop Theobald, standing upon a piece of ice to cool his feet, was nearer purgatory than he was aware, and was convinced of it, when he heard a poor soul telling him, that under that ice he was tormented; and that he should be delivered, if for thirty days continual, he would say for him thirty masses. And some such thing was seen by Conrade and Udalric in a pool of water; for the place of purgatory was not yet resolved on, till St. Patrick had the key of it delivered to him, which when one Nicholas borrowed of him, he saw as strange and true things there, as ever Virgil dreamed of in his purgatory, or Cicero in his dream of Scipio, or Plato in his Gorgias, or Phædo, who indeed are the surest authors to prove purgatory."—*Jer. Taylor, Works*, vol. x. pp. 151, 152.

Another specimen of doctrine, which no one will attempt to prove from Scripture, is the following :—

" Returning to the first Church, there they found St. Michael the Archangel and the Apostles Peter and Paul. St. Michael caused all the white souls to pass through the flames, unharmed, to the mount of joy; and those that had black and white spots, St. Peter led into purgatory to be purified.

" In one part sate St. Paul, and the devil opposite to him with his guards, with a pair of scales between them, weighing all such souls as were all over black; when upon turning a soul, the scale turned towards St. Paul, he sent it to purgatory, there to expiate its sins; when towards the devil, his crew, with great triumph, plunged it into the flaming pit. . . . .

" The rustic likewise saw near the entrance of the town-hall, as it were, four streets; the first was full of innumerable furnaces and cauldrons filled with flaming pitch and other liquids, and boiling of souls, whose heads were like those of black fishes in the seething liquor. The second had its cauldrons stored with snow and ice, to torment souls with horrid cold. The third had thereof boiling sulphur and other materials, affording the worst of stinks, for the vexing of souls that had wallowed in the filth of lust. The fourth had cauldrons of a most horrid salt and black water. Now sinners of all sorts were alternately tormented in these cauldrons."—*Purgatory proved by Miracle, by S. Johnson*, pp. 8—10.

2. Pardons, or Indulgences.

Burnet says,—

"The virtue of indulgences is the applying the treasure of the Church upon *such terms* as Popes shall think fit to prescribe, in order to the redeeming souls from purgatory, and from all other temporal punishments, and that for such a number of years as shall be specified in the bulls; some of which have gone to thousands of years; one I have seen to ten hundred thousand: and as these indulgences are sometimes granted by special tickets, like tallies struck on that treasure; so sometimes they are affixed to particular churches and altars, to particular times, or days, chiefly to the year of jubilee; they are also affixed to such things as may be carried about, to Agnus Dei's, to medals, to rosaries, and scapularies; they are also affixed to some prayers, the devout saying of them being a mean to procure great indulgences. The granting these is left to the Pope's discretion, who ought to distribute them as he thinks may tend most to the honour of GOD and the good of the Church; and he ought not to be too profuse, much less to be too scanty in dispensing them.

"This has been the received doctrine and practice of the Church of Rome since the twelfth century: and the Council of Trent, in a hurry, in its last session, did, *in very general words*, approve of the practice of the Church in this matter, and decreed that indulgences should be continued; only *they restrained some abuses*, in particular that of *selling* them."—*Burnet on Article XXII.* p. 305; also on *Art. XIV.* p. 190.

If it be necessary to say more on the subject, let us attend to the following passage from Jeremy Taylor:—

"1. That a most scandalous and unchristian dissolution and death of all ecclesiastical discipline, is consequent to the making all sin so cheap and trivial a thing; that the horrible demerits and exemplary punishment and remotion of scandal and satisfactions to the Church, are indeed reduced to trifling and mock penances. He that shall send a servant with a candle to attend the holy Sacrament, when it shall be carried to sick people, or shall go himself; or, if he can neither go nor send, if he say a 'Pater Noster' and an 'Ave,' he shall have a hundred years of true pardon. This is fair and easy. But then,—

"2. It would be considered what is meant by so many years of pardon, and so many years of true pardon. I know but of one natural interpretation of it; and that it can mean nothing, but that some of the pardons are but fantastical, and not true; and in this I find no fault, save only that it ought to have been said, that all of them are fantastical.

"3. It were fit we learned how to compute four thousand and eight hundred years of quarantines, and a remission of a third part of all their sins; for so much is given to every brother and sister of this fraternity, upon Easter-day, and eight days after. Now if a brother needs not thus many, it would be considered whether it did not encourage a brother or a frail sister to use all their medicine, and sin more freely, lest so great a gift become useless.

"4. And this is so much the more considerable because the gift is vast beyond all imagination. The first four days in Lent they may purchase thirty-three thousand years of pardon, besides a plenary remission of all their sins over and above. The first week of Lent a hundred and three-and-thirty thousand years of pardon, besides five plenary remissions of all their sins, and two third parts besides, and the delivery of one soul out of purgatory. The second week in Lent a hundred and eight-and-fifty thousand years of pardon, besides the remission of all their sins, and a third part besides; and the delivery of one soul. The third week in Lent, eight thousand years, besides a plenary remission, and the delivery of one soul out of purgatory. The fourth week in Lent, threescore thousand years of pardon, besides a remission of two-thirds of all their sins, and one plenary remission, and one soul delivered. The fifth week, seventy-nine thousand years of pardon, and the deliverance of two souls; only the two thousand seven hundred years that are given for the Sunday, may be had twice that day, if they will visit the altar twice, and as many quarantines. The sixth week, two hundred and five thousand years, besides quarantines, and four plenary pardons. Only on Palm Sunday, whose portion is twenty-five thousand years, it may be had twice that day. And all this is the price of him that shall, upon these days, visit the altar in the church of St. Hilary. And this runs on to the Fridays, and many Festivals, and other solemn days in the other parts of the year."—*Jer. Taylor*, vol. xi. pp. 53—56.

The pardons then, spoken of in the Article, are large and reckless indulgences from the penalties of sin obtained on money payments.

3. Veneration and worshipping of Images and Relics.

That the Homilies do not altogether discard reverence towards relics, has already been shown. Now let us see what they do discard.

"What meaneth it that Christian men, after the use of the Gentiles idolaters, *cap and kneel* before images? which, if they had any sense and gratitude, would kneel before men, carpenters, masons, plasterers, founders, and goldsmiths, their makers and framers, by whose means they have attained this honour, which else should have been evil-favoured, and rude lumps of clay or plaster, pieces of timber, stone, or metal, without shape or fashion, and so without all estimation and honour, as that idol in the Pagan poet confesseth, saying, 'I was once a vile block, but now I am become a god,' &c. What a fond thing is it for man, who hath life and reason, to bow himself to a dead and insensible image, the work of his own hand! Is not this stooping and kneeling before them, which is forbidden so earnestly by GOD's word? Let such as so fall down before images of saints, know and confess that they exhibit that honour to dead stocks and stones, which the saints themselves, Peter, Paul, and Barnabas, would not to be given to them, being alive; which the angel of GOD forbiddeth to be given to him. And if they say they exhibit such honour not to the image, but to the saint whom it representeth, they are convicted of folly, to believe that they please saints with that honour, which they abhor as a spoil of GOD's honour."—*Homily on Peril of Idolatry*, p. 191.

Again:—

"Because Relics were so gainful, few places were there but they had Relics provided for them. And for more *plenty* of Relics, some one saint had many heads, one in one place, and another in another place. Some had six arms, and twenty-six fingers. And where our LORD bare His cross alone, if all the pieces of the relics thereof were gathered together, the greatest ship in England would scarcely bear them; and yet the greatest part of it, they say, doth yet remain in the hands of the Infidels; for the which they pray in their beads-bidding, that they may get it also into their hands, for such godly use and purpose. And not only the bones of the saints, but everything appertaining to them, was a holy relic. In some place they offer a sword, in some the scabbard, in some a shoe, in some a saddle that had been set upon some holy horse, in some the coals wherewith St. Laurence was roasted, in some place the tail of the ass which our LORD JESUS CHRIST sat on, to be *kissed and offered unto* for a relic. For rather than they would lack a relic, they would offer you *a horse-bone instead of a virgin's arm,* or the tail of the ass to be kissed and offered unto for relics. O wicked, impudent, and most shameless men, the devisers of these things! O silly, foolish, and dastardly daws, and more beastly than the ass whose tail they kissed, that believe such things!"—*Ibid.* pp. 193-97.

In another place the Homilies speak as follows:—

"Our churches stand full of such great puppets, *wondrously decked and adorned;* garlands and coronets be set on their heads, precious pearls hanging about their necks; their fingers shine with rings, set with precious stones; their dead and stiff bodies are clothed with garments stiff with gold. You would believe that the images of our men-saints were some princes of Persia land with their proud apparel; and the idols of our women-saints were *nice and well-trimmed harlots, tempting their paramours to wantonness:* whereby the saints of GOD are not honoured, but most dishonoured, and their godliness, soberness, chastity, contempt of riches, and of the vanity of the world, defaced and brought in doubt by such *monstrous decking,* most differing from their sober and godly lives. And because the whole pageant must thoroughly be played, it is not enough thus to deck idols, but at last come in the priests themselves, likewise decked with gold and pearl, that they may be meet servants for such lords and ladies, and fit worshippers of such gods and goddesses. And with a solemn pace they pass forth before these *golden puppets,* and *fall down* to the ground on their marrow-bones before these honourable idols." . . . . . . "O books and scriptures, in the which the devilish schoolmaster, Satan, hath penned the lewd lessons of wicked idolatry, for his dastardly disciples and scholars to behold, read, and learn, to GOD's most high dishonour, and their most horrible damnation!"—*Homily on Peril of Idolatry,* pp. 219—222.

Again:—

"Sects and feigned religions were neither the fortieth part so many among the Jews, nor more superstitiously and ungodly abused, than of late years they have been among us: which sects and religions had so many hypocritical and feigned works in their state of religion, as they arrogantly named it, that their lamps, as they said, ran always over able to satisfy not only for their own sins, but also for all other their benefactors, brothers, and sisters of religion, as most ungodly and craftily they had persuaded the multitude of ignorant people; keeping in divers places, as it were, marts or markets of merits, being full of their holy relics, images, shrines, and works of overflowing abundance, ready to be sold; and all things which they had were called holy—holy cowls, holy girdles, holy pardons, holy beads, holy shoes, holy rules; and all full of holiness. And what thing can be more foolish, more superstitious, or ungodly, than that men, women, and children, should wear a friar's coat to deliver them from agues or pestilence; or when they die, or when they be buried, cause it to be cast upon them, *in hope thereby to be saved?*"—*Homily on Good Works,* pp. 45, 46, also p. 223.

Now the veneration and worship condemned in these and other passages are observances such as these: kneeling before images, lighting candles to them, offering them incense, going on pilgrimage to them, hanging up crutches, &c., before them, lying legends about them, belief in miracles as if wrought by them through illusion of the devil, decking them up immodestly, and providing incentives by them to bad passions; and, in like manner, merry music and minstrelsy and licentious practices in honour of relics, counterfeit relics, multiplication of them, absurd pretences about them. This is what the Article means by "the Romish doctrine," which, in agreement to one of the above extracts, it calls "a fond thing," *res futilis;* for who can ever hope, except the grossest and most blinded minds, to be gaining the favour of the blessed saints, while they come with unchaste thoughts and eyes, that cannot cease from sin; and to be profited by "pilgrimage-going," in which "Lady Venus and her son Cupid were rather worshipped wantonly in the flesh, than God the Father, and our Saviour Christ His Son, truly worshipped in the Spirit?"

Here again it is remarkable that, urged by the truth of the allegation, the Council of Trent is obliged, both to confess the above-mentioned enormities in the veneration of relics and images, and to forbid them:—

"Into these holy and salutary observances should any abuses have crept, of these the Holy Council strongly [vehementer] desires the utter extinction; so that no images of a false doctrine, and supplying to the uninstructed opportunity of perilous error, should be set up. .... All superstition also in invocation of saints, veneration of relics, and religious use of images, be put away; all *filthy lucre* be cast out of doors; and *all wantonness* be avoided; *so that images be not painted or adorned with an immodest beauty;* or the celebration of Saints and attendance on Relics *be abused to revelries and drunkennesses;* as though festival days were kept in honour of saints by *luxury and lasciviousness."—Sess.* 25.

4. Invocation of Saints.

By "invocation" here is not meant the mere circumstance of addressing beings out of sight, because we use the Psalms in our daily service, which are frequent in invocations of Angels to praise and bless GOD. In the Benedicite too we address "the spirits and souls of the righteous."

Nor is it a "fond" invocation to pray that unseen beings may bless us; for this Bishop Ken does in his Evening Hymn:

> O may my Guardian, while I sleep,
> Close to my bed his vigils keep,
> His love angelical *instil,*
> Stop all the avenues of ill, &c.

Indeed, it is not unnatural, if "the seven spirits before the Throne" have sent us through St. John the Evangelist, "grace and peace," that we, in turn, should send up our thoughts and desires to them.

On the other hand, judging from the example set us in the Homilies themselves, invocations are not censurable if we mean nothing definite by them, addressing them to beings which we *know* cannot hear, and using them as interjections. The Homily seems to avail itself of this proviso in a passage, which will serve to begin our extracts in illustration of the superstitious use of invocations :—

"We have left Him neither heaven, nor earth, nor water, nor

country, nor city, peace nor war to rule and govern, neither men, nor beasts, nor their diseases to cure; that a godly man might justly, for zealous indignation, cry out, O heaven, O earth, and seas,[2] what madness and wickedness against GOD are men fallen into! What dishonour do the creatures to their Creator and Maker!"—*Homily on Peril of Idolatry*, p. 189.

Again, just before :—

"Terentius Varro sheweth, that there were three hundred Jupiters in his time: there were no fewer Veneres and Dianæ: we had no fewer Christophers, Ladies, and Mary Magdalens, and other saints. Œnomaus and Hesiodus show, that in their time there were thirty thousand gods. I think we had no fewer saints, to whom we gave the honour due to GOD. And they have not only spoiled the true living GOD of his due honour in temples, cities, countries, and lands, by such devices and inventions as the Gentiles idolaters have done before them: but the sea and waters have as well special saints with them, as they had gods with the Gentiles, Neptune, Triton, Nereus, Castor and Pollux, Venus, and such other: in whose places become St. Christopher, St. Clement, and divers others, and specially our Lady, to whom shipmen sing, 'Ave, maris stella.' Neither hath the fire escaped their idolatrous inventions. For, instead of Vulcan and Vesta, the Gentiles' gods of the fire, our men have placed St. Agatha, and make litters on her day for to quench fire with. Every artificer and profession hath his special saint, as a peculiar god. As for example, scholars have St. Nicholas and St. Gregory: painters, St. Luke; neither lack soldiers their Mars, nor lovers their Venus, amongst Christians. All diseases have their special saints, as gods the curers of them; .... the falling-evil St. Cornelio, the tooth-ache St. Apollin, &c. Neither do beasts nor cattle lack their gods with us; for St. Loy is the horse-leech, and St. Anthony the swineherd."—*Ibid.* p. 188.

The same subject is introduced in connexion with a lament over the falling off of attendance on religious worship consequent upon the Reformation :—

"GOD's vengeance hath been and is daily provoked, because much wicked people pass nothing to resort to the Church, either for that they are so sore blinded, that they understand nothing of GOD and godliness, and care not with devilish example to offend their neighbours; or else for that they see the Church altogether scoured of such *gay gazing sights*, as their gross fantasy was greatly delighted with,

---

[2] O cœlum, o terra, o maria Neptuni.—*Terent. Adelph.* v. 3.

because they see the false religion abandoned, and the true restored, which seemeth an unsavoury thing to their unsavoury taste; as may appear by this, that a woman said to her neighbour, 'Alas, gossip what shall we now do at Church, since all the saints are taken away, since all the *goodly sights* we were wont to have are gone, since we cannot hear the like *piping, singing, chanting,* and *playing upon the organs,* that we could before?' But, dearly beloved, we ought greatly to rejoice, and give GOD thanks, that our churches are delivered of all those things which displeased GOD so sore, and *filthily defiled* His house and His place of prayer."—*On the Place and Time of Prayer,* pp. 293, 294.

Again:—

"CHRIST, sitting in heaven, hath an everlasting priesthood, and always prayeth to His FATHER for them that be penitent, obtaining, by virtue of His wounds, which are evermore in the sight of GOD, not only perfect remission of our sins, but also all other necessaries that we lack in this world; so that this Holy Mediator is sufficient in heaven, and needeth no others to help Him.

"Invocation is a thing *proper unto* GOD, which if we attribute unto the saints, it soundeth unto their reproach, neither can they well bear it at our hands. When Paul healed a certain lame man, which was impotent in his feet, at Lystra, the people would have *done sacrifice* unto him and Barnabas; who, rending their clothes, refused it, and exhorted them to *worship* the true GOD. Likewise in the Revelation, when St. John *fell before the angel's feet to worship him,* the angel would not permit him to do it, but commanded him that he should worship GOD. Which examples declare unto us, that the saints and angels in heaven will not have us to do *any honour* unto them, *that is due and proper unto* GOD."—*Homily on Prayer,* pp. 272—277.

Whereas, then, it has already been shown that not *all* invocation is wrong, this last passage plainly tells us *what kind* of invocation is not allowable, or what is meant by invocation in its exceptionable sense: viz. "a thing proper to GOD," as being part of the "honour that is due and proper unto GOD." And two instances are specially given of such calling and invocating, viz. *sacrificing,* and *falling down in worship.* Besides this, the Homily adds, that it is wrong to pray to them for "necessaries in this world," and to accompany their services with "piping, singing, chanting, and playing" on the organ, and of invoking saints as patrons of particular elements, countries, arts, or remedies.

Here, again, as before, the Article gains a witness and concurrence from the Council of Trent. "Though," say the divines there assembled, "the Church has been accustomed sometimes to celebrate a few masses to the honour and remembrance of saints, yet she *doth not teach that sacrifice is offered to them*, but to GOD alone, who crowned them; wherefore neither is the priest wont to say, *I offer sacrifice to thee, O Peter, or O Paul*, but to GOD." (Sess. 22.)

Or, to know what is meant by fond invocations, we may refer to the following passage of Bishop Andrewes's answer to Cardinal Perron :—

"This one point is needful to be observed throughout all the Cardinal's answer, that he hath framed to himself five distinctions:—(1.) Prayer *direct*, and prayer *oblique*, or indirect. (2.) Prayer *absolute*, and prayer *relative*. (3.) Prayer *sovereign*, and prayer *subaltern*. (4.) Prayer *final*, and prayer *transitory*. (5.) Prayer *sacrificial*, and prayer *out of*, or *from the sacrifice*. Prayer *direct, absolute, final, sovereign, sacrificial*, that must not be made to the saints, but to GOD only : but as for *prayer oblique, relative, transitory, subaltern, from*, or *out of the sacrifice*, that (saith he) we may make to the saints. . . .

"Yet it is sure, that in these distinctions is the whole substance of his answer."—*Andrewes's Answer to Perron's Reply*, c. 20, pp. 57—62.

Bellarmine's admissions quite bear out the principles laid down by Bishop Andrewes and the Homily :—

"It is not lawful," he says, "to ask of the saints to grant to us, as if they were the *authors* of divine benefits, glory or grace, or the other means of blessedness. . . . This is proved, first, from Scripture, 'The LORD will give grace and glory.' (Psal. lxxxiv.) . . . Secondly, from the usage of the Church; for in the mass-prayers, and the saints' offices, we never ask anything else, but that, at their prayers, benefits may be granted to us by GOD. Thirdly, from reason : for *what we need surpasses the powers of the creature*, and therefore even of saints; therefore we ought to ask nothing of saints beyond their impetrating from GOD what is profitable for us. Fourthly, from Augustine and Theodoret, who expressly teach that saints are not to be invoked *as gods*, but as able to gain from GOD what they wish. However, it must be observed, when we say that nothing should be asked of saints but their prayers for us, the question is not about the words, but the *sense* of the words. For, as far as the words go, *it is lawful* to say : 'St. Peter, pity me, save me, open for me the gate of heaven ;' also, 'give me health of body, patience, fortitude,' &c., provided that we mean 'save and pity me *by praying for me;*' 'grant me this or that *by thy prayers and merits.*' For so speaks Gregory Nazianzen, and many others of the ancients, &c.—*Ds Sanct. Beat.* i. 17.

§ 7.—*The Sacraments.*

Art. xxv.—" Those five, commonly called Sacraments, that is to say, Confirmation, Penance, Orders, Matrimony, and Extreme Unction, are not to be counted for Sacraments of the Gospel, being such as have grown, partly of the corrupt following (pravâ imitatione) of the Apostles, partly from states of life allowed in the Scriptures; but yet have not like nature of sacraments, (sacramentorum eandem rationem,) with Baptism and the LORD's Supper, for that they have not any visible sign or ceremony ordained of GOD."

This Article does not deny the five rites in question to be sacraments, but to be sacraments in *the sense* in which Baptism and the LORD's Supper are sacraments; " sacraments of *the Gospel,*" sacraments *with an outward sign ordained of* GOD.

They are not sacraments in *any* sense, *unless* the Church has the power of dispensing grace through rites of its own appointing, or is endued with the gift of blessing and hallowing the " rites or ceremonies " which, according to the twentieth article, it " hath power to decree." But we may well believe that the Church has this gift.

If, then, a sacrament be merely *an outward sign of an invisible grace given under it,* the five rites may be sacraments; but if it must be an outward sign *ordained by* GOD *or* CHRIST, then only Baptism and the LORD's Supper are sacraments.

Our Church acknowledges both definitions;—in the Article before us, *the stricter;* and again in the Catechism, where a sacrament is defined to be " an outward visible sign of an inward spiritual grace, given unto us, *ordained by* CHRIST *himself.*" And this, it should be remarked, is a characteristic of our formularies in various places, not to deny the *truth* or *obligation* of certain doctrines or ordinances, but simply to deny, (what no Roman opponent now can successfully maintain,) that CHRIST for certain directly ordained them. For instance, in regard to the visible Church it is sufficient that the ministration of the sacraments should be "*according to* CHRIST's *ordinance.*" Art. xix.—And it is added, "in all those things that *of necessity* are requisite to the same." The question entertained is, what is *the least* that GOD requires of us. Again, "the baptism of young children is to be retained, as most agreeable to *the institution of* CHRIST." Art. xxvii.—Again, "the sacrament of the Lord's Supper was not by CHRIST's *ordinance* reserved, carried about, lifted up, or worshipped." Art. xxviii.—Who will maintain the paradox that what the Apostles "set in order when they came" had been already done by CHRIST? Again, "both parts of the LORD's sacrament, *by* CHRIST's *ordinance and commandment*, ought to be administered to all Christian men alike." Art. xxx.—Again, "bishops, priests, and deacons, *are not commanded by* GOD's *law* either to vow the estate of single life or to abstain from marriage." Art. xxxii.—In making this distinction, however, it is not here insinuated, (though the question is not entered on in these particular articles,) that every one of these points, of which it is only said that they are not ordained by CHRIST, is justifiable on grounds short of His appointment.

On the other hand, our Church takes the *wider* sense of the meaning of the word *Sacrament* in the Homilies; observing,—

"In the second Book against the Adversary of the Law and the Prophets, he [St. Augustine] calleth sacraments *holy signs*. And writing to Bonifacius of the baptism of infants, he saith, 'If sacraments had not a certain similitude of those things whereof they be sacraments, they should be no sacraments at all. And of this similitude they do for the most part receive the names of the selfsame things they signify.' By these words of St. Augustine it appeareth, that he alloweth the common description of a sacrament, which is, that it is *a visible sign of an invisible grace;* that is to say, that setteth out to the eyes and other outward senses the inward working of God's free mercy, and doth, as it were, seal in our hearts the promises of God."—*Homily on Common Prayer and Sacraments*, pp. 296, 297.

Accordingly, starting with this definition of St. Augustine's, the writer is necessarily carried on as follows:—

"You shall hear how many sacraments there be, that were instituted by our SAVIOUR CHRIST, and are to be continued, and received of every Christian in due time and order, and for such purpose as our SAVIOUR CHRIST willed them to be received. And as for the number of them, if they should be considered according to the *exact* signification of a sacrament, namely, for visible signs expressly commanded in the New Testament, whereunto is annexed the promise of free forgiveness of our sins, and of our holiness and joining in CHRIST, there be but two; namely, Baptism, and the Supper of the Lord. For although absolution hath the promise of forgiveness of sin; yet by the *express* word of the New Testament, it hath not this promise annexed and tied to the visible sign, which is imposition of hands. For this visible sign (I mean laying on of hands) is not *expressly* commanded in the New Testament to be used in absolution, as the visible signs in Baptism and the LORD'S Supper are: and therefore absolution is no *such* sacrament as Baptism and the Communion are. And though the ordering of ministers hath this visible sign and promise; yet it lacks the promise of remission of sin, as all other sacraments besides the two above named do. Therefore neither it, nor any *other* sacrament, be *such* sacraments as Baptism and the Communion are. But in a general acception, the name of a sacrament may be attributed to anything, whereby an holy thing is signified. In which understanding of the word, the ancient writers have given this name, not only to the other five, commonly of late years taken and used for supplying the number of the seven sacraments; but also to divers and sundry other ceremonies, as to oil, washing of feet, and such like; not meaning thereby to repute them as sacraments, *in the same signification* that the two forenamed sacraments are. And therefore St. Augustine, weighing the true signification and exact meaning of the word, writing to Januarius, and also in the third Book of Christian Doctrine, affirmeth, that the sacraments of the Christians, as they are most excellent in signification, so are they most few in number, and in both places maketh mention expressly of two, the sacrament of Baptism, and the Supper of the LORD. And although there are retained by order of the Church of England, besides these two, certain other rites and ceremonies, about the institution of ministers in the the Church, Matrimony, Confirmation of Children, by examining them of their knowledge in their Articles of the Faith, and joining thereto the prayers of the Church for them, and likewise for the Visitation of the Sick; yet no man ought to take these for sacraments, in *such* signification and meaning as the sacraments of Baptism and the LORD's Supper are: but either for godly states of life, necessary in Christ's Church, and therefore worthy to be set forth by public action and solemnity, by the ministry of the Church, or else judged to be such ordinances as may make for the instruction, comfort, and edification of CHRIST's Church."—*Homily on Common Prayer and Sacraments*, pp. 298—300.

Another definition of the word *Sacrament*, which equally succeeds in limiting it to the two principal rites of the Christian Church, is also contained in the Catechism, as well as implied in the above passage :—"Two only, as *generally necessary* to salvation, Baptism and the Supper of the LORD." On this subject the following remark has been made :—

"The Roman Catholic considers that there are seven [sacraments]; we do not strictly determine the number. We define the word generally to be an 'outward sign of an inward grace,' without saying to how many ordinances this applies. However, what we do determine is, that CHRIST has ordained two special sacraments, as *generally necessary to salvation*. This, then, is the characteristic mark of those two, separating them from all other whatever; and this is nothing else but saying in other words that they are the only *justifying* rites, or instruments of communicating the

Atonement, which is the one thing necessary to us. Ordination, for instance, gives *power*, yet without making the soul *acceptable* to GOD; Confirmation gives *light and strength*, yet is the mere *completion* of Baptism; and Absolution may be viewed as a negative ordinance removing the *barrier* which sin has raised between us and that grace, which by inheritance is ours. But the two sacraments 'of the Gospel,' as they may be emphatically styled, are the instruments of inward *life*, according to our LORD's declaration, that Baptism is a new *birth*, and that in the Eucharist we eat the *living* bread."[1]

[1] [Lect. on Justification vi., fin.]

§ 8.—*Transubstantiation.*

Article xxviii.—" Transubstantiation, or the change of the substance of bread and wine, in the Supper of the Lord, cannot be proved by Holy Writ; but is repugnant to the plain words of Scripture, overthroweth the nature of a sacrament, and hath given occasion to many superstitions."

What is here opposed as " Transubstantiation," is the shocking doctrine that " the body of CHRIST, as the Article goes on to express it, is *not* " given, taken, and eaten, after an heavenly and spiritual manner, but is carnally pressed with the teeth ;" that It is a body or substance of a certain extension and bulk in space, and a certain figure and due disposition of parts, whereas we hold that the only substance such, is the bread which we see.

This is plain from Article xxix., which quotes St. Augustine as speaking of the wicked as " carnally and visibly pressing with their teeth the *sacrament* of the body and blood of CHRIST," not the real substance, a statement which even the Breviary introduces into the service for Corpus Christi day.

This is plain also from the words of the Homily:— "Saith Cyprian, ' When we do these things, *we need not whet our teeth*, but with sincere faith we break and divide that holy bread. It is well known that the meat we seek in this supper is spiritual food, the nourishment of the soul, a heavenly refection, *and not earthly;* an invisible meat, *and not a bodily:* a ghostly substance, *and not carnal.'* "

An extract may be quoted to the same effect from Bishop Taylor. Speaking of what has been believed in the Church of Rome, he says,—

"They that *deny the spiritual sense,* and affirm the natural, are to remember that CHRIST reproved all senses of these words that were not *spiritual.* And by the way let me observe, that the expressions of some chief men among the Romanists are so rude and crass, *that it will be impossible to excuse them from the understanding the words in the sense of the men of Capernaum;* for, as they understood CHRIST to mean His 'true flesh natural and proper,' so do they: as they thought CHRIST intended they should *tear Him with their teeth and suck His blood,* for which they were offended; so do these men not only think so, but say so, and are not offended. So said Alanus, 'Assertissime loquimur, corpus Christi vere a nobis contrectari, manducari, circumgestari, *dentibus teri [ground by the teeth]*, *sensibiliter sacrificari [sensibly sacrificed]*, non minus quam ante consecrationem panis,' [not less than the bread before consecration] .... I thought that the Romanists had been glad to separate their own opinion from the carnal conceit of the men of Capernaum and the offended disciples .... but I find that Bellarmine owns it, even in them, in their rude circumstances, for he affirms that 'CHRIST corrected them *not for supposing so,* but reproved them *for not believing it to be so.*' And indeed himself says as much: 'The body of CHRIST is *truly and properly manducated or chewed* with the bread in the Eucharist;' and to take off the foulness of the expression, by avoiding a worse, he is pleased to speak nonsense: 'A thing may be manducated or chewed, though it be not attrite or broken.' ... But Bellarmine adds, that if you will not allow him to say so, then he grants it in plain terms, that CHRIST's body is chewed, *is attrite, or broken with the teeth,* and that not tropically, *but properly ....* How? under the species of bread, and invisibly."[1]—*Taylor, Real Presence,* iii. 5; also *Dedic.* x. 8, xi. 18.

Take again the statement of Ussher:—

"Paschasius Radbertus, who was one of the first setters forward of this doctrine in the West, spendeth a large chapter upon this point, wherein he telleth us, that CHRIST in the sacrament did show himself 'oftentimes in a visible shape, either in the form of a lamb, or in the colour of flesh and blood; so that while the

---

[1] [This is not fair to Bellarmine. He says, in explanation, "Non dicimus corpus Christi *absolutè* manducari, sed manducari *sub specie* panis; quæ sententia significat ipsas species manducari *visibiliter* ac *sensibiliter*, ac proinde *ipsas* dentibus atteri, ʀed *sub* illis *invisibiliter* sumitur et transmittitur in stomachum corpus Christi."—*Euch.* i. 11, col. 390.]

host was a breaking or an offering, a lamb in the priest's hands, and blood in the chalice should be seen as it were flowing from the sacrifice, that what lay hid in a mystery might to them that yet doubted be made manifest in a miracle.' " [2]—*Ussher's Answer to a Jesuit*, pp. 62—64. *Johnson's Miracles*, pp. 27, 28.

The same doctrine was imposed by Nicholas the Second on Berengarius, as the confession of the latter shows, which runs thus :—

" I, Berengarius .... anathematize every heresy, and more particularly that of which I have hitherto been accused .... I agree with the Roman Church .... that the bread and wine which are placed on the altar are, after consecration, not only a sacrament, but even the true body and blood of our LORD JESUS CHRIST; and that these are *sensibly*, and not merely sacramentally, but in truth, *handled and broken* by the hands of the priest, and *ground by the teeth* of the faithful." [3]—*Bowden's Life of Gregory VII.*, vol. ii. p. 243.

Another illustration of the sort of doctrine opposed in the Article, may be given from Bellarmine, whose controversial statements have already been introduced in the course of the above extracts. He thus opposes the doctrine of *introsusception*, which the spiritual view of the Real Presence naturally suggests :—

He observes that there are " two particular opinions, false and erroneous, excogitated in the schools : that of Durandus, who thought it probable that the substance of the body of CHRIST in the Eucharist was *without magnitude;* and that of certain ancients, which Occam seems afterwards to have followed, that though it has magnitude, (which they think not really separable from substance,) yet every part is so penetrated by every other, that the body of CHRIST is

---

[2] [Such appearances were apparitions or visions, vouchsafed in order to impress the hidden truth upon the mind.]

[Afterwards " sacramentally " was the received word ; vid. *supr.* p. 224, no c, " in multis aliis locis *sacramentaliter* præsens." The modern term " Sacramentalists," as the title of the Zwinglians, illustrates how Berengarius used the word.]

without figure, without distinction and order of parts." With this he contrasts the doctrine which, he maintains, is that of the Church of Rome as well as the general doctrine of the schools, that "in the Eucharist whole CHRIST exists *with magnitude* and *all accidents,* except that relation to a heavenly location which He has as He is in heaven, and those things which are concomitants on His existence in that location; and that the parts and members of CHRIST's body do *not* penetrate each other, but are so distinguished and arranged one with another, as to have a *figure and order* suitable to a human body."—*De Euchar.* iii. 5.

We see then, that, by transubstantiation, our Article does not confine itself to any abstract theory, nor aim at any definition of the word substance, nor in rejecting it, rejects a word, nor in denying a " mutatio panis et vini," is denying *every kind* of change, but opposes itself to a certain plain and unambiguous statement, not of this or that Council, but one generally received or taught both in the schools and in the multitude, that the material elements are changed into an earthly, fleshly, and organized body, extended in size, distinct in its parts, which is there where the outward appearances of bread and wine are, and only does not meet the senses, nor even withdrawn from the senses always.

Objections against "substance," "nature," "change," "accidents," and the like, seem more or less questions of words, and inadequate expressions of the great offence which we find in the received Roman view of this sacred doctrine.[4]

In this connexion it may be suitable to quote and observe upon the Explanation appended to the Communion Service, of our practice of kneeling at the LORD's Supper,

---

[4] [On this subject, vid. *supr.* p. 228, note, and p. 231, note.]

which requires explanation itself, more perhaps than any part of our formularies. It runs as follows :—

"Whereas it is ordained in this office for the Administration of the LORD's Supper, that the communicants should receive the same kneeling: (which order is well meant, for a signification of our humble and grateful acknowledgment of the benefits of CHRIST therein given to all worthy receivers, and for the avoiding of such profanation and disorder in the holy communion, as might otherwise ensue;) yet, lest the same kneeling should by any persons, either out of ignorance and infirmity, or out of malice and obstinacy, be misconstrued and depraved,—It is hereby declared, that thereby no adoration is intended, or ought to be done, either unto the sacramental bread or wine there bodily received, or unto any corporal presence of CHRIST's natural flesh and blood. For the sacramental bread and wine remain still in their very natural substances, and therefore may not be adored, (for that were idolatry, to be abhorred of all faithful Christians); and the natural body and blood of our SAVIOUR CHRIST are in heaven, and not here, it being against the truth of CHRIST's natural body to be at one time in more places than one."

Now it may be admitted without difficulty,—1. That "no adoration ought to be done unto the sacramental bread and wine there bodily received." 2. Nor "unto any *corporal* (*i.e.* carnal) presence of CHRIST's natural flesh and blood." 3. That "the sacramental bread and wine remain still in their very natural substances." 4. That to adore *them* "were idolatry to be abhorred of all faithful Christians;" and 5. That "the natural body and blood of our SAVIOUR CHRIST are in heaven."

But "to heaven" is added, "*and not here.*" Now, though it be allowed that there is no "*corporal* presence," *i.e.* carnal, of "CHRIST's natural flesh and blood" here, it is a further point to allow that "CHRIST's natural body and blood" are "*not here.*" And the question is, how can there be any *presence* at all of His Body and Blood, yet a presence such, as not to be *here?* That is, in other words, how can there be any *presence*, yet not *local?*

Yet that this is the meaning of the paragraph in question is plain, from what it goes on to say in proof of its position: "It being against the truth of CHRIST's natural body to be at one time in more places than one." It is here asserted then, 1. Generally, "no natural body can be in more places than one;" therefore, 2. CHRIST's natural body cannot be in the bread and wine, or there where the bread and wine are seen. In other words, there is no local presence in the Sacrament. Yet, that there is a presence is asserted in the Homilies, as quoted above, and the question is, as just stated, "How can there be a presence, yet not a local one?"

Now, first, let it be observed that the question to be solved is the truth of a certain philosophical deduction, not of a certain doctrine of Scripture. That there is a real presence, Scripture asserts, and the Homilies, Catechism, and Communion Service confess; but the explanation before us adds, that it is philosophically impossible that it should be a particular kind of presence, viz. a presence of which one can say "it is here," or which is "local." It states then a philosophical deduction; but to such deduction none of us have subscribed. We have professed in the words of the Canon: "That the Book of Prayer, &c., containeth in it *nothing contrary to the word of God.*" Now, a position like this may not be, and is not, "contrary to the word of God," and yet need not be true. *E.g.* we may accept St. Clement's Epistle to the Corinthians, as containing nothing contrary to Scripture, nay, as altogether most scriptural, and yet this would not hinder us from rejecting his account of the Phœnix—as contrary,.

not to GOD's word, but to matter of fact. Even the infallibility of the Roman see is not considered to extend to matters of fact or points of philosophy. Nay, we commonly do not consider that we need take the words of Scripture itself literally about the sun's standing still, or the earth being fixed, or the firmament being above. Those at least who distinguish between what is theological in Scripture and what is scientific, and yet admit that Scripture is true, have no ground for wondering at such persons as subscribe to a paragraph, of which at the same time they disallow the philosophy; especially considering they expressly subscribe it only as not "contrary to the word of GOD." This then is what must be said first of all.

However, the philosophical position is itself capable of a very specious defence. The truth is, we do not at all know what is meant by distance or intervals absolutely, any more than we know what is meant by absolute time. Late discoveries in geology have tended to make it probable that time may under circumstances go indefinitely faster or slower than it does at present; or, in other words, that indefinitely more may be accomplished in a given portion of it. What Moses calls a day, geologists wish to prove to be thousands of years, if we measure time by the operations at present effected in it. It is equally difficult to determine what we mean by distance, or why we should not be at this moment close to the throne of GOD, though we seem far from it. Our measure of distance is our hand or our foot; but as an object a foot off is not called distant, though the interval is indefinitely divisible, neither need it be distant, even after it has been multiplied indefinitely. Why should any conventional measure of ours—why should the perception of our eyes or our ears, be the standard of presence or distance? CHRIST may really be close to us, though in heaven, and His presence in the Sacrament may be but a realizing to the worshipper of that nearness, not a change of place, which may be unnecessary. But on this subject some extracts may be suitably made from a pamphlet published several years since, and admitting of some verbal corrections, which, as in the case of other similar quotations above, shall here be made without scruple : [5]—

"It may be asked, What is the meaning of saying that CHRIST is really present, yet not locally? I will make two suggestions on the subject," &c., &c.

There is nothing, then, in the Explanatory Paragraph which has given rise to these remarks, to interfere with the doctrine, elsewhere taught in our formularies, of a real super-local Presence in the Holy Sacrament.

---

[5] [Vid. for the whole passage, *supr.* pp. 235—237, where other "corrections" in addition (bearing on its perspicuity, not its sense) have been made].

§ 9.—*Masses*.[1]

Article xxxi.—" The sacrifice (sacrificia) of Masses, in which it was commonly said, that the priests did offer CHRIST for the quick and the dead, to have remission of pain or guilt, were blasphemous fables and dangerous deceits (perniciosæ imposturæ)."

Nothing can show more clearly than this passage that the Articles are not written against the creed of the Roman Church, but against actual existing errors in it, whether taken into its system or not. Here the sacrifice of the *Mass* is not spoken of, in which the special question of doctrine would be introduced; but "the sacrifice of *Masses*," certain observances, for the most part private and solitary, which the writers of the Articles knew to have been in force in time past, and saw before their eyes, and which involved certain opinions and a certain teaching. Accordingly the passage proceeds, " in which it *was commonly said;*" which surely is a strictly historical mode of speaking.

If any testimony is necessary in aid of what is so plain from the wording of the Article itself, it is found in the drift of the following passage from Burnet :—

" It were easy from all the rituals of the ancients to show, that they had none of those ideas that are now in the Roman Church. They had but one altar in a Church, and probably but one in a city: they had but one communion in a day at that altar: so far were they from the many altars in every church, and *the many masses* at every altar, that are now in the Roman Church. They did not know what *solitary masses* were, without a communion. All the liturgies and all the writings of ancients are as express in this matter as is possible. The whole constitution of their worship and discipline shows it. Their worship always concluded with the Eucharist: such as were not capable of it, as the catechumens, and

[1] [Vid. *infr.*, Note 2, p. 351 at the end of this Tract.]

those who were doing public penance for their sins, assisted at the more general parts of the worship; and so much of it was called their mass, because they were dismissed at the conclusion of it. When that was done, then the faithful stayed, and did partake of the Eucharist; and at the conclusion of it they were likewise dismissed, from whence it came to be called the mass of the faithful."—*Burnet on the XXXIst Article*, p. 482.

These sacrifices (Missæ) are said to be "blasphemous fables and pernicious impostures. Now the "blasphemous fable" is the teaching that there are sacrifices for sin other than CHRIST'S death, and that masses are those other sacrifices. And the "pernicious imposture" is the turning this belief into a means of filthy lucre.

I. That the "blasphemous fable" is the teaching that masses are sacrifices for sin distinct from the sacrifice of CHRIST'S death, is plain from the first sentence of the Article. "The offering of CHRIST *once made*, is that perfect redemption, propitiation, and satisfaction for *all* the sins of the *whole world, both original and actual*. And *there is none other* satisfaction for sin, but *that alone*. Wherefore the sacrifice of masses, &c." It is observable too that the heading of the Article runs, "Of the one oblation of CHRIST finished upon the Cross," which interprets the *drift* of the statement contained in it about masses.

Our Communion Service shows it also, in which the prayer of consecration commences pointedly with a declaration, which has the force of a protest, that CHRIST made on the cross "by His *one* oblation of Himself *once* offered, a *full, perfect*, and *sufficient* sacrifice, oblation, and *satisfaction* for the sins of the whole world."

And again in the offering of the sacrifice: "We entirely desire thy fatherly goodness mercifully to accept our sacrifice of praise and thanksgiving, most humbly beseeching Thee to grant that *by the merits and death of Thy* SON JESUS CHRIST, and through faith in His blood, we and all

Thy whole Church may obtain *remission of our* sins and all *other benefits* of His passion."

But the popular charge still urged against the Roman system as introducing in the Mass a second or rather continually recurring atonement, is a sufficient illustration, without further quotations, of this part of the Article.[2]

2. That the "blasphemous and pernicious imposture" is the turning the Mass into a gain is plain from such passages as the following:—

"With what earnestness, with what vehement zeal, did our SAVIOUR CHRIST drive the buyers and sellers out of the temple of GOD, and hurled down the tables of the changers of money, and the seats of the dove-sellers, and could not abide that a man should carry a vessel through the temple. He told them, that they made His FATHER'S house a den of thieves, partly through their superstition, hypocrisy, false worship, false doctrine, and insatiable covetousness, and partly through contempt, abusing that place with walking and talking, with worldly matters, without all fear of GOD, and due reverence to that place. What dens of thieves the Churches of England have been made by the *blasphemous buying and selling the most precious body and blood of* CHRIST *in the Mass*, as the world was made to believe, at dirges, at month's minds, at trentalls, in abbeys and chantries, besides other horrible abuses, (GOD's holy name be blessed for ever,) which we now see and understand. All these abominations they that supply the room of CHRIST have cleansed and purged the Churches of England of, taking away all such fulsomeness and filthiness, as through blind devotion and ignorance hath crept into the Church these many hundred years."
—*On repairing and keeping clean of Churches*, pp. 229, 230. *Place and Time of Prayer*, p. 293. *Sacrament*, pp. 377, 378. *Bull's Sermons*, p. 10. *Burnet, Article XXII.*, pp. 303, 304.

The truth of representations such as these cannot be better shown than by extracting the following passage from the Session 22 of the Council of Trent:—

[2] [But we say that the charge is a calumny, and ask for proof.]

"Whereas many things appear to have crept in heretofore, whether by the fault of the times or by the neglect and wickedness of men, foreign to the dignity of so great a sacrifice, in order that it may regain its due honour and observance, to the glory of GOD and the edification of His faithful people, the Holy Council decrees, that the bishops, ordinaries of each place, diligently take care and be bound, to forbid and put an end to all those things, which either *avarice*, which is idolatry, or *irreverence*, which is scarcely separable from impiety, or *superstition*, the pretence of true piety, has introduced. And, to say much in a few words, first of all, as to avarice, let them altogether forbid agreements, and bargains of *payment* of whatever kind, and *whatever is given for celebrating new masses;* moreover importunate and mean extortion, rather than petition of alms, and such like practices, which border on simoniacal sin, certainly on *filthy lucre.* . . . And let them banish from the churches those musical performances, *when with the organ or with the chant anything lascivious or impure is mingled;* also all secular practices, idle and therefore profane conversations, promenadings, bustle, clamour; so that the house of GOD may truly seem and be called the house of prayer. Lastly, lest any opening be given to superstition, let them forbid by edict and punishments appointed, the priests to celebrate at any other than the due hours, or to use rites or ceremonies and prayers in the celebration of masses, other than those which have been approved by the Church, and received on frequent and laudable use. And let them altogether remove from the Church a *set number of certain masses and candles*, which has proceeded rather from *superstitious observance* than from true religion, and teach the people in what consists, and from whom, above all, proceeds the so precious and heavenly fruit of this most holy sacrifice. And let them admonish the same people to come frequently to their parish Churches, at least on Sundays and the greater feasts," &c.

On the whole, then, it is conceived that the Article before us neither speaks against the Mass in itself, nor against its being an offering for the quick and the dead for the remission of sin; but against its being viewed, on the one hand, as independent of or distinct from the Sacrifice on the Cross, which is blasphemy, and, on the other, its being directed to the emolument of those to whom it pertains to celebrate it, which is imposture in addition.

§ 10.—*Marriage of Clergy.*

Article xxxii.—" Bishops, Priests, and Deacons, are not commanded by God's law, either to vow the estate of single life, or to abstain from marriage."

There is literally no subject for controversy in these words, since even the most determined advocates of the celibacy of the clergy admit their truth. Clerical celibacy, as a duty, is grounded not on GOD's law, but on the Church's rule, or on vow. No one, for instance, can question the vehement zeal of St. Jerome in behalf of this observance, yet he makes the following admission in his attack upon Jovinian:—

"Jovinian says, 'You speak in vain, since the Apostle appointed Bishops, and Presbyters, and Deacons, the husbands of one wife, and having children.' But, as the Apostle says, that he has not a precept concerning virgins, yet gives a counsel, as having received mercy of the Lord, and urges throughout that discourse a preference of virginity to marriage, and *advises what he does not command*, lest he seem to cast a snare, and to impose a burden too great for man's nature; *so also*, in ecclesiastical order, seeing that an infant Church was then forming out of the Gentiles, he gives the lighter precepts to recent converts, lest they should fail under them through fear."—*Adv. Jovinian*, i. 34.

And the Council of Trent merely lays down :—

" If any shall say that clerks in holy orders, or regulars, who have solemnly professed chastity, can contract matrimony, and that the contract is valid *in spite of ecclesiastical law or vow*, let him be anathema."—*Sess.* 24, *Can.* 9.

Here the observance is placed simply upon rule of the Church or upon vow, neither of which exists in the English Church; "*therefore,*" as the Article logically proceeds, " it *is* lawful for them, as for all other Christian men, to marry *at their own discretion*, as they shall judge the same to serve better to godliness." Our Church leaves the discretion with the clergy; and most persons will allow that, *under our circumstances*, she acts wisely in doing so. That she has *power*, did she so choose, to take from them this discretion, and to oblige them either to marriage (as is said to be the case as regards the parish priests of the Greek Church) or to celibacy, would seem to be involved in the doctrine of the following extract from the Homilies; though, whether an enforcement either of the one or the other rule would be expedient and pious, is another matter. Speaking of fasting, the Homily says,—

"God's Church ought not, neither may it be so tied to that or any other order now made, or hereafter to be made and devised by the authority of man, but that *it may lawfully, for just causes, alter, change, or mitigate* those ecclesiastical decrees and orders, yea, *recede wholly from them, and break them,* when they tend either to superstition or to impiety; when they draw the people from God rather than work any edification in them. This authority Christ Himself used, and *left it to His Church.* He used it, I say, for the order or decree made by the elders for washing ofttimes, which was diligently observed of the Jews; yet tending to superstition, our Saviour Christ altered and changed the same in His Church into a profitable sacrament, the sacrament of our regeneration, or new birth. This authority to mitigate laws and decrees ecclesiastical, the Apostles practised, when they, writing from Jerusalem unto the congregation that was at Antioch, signified unto them, that they would not lay any further burden upon them, but these necessaries: that is, 'that they should abstain from things offered unto idols, from blood, from that which is strangled, and from fornication;' notwithstanding that Moses's law required many other observances. This authority to change the orders, decrees, and constitutions of the Church, was, after the Apostles' time, used of the fathers about the manner of fasting, as it appeareth in the Tripartite History. . . Thus ye have heard, good people, first, that Christian subjects are bound even in conscience to obey princes' laws, which are not repugnant to the laws of God. Ye have also heard that Christ's Church is not so bound to observe any order, law, or decree made by man, to prescribe a form in religion, but that the Church hath full power and authority from God to change and alter the same, when need shall require; which hath been showed you by the example of our SAVIOUR CHRIST, by the practice of the Apostles, and of the Fathers since that time." *Homily on Fasting*, p. 242—244.

To the same effect the Thirty-fourth Article declares, that—

"It is not necessary that traditions and ceremonies be in all places one, and utterly like; for at all times they have been divers, and *may be changed* according to diversities of countries, times, and men's manners, so that nothing be ordained against God's Word. Whosoever, *through his private judgment*, willingly and purposely doth openly *break* the traditions and ceremonies of the Church, which be not repugnant to the Word of GOD, and be ordained and approved by common authority, ought to be rebuked openly."

§ 11.—*The Homilies.*

Article xxxv.—"The second Book of Homilies doth contain a godly and wholesome doctrine, and necessary for these times, as doth the former Book of Homilies."

This Article has been treated of in No. 82 of these Tracts,[1] in the course of an answer given to an opponent, who accused its author of not fairly receiving the Homilies, because he dissented from their doctrine, that the Bishop of Rome is Antichrist, and that regeneration was vouchsafed under the law. Some portions of the passage in the Tract shall here be inserted.

"I say plainly, then, I have not *subscribed* the Homilies, nor was it ever intended that any member of the English Church should be subjected to what, if considered as an extended confession, would indeed be a yoke of bondage. Romanism surely is innocent, compared with that system which should impose upon the conscience a thick octavo volume, written flowingly and freely by fallible men, to be received exactly, sentence for sentence; I cannot conceive any grosser instance of a pharisaical tradition than this would be, &c.

"How then are we bound to the Homilies? By the Thirty-fifth Article, which speaks as follows:—'The second Book of Homilies . . . doth *contain* a godly and wholesome *doctrine*, and necessary for these times, as doth the former *Book of Homilies.*' Now, observe, this Article does not speak of every statement made in them, but of the '*doctrine.*' It speaks of the *view or cast, or body of doctrine* contained in them. In spite of ten thousand incidental propositions, as in any large book, there is, it is

---

[1] [Vid. *supr.* pp. 17 –185.]

obvious, a certain line of doctrine, which may be contemplated continuously in its shape and direction," &c. . . .

This illustration of the subject may be thought enough; yet it may be allowable to add from the Homilies a number of propositions or statements of more or less importance, which are too much forgotten at this day, and are decidedly opposed to the views of certain schools of religion, which at the present moment are so eager in claiming the Homilies for themselves. This is not done, as the extract already read will show, with the intention of maintaining that they are one and all binding on the conscience of those who subscribe the Thirty-fifth Article; but, since the strong language of the Homilies against the Bishop of Rome is often quoted, as if it were thus proved to be the doctrine of our Church, it may be as well to show that, following the same rule, we shall be also introducing Catholic doctrines, which indeed it far more belongs to a Church to profess than a certain view of prophecy, but which do not approve themselves to those who hold that view. For instance, we read as follows:—

1. "The great clerk and godly preacher, St. John Chrysostom."—1 B. i. 1. And, in like manner, mention is made elsewhere of St. Augustine, St. Ambrose, St. Hilary, St. Basil, St. Cyprian, St. Hierome, St. Martin, Origen, Prosper, Ecumenius, Photius, Bernardus, Anselm, Didymus, Theophylactus, Tertullian, Athanasius, Lactantius, Cyrillus, Epiphanius, Gregory, Irenæus, Clemens, Rabanus, Isidorus, Eusebius, Justinus Martyr, Optatus, Eusebius Emissenus, and Bede.

2. "Infants, being baptized, and dying in their infancy, are by this Sacrifice washed from their sins . . . and they which in act or deed do sin after this baptism, when they turn to GOD, unfeignedly, they are *likewise* washed by this Sacrifice," &c.—1 B. iii. 1. *init.*

3. "Our office is, not to pass the time of this present

life unfruitfully and idly, after that we are *baptized or justified,*" &c.—1 B. iii. 3.

4. "By holy promises, we be made lively members of CHRIST, receiving the Sacrament of Baptism. By like holy promises *the sacrament of Matrimony* knitteth man and wife in perpetual love."—1 B. vii. 1.

5. "Let us learn also here [in the Book of Wisdom] by *the infallible and undeceivable Word of* GOD, that," &c.—1 B. x. 1.

6. "The due receiving of His blessed Body and Blood, *under the form* of bread and wine."—*Note at end of* Book i.

7. "In the Primitive Church, *which was most holy and godly* . . . open offenders were not suffered once to enter into the house of the LORD . . . until they had done open penance . . . but this was practised, not only upon mean persons, but also upon the *rich, noble, and mighty persons,* yea, upon Theodosius, *that puissant and mighty Emperor,* whom . . St. Ambrose . . did . . excommunicate."—2 B. i. 2.

8. "Open offenders were not . . admitted to common prayer, and the use of the holy *sacraments.*"—*Ibid.*

9. "Let us amend this our negligence and contempt in coming to the house of the LORD; and resorting thither diligently together, let us there . . . celebrating also reverently the LORD's holy *sacraments,* serve the LORD in His holy house."—*Ibid.* 5.

10. "Contrary to the . . . most manifest doctrine of the Scriptures, and contrary to the usage of the Primitive Church, *which was most pure and uncorrupt,* and contrary to the sentences and judgments of the *most ancient, learned, and godly* doctors of the Church."—2 B. ii. 1. *init.*

11. "This truth . . . was believed and taught by the *old holy fathers,* and *most ancient learned doctors,* and received by the old Primitive Church, *which was most uncorrupt and pure.*"—2 B. ii. 2. *init.*

12. "Athanasius, a very ancient, holy, and learned bishop and doctor."—*Ibid.*
13. "Cyrillus, an old and holy doctor."—*Ibid.*
14. "Epiphanius, Bishop of Salamine, in Cyprus, a very holy and learned man."—*Ibid.*
15. "To whose (Epiphanius's) judgment you have ... all the learned and godly bishops and clerks, yea, and the whole Church of that age" [the Nicene] "and so upward to our SAVIOUR CHRIST's time, by the space of about four hundred years, consenting and agreeing."—*Ibid.*
16. "Epiphanius, a bishop and doctor of such antiquity, holiness, and authority."—*Ibid.*
17. "St. Augustin, the best learned of all ancient doctors."—*Ibid.*
18. "That ye may know why and when, and by whom images were first used privately, and afterwards not only received into Christian churches and temples, but, in conclusion, worshipped also; and how the same was gainsaid, resisted and forbidden, as well by *godly bishops and learned doctors*, as also by sundry Christian princes, I will briefly collect," &c. The bishops and doctors which follow are: "St. Jerome, Serenus, Gregory, the Fathers of the Council of Eliberis."
19. "Constantine, Bishop of Rome, assembled a Council of bishops of the West, and did condemn Philippicus, *the Emperor*, and John, Bishop of Constantinople, of the *heresy of the Monothelites*, not without a cause indeed, but *very justly.*"—*Ibid.*
20. "Those six Councils, *which were allowed and received of all men.*"—*Ibid.*
21. "There were no images publicly by the space of almost *seven hundred* years. And there is *no doubt* but the Primitive Church, next the Apostles' times, was *most pure.*"—*Ibid.*
22. "Let us beseech GOD that we, being *warned* by His

holy Word . . . and by *the writings of old godly doctors and ecclesiastical histories,*" &c.—*Ibid.*

23. "It shall be declared, both by GOD's Word, and the *sentences* of the ancient doctors, and *judgment* of the Primitive Church," &c.—2 B. ii. 3.

24. "Saints, whose souls *reign* in joy with GOD."—*Ibid.*

25. "That the law of GOD is likewise to be *understood* against all our images . . . appeareth further by the *judgment* of the old doctors and the Primitive Church."—*Ibid.*

26. "The Primitive Church, *which is specially to be followed,* as most incorrupt and pure."—*Ibid.*

27. "Thus it is declared by GOD's Word, the *sentences* of the doctors, and the *judgment* of the Primitive Church." —*Ibid.*

28. "The rude people, who specially as the *Scripture* teacheth, are in danger of superstition and idolatry; viz. Wisdom xiii. xiv."—*Ibid.*

29. "They [the 'learned and holy bishops and doctors of the Church' of the eight first centuries] were the preaching bishops. . . . And as they were most zealous and diligent, so were they of excellent learning and godliness of life, and by both of great authority and credit with the people."—*Ibid.*

30. "The most virtuous and best learned, the most diligent also, and in number almost infinite, ancient fathers, bishops, and doctors . . . could do nothing against images and idolatry."—*Ibid.*

31. "As the *Word of God* testifieth, Wisdom xiv."— *Ibid.*

32. "The saints, *now reigning in heaven* with GOD."— *Ibid.*

33. "The *fountain of our regeneration* is there [in GOD's house] presented unto us."—2 B. iii.

36. "Somewhat shall now be spoken of one particular

good work, whose commendation is both in the law and in the Gospel [fasting]."—2 B. iv. 1.

37. " If any man shall say . . . we are not now under the yoke of the law, we are set at liberty by the freedom of the Gospel ; therefore these rites and customs of the old law bind not us, except it can be showed by the Scriptures of the New Testament, or by examples out of the same, that fasting, now under the Gospel, is a *restraint of meat, drink, and all bodily food and pleasures from the body,* as before : first, that we ought to fast, is a *truth more manifest, than it should here need to be proved.* . . . Fasting, even by CHRIST's assent, is a withholding meat, drink, and all natural food from the body," &c.—*Ibid.*

38. " That it [fasting] was used in the Primitive Church, appeareth most evidently by the Chalcedon Council, one of the *four first general councils.* The fathers assembled there . . . decreed in that council that every person, as well in his private as public fast, should continue all the day without meat and drink, till after the evening prayer. . . This Canon teacheth how fasting was used in the *Primitive* Church."—*Ibid.* [This Council was A.D. 451.]

39. " Fasting then, by the *decree* of those 630 fathers, *grounding* their determinations in this matter upon the sacred Scriptures . . . is a withholding of meat, drink, and all natural food from the body, from the determined time of fasting."—*Ibid.*

40. " The order or decree made by the elders for washing ofttimes, tending to superstition, our SAVIOUR CHRIST altered and changed the same in His Church, into a profitable sacrament, the sacrament of our *regeneration* or *new birth.*"—2 B. iv. 2.

41. " Fasting thus used with prayer is of *great efficacy* and *weigheth much* with God, so the angel Raphael told Tobias."—*Ibid.*

42. "As he" [St. Augustine] "witnesseth in another place, the martyrs and holy men in times past, were wont after their death to be *remembered* and *named* of the priest at divine service; but never to be invocated or called upon."—2 B. vii. 2.

43. "Thus you see that the *authority both* of Scripture and *also* of Augustine, doth not permit that we should pray to them."—*Ibid.*

44. "To temples have the *Christians* customably used to resort from time to time as to most meet places, where they might . . . receive His holy *sacraments* ministered unto them duly and purely."—2 B. viii. 1.

45. "The which thing both CHRIST and His apostles, *with all the rest of the holy fathers*, do sufficiently declare so."—*Ibid.*

46. "Our godly *predecessors*, and the *ancient* fathers of the Primitive Church, spared not their goods to build Churches."—*Ibid.*

"If we will show ourselves true Christians, if we will be followers of CHRIST our MASTER, and of those *godly fathers* who have lived before us, and now have received the reward of true and faithful Christians," &c.—*Ibid.*

48. "We must . . . come unto the material churches and temples to pray . . . whereby we may reconcile ourselves to GOD, be partakers of His holy *sacraments*, and be devout hearers of His holy Word," &c.—*Ibid.*

49. "It [ordination] lacks the promise of remission of sin, as all *other* sacraments besides the two above named do. Therefore neither it, nor any *other* sacrament else, be *such* sacraments as Baptism and the Communion are."—2 *Hom.* ix.

50. "Thus we are taught, both by the Scriptures and ancient doctors, that," &c.—*Ibid.*

51. "The holy apostles and disciples of CHRIST . . . the godly fathers also, that were both *before* and *since* CHRIST,

endued without doubt with the HOLY GHOST, . . . they both do most earnestly exhort us, &c. . . that we should remember the poor . . St. Paul crieth unto us after this sort . . Isaiah the Prophet teacheth us on this wise . . And the holy father *Tobit* giveth this counsel. And *the learned and godly doctor Chrysostom* giveth this admonition. . . But what mean these often admonitions and earnest exhortations of the prophets, apostles, fathers, and holy doctors?"—2 B. xi. 1.

52. "The holy fathers, Job and Tobit."—*Ibid.*

53. " CHRIST, whose especial *favour* we may be assured by *this means* to *obtain,*" [viz. by almsgiving]—2 B. xi. 2.

54. " Now will I . . . show unto you how *profitable* it is for us to exercise them [alms-deeds] . . . [CHRIST'S saying] serveth to . . . prick us forwards . . . to learn . . . *how* we may *recover* our health, if it be lost or impaired, and how it may be defended and maintained if we have it. Yea, He teacheth us also therefore to esteem that as a *precious medicine* and an *inestimable jewel,* that hath such *strength and virtue* in it, that can either *procure* or preserve so incomparable a treasure."—*Ibid.*

55. "Then He and His disciples were grievously accused of the Pharisees, . . . because they went to meat and washed not their hands before, . . . CHRIST, answering their *superstitious* complaint, teaching them an especial *remedy* how to *keep clean* their souls, . . . Give alms," &c. —*Ibid.*

56. " Merciful alms-dealing is *profitable* to *purge* the soul from the *infection and filthy spots of sin.*"—*Ibid.*

57. " The same lesson *doth the* HOLY GHOST *teach* in sundry places of the *Scripture,* saying, ' Mercifulness and alms-giving,' &c. [Tobit iv.] . . . The wise preacher, the son of Sirach, confirmeth the same, when he says, that ' as water quencheth burning fire,' " &c.—*Ibid.*

58. " A great *confidence* may they have *before the high*

God, that show mercy and compassion to them that are afflicted."—*Ibid.*

59. "If ye have by any infirmity or weakness been touched and annoyed with them . . . straightway shall mercifulness *wipe and wash them away*, as *salves and remedies* to heal their *sores and grievous diseases*."—*Ibid.*

60. "And therefore that *holy father* Cyprian admonisheth to consider how *wholesome* and *profitable* it is to relieve the needy, &c. . . . by *the which* we may *purge our sins* and *heal our wounded souls*."—*Ibid.*

61. "We be therefore *washed* in our baptism from the *filthiness of sin*, that we should live afterwards in the pureness of life."—2 B. xiii. 1.

62. "By these means [by love, compassion, &c.] shall we *move* God to be *merciful to our sins*."—*Ibid.*

63. "'He was dead,' saith St. Paul, 'for our sins, and rose again for our *justification*' . . . He died to destroy the rule of the devil in us, and He rose again to send down His HOLY SPIRIT *to rule in our hearts*, to endue us with *perfect righteousness*."—2 B. xiv.

64. "The *ancient Catholic fathers*," (in marg.) Irenæus, Ignatius, Dionysius, Origen, Optatus, Cyprian, Athanasius, ... "were not afraid to call this supper, some of them, *the salve of immortality and sovereign preservative against death*; other, the sweet dainties of our SAVIOUR, the pledge of eternal health, the defence of faith, the hope of the resurrection; other, the *food of immortality*, the healthful grace, and the conservatory to everlasting life."—2 B. xv. 1.

65. "The meat we seek in this supper is spiritual food, the nourishment of our soul, a heavenly refection, and not earthly; an *invisible meat*, and not bodily; a *ghostly substance*, and not carnal."—*Ibid.*

66. "Take this lesson . . . of Emissenus, a godly father that . . . . thou *look up* with faith upon the *holy body and blood of thy* God, thou marvel with reverence, thou *touch* it

with thy mind, thou receive it with the hand of thy heart, and thou take it fully with thy inward man."—*Ibid.*

67. "The saying of the holy martyr of GOD, St. Cyprian."—2 B. xx. 3.

Thus we see the authority of the Fathers, of the six first councils, and of the judgments of the Church generally, the holiness of the Primitive Church, the inspiration of the Apocrypha, the sacramental character of Marriage and other ordinances, the Real Presence in the Eucharist, the Church's power of excommunicating kings, the profitableness of fasting, the propitiatory virtue of good works, the Eucharistic commemoration, and justification by inherent righteousness, are taught in the Homilies. Let it be said again, it is not here asserted that a subscription to all and every of these quotations is involved in the subscription of an Article which does but generally approve the Homilies; but they who insist so strongly on our Church's holding that the Bishop of Rome is Antichrist because the Homilies declare it, should recollect that there are other doctrines contained in them beside it, which they should be understood to hold, before their argument has the force of consistency.

§ 12.—*The Bishop of Rome.*

Article xxxviii.—"The Bishop of Rome hath no jurisdiction in this realm of England."

By " hath " is meant " ought to have," as the Article in the 36th Canon and the Oath of Supremacy show, in which the same doctrine is drawn out more at length. " No foreign prince, person, prelate, state, or potentate, hath, *or ought to have,* any jurisdiction, power, superiority, pre-eminence, or authority, ecclesiastical or spiritual, within this realm."

This is the profession which every one must in consistency make, who does not join the Roman Church. If the Bishop of Rome has jurisdiction and authority here, why do we not acknowledge it, and submit to him? To use then the above words, is nothing more or less than to say " I am not a Roman Catholic ;" and whatever reasons there are against using them, are so far reasons against remaining in the English Church. They are a mere enunciation of the principle of Anglicanism.

Anglicans maintain that the supremacy of the Pope is not directly from revelation, but an event in Providence. All things may be undone by the agents and causes by which they are done. What revelation gives, revelation takes away; what Providence gives, Providence takes away. GOD ordained by miracle, He reversed by miracle, the Jewish election; He promoted in the way of Providence, and He cast down by the same way, the Roman empire. "The powers that be, are ordained of GOD," *while* they be, and thereby have a claim on our obedience. When they cease to be, they cease to have a claim. They cease to be, when GOD removes them. He may be considered to remove them when He undoes what

He had done. The Jewish election did not cease to be, when the Jews went into captivity : this was an event in Providence; and what miracle had ordained, it was miracle that annulled. But the Roman power ceased to be when the barbarians overthrew it ; for it rose by the sword, and it therefore perished by the sword. The Gospel Ministry began in CHRIST and His Apostles ; and what they began they only can end. The Papacy began in the exertions and passions of man ; and what man can make, man can destroy. Its jurisdiction, while it lasted, was "ordained of GOD;" when it ceased to be, it ceased to claim our obedience; and it ceased to be·at the Reformation. The Reformers, who could not destroy a Ministry, which the Apostles began, could destroy a Dominion which the Popes founded.

Perhaps the following passage will throw additional light upon this point:—

" The Anglican view of the Church has ever been this : that its portions need not otherwise have been united together for their essential completeness, than as being descended from one original. They are like a number of colonies sent out from a mother-country. . . . . Each Church is independent of all the rest, and is to act on the principle of what may be called Episcopal independence, except, indeed, so far as the civil power unites any number of them together. . . . . Each diocese is a perfect independent Church, is sufficient for itself; and the communion of Christians one with another, and the unity of them altogether, lie, not in a mutual understanding, intercourse, and combination, not in what they do in common, but in what they are and have in common, in their possession of the Succession, their Episcopal form, their Apostolical faith, and the use of the Sacraments. . . . . Mutual intercourse is but an *accident* of the Church, not of its essence. . . . . Intercommunion is a duty, as other duties, but is not the tenure of instrument of the communion between the unseen world and this ; and much more the confederacy of sees and churches, the metropolitan, patriarchal, and papal systems, are matters of expedience or of natural duty from long custom, or of propriety from gratitude and reverence, or of necessity from voluntary oaths and engagements, or of ecclesiastical force from the canons of Councils, but not necessary in order to the conveyance of grace, or for fulfilment of the ceremonial law, as it may be called, of unity. Bishop is superior to bishop only in rank, not in real power; and the Bishop of Rome, the head of the Catholic world, is not the centre of unity, except as having a primacy of order. Accordingly, even granting, for argument's sake, that the English Church violated a duty in the 16th century, in releasing itself from the Roman supremacy, still it did not thereby commit that special sin, which cuts off from it the fountains of grace, and is called schism. It was essentially complete without Rome, and naturally independent of it; it had, in the course of years, whether by usurpation or not, come under the supremacy of Rome ; and now, whether by rebellion or not, it is free from it: and as it did not enter into the Church invisible by joining Rome, so it was not cast out of it by breaking from Rome. These were accidents in its history, involving, indeed, sin in individuals, but not affecting the Church as a Church.

"Accordingly, the Oath of Supremacy declares ' that no foreign prelate hath or ought to have any jurisdiction, power, pre-eminence, or authority within this realm.' In other words, there is nothing in the Apostolic system which gives an authority to the Pope over the Church, such as it does not give to a Bishop. It is altogether an ecclesiastical arrangement ; not a point *de fide*, but of expedience, custom, or piety, which cannot be claimed as if the Pope *ought* to have it, any more than, on the other hand, the King could of Divine right claim the supremacy ; the claim of both one and the other resting, not on duty or revelation, but on specific engagement. We find ourselves, as a Church, under the King now, and we obey him; we were under the Pope formerly, and we obeyed him. 'Ought' does not, in any degree, come into the question."[1]

[1] British Critic, Jan. 1840, pp. 54—58 : [Essays, vol. ii. ix. 4.]

Conclusion.

One remark may be made in conclusion. It may be objected that the tenor of the above explanations is anti-Protestant, whereas it is notorious that the Articles were drawn up by Protestants, and intended for the establishment of Protestantism; accordingly, that it is an evasion of their meaning to give them any other than a Protestant drift, possible as it may be to do so grammatically, or in each separate part.

But the answer is simple :—

1. In the first place, it is a *duty* which we owe both to the Catholic Church and to our own, to take our reformed confessions in the most Catholic sense they will admit; we have no duties towards their framers. Nor do we receive the Articles from their original framers, but from several successive Convocations after their time; in the last instance, from that of 1662.

2. In giving the Articles a Catholic interpretation, we bring them into harmony with the Book of Common Prayer, an object of the most serious moment for those who have given their assent to both formularies.

3. Whatever be the authority of the Declaration prefixed to the Articles, so far as it has any weight at all, it sanctions the mode of interpreting them above given. For its enjoining the "literal and grammatical sense," relieves us from the necessity of making the known opinions of their framers, a comment upon their text; and its forbidding any person to "affix any *new* sense to any Article," was promulgated at a time when the leading men of our Church were especially noted for those Catholic views which have been here advocated.

4. It may be remarked, moreover, that such an interpretation is in accordance with the well-known general leaning

of Melanchthon, from whose writings our Articles are principally drawn, and whose Catholic tendencies gained for him that same reproach of popery, which has ever been so freely bestowed upon members of our own reformed Church.

"Melanchthon was of opinion," says Mosheim, "that for the sake of peace and concord many things might be given up and tolerated in the Church of Rome, which Luther considered could by no means be endured. . . . In the class of matters indifferent, this great man and his associates placed many things which had appeared of the highest importance to Luther, and could not of consequence be considered as indifferent by his true disciples. For he regarded as such, the doctrine of justification by faith alone; the necessity of good works to eternal salvation; the number of the sacraments; the jurisdiction claimed by the Pope and the Bishops; extreme unction; the observation of certain religious festivals, and several superstitious rites and ceremonies."—*Cent.* XVI. § 3. part 2. 27, 28.

5. Further: the Articles are evidently framed on the principle of leaving open large questions, on which the controversy hinges. They state broadly extreme truths, and are silent about their adjustment. For instance, they say that all necessary faith must be proved from Scripture, but do not say *who* is to prove it. They say that the Church has authority in controversies, they do not say *what* authority. They say that it may enforce nothing beyond Scripture, but do not say *where* the remedy lies when it does. They say that works *before* grace *and* justification are worthless and worse, and that works *after* grace *and* justification are acceptable, but they do not speak at all of works *with* GOD's grace, *before* justification. They say that men are lawfully called and sent to minister and preach who are chosen and called by men who have public authority *given* them in the congregation to call and send; but they do not add *by whom* the authority is to be given. They say that Councils called *by princes* may err; they do not determine whether Councils called *in the name of* CHRIST will err.

6. The variety of doctrinal views contained in the Homilies, as above shown, views which cannot be brought under Protestantism itself, in its greatest comprehension of opinions, is an additional proof, considering the connexion of the Articles with the Homilies, that the Articles are not framed on the principle of excluding those who prefer the theology of the early ages to that of the Reformation; or rather let it be considered whether, considering both Homilies and Articles appeal to the Fathers and Catholic Antiquity, in interpreting them by these witnesses, we are not going to the very authority to which they profess to submit.

7. Lastly, their framers constructed them in such a way as best to comprehend those who did not go so far in Protestantism as themselves. Anglo-Catholics then are but the successors and representatives of those moderate reformers; and their case has been directly anticipated in the wording of the Articles. It follows that they are not perverting, they are using them for an express purpose for which among others their authors framed them. The interpretation Anglo-Catholics take was intended to be admissible; though not that which those authors took themselves. Had it not been provided for, possibly the Articles never would have been accepted by our Church at all. If, then, their framers have gained their side of the compact in effecting the reception of the Articles, let Catholics have theirs too in retaining their own Catholic interpretation of them.

An illustration of this occurs in the history of the 28th Article. In the beginning of Elizabeth's reign a paragraph formed part of it, much like that which is now appended to the Communion Service, but in which the Real Presence was *denied in words*. It was adopted by the clergy at the first Convocation, but not published. Burnet observes on it thus:—

"When these Articles were at first prepared by the Convocation in Queen Elizabeth's reign, this paragraph was made a part of them; for the original subscription by both houses of Convocation, yet extant, shows this. But the *design of the government* was at that time much turned *to the drawing over the body of the nation to the Reformation*, in whom the old leaven had gone deep; and no part of it deeper than the belief of the corporeal presence of CHRIST in the Sacrament; therefore it was *thought not expedient* to *offend* them by so particular a definition in this matter; in which the very word Real Presence was rejected. It might, perhaps, be also suggested, that here a definition was made that went too much upon the principles of natural philosophy; which how true soever, they might not be the proper subject of an article of religion. Therefore it was thought fit to suppress this paragraph; though it was a part of the Article that was subscribed, yet it was not published, but the paragraph that follows, 'The Body of CHRIST,' &c., was put in its stead, and was received and published by the next Convocation; which upon the matter was a full explanation of the way of CHRIST's presence in this Sacrament; that 'He is present in a heavenly and spiritual manner, and that faith is the mean by which he is received.' This seemed to be more theological; and it does indeed amount to the same thing. But howsoever we see what was the sense of the first Convocation in Queen Elizabeth's reign; it differed in nothing from that in King Edward's time: and therefore though this paragraph is now no part of our Articles, yet we are certain that the clergy at that time did not at all doubt of the truth of it; we are sure it was their opinion; since they subscribed it, though *they did not think fit* to publish it at first; and though it was afterwards changed for another, that was the same in sense."—*Burnet on Article XXVIII.*, p. 416.

What has lately taken place in the political world will afford an illustration in point. A French minister, desirous of war, nevertheless, as a matter of policy, draws up his state papers in such moderate language, that his successor who is for peace, can act up to them, without compromising his own principles. The world, observing this, has considered it a circumstance for congratulation; as if the former minister, who acted a double part, had been caught in his own snare. It is neither decorous, nor necessary, nor altogether fair, to urge the parallel rigidly; but it will explain what it is here meant to convey. The Protestant

Confession was drawn up with the purpose of including Catholics; and Catholics now will not be excluded. What was an economy in the Reformers, is a protection to us. What would have been a perplexity to us then, is a perplexity to Protestants now. We could not then have found fault with their words; they cannot now repudiate our meaning.

OXFORD.
The Feast of the Conversion of St. Paul.
1841.

NOTE 1 ON *Section* 6, *p.* 294 *of the above Tract.*

[May 26, 1877.—Section 6th of the above Tract, on its first publication was selected as an object for the remonstrance of Four College Tutors, which will be found *infra*, p. 359, and towards which I feel very much as I did when I first read it.

The Tutors speak of the "painful character of the impression" which "the contents of the Tract had produced on their minds," inasmuch as "it has to their apprehension a highly dangerous tendency from its suggesting that certain very important errors are not condemned by the Articles of the Church of England as they are taught authoritatively by the Church of Rome, but only certain practices and opinions which intelligent Romanists repudiate as much as we do."

The best answer to this representation is, that (in 1868) at the end of twenty-seven years, the lamented Dr. Forbes, the Anglican Bishop of Brechin, was suffered to repeat the very same statements without protest, which were considered so disingenuous and disgraceful in Tract 90. Prævalebit veritas. It may be interesting to place his statements and those of the Tract in juxtaposition.

1. "The Romish doctrine :"—

The Tract.—" By the Romish doctrine is not meant the Tridentine, because this Article was drawn up before the Decree of the Council of Trent," *supr.* p. 287.

Dr. Forbes.—" The questions of Purgatory and Pardons were not discussed [in the Tridentine Council] for many months after the publication of the Article . . . and we must come to the conviction that it was not the formularized doctrine, but a current and corrupt practice in the Latin or Western Church, which is here declared to be 'fond' and 'vainly' invented.'"
—*On the Thirty-nine Articles,* p. 302.

2. Purgatory :—

The Tract.—" There was a primitive doctrine, concerning the fire of judgment . . . through which all men will pass. . . . Here is one purgatorial doctrine, not 'Romish.' Another, said to be maintained by the Greeks at Florence, in which the cleansing, though a punishment, was but *pœna damni*, not a *pœna sensûs*. . . . And another is that in which the cleansing is but progressive sanctification, and has no pain at all. None of these doctrines does the Article condemn."—pp. 288-9.

Dr. Forbes.—" There are . . . two sets of statements, both founded on Holy Scripture. The one, . . St. Paul's description of that fire which shall try every man's work . . . the other, our Blessed Lord's words of that prison into which they who shall be cast shall not come forth, till they have paid the uttermost farthing, ... (p. 328). "While our Church has justly stigmatized popular practices which had become gainful superstitions, she has not condemned either the devotions of the Primitive Church, or the deep truths on which those devotions are grounded. ... With regard to the imperfect Christian ... we may rejoice in the thought that, ... through the fire of suffering and the water of affliction, [God] is bringing him into a wealthy place."—p. 346.

3. Pardons :—

The Tract.—" The Pardons, spoken of in the Article, are large and reckless indulgences from the penalties of sin obtained on money payments," p. 293.

Dr. Forbes.—" It was the shameless traffic in indulgences which burst the barrier, &c. ... A doctrine, which had its roots in primitive Antiquity was preached in a way to destroy all Christian morality. ... To call this a 'fond thing,' &c., is a mild censure," p. 352. "When the Articles were promulgated, they were all in their abomination. ... The Council of Trent, while it maintained the practice as being the exercise of a power given to the Church by God, and used in the most ancient times also, set itself to check the abuses which it acknowledged."—p. 356.

4. Images :—

The Tract.—" The veneration and worship condemned ... are such as these; kneeling before images, lighting candles to them, offering them incense, going on pilgrimage to them, hanging up crutches, &c., before them, lying tales about them, belief in miracles ... decking them up immodestly," &c., &c.—p. 296.

Dr. Forbes.—" There is always a danger of religion among the unlettered becoming superstitious. ... As a matter of fact, a *cultus* of images had grown up which required to be checked and all its coarser manifestations to be condemned," p. 361. "Of the having images or pictures nothing is said in the Article, only of worshipping them," p. 367. "The Homilies illustrate what it was, in regard to the veneration or worship of images, which the framers of the Articles had before their eyes. The Council of Trent reformed in the direction which our writers wished."—p. 369.

5. Relics :—

The Tract.—" In some sentences in the Homily on Peril of Idolatry, ... as far as regards Relics, a certain veneration is sanctioned by its tone in speaking of them, though not of course the Romish veneration."— p. 286.

Dr. Forbes.—" People kiss the picture or some relic of one whom they deeply love, as if it were the person," p. 369. "The principle that lay at the bottom of the sentiment was not in itself vicious, and had early established itself in the Church," p. 370. "The coarse attack of the innkeeper Vigilantius was not of a nature to gain him followers, or to disturb the tide of pious feeling," p. 373. "But where will not the idolatry of gain creep in ? Even St. Augustine had to complain of the sale of relics, probably fictitious. . . . The Article relates, not to the reverence of the relics . . . but to 'superstitions in their veneration,' which the Council of Trent had to forbid."—p. 376.

6. Images:—

The Tract.—" By 'invocation,' here, is not meant the mere circumstance of addressing beings out of sight, because we use the Psalms in our Daily Service, which are frequent in invocations of Angels to praise and bless God. In the Benedicite, too, we address 'the spirits and souls of the righteous.' Nor is it a 'fond' invocation to pray that unseen beings may bless us, for this Bishop Ken does in his Evening Hymn," p. 297. "This last passage plainly tells us . . . what is meant by invocation in its exceptionable sense . . . sacrificing and falling down in worship."—p. 299.

Dr. Forbes.—" In principle there is no question herein between us and any other portion of the Catholic Church. . . . Prayer to the Saints in heaven is explained again and again to be the same in kind as the prayers to the Saints on earth. . . . Had this been all, the Article never could have been written. . . . The Church of Rome has not stated the practice to be necessary to salvation, nor required it of any, so that he deny not that, as above explained, it is in itself good and useful. . . . We shall be disposed to accept the conclusion of a pious divine. . . . Let not that most ancient custom, common in the Universal Church, as well Greek as Latin, of addressing Angels and Saints in the way we have said, be condemned or rejected as impious, or as vain and foolish," &c.—p. 422.]

NOTE 2 ON *Section 9, p. 323 of the above Tract.*

[June 14, 1883.—The reasoning in this Section is not satisfactory. The Tract, as a whole, I have been able to defend, but not this portion of it. It argues that what the Article condemns is not the authoritative teaching of Rome, but only the common belief and practice of Catholics, as regards Purgatory and private Masses. But the words in which the Article condemns the so-called abuse are *ipso facto* a condemnation also of the ordinance itself which is abused. This will be seen at once by comparing the language of the Article with the language of Pope Pius IV. and the Council of Trent. What the Article abjures as a lie, is just that which Pope and Council declare to be a divine truth. The Pope says in his Creed, "I profess that in the Mass there is offered to God a true, proper, and propitiatory sacrifice for the living and the dead." And the Council, " In this divine sacrifice which is performed in the Mass, that same Christ is contained and immolated bloodlessly who did once offer Himself in blood." " And it is offered not only for the sins, pains, &c., of the living, but for the dead in Christ," &c. . . . On the other hand, the Article says " The sacrifices of Masses in the which it was commonly said that the Priest did offer Christ for the quick and the dead, to have remission of pain or guilt, were blasphemous fables and dangerous deceits." There is no denying then that these audacious words apply to the doctrinal teaching as well as to the popular belief of Catholics. What was "commonly said," was also formally enunciated by the Ecumenical Hierarchy in Council assembled.

This distinction between what is dogmatic and what is popular being untenable here, nothing can come of the suggested distinction between Mass and Masses, as if "the Mass" was the aboriginal divine Rite, which the Article left alone, and "the Masses" were those private superstitions which the Article denounced. However, this suggestion in aid is as unfounded as the original thesis. "Mass" and "Masses" do but respectively denote abstract and concrete, as can easily be shown.

Thus, in the Rubrics of the Missal we find "de Missis votivis S. Maria" followed by "dicitur Missa de S. Maria;" and "Vigiliis quando Missa dicenda est," by "Vigilias quæ habent Missas proprias," and "Benedictio semper data in Missa, præterquam in Missis defunctorum." Moreover the Council of Trent has distinctly sanctioned private Masses, on which it is attempted to throw the foul language of the Article, in these words : "Nec Missas illas, in quibus solus sacerdos sacramentaliter communicat, ut privatas et illicitas damnat, sed probat, Sacrosancta Synodus."

What then the 31st Article repudiates is undeniably the central and most sacred doctrine of the Catholic Religion ; and so its wording has ever been read since it was drawn up. And conformable to it has been the doctrine of Anglican divines, even of those who hold that there was a sacrifice in the Eucharist. They might not like the outrageous language of the Article, but, as far as I know and believe, none of these have maintained with the Church that Christ is really offered up in sacrifice in the Eucharistic Rite. As this appears lately to have been questioned, I think it well here to enlarge upon it.

1. The Tracts of the Times are no exception to their rule. Dr. Pusey is considered to be the author of Trac 81, an whatever he may have held at a later date, which I do not know, his antagonism in it to the Catholic dogma is unequivocal. He distinctly denies that our Lord is literally offered up in the Mass. According to him the real Presence lies, not in the oblation but in the communion. He recognizes this distinction as constituting the cardinal difference between the Roman and the Anglican belief. In the Introduction to the Tract he says, p. 13, "The *false doctrine* was that ordinary persuasion, that in the Mass the Priest did offer Christ for the quick and dead." And this "false doctrine" was founded, he says, on the doctrine of Transubstantiation, so much so that, when there was no Transubstantiation, there was no real and literal offering of Christ; for he says, p. 7, "By *combining* the doctrine of Transubstantiation with that of the Sacrifice of the Eucharist, the laity were persuaded that not only a commemorative Sacrifice but that Christ was offered." Accordingly at

p. 47 he puts into capital letters these words, "The doctrine of the Sacrifice cannot be the same where Transubstantiation is held and where it is not." This, I suppose, was my own view also; and it explains a passage in my *Apologia* in which I say, "I claimed" [as an Anglican] "in behalf of who would, the right of holding the Mass *all but* Transubstantiation, with Andrewes;" but without Transubstantiation, says Dr. Pusey, Christ was not literally offered.

The process then of sacrificing, that is, of offering and of communicating according to the Tractarian doctrine was this: The first solemn act was oblation, the formal oblation of Bread and Wine in their proper nature; thus the material elements went up to God. This was a human act; the second was divine, it was the return of the elements from the Heavenly Throne for communion, permeated and laden with Divine Grace so abundant and special, that it was, or at least might be truly called, the Very Body and Blood of the Redeemer, and His Personal Presence; but from first to last there was no real offering up of Christ, because there was no Transubstantiation. He was really present, but as our spiritual food, and as the Lamb that had been offered once, but not as then being offered; not as the Lamb of the Mass.

This is the categorical teaching of the Tracts. "The early Christians," says Dr. Pusey, p. 5, 6, "presented to the Almighty Father the *symbols* and *memorials* of the meritorious Death and Passion, &c., . . . they *first offered* to God His *gifts,* and placed them on His Altar here . . . and then trusted to receive them *back, conveying* to them the life-giving Body and Blood."

According then to Tract 81, there was no Christ present in the Eucharist till after the offering, oblation, or sacrifice, which sacrifice consisted in bread and wine in their natural substances; and thus there was not even the slightest approximation to that doctrine of Christ offered in the Mass for the quick and dead, which was condemned in the 31st Article.

2. The party of Non-jurors and others at the end of the 17th century are considered to have followed the doctrine of the early Church more closely than other Anglicans; but they, as to the doctrine of the Holy Eucharist, though they sometimes used more emphatic words, did not rise much higher in doctrine than the Tractarians. The latter held that in the Eucharistic Rite there was an oblation of Bread and Wine, which was representative and commemorative of the sacrifice of our Lord's Body and Blood upon the Cross. And the Non-jurors too held that there was no literal offering of our Lord in the Eucharist, as on the Cross; the rite indeed was more than a type and symbol of that sacrifice; but not more than a commemoration and a pleading of it; still, though in its nature merely Bread and Wine, it was endued with the power of a propitiatory and expiatory Sacrifice.

Johnson, who, though not a Non-juror himself, was of their school, writes as follows:—

"If the Holy Eucharist, as it is an oblation of Bread and Wine, and as that Bread and Wine are types and symbols of Christ's death, do not expiate and atone for sin, yet . . . it does this as it is a full and perfect *representation* of the sacrifice of Christ's Body and Blood. . . . I rather choose the word "representation" as being known to denote in our language not only that which resembles and puts us in mind of something else, but what is *deputed* or *substituted* in the stead of another, and is to us what the principal *would* be, *if* it were present. They are instituted by Christ, not only to call Him and His sufferings to remembrance, but to be to us all that His natural Body and Blood, crucified and poured out for us, *could* be *if* we had them *actually* lying on our altars. . . . When St. Paul says that ignorant and profane communicants "do not discern the Lord's body" in the holy Eucharist, he surely takes it for granted that the Body and Blood are actually[1] there, whether they discern it or not. . . . Such a representation we now see of that which God "set in the clouds," in the time of Noah . . . so, though the evangelical Covenant was effectually confirmed by Christ's death on the Cross, yet God has thought fit, for the supporting our faith and hope, to have the representative Sacrifice of His Body and Blood often repeated, and the Gospel Covenant by this means renewed. . . . *I have already declared against the Personal Presence or Sacrifice* of Christ in the Eucharistical elements. Nor do I suppose that the Bread and Wine *represent* His Whole Person, as He is God and man, but only His sacrificed Body and His effused Blood. . . . Since they are representatives of the only truly propitiatory and expiatory Sacrifice of the Cross, I suppose it clearly follows that they also are a propitiatory and expiatory sacrifice. . . . The Bread and Wine are divinely authorized *substitutes* for the Body and Blood of Christ Jesus, and therefore may *justly have the names* and titles of their principals," p. 305-8.

This is his positive doctrine, and to make still clearer its agreement with Article 31, we may, on the other hand, add to it his direct repudiation of the Roman doctrine, as being irreconcilable with his own.

1. The Papists hold that in the sacrifice of the Mass the whole Christ, God and man, is offered up hypostatically to the Father in the Eucharist, and is to be worshipped there by men under the species of Bread and Wine. This doctrine is utterly renounced by all Protestants, by those who assert the Eucharistic Oblation as well as those who deny it.

2. The Papists do maintain that the Sacrifice of the Mass is available for remission of sins to the dead as well as to the living. And as this is not asserted by any of our Church, so it is heartily detested by the author of this Treatise.

"The Papists have private Masses, in which the Priest pretends to make the oblation without distributing either the Body or Blood to

---

[1] I print this as I find it in Tract 81. The author presently says, "The Bread and Wine may justly have the *names* of their principals."

the people. . . . All this is condemned by those who defend the Eucharistical Oblation here in England," *ibid.* pp. 299, 300.

And to the same effect the Non-juring Bishop Hickes,—

"According to the Ancient Church the Bread and Wine were . . . the matter which the Bishop solemnly offered up to God by consecration for the heavenly banquet of the Lord's Supper, and which, as they were in the literal sense a proper, external, material offering for sacrifice, which succeeded in the place of the legal sacrifices, so in the sacramental or mystical they were the Body and Blood of Christ, of which they were the *representatives*," *ibid.* p. 264.

"The Bread and Wine . . . are the *symbols* of His natural Body and Blood, and by His appointment are to be *deemed, reputed,* and *received* as His natural Flesh and Blood," p. 270.

"The ancient notion of this holy Sacrament's being a *commemorative* Sacrifice, in which we *represent* before God the Sacrifice of Christ upon the Cross, perfectly secures the holy mystery from that corrupt and absurd notion" [Popish], "it being impossible that a solemn commemoration of a fact or thing should be the fact or thing itself," p. 272.

"Mystical and real differ as much as the substance and its shadow, the verity and its type, or a thing . . . from its image," p. 282.

I will add some sentences from Brett, another Non-juring divine, which give the same view of the Eucharistic Sacrifice.

"It is evident from the Scriptures that it is not the Christ, body, soul, and divinity hypostatically united, as the Papists also blasphemously teach, and from thence as blasphemously infer that it is to be worshipped. That which is *represented* in the Eucharist is neither the divinity nor the human soul of Christ, but only His Body and Blood separated from both and one another. . . . The Bread and Wine . . . are so full and perfect *representatives* thereof, that our Lord Himself thought fit to give to the Bread and Wine the *name* of His Body and Blood," *ibid.* p. 376.

3. If the Non-juring and Tractarian divinity may not be taken, as regards the Eucharist, as the measure of the nearest approximation of Anglicans to Rome, I do not know where to look for it; however, that the inquiry into it may be taken out of my hands, I will refer the decision to the exact Waterland. This writer, in a question of fact, surely may be trusted, and the more so, if, as I believe, he has been contradicted by no later authority. He writes thus :—

"That the Sacrament of the Eucharist, in whole or in part, in a sense proper or improper, is a Sacrifice of the Christian Church, is a point agreed upon among all knowing and sober divines; but the Romanists have so often and so grievously abused the once innocent names of *oblation, sacrifice, propitiation* . . . that the Protestants have been justly jealous, &c. . . . The general way, among both Lutheran and Reformed, has been to reject any proper propitiation or proper sacrifice in the Eucharist, admitting however of some kind of propitiation in a qualified sense, and of sacrifice also, but of a spiritual kind, and therefore styled improper or metaphorical. Nevertheless Mr. Mede, a very learned and judicious divine and Protestant, scrupled not to assert a proper sacrifice in the Eucharist (as he termed it), a material sacrifice, the sacrifice of Bread and Wine, analogous to the *Mincha* of the Old Law. This doctrine he delivered in the College Chapel, A.D. 1635, which was afterwards published with improvements, under the title of 'The Christian Sacrifice.'

"In the year 1642, the no less learned Dr. Cudworth printed his well-known treatise on the same subject, wherein he as plainly denies any proper, or any material sacrifice in the Eucharist, but admits of a symbolical feast upon a sacrifice, that is to say, upon the Grand Sacrifice itself, commemorated under certain symbols. This appears to have been the prevailing doctrine of our divines, both before and since. There can be no doubt of the current doctrine down to Mr. Mede; and as to what has most prevailed since" [i.e. from 1635 to 1737] "I need only refer to three eminent divines, who wrote in the years 1685, 1686, and 1638.

"In the year 1702, the very pious and learned Dr. Grabe published his Irenæus, and in his notes upon the author fell in with the sentiments of Mr. Mede, so far as concerns a proper and material sacrifice in the Eucharist; and after him our incomparably learned and judicious Bishop Bull, in an English treatise, gave great countenance to the same."—Vol. vii. pp. 341—343.

4. I will conclude with a passage from Mr. William Palmer's "Notes of a Visit to the Russian Church," in which he gives an account of Dr. Routh's virtual interpretation of the 31st Article, on occasion of his reading a comment of Mr. Palmer's on the xxxix., written in the same spirit as No. 90. This brings up the teaching of the Church of England upon it up to the year 1840.

"He had marked a passage," says Mr. Palmer, "in which I said of the Anglican Liturgy that in it, notwithstanding these changes, by which it now differs from the Roman, 'the Mystical Lamb is still truly immolated, and a sacrifice is offered propitiatory for the quick and for the dead.' Turning to his mark at this page, and pointing with his finger to the passage, he asked, 'What do you say to the Article, sir ?' I replied, 'Since this is certainly the doctrine of the Fathers, with which the English canon of 1571 required all preachers to agree,' &c., &c. . . . He repeated, ' I say nothing about the doctrine, sir, but what do *you* say to the *Article ?* ' " p. 45.

P.S.—Johnson, I should observe, brings out his theory of "offering" most clearly and completely at *Unbl. Sacr.* ch. ii. § 1, p. 214, where, as in other places, he insists on (what by itself utterly separates him from Catholics) that "the offering of the Body and Blood" is not only not "the substantial Body and Blood of Christ," but "much less His divinity."]

VIII.

DOCUMENTARY MATTER

CONSEQUENT UPON THE

FOREGOING REMARKS ON THE THIRTY-NINE ARTICLES.

DOCUMENTARY MATTER,
&c.

LETTER OF FOUR COLLEGE TUTORS.
To the Editor of the TRACTS FOR THE TIMES.

SIR,—Our attention having been called to No. 90 in the Series of "Tracts for the Times by Members of the University of Oxford," of which you are the Editor, the impression produced on our minds by its contents is of so painful a character, that we feel it our duty to intrude ourselves briefly on your attention.

This publication is entitled "Remarks on certain Passages in the Thirty-nine Articles;" and, as these Articles are appointed by the Statutes of the University to be the text-book for Tutors in their theological teaching, we hope that the situations we hold in our respective Colleges will secure us from the charge of presumption in thus coming forward to address you.

The Tract has in our apprehension a highly dangerous tendency from its suggesting that certain very important errors of the Church of Rome are not condemned by the Articles of the Church of England; for instance, that those Articles do not contain any condemnation of the doctrines, 1, of Purgatory; 2, of Pardons; 3, of the worship and adoration of Images and Relics; 4, of the Invocation of Saints; 5, of the Mass, as they are taught authoritatively by the Church of Rome, but only of certain absurd practices and opinions which intelligent Romanists repudiate as much as we do.

It is intimated, moreover, that the Declaration prefixed to the Articles, so far as it has any weight at all, sanctions this mode of interpreting them; as it is one which takes them in their "literal and grammatical sense," and does not "affix any new sense" to them.

The Tract would thus appear to us to have a tendency

to mitigate, beyond what charity requires, and to the prejudice of the pure truth of the Gospel, the very serious differences which separate the Church of Rome from our own; and to shake the confidence of the less learned members of the Church of England in the spiritual character of her formularies and teaching.

We readily admit the necessity of allowing that liberty in interpreting the formularies of our Church, which has been advocated by many of its most learned Bishops and other eminent divines; but this Tract puts forward new and startling views as to the extent to which that liberty may be carried. For if we are right in our apprehension of the Author's meaning, we are at a loss to see what security would remain, were his principles generally recognized, that the most plainly erroneous doctrines and practices of the Church of Rome might not be inculcated in the lecture-rooms of the University and from the pulpits of our Churches.

In conclusion we venture to call your attention to the impropriety of such questions being treated in an anonymous publication, and to express an earnest hope that you may be authorized to make known the writer's name. Considering how very grave and solemn the whole subject is, we cannot help thinking, that both the Church and the University are entitled to ask that some person, besides the printer and publisher of the Tract, should acknowledge himself as responsible for its contents. We are, Sir, your obedient, humble servants,

T. T. CHURTON, M.A.,
Vice-Principal and Tutor of Brasen-Nose College.

H. B. WILSON, B.D.,
Senior Tutor of St. John's College.

JOHN GRIFFITHS, M.A.,
Subwarden and Tutor of Wadham College.

A. C. TAIT,
Fellow and Senior Tutor of Balliol College.

OXFORD, *March* 8, 1841.

*Answer by the Author of Tract No. 90
to the above Letter.*

The Editor of the Tracts for the Times begs to acknowledge the receipt of the very courteous communication of Mr. Churton, Mr. Wilson, Mr. Griffiths, and Mr. Tait, and receives it as expressing the opinion of persons for whom he has much respect, and whose names carry great weight.

To the Rev. T. T. Churton, &c.

March 8, 1841.

At a meeting of the Vice-Chancellor, Heads of Houses, and Proctors, in the Delegates' Room, March 15, 1841.

Considering that it is enjoined in the STATUTES of this University, (TIT. iii. SECT. 2. TIT. ix. SECT. ii. § 3. SECT. v. § 3), that every student shall be instructed and examined in the Thirty-nine Articles, and shall subscribe to them; considering also that a Tract has recently appeared, dated from Oxford, and entitled "Remarks on certain Passages in the Thirty-nine Articles," being No. 90 of the Tracts for the Times, a series of Anonymous Publications purporting to be written by members of the University, but which are in no way sanctioned by the University itself;

RESOLVED, That modes of interpretation such as are suggested in the said Tract, evading rather than explaining the sense of the Thirty-nine Articles, and reconciling subscription to them with the adoption of errors, which they were designed to counteract, defeat the object, and are inconsistent with the due observance of the above-mentioned STATUTES.

P. WYNTER,
Vice-Chancellor.

[Promulgated March 16, 1841.]

*Letter of the Author of Tract No. 90
to the Vice-Chancellor.*

MR. VICE-CHANCELLOR.—I write this to inform you respectfully, that I am the author, and have the sole responsibility of the Tract, on which the Hebdomadal Board has just now expressed an opinion; and that I have not given my name hitherto, under the belief that it was desired I should not do so.

I hope it will not surprise you if I say, that my opinion remains unchanged of the truth and honesty of the principle maintained in the Tract, and of the necessity of putting it forth.

At the same time I am prompted by my feelings to express my deep consciousness, that everything I attempt might be done in a better spirit, and in a better way; and, while I am sincerely sorry for the trouble and anxiety I have given to the members of the Board, I beg to return my thanks to them for an act, which, even though founded on misapprehension, may be made as profitable to myself, as it is religiously and charitably intended.

I say all this with great sincerity, and am,
   Mr. VICE-CHANCELLOR,
    Your obedient servant,
      JOHN HENRY NEWMAN.

ORIEL COLLEGE, *March* 16, 1841.

IX.

A LETTER ADDRESSED TO

THE REV. R. W. JELF, D.D.,

CANON OF CHRIST CHURCH,

IN EXPLANATION OF THE NINETIETH TRACT

IN THE SERIES CALLED

THE TRACTS FOR THE TIMES.

1841.

A LETTER,

&c.

My dear Dr. Jelf,

I have known you so many years that I trust I may fitly address the present pages to you, on the subject of my recent Tract, without seeming to imply that one like yourself, who from circumstances has taken no share whatever in any of the recent controversies in our Church, is implicated in any approval or sanction of it. It is merely as a friend that I write to you, through whom I may convey to others some explanations which seem necessary at this moment.

Four Gentlemen, Tutors of their respective Colleges, have published a protest against the Tract in question. I have no cause at all to complain of their so doing, though as I shall directly say, I consider that they have misunderstood me. They do not, I trust, suppose that I feel any offence or soreness at their proceeding; of course I naturally think that I am right and they are wrong; but this persuasion is quite consistent both with my honouring their zeal for Christian truth and their anxiety for the welfare of our younger members, and with my very great consciousness that, even though I be right in my principle, I may have advocated truth in a wrong way. Such acts as theirs when done honestly, as they have done them, must benefit all parties, and draw them nearer to each other in good will, if not in opinion. But to proceed to the subject of this letter.

I propose to offer some explanation of the Tract in two respects,—as to the hypothesis on which it is written and as to its object.

2.

I. These Four Gentlemen, whom I have mentioned, have misunderstood me in so material a point, that it certainly is necessary to enter into the subject at some length. They consider that the Tract asserts that the Thirty-nine Articles

" do not contain any condemnation of the doctrines of Purgatory, of Pardons, of the Worship and Adoration of Images and Relics, of Invocation of Saints, of the Mass, as they are *taught authoritatively* by the Church of Rome, but only of certain absurd practices and opinions, which intelligent Romanists repudiate as much as we do."

On the contrary I consider that the Articles *do* contain a condemnation of the authoritative teaching of the Church of Rome on these points; I only say that, whereas they were written before the decrees of Trent, they were not directed against those decrees. The Church of Rome taught authoritatively before those decrees as well as since. Those decrees expressed her authoritative teaching, and they will continue to express it, while she so teaches. The simple question is, whether, taken by themselves in their mere letter, they express it; whether in fact other senses, short of the sense conveyed in the present authoritative teaching of the Roman Church will not fulfil their letter, and may not even now in point of fact be held in that Church.

As to the present authoritative teaching of the Church of Rome, to judge by what we see of it in public, I think it goes very far indeed to substitute another Gospel for the true one. Instead of setting before the soul the Holy Trinity, and heaven and hell; it does seem to me, as a popular system, to preach the Blessed Virgin and the Saints, and Purgatory.[1] If there ever was a system which required reformation, it is that of Rome at this day, or in other words (as I should call it) Romanism or Popery. Or, to use words in which I have only a year ago expressed myself, when contrasting Romanism with the teaching of the ancient Church,—

"In Antiquity, the main aspect in the economy of redemption contains Christ, the Son of God, the Author and Dispenser of all grace and pardon, the Church His living representative, the Sacraments her instruments, Bishops her rulers, their collective decisions her voice, and Scripture her standard of truth. In the Roman Schools we find St. Mary and the Saints the prominent objects of regard and dispensers of mercy, Purgatory or Indulgences the means of obtaining it, the Pope the ruler and teacher of the Church, and miracles the warrant of doctrine.[2] As to the doctrines of Christ's merits and eternal life and death, these are points not denied (God forbid), but taken for granted and passed by, in order to make way for others of more present, pressing, and lively interest. That a certain change then in objective and external religion has come over the Latin, nay, and in a measure over the Greek Church, we consider to be a plain historical fact; a change

[1] ["I had a great and growing dislike, after the summer of 1839, to speak against the Roman Church herself or her formal doctrines. I was very averse to speaking against doctrines, which might possibly turn out to be true, though at the time I had no reason for thinking they were; or against the Church, which had preserved them.... However, on occasions which demanded it, I felt it a duty to give out plainly all that I thought, though I did not like to do so. One such instance occurred, when I had to publish a Letter about Tract 90. In that Letter I said, 'Instead of setting before the soul,' &c." (as in the text). "On this occasion I recollect expressing to a friend the distress it gave me thus to speak; but I said, 'How can I help saying it, if I think it? and I *do* think it; my Bishop calls on me to say out what I think; and that is the long and the short of it.'"—*Apolog.* pp. 121—123.]

[2] [*Vid.* Note at the end of this Letter, p. 392, and on the whole subject of this Letter, *vid.* the answer given *supr.* in Preface to vol. i.]

.... sufficiently startling to recall to our minds, with very unpleasant sensations, the awful words, 'Though we, or an Angel from Heaven, preach any other gospel unto you, than that ye have received, let him be accursed.'"

3.

1. On the doctrine of Purgatory the received Romanism goes beyond the Decrees of Trent thus: the Council of Trent says,—

"There is a Purgatory, and the souls there detained are helped by the suffrages of the faithful, and especially by the acceptable sacrifice of the Altar."

This definition does not explain the meaning of the word Purgatory—and it is not incompatible with the doctrine of the Greeks;—but the Catechism of Trent, which expresses the existing Roman doctrine says,—

"There is a Purgatorial *fire*, in which the souls of the pious are *tormented* for a certain time, and expiated (expiantur) in order that an entrance may lie open to them into their eternal home, into which nothing defiled enters."

And the popular notions go very far beyond this, as the extracts from the Homilies, Jeremy Taylor, &c., in the Tract show.

2. Again, the doctrine of Pardons, is conveyed by the Divines of Trent in these words:—

"The use of Indulgences, which is most salutary to the Christian people, and approved by the authority of Councils, is to be retained in the Church;"

it does not explain what the word Indulgence means:— it is necessary to observe how very definite and how monstrous is the doctrine which Luther assailed.

3. Again, the Divines at Trent say that "to Images are to be paid due honour and veneration;" and to those who honour the sacred volume, pictures of friends and the like, as we all do, I do not see that these very words can of themselves afford matter of objection. Far other-

wise when we see the comment which the Church of Rome has put on them in teaching and practice. I consider its existing creed and popular worship to be as near idolatry as any portion of that Church can be, from which it is said that "the idols" shall be "utterly abolished."

4. Again, the Divines of Trent say that "it is good and useful suppliantly to invoke the saints ;" it does not even command the practice. But the actual honours paid to them in Roman Catholic countries are in my judgment, as I have already said, a substitution of a wrong object of worship for a right one.

5. Again, the Divines at Trent say that the Mass is "a sacrifice truly propitiatory :" words which (considering they add, " The fruits of the Bloody Oblation are through the Mass most abundantly obtained,—so far is the latter from derogating in any way from the former,") to my mind have no strength at all compared with the comment contained in the actual teaching and practice of the Church, as regards private masses.

This distinction between the words of the Tridentine divines and the authoritative teaching of the present Church, is made in the Tract itself, and would have been made in far stronger terms, had I not often before spoken against the actual state of the Church of Rome, or could I have anticipated the sensation which the appearance of the Tract has excited. I say there,—

" By 'the Romish doctrine' is not meant the Tridentine doctrine, because this article was drawn up before the decree of the Council of Trent. What *is* opposed is the *received doctrine of that day*, and *unhappily of this day too*, or the *doctrine of the Roman Schools.*"—§ 6.

This doctrine of the Schools is at present, on the whole, the established creed of the Roman Church, and this I call Romanism or Popery, and against this I think the Thirty-nine Articles speak. I think they speak, not of certain accidental practices, but of a *body* and *substance* of divinity, and that traditionary, an existing ruling spirit and view in the Church ; which, whereas it is a corruption and perversion of the truth, is also a very active and energetic principle, and, whatever holier manifestations there may be in the same Church, manifests itself in ambition, insincerity, craft, cruelty, and all such other grave evils as are connected with these.

Further, I believe that the decrees of Trent, though not necessarily in themselves tending to the corruptions which we see, yet considering these corruptions exist, will ever tend to foster and produce them, as if principles and elements of them—that is, while these decrees remain unexplained in any truer and more Catholic way.

4.

The distinction I have been making, is familiar with our controversialists. Dr. Lloyd, the late Bishop of Oxford, whose memory both you and myself hold in affection and veneration, brings it out strongly in a review which he wrote in the British Critic in 1825. Nay he goes further than anything I have said on one point, for he thinks the Roman Catholics are not what they once were, at least among ourselves. I pronounce no opinion on this point; nor do I feel able to follow his revered guidance in some other things which he says, but I quote him in proof that the Reformers did not aim at decrees or abstract dogmas, but against a living system, and a system which it is quite possible to separate from the formal statements which have served to represent it.

"Happy was it," he says, "for the Protestant controversialist, when his own eyes and ears could bear witness to the doctrine of Papal satisfactions and meritorious works, when he could point to the benighted wanderer, working his way to the shrine of our Lady of Walsingham or Ipswich, and hear him confess with his own mouth that he trusted to such works for the expiation of his sins; or when every eye could behold 'our churches full of images, wondrously decked and adorned, garlands and coronets set on their heads, precious pearls hanging about their necks, their fingers shining with rings, set with precious stones; their dead and still bodies, clothed with garments stiff with gold,' *Hom.* 3, *ag. Idol.*"—p. 97.

On the other hand he says,—

"Our full belief is that the Roman Catholics of the United Kingdom, from their long residence among Protestants, their disuse of processions and other Romish ceremonies, have been brought gradually and almost unknowingly to a more spiritual religion and a purer faith,—that they themselves see with sorrow the disgraceful tenets and principles that were professed and carried into practice by their forefathers,—and are too fond of removing this disgrace from them, by denying the former existence of these tenets, and ascribing the imputation of them to the calumnies of the Protestants. This we cannot allow; and while we cherish the hope that they are now gone for ever, we still assert boldly and fearlessly, that they did once exist."—p. 148.

Again,—

"That latria is due only to the Trinity, is continually asserted *in the Councils;* but the terms of dulia and hyperdulia, *have not been adopted or acknowledged by them in their public documents;* they are, however, *employed unanimously by all the best writers of the Romish Church*, and their use is maintained and defended by them."—p. 101.

I conceive that what "all the best writers" say is authoritative teaching, and a sufficient object for the censures conveyed in the Articles, though the decrees of Trent, taken by themselves, remain untouched.

"This part of the inquiry," [to define exactly the acts peculiar to the different species of worship] " however, is more theoretical than useful; and, as everything that can be said on it must be derived, *not from Councils*, but from *Doctors* of the Romish Church, whose authority would be called in question, it is not worth while to enter upon it now. And therefore, observing only that the *Catechism of Trent* still retains the term of *adoratio angelorum*, we pass on," &c.—p. 102.

Again :—

"On the question whether the Invocation of Saints, professed and practised by the Church of Rome, is idolatrous or not, our opinion is this; that in *the public formularies* of their Church, and even in the belief and practice of the best informed among them, there is *nothing of idolatry*, although, as we have said, we deem that practice altogether unscriptural and unwarranted; but we do consider the principles relating to the worship of the Virgin, calculated to lead in the end to positive idolatry; and we are well convinced, and we have strong grounds for our conviction, that a large portion of the lower classes are in this point guilty of it. Whether the Invocation of Angels or of Saints has produced the same effect, we are not able to decide."—p. 113.

I accept this statement entirely with a single explanation. By "principles" relating to the worship of the Blessed Virgin, I understand either the *received* principles as distinct from those laid down in the Tridentine statements; or the principles contained in those statements, viewed as *practically* operating on the existing feelings of the Church.

Again :—

"She [the Church of England] is unwilling to fix upon the *principles* of the Romish Church the charge of positive idolatry; and contents herself with declaring that 'the Romish doctrine concerning the Adoration as well of Images as of Relics, is a fond thing,' &c. &c. But in regard to the universal *practice* of the Romish Church, *she adheres to the declaration of her Homilies;* and professes her conviction that this fond and unwarranted and unscriptural doctrine has at all times produced, and will hereafter, as long as it is suffered to prevail, produce the sin of *practical* idolatry."—p. 121.

I will add my belief that the only thing which can stop this tendency in the decrees of Rome, as things are, is its making some formal declaration the other way.

Once more :—

"We reject the second [Indulgences] not only because they are

altogether unwarranted by any word of Holy Writ, and contrary to every principle of reason, but because we conceive the *foundations* on which they rest to be, in the highest degree, blasphemous and absurd. These *principles* are, 1. That the power of the Pope, great as it is, does not properly extend beyond the limits of this present world. 2. That the power which he possesses of releasing souls from Purgatory arises out of the treasure committed to his care, a treasure consisting of the supererogatory merits of our blessed Saviour, the Virgin, and the Saints. . . . . . This is the treasure of which Pope Leo, in his Bull of the present year, 1825, speaks in the following terms : ' We have resolved, in virtue of the authority given to us by Heaven, fully to unlock that sacred treasure, composed of the merits, sufferings, and virtues of Christ our Lord, and of His Virgin Mother, and of all the Saints, which the Author of human salvation has entrusted to our dispensation.' "
—p. 143.

This is what our Article means by Pardons; but it is more than is said in the Council of Trent.

5.

Dr. Lloyd is not the only writer who distinguishes between the doctrine and the practical teaching of Rome. Bramhall says,—

" A comprecation [with the Saints] both the Grecians and we do allow ; an ultimate invocation both the Grecians and we detest; so do the Church of Rome *in their doctrine*, but they vary from it in their practice."—*Works*, p. 418.

And Bull :—

" This Article [the Tridentine] of a Purgatory after this life, *as it is understood* and *taught* by the Roman Church (*that is*, to be a place and state of misery and torment, whereunto many faithful souls go presently after death, and there remain till they are thoroughly purged from their dross, or *delivered thence by Masses, Indulgences*, &c.) is contrary to Scripture, and the sense of the Catholic Church for at least the first four Centuries, &c."—*Corrupt. of Rom.* § 3.

And Wake :—

" The Council of Trent has spoken *so uncertainly* in this point [of Merits] as plainly shows that they in this did not know themselves,

what they would establish, or were unwilling that others should."
—*Def. of Expos.* 5.

I have now said enough on the point of distinction between the existing creed, or what the Gentlemen who signed the protest call the "authoritative teaching" of the Church of Rome, and its decrees on the matters in question. And while this distinction seems acknowledged by our controversialists, it is a *fact* ever to be insisted on, that our Articles were written *before* those decrees, and therefore are levelled not against them, but against the authoritative teaching.

6.

I will put the subject in another way, which will lead us to the same point. If there is one doctrine more than another which characterizes the present Church of Rome, and on which all its obnoxious tenets depend, it is the doctrine of its *infallibility*. Now I am not aware that this doctrine is anywhere embodied in its formal decrees. Here then is a critical difference between its decrees and its received and established creed. Any one who believed that the Pope and Church of Rome are the seat of the infallibility of the Catholic Church, ought to join their communion. If a person remains in our Church, he thereby disowns the infallibility of Rome—and is its infallibility a slight characteristic of the Romish, or Romanistic, or Papal system, by whatever name we call it? is it not, I repeat, that on which all the other errors of its received teaching depend?

The Four Gentlemen

"are at a loss to see what security would remain, were his [the Tract-writer's] principles generally recognized, that the most plainly erroneous doctrines and practices of the Church of Rome might not be inculcated in the lecture-rooms of the University and from the pulpits of our Churches."

Here is a doctrine, which could not enter our lecture-rooms and pulpits—Rome's infallibility—and if this is excluded, then also are excluded those doctrines which depend, I may say, solely on it, not on Scripture, not on reason, not on Antiquity, not on Catholicity. For who is it that gives the doctrine of Pardons their existing meaning which our Article condemns? The Pope; as in the words of Leo in 1825, as above quoted from Bishop Lloyd. Who is it that has exalted the honour of the Blessed Virgin into worship of an idolatrous character? The Pope; as when he sanctioned Bonaventura's Psalter.[3] In a word, who is the recognized interpreter of all the Councils but the Pope?

On this whole subject I will quote from a work, in which, with some little variation of wording, I said the very same thing four years ago without offence.

"There are in fact two elements in operation within the system. As far as it is Catholic and Spiritual, it appeals to the Fathers; as far as it is a corruption, it finds it necessary to supersede them. Viewed in its *formal principles* and authoritative statements, it professes to be the champion of past times; viewed as an active and political power, as a ruling, grasping, and ambitious principle, in a word, what is expressively called Popery, it exalts the will and pleasure of the existing Church above all authority, whether of Scripture or Antiquity, interpreting the one and disposing of the other by its absolute and arbitrary decree.... We must deal with her as we would towards a friend who is visited by derangement... she is her real self only in name.... Viewed as a practical system, its main tenet, which gives a colour to all its parts, is the Church's infallibility, as on the other hand the principle of that genuine theology out of which it has arisen is the authority of Catholic antiquity."—*On Romanism*, pp. 102-4.

---

[3] [This Psalter is not generally received as genuine. In the *Biographie Univ.* we are told "Il est douteux que ce dernier ouvrage (*le Psautier de la Vierge*) soit de S. Bonaventure." t. 5. p.89. The Venice Edition, 1751, speaks out, " Nemo sit qui nobis persuadeat, absurdum hoc Psalterium, quod vocant Majus, Bonaventuræ manu compositum fuisse," t. i. p. 131. Canisius, taking its genuineness for granted, makes a common-sense defence of it. *De Deip.* p. 592-3.]

7.

Nothing more then is maintained in the Tract than that Rome is *capable* of a reformation; its corrupt system indeed cannot be reformed; it can only be destroyed; and that destruction is *its* reformation. I do not think that there is anything very erroneous or very blameable in such a belief; and it seems to be a very satisfactory omen in its favour, that at the Council of Trent, such protests, as are quoted in the Tract, were entered against so many of the very errors and corruptions which our Articles and Homilies also condemn. I do not think it is any great excess of charity towards the largest portion of Christendom, to rejoice to detect such a point of agreement between them and us, as a joint protest against some of their greatest corruptions, though they in practice cherish them, and though there are still other points in which they differ from us. That I have not always consistently kept to this view in all that I have written, I am well aware; yet I have made very partial deviations from it.

I should not be honest if I did not add, that I consider our own Church, on the other hand, to have in it a traditionary system, as well as the Roman, beyond and beside the letter of its formularies, and to be ruled by a spirit far inferior to its own nature. And this traditionary system, not only inculcates what I cannot receive, but would exclude any difference of belief from itself. To this exclusive modern system, I desire to oppose myself; and it is as doing this, doubtless, that I am incurring the censure of the Four Gentlemen who have come before the public. I want certain points to be left open which they would close. I am not here speaking for myself in one way or another; I am not examining the scripturalness, safety, propriety, or expedience of the points in question; but I desire that it may not be supposed as utterly unlawful for such private Christians as feel they can do it with a clear conscience, to allow a comprecation with the Saints as Bramhall does, or to hold with Andrewes that, taking away the doctrine of Transubstantiation from the Mass, we shall have no dispute about the Sacrifice; or with Hooker to treat even Transubstantiation as an opinion which by itself need not cause separation; or to hold with Hammond that no General Council, truly such, ever did, or shall err in any matter of faith; or with Bull, that man was in a supernatural state of grace before the fall, by which he could attain to immortality, and that he has recovered it in Christ; or with Thorndike, that works of humiliation and penance are requisite to render God again propitious to those who fall from the grace of Baptism; or with Pearson that the Name of Jesus is no otherwise given under Heaven than in the Catholic Church.

8.

In thus maintaining that we have open questions, or as I have expressed it in the Tract "ambiguous formularies," I observe, first, that I am introducing no novelty. For instance, it is commonly said that the Articles admit both Arminians and Calvinists; the principle then is admitted, as indeed the Four Gentlemen, whose remonstrance I am meeting, themselves observe. I do not think it a greater latitude than this, to admit those who hold, and those who do not hold, the points of doctrine on which I have been dwelling.

Nor, secondly, can it be said that such an interpretation throws any uncertainty upon the primary and most sacred doctrines of our religion. These are consigned to the Creed; the Articles did not define them; they existed before the Articles; they are referred to in the Articles as existing *facts*, just as the broad Roman errors are referred to; but the decrees of Trent were drawn up after the Articles.

On these two points I may be allowed to quote what I said four years ago in a former Tract.

"The meaning of the Creed... is known; there is no opportunity for doubt here; it means but one thing, and he who does not hold that one meaning, does not hold it at all. But the case is different (to take an illustration) in the drawing up of a Political Declaration or a Petition to Parliament. It is composed by persons, differing in matters of detail, agreeing together to a certain point and for a certain end. Each narrowly watches that nothing is inserted to prejudice his own particular opinion, or stipulates for the insertion of what may rescue it. Hence general words are used, or particular words inserted, which by superficial inquirers afterwards are criticized as vague and indeterminate on the one hand, or inconsistent on the other; but in fact, they all have a meaning and a history, could we ascertain it. And if the parties concerned in such a document are legislating and determining for posterity, they are respective representatives of corresponding parties in the generations after them. Now the Thirty-nine Articles lie between these two, between a Creed and a mere joint Declaration; to a certain point they have one meaning, beyond that they have no one meaning. They have one meaning so far as they embody the doctrine of the Creed; they have different meanings, so far as they are drawn up by men influenced by the discordant opinions of the day."—*Tract* 82.[4]

9.

These two points—that our Church allows (1) a great diversity in doctrine, (2) except as to the Creed,—are abundantly confirmed by the following testimonies of Bramhall, Laud, Hall, Taylor, Bull, and Stillingfleet, which indeed go far beyond anything I have said.

For instance, Bull:—

"What next he [a Roman Catholic objector] saith concerning our notorious prevarication from the Articles of our Church, I do not perfectly understand. He very well knows, that all our Clergy doth still subscribe them: and if any man hath dared *openly to oppose* the

---

[4] [Vid. *supr.* pp. 187-8.]

declared sense of the Church of England in any one of those Articles he is liable to ecclesiastical censure, which would be more duly passed and executed, did not the divisions and fanatic disturbances, first raised and still fomented by the blessed emissaries of the Apostolic See, hinder and blunt the edge of our discipline. But possibly he intends that latitude of sense, which our Church, as an indulgent mother, allows her sons in some abstruser points, (such as Predestination, &c.) not particularly and precisely defined in her Articles, but in general words capable of an indifferent construction. If this be his meaning, this is so far from being a fault, that it is the singular praise and commendation of our Church. As for our being concluded by the Articles of our Church, if he means our being obliged to give our internal assent to everything delivered in them upon peril of damnation, it is confessed that few, yea none of us, that are well advised, will acknowledge ourselves so concluded by them, nor did our Church ever intend we should. For she professeth not to deliver all her Articles (all I say, for *some* of them are coincident with the *fundamental* points of Christianity) as essentials of faith, without the belief whereof no man can be saved; but only propounds them as a body of safe and pious principles, *for the preservation of peace to be subscribed*, and not openly contradicted by her sons. And therefore she requires subscription to them only from the Clergy, and not from the laity, who yet are obliged to acknowledge and profess all the fundamental Articles of the Christian faith, no less than the most learned Doctors. This hath often been told the Papists by many learned writers of our Church. I shall content myself (at present) only with two illustrious testimonies of two famous prelates. The late terror of the Romanists, Dr. Usher [Bramhall?], the most learned and reverend Primate of Ireland, thus expresseth the sense of the Church of England, as to the subscription required to the Thirty-nine Articles: 'We do not suffer any man to reject the Thirty-nine Articles of the Church of England at his pleasure, yet neither do we look upon them as essentials of saving faith, or legacies of Christ and His Apostles; but in a mean, as pious opinions, *fitted for the preservation of peace and unity; neither do we oblige any man to believe them*, but only not to contradict them.'

"So the excellent Bishop Hall, in his *Catholic Propositions*, (truly so called,) denieth, in general, that any Church can lawfully propose any Articles to her sons, besides those contained in the common rule of faith, to be believed under pain of damnation. His third proposition is this: 'The sum of the Christian faith are those principles of the Christian religion, and fundamental grounds and points of faith, which are undoubtedly contained and laid down in the canonical Scriptures, whether in express terms or by necessary consequence, and in the ancient Creeds universally received and allowed by the whole Church of God.' And then in the seventh and eighth Propositions, he speaks fully to our purpose :—Prop. 7: 'There are and may be many theological points, which are wont to be believed and maintained, and so may lawfully be, of this or that particular Church, or the Doctors thereof, or their followers, as godly doctrines and profitable truths, besides those other essential and main matters of faith, without any prejudice at all of the common peace of the Church.' Prop. 8: 'Howsoever it may be lawful for learned men and particular Churches to believe and maintain those probable or (as they may think) certain points of theological verities, yet *it is not lawful for them to impose and obtrude the same doctrines upon any Church or person*, to be believed and held, as upon the necessity of salvation; or to anathematize or eject out of the Church any person or company of men that think otherwise.'

"As for the fundamental principles of the Christian religion, undoubtedly delivered in the Scriptures, and allowed (except the Romanists, who have so affected singularity, as to frame to themselves a new Christianity) by the whole Church of God, they are by the consent of all Christians acknowledged to be contained in that called the Creed, or rule of faith.

"This rule of faith, and that also as it is more fully explained by the first General Councils, our Church heartily embraceth, and hath made a part of her Liturgy, and so hath obliged all her sons to make solemn profession thereof. To declare this more distinctly to your ladyship, our Church receiveth that which is called the Apostles' Creed, and enjoins the public profession thereof to all her sons in her daily Service. And if this Creed be not thought express enough fully to declare the sense of the Catholic Church in points of necessary belief, and to obviate the perverse interpretations of heretics, she receiveth also that admirable summary of the Christian faith, which is called the Nicene Creed, (but is indeed the entire ancient creed of the Oriental Churches, together with the necessary additional explications thereof, made by Fathers both of the Council of Nice against Arius, and the Council of Constantinople against Macedonius,) the public profession whereof she also enjoins all her sons (without any exception) to make in the Morning Service of every Sunday and holy day. This creed she professeth (consentaneously to her own principles) to receive upon this ground primarily, because she finds that the articles thereof may be proved by most evident testimonies of Scripture; although she deny not, that she is confirmed in her belief of this creed, because she finds all the articles thereof, in all ages, received by the Catholic Church."—*Vindication of the Church of England*, 27.

And Stillingfleet :—

"The Church of England makes no Articles of Faith, but such as have the testimony and approbation of the whole Christian world of all ages, and are acknowledged to be such by Rome itself, and in other things she requires *subscription* to them not as Articles of Faith, but as inferior Truths which she expects a submission to, *in order to her Peace and Tranquillity*. So the late learned L. Primate of Ireland [Bramhall] often expresseth the sense of the Church of England, as to her Thirty-nine Articles. 'Neither doth the Church of England,' saith he, 'define any of these questions, as necessary to be believed, either necessitate medii, *or* necessitate præcepti, which is much less; *but only bindeth her sons for peace sake, not to oppose them.*' And in another place more fully. 'We do not suffer any man to reject the Thirty-nine Articles of the Church of England at his pleasure; yet neither do we look upon them as Essentials of saving Faith, or Legacies of Christ and His Apostles : but in a mean, *as pious Opinions fitted for the preservation of Unity; neither do we oblige any man to believe them*, but only not to contradict them.' By which we see, what a vast difference there is between those things which are required by the Church of England, *in order to Peace;* and those which are imposed by the Church of Rome, as part of that Faith, *extra quam non est salus*, without the belief of which there is no salvation. In which she hath as much violated the Unity of the Catholic Church, as the Church of England by her Prudence and Moderation hath studied to preserve it."—*Grounds of Protestant Rel*. part i. chap. 11.

And Laud :—

"A. C. will prove the Church of England a Shrew, and such a Shrew. For in her Book of Canons she excommunicates every man, who shall hold anything contrary to any part of the said Articles. So A. C. But surely these are not the very words of the Canon nor perhaps the sense. Not the words; for they are : Whosoever shall affirm that the Articles are in any part superstitious or erroneous, &c. And perhaps not the sense. For it is one thing for a man to *hold an opinion privately within himself*, and another thing *boldly and publicly to affirm it.* And again, 'tis one thing to hold contrary to some part of an Article, which perhaps may be but in the manner of Expression, and another thing positively to affirm, that the Articles in any part of them are superstitious, and erroneous.—*On Tradition,* xiv. 2.

And Taylor :—

"I will not pretend to believe that those doctors who first framed the article, did all of them mean as I mean; I am not sure they did, or that they did not; but this I am sure, that they framed the words with much caution and prudence, and so as might abstain from grieving the contrary minds of differing men. . . . . . . It is not unusual for Churches, in matters of difficulty, to frame their articles so as *to serve the ends of peace,* and yet not to endanger truth, or to destroy liberty of improving truth, or a further reformation. And since there are so very many questions and opinions in this point, either all the Dissenters must be allowed to reconcile the article and their opinion, or must refuse her communion; which whosoever shall enforce, is a great schismatic and an uncharitable man. This only is certain, that to tie the article and our doctrine together, is an excellent art of peace, and a certain signification of obedience; and yet is a security of truth, and that just liberty of understanding, which, because it is only God's subject, is then sufficiently submitted to men, when we consent in the same form of words."—*Further Explic. Orig. Sin.* § 6.

The view of the Articles conveyed in these extracts evidently allows, as I have said above, of much greater freedom in the private opinions of individuals, subscribing them, than I have contended for.

10.

While I am on this subject, I will make this remark in addition:—That though I consider that the wording of the Articles is wide enough to admit persons of very different sentiments from each other in detail, provided they agree in some broad general sense of them—(for instance, as differing from each other whether or not there is *any* state of purification after death, or whether or not *any* addresses are allowable to Saints departed, provided they one and all condemn the Roman doctrine of Purgatory and of Invocation as actually taught and carried into effect) nevertheless I do not leave the Articles without their *one legitimate sense* in preference to all other senses. The only peculiarity of the view I advocate, if I must so call it, is this, that whereas it is usual at this day to make the particular *belief of their writers* their true interpretation, I would make the *belief of the Catholic Church* such. That is, as it is often said that infants are regenerated in Baptism, not on the faith of their *parents*, but of the *Church*, so in like manner I would say the Articles are received, not in the sense of their framers, but (as far as the wording will admit, or any ambiguity requires it,) in the one Catholic sense. For instance as to Purgatory, I consider (with the Homily) that the Article opposes the main idea really encouraged by Rome, that temporary punishment is a substitute for hell in the case of the unholy, and all the superstitions consequent thereupon. As to Invocation, that the Article opposes, not every sort of calling on beings short of God, (for certain passages in the Psalms do this) but all that *trenches on worship*, (as the Homily puts it,) the question whether *ora pro nobis* be such, being open—open, not indifferent, but a most grave and serious one for any individual who feels drawn to it, but still undecided by the Article. As to Images, the Article condemns all approach to idolatrous regard, such as Rome does in point of fact encourage. As to the Mass, all that impairs or obscures the doctrine of the one Atonement, once offered, which Masses, as observed in the Church of Rome, actually have done.

11.

II. And now, if you will permit me to add a few words more, I will briefly state *why* I am anxious about securing this liberty for us.

Every one sees his own portion of society; and, judging of a measure by its effect upon that portion, comes to a conclusion different from that of others about its utility, expedience, and propriety. That the Tract in question has been very inexpedient as addressed to one class of persons is quite certain; but it was meant for another, and I sincerely think is necessary for them. And in giving the reason, I earnestly wish even those who do not admit or feel it, yet to observe that I *had* a reason.

In truth there is at this moment a great progress of the religious mind of our Church to something deeper and truer than satisfied the last century. I always have contended, and will contend, that it is not satisfactorily accounted for by any particular movements of individuals on a particular spot. The poets and philosophers of the age have borne witness to it for many years. Those great names in our literature, Sir Walter Scott, Mr. Wordsworth, Mr. Coleridge, though in different ways and with essential differences one from another, and perhaps from any Church system, still all bear witness to it. Mr. Alexander Knox in Ireland bears a most surprising witness to it. The system of Mr. Irving is another witness to it. The age is moving towards something, and most unhappily the one religious communion among us which has of late years been practically in possession of this something, is the Church of Rome. She alone, amid all the errors and evils of her practical system, has given free scope to the feelings of awe, mystery, tenderness, reverence, devotedness, and other feelings which may be especially called Catholic. The question then is, whether we shall give them up to the Roman Church or claim them for ourselves, as we well may, by reverting to that older system, which has of late years indeed been superseded, but which has been, and is, quite congenial (to say the least), I should rather say proper and natural, or even necessary to our Church. But if we do give them up, then we must give up the men who cherish them. We must consent either to give up the men, or to admit their principles.

12.

Now, I say, I speak of what especially comes under my eye, when I express my conviction that this is a very serious question at this time. It is not a theoretical question at all. I may be wrong in my conviction, I may be wrong in the mode I adopt to meet it, but still the Tract is grounded on the belief that the Articles *need* not be so closed as the received method of teaching closes them, and *ought* not to be for the sake of many persons. If we will close them, we run the risk of subjecting persons whom we should least like to lose or distress, to the temptation of joining the Church of Rome, or to the necessity of withdrawing from the Church as established, or to the misery of subscribing with doubt and hesitation. And, as to myself, I was led especially to exert myself with reference to this difficulty, from having had it earnestly set before me by parties I revere, to do all I could to keep members of our Church from straggling in the direction of Rome ; and, as not being able to pursue the methods commonly adopted, and as being persuaded that the view of the Articles I have taken is true and honest, I was anxious to set it before them. I thought it would be useful to them without hurting any one else.

I have no wish or thought to do more than to claim an admission for these persons to the right of subscription. Of course I should rejoice if the members of our Church were all of one mind ; but they are not; and till they are, one can but submit to what is at present the will, or rather the chastisement of Providence. And let me now implore my brethren *to* submit, and not to force an agreement at the risk of a schism.

In conclusion, I will but express my great sorrow that I have at all startled or offended those for whom I have nothing but respectful and kind feelings. That I am startled myself in turn, that persons, who have in years past and present borne patiently disclaimers of the Athanasian Creed, or of the doctrine of Baptismal Regeneration, or of belief in many of the Scripture miracles, should now be alarmed so much, when a private Member of the University, without his name, makes statements in an opposite direction, I must also avow. Nor can I repent of what I have published. Still, whatever has been said, or is to be done in consequence, is, I am sure, to be ascribed to the most conscientious feelings; and though it may grieve me, I trust it will not vex me, or make me less contented and peaceful in myself.

Ever yours most sincerely,

J. H. N.

Saturday, March 13*th*, 1841.

P.S.—Since the above was in type, it has been told me that the Hebdomadal Board has already recorded its opinion about the Tract.

POSTSCRIPT.

I am led by circumstances, in order to explain the Tract more fully, to add,—

1. That I have most honestly stated in the above Letter what was intended, though not expressed in the Tract, about the actual dominant errors of the Church of Rome. The Tract was no *feeler*, as it is called, put forth to see how far one might go without notice, nor is the Letter a retractation. Those who are immediately about me, know that in the interval between the printing and publication of the Tract, I was engaged in writing some Letters about Romanism in which I spoke of the impossibility of any approach of the English towards the Roman Church, arising out of the present state of the latter, as strongly as I did a year ago, or as I do now in my Letter.

2. Again as to the object of my Pamphlet. I can declare most honestly that my reason for writing and publishing it, without which I should not have done it, and which was before my mind from first to last, was, as I have stated it in my Letter, the quieting the consciences of persons who considered (falsely as I think) that the Articles prevent them from holding views found in the Primitive Church. That while I was writing it, I was not unwilling to show that the Decrees of Trent were but partially, if at all, committed to certain popular errors, I fully grant; but even this I did with reference to others.

In explanation of the sensation which the Tract has caused (as far as it arises from the Tract itself), I observe,—

1. The Tract was addressed to one set of persons, and has been used and commented on by another.

2. As its Author had very frequently and lately entered his protest against many things in the Roman system, he did not see that it was necessary to repeat them, when that system did not form the direct object of the Tract; and the consciousness how strongly he had pledged himself against Rome, as it is, made him, as persons about him know full well, quite unsuspicious of the possibility of any sort of misunderstanding arising out of his statements in it.

3. Those who had happened to read his former publications, understanding him to *identify* rather than *connect* the Decrees of Trent with the peculiar Roman errors, were led perhaps to think, that in speaking charitably of those decrees he was speaking tenderly of those errors. And it must be confessed that, though he has uniformly maintained the existence of the errors in the Church of Rome both before and after the Tridentine Council, yet he has sometimes spoken of the decrees rather as the essential development, than the existing symbol and index of the errors.

4. There was, confessedly, a vagueness and deficiency in some places as to the conclusions he would draw from the premisses stated, and a consequent opening to the charge of a disingenuous understatement of the contrariety between the Articles and the actual Roman system. This arose in great measure from his being more bent on laying down his principle than defining its results.

5. It arose also from the circumstance that, the main drift of the Tract being that of illustrating the Articles from the *Homilies*, the doctrines of the Articles are sometimes brought out only so far as the Homilies explain them, which is in some cases an inadequate representation. I will add, moreover, 1. That in the expression "ambiguous Formularies," I did not think of referring to the

Prayer Book. And I suppose all persons will grant, that if the Articles treat of Predestination, and yet can be signed by Arminians and Calvinists, they are not clear on all points. But I gladly withdraw the phrase. And I express now, as I often have done before, my great veneration for those ancient forms of worship which, by God's good providence, are preserved to us.

2. That I did not mean at all to assert that persons called High Churchmen have a difficulty in holding Catholic principles consistently with a subscription to the Articles; on the contrary, I observe in the Tract, that "the objection" on this score "is groundless;" yet that there are many who have felt it, however causelessly, I know, and certainly *have* said.

3. That I had no intention whatever of implying that there are not many persons of Catholic views in our Church, and those more worthy of consideration than myself, who deny that the Reformers were uncatholic. I consider the question quite an open one.

4. That, in implying that certain modified kinds of Invocation, veneration of Relics, &c., might be Catholic, I did not mean to rule it, that they were so; but considered it an open question, whether they were or not, which I did not wish decided one way or the other, and which I considered the Articles left open. At the same time it is quite certain, that such practices as the Invocation of Saints, cannot justly be called Catholic in the same sense in which the doctrine of the Incarnation is, or the Episcopal principle.

5. That my mode of interpreting the Articles is not of a lax and indefinite character, but one which goes upon a plain and intelligible principle, viz., that of the Catholic sense; or, in the words of the Tract, "in the most Catholic sense they will admit."

Note on p. 369 of Letter to Dr. Jelf.

[As to the theological contrast presented to us on a comparison of the external aspect of primitive with that of modern Catholicity, I do not deny that, *primâ facie,* it exists, that is, in the eyes of a superficial observer, who passes through foreign countries on a tour, and learns about Antiquity, as for the most part he must learn about it, from patristical treatises. It is unfair to put side by side an every-day religion and a religion of books. Compare St. Augustine or St. Chrysostom with Bossuet or Lambertini, and Antioch or Carthage with Bruges or Naples, compare doctrine with doctrine and devotions with devotions, and, though a contrast between old times and modern times undoubtedly will remain, it will have lost much of its sharpness.

As to this day's Catholicity, it is strange that in the charges made in the foregoing Letter no notice is taken of the Sacraments, as one of the chief features of the modern as of the old Religion; and with the Sacraments, the sole channels of spiritual life, the Blessed Virgin has no concern whatever. Our Lord is the first and the last in these appointed means of grace. Surely Confessionals, not Images of Saints, are in a Catholic Church the "prominent dispensers of mercy;" and neither "Purgatory nor Indulgences" are within the Priest's jurisdiction. And, while every altar has in its crucifix the "prominent object of regard," so again in the perpetual Mass, in the abiding Sacramental Presence, and in Its Exposition and Benediction our Lord vindicates and exercises His prerogative of Sovereignty and loving Providence. It is true that there are additions to these primary elements in the popular Religion, but they are not more than additions; and though it is fair to object that they are dangerous additions, it is not true to say that they are substitutes.

So much on the popular Religion in the Catholic Church of this day; if we would have a view of that of the early times, we should turn to a paper of Cardinal Wiseman's, a review of a publication entitled "*A Voice from Rome.*" Some paragraphs from it shall here be given: [1]—

"We may imagine, if we please, some Persian gentleman of ancient days, going on his travels through Christian countries," [in the fourth or fifth century] "with that instinctive horror of idolatry and of worship through visible symbols, which becomes one accustomed to feed his piety only on the ethereal subtlety of the solar rays; most anxious to collect all possible evidence why he should not be a Christian. It is true, he understands very little of the languages of the countries through which he passes, and cannot be supposed to enter much into the habits, the ideas, and the feelings of their inhabitants, but, with the help of a dictionary, and a *valet de place,* he can make his way; and, at any rate, he can see what the people do, and read their books and inscriptions.

---

[1] *Vid.* Dublin Review, Dec. 1843, and Wiseman's Essays, vol. i. pp. 545—563.

"What place does Christ hold in their worship? How does God appear in relation to man? Surely, we could easily imagine him struck with the prominent place which the Martyrs occupy in all the worship, in the thoughts, and words and feelings of Christians; whether clergy or laity, learned or simple. Not a town does he come to, but he finds the Church, most frequented, nay, crowded by worshippers, to be that of some Martyr: while smaller oratories, in every direction, are favourite places of prayer, because they commemorate some other Saint, or contain a portion of his ashes. Not an altar does he see anywhere, which is not consecrated by their relics. Before them hang lamps, garlands, and votive offerings; around them are palls of silk and richer stuffs; their shrines are radiant with gold and jewels; the pavement of the temple is covered with prostrate suppliants, with the sick and afflicted, come to ask health and consolation from Christ's servant. The pilgrim from afar scrapes with simple faith some of the dust from the floor or from the tomb; the preacher, ay, a Basil or a Gregory, or a Chrysostom, or an Ambrose, instead of cooling their fervour, adds confidence, earnestness and warmth to it by a glowing and impassioned discourse in its favour. And if he afterwards goes and interrogates these holy men he receives some such answer as this: 'What! will you not reverence, but rather contemn those by whom evil spirits are expelled, and diseases cured; who appear in visions and foretell in prophecy; whose very bodies, if touched &c., the drops of whose blood,' &c., (Greg. Naz. Orat. t. 1. p. 76) . . . . . Again, he looks about him. At Antioch, he finds the Church of St. Barlaam richly decorated with paintings; but all representing the life and death of a Saint; Christ is introduced, but as if in illustration or by chance into the picture. At Nola he finds a magnificent basilica, literally covered with mosaics and inscriptions, full of the praises of Saints, and especially Martyrs. At Rome he sees the basilicas of the Apostles, of St. Laurence and others, adorned with similar encomiastic verses . . . . If he descends into the catacombs, the favourite retreat of devout Christians, what does he find? Martyrs everywhere, their tombs hallow each maze of those sacred labyrinths and form the altar of every chapel. Their effigies and praises cover the walls, prayers for their intercession are inscribed on their tablets. He goes into the houses of believers; memorials of the Saints everywhere. Their cups and goblets are adorned with their pictures; for one representation of Our Saviour, he finds twenty of the Blessed Virgin, or of St. Agnes, or St. Laurence, or the Apostles Peter and Paul . . . .

"Let any one take the trouble to read any of the miracles recorded by St. Augustine, &c. . . . Take for instance, the history which he gives of a certain poor tailor at Hippo, &c. . . . " There was a man at Calama of high rank, named Martial, advanced in years, &c., &c.

"On entering the convent, Gregory Nyssen found his sister very ill in her cell; instead of a bed, she lay upon a plank upon the ground, with another for her pillow," &c.]

X.

A LETTER ADDRESSED TO

THE RIGHT REVEREND FATHER IN GOD,

RICHARD, LORD BISHOP OF OXFORD,

ON OCCASION OF THE NINETIETH TRACT

IN THE SERIES CALLED

THE TRACTS FOR THE TIMES.

1841.

A LETTER,

&c.

My dear Lord,

It may seem strange that, on receipt of a message from your Lordship, I should proceed at once, instead of silently obeying it, to put on paper some remarks of my own on the subject of it; yet, as you kindly permit me to take such a course with the expectation that I may thereby succeed in explaining to yourself and others my own feelings and intentions in the occurrence which has given rise to your interposition, I trust to your Lordship's indulgence to pardon me any discursiveness in my style of writing, or appearance of familiarity, or prominent introduction of myself, which may be incidental to the attempt.

Your Lordship's message is as follows: That you consider that the Tract No. 90 in the Series called the Tracts for the Times, is "objectionable, and may tend to disturb the peace and tranquillity of the Church," and that it is your Lordship's "advice that the Tracts for the Times should be discontinued."

Your Lordship has, I trust, long known quite enough of my feelings towards any such expression of your Lordship's wishes to be sure I should at once obey it, though it were ever so painful to me, or contrary to the course I should have taken if left to myself. And I do most readily and cheerfully obey you in this instance; and at the same time I express my great sorrow that any writing of mine should be judged objectionable by your Lordship, and of a disturbing tendency, and my hope that in what I write in future I shall be more successful in approving myself to your Lordship.

I have reminded your Lordship of my willingness on a former occasion to submit myself to any wishes of your Lordship, had you thought it advisable at that time to signify them. In your Charge in 1838, an allusion was made to the Tracts for the Times. Some opponents of the Tracts said that your Lordship treated them with undue indulgence. I will not imply that your Lordship can act otherwise than indulgently to any one, but certainly I did feel at the time, that in the midst of the kindness you showed to me personally, you were exercising an anxious vigilance over my publication, which reminded me of my responsibility to your Lordship. I wrote to the Archdeacon on the subject, submitting the Tracts entirely to your Lordship's disposal. What I thought about your Charge will appear from the words I then used to him. I said, "A Bishop's lightest word *ex Cathedrâ*, is heavy. His judgment on a book cannot be light. It is a rare occurrence." And I offered to withdraw any of the Tracts over which I had control, if I was informed which were those to which your Lordship had objections. I afterwards wrote to your Lordship to this effect: that "I trusted I might say sincerely, that I should feel a more lively pleasure in knowing that I was submitting myself to your Lordship's expressed judgment in a matter of that kind, than I could have even in the widest circulation of the volumes in question." Your Lordship did not think it necessary to proceed to such a measure, but I felt and always have felt, that, if ever you determined on it, I was bound to obey.

Accordingly on the late occasion, as soon as I heard that you had expressed an unfavourable opinion of Tract

90, I again placed myself at your disposal, and now readily submit to the course on which your Lordship has finally decided in consequence of it. I am quite sure that in so doing I am not only fulfilling a duty I owe to your Lordship, but consulting for the well-being of the Church and benefiting myself.

And now, in proceeding to make some explanations in addition, which your Lordship desires of me, I hope I shall not say a word which will seem like introducing discussion before your Lordship. It would ill become me to be stating private views of my own, and defending them, on an occasion like this. If I allude to what has been maintained in the Tracts, it will not be at all by way of maintaining it in these pages, but in illustration of the impressions and the drift with which they have been written. I need scarcely say they are thought by many to betray a leaning towards Roman Catholic error, and a deficient appreciation of our own truth; and your Lordship wishes me to show that these apprehensions have no foundation in fact. This I propose to do, and that by extracts from what I have before now written on the subject, which, while they can be open to no suspicion of having been provided to serve an occasion, will, by being now cited, be made a second time my own.

2.

11. First, however, I hope to be allowed to make one or two remarks by way of explaining some peculiarities in the Tracts which at first sight might appear, if not to tend toward Romanism, at least to alienate their readers from that favoured communion in which God's good providence has placed us.

I know it is a prevalent idea, and entertained by persons of such consideration that it cannot be lightly treated, that many of the Tracts are the writing of persons who either are ignorant of what goes on in the world, and are gratifying their love of antiquarian research or of intellectual exercise at any risk; or, who are culpably reckless of consequences, or even find a satisfaction in the sensation or disturbance which may result from such novelties or paradoxes as they may find themselves in a condition to put forward. It is thought, that the writers in question often have had no aim at all in what they have hazarded, that they did not mean what they said, that they did not know the strength of their own words, and that they were putting forth the first crude notions which came into their minds; or that they were pursuing principles to their consequences as a sort of pastime, and developing their own theories in grave practical matters, in which no one should move without a deep sense of responsibility. In fact, that whatever incidental or intrinsic excellence there may be in the Tracts, and whatever direct or indirect benefits have attended them, there is much in them which is nothing more or less than mischievous, and convicts its authors of a wanton inconsiderateness towards the feelings of others.

I am very far from saying that there is any one evil temper or motive which may not have its share in anything that I write myself; and it does not become me to deny the charge as far as it is brought against me, though I am not conscious of its justice. But still I would direct attention to this circumstance, that what persons who are not in the position of the writers of the Tracts set down to wantonness, may have its definite objects, though those objects be not manifest to those who are in other positions. I am not maintaining that those objects are real, or important, or defensible, or pursued wisely or seasonably; but if they exist in the mind of the writers, I trust they will serve so far as to relieve them from the odious charge of scattering firebrands about without caring for or apprehending consequences.

May I then, without (as I have said) at all assuming e soundness of the doctrines to be mentioned, or by mentioning them seeking indirectly a sanction for them from your Lordship, be allowed to allude to one or two Tracts, merely in illustration of what I have said?

3.

One of the latest Tracts is written upon "The Mysticism attributed to the Early Fathers of the Church." It discusses the subject of the mystical interpretation of nature and Scripture with a learning and seriousness which no one will wish to deny; but the question arises, and has actually been asked, why discuss it at all? why startle and unsettle the Christian of this age by modes of thought which are now unusual and strange; and which being thus fixed upon the Fathers, serve but to burden with an additional unpopularity an authority which the Church of England has ever revered, ever used in due measure in behalf of her own claims upon the loyalty of her children? But the state of the case has been this. For some years the argument in favour of our Church drawn from Antiquity has been met by the assertion, that that same Antiquity held also other opinions which no one now would think of maintaining; that if it were mistaken in one set of opinions, it might be in the other; that its mistakes were of a nature which argued feebleness of intellect, or unsoundness of judgment, or want of logical acumen in those who held them, which would avail against its authority in the instances in which it was used, as well as in those in which it had been passed over. Moreover it was said that those who used it in defence of the Church knew this well, but were not honest enough to confess it. They were challenged to confess or deny the charges thus brought against the Fathers; and, since to deny the fact was supposed impossible, they were bid to draw out a case, such, as either would admit of a defence of the fact on grounds of reason, or of its surrender without surrendering the authority of the Fathers altogether.

Such challenges, and they have not been unfrequent, afford, I conceive, a sufficient reason for any one who considers that the Church of England derives essential assistance from Christian Antiquity in her interpretation of Scripture, to enter upon the examination of the particular objections by which certain authors have assailed its authority. Yet it is plain that by those who had not heard of the writings of these persons, such an examination would be considered a wanton mooting of points which no one had called in question.

4.

Again, much animadversion has been expressed, and in quarters which claim the highest deference, upon the Tract upon "Reserve in Communicating Religious Knowledge." Yet I do not think it will be called a wanton exercise of ingenuity. Not only does it bear marks, which no reader can mistake, of deep earnestness, but it in fact originated in a conviction in the mind of the writer of certain actual moral evils at present resulting from the defective appreciation which the mass of even religious men have of the mysteries and privileges of the Gospel.

And another Tract, which has experienced a great deal of censure, is that which is made up of Selections from the Roman Breviary. I will not here take upon me to say a word in its defence, except to rescue its author from the charge of wantonness. He had observed what a very powerful source of attraction the Church of Rome possessed in her devotional Services, and he wished, judiciously or not, to remove it by claiming it for ourselves. He was desirous of showing, that such Devotions would be but a continuation in private of those public Services which we use in Church ; and that they might be used by individuals with a sort of fitness, (removing such portions as were inconsistent with the Anglican creed or practice,) *because* they were a continuation. He said, in the opening of the Tract,—

"It will be attempted to wrest a weapon out of our adversaries' hands; who have in this, as in many other instances, appropriated to themselves a treasure which was ours as much as theirs. . . . It may suggest . . . . character and matter for our private devotions, over and above what our Reformers have thought fit to adopt into our public Services; a use of it which will be but carrying out and completing what they have begun."—*Tract* 75.

I repeat it, that I have no intention here of defending the proceeding except from the charge of wantonness; and with that view I would add, that though there is a difference not to be mistaken between a book published by authority and an anonymous Tract, yet, as far as its object is concerned, it is not very unlike Bishop Cosin's Hours of Prayer, of which I hope I may be permitted to remind your Lordship in the words of the recent Editor.

"At the first coming of the Queen Henrietta into England, she and her French ladies, it appears, were equally surprised and dissatisfied at the disregard of the hours of Prayer, and the want of Breviaries. Their remarks, and perhaps the strength of their arguments, and the beauty of many of their books, induced the Protestant ladies of the household to apply to King Charles. The King consulted Bishop White as to the best plan of supplying them with Forms of Prayer, collected out of already approved Forms. The Bishop assured him of the ease and the great necessity of such a work, and chose Cosin as the fittest person to frame the Manual. He at once undertook it, and in three months finished it and brought it to the King. The Bishop of London (Mountain), who was commanded to read it over and make his report, is said to have liked it so well, that instead of employing a Chaplain as was usual, he gave it an "*imprimatur*" under his own hand. There were at first only two hundred copies printed. There was, as Evelyn tells us, nothing of Cosin's own composure, nor any name set as author to it, but those necessary prefaces, &c., touching the times and seasons of Prayer, all the rest being entirely translated and collected out of an Office published by authority of Queen Elizabeth and out of our own Liturgy. 'This,' adds Evelyn, 'I rather mention to justify that industrious and pious Dean, who had exceedingly suffered by it, as if he had done it of his own head to introduce Popery, from which no man was more averse, and who was one who, in this time of temptation and apostasy, held and confirmed many to our Church.'

"The book soon grew into esteem, and justified the judgment which had been passed upon it, so that many who were at first startled at the title, 'found in the body of it so much piety, such regular forms of divine worship, such necessary consolations in special exigencies, that they reserved it by them as a jewel of great price and value.' 'Not one book,' it was said, 'was in more esteem with the Church of England, next to the Office of the Liturgy itself.' It appears, in fact, to have become exceedingly popular, and ran through ten editions, the last of which was published in 1719." *Preface to Cosin's Devotions,* p. xi—xiii.

5.

III. There has been another, and more serious peculiarity in the line of discussion adopted in the Tracts, which, whatever its merits or demerits, has led to their being charged, I earnestly hope groundlessly, with wanton innovation on things established. I mean the circumstance that they have attempted to defend our Ecclesiastical system upon almost first principles. The immediate argument for acquiescing in what is established is that it *is* established: but when what has been established is in course of alteration, (and this evil was partly realized, and feared still more, eight years since,) the argument ceases, and then one is driven to considerations which are less safe because less investigated, which it is impossible at once to survey in all their bearings, or to use with a sure confidence that they will not do a disservice to the cause for which they are adduced rather than a benefit. It seemed safe at the period in question, when the immediate and usual arguments failed, to recur to those which were used by our divines in the seventeenth century, and by the most esteemed writers in the century which followed, and down to this day. But every existing establishment, whatever be its nature, is a *fact*, a thing *sui simile*, which cannot be resolved into any one principle, nor can be defended and built up upon one idea. Its position is the result of a long history, which has moulded it and stationed it in the form and place which characterize it. It has grown into what it is by the influence of a number of concurrent causes in time past, and in consequence no one fundamental truth can be urged in its defence, but what in some other respect or measure may also possibly admit of being urged against it. This applies, I conceive, as to other social institutions, so to the case of our religious establishment and system at this day. It is a matter of extreme difficulty and delicacy, to say the least, so to defend them in an argumentative discussion in one respect as not to tend to unsettle them in another. And none but minds of the greatest powers, or even genius, will find it possible, if they do attempt it, to do more than to strike a balance between gain and loss, and to aim at the most good on the whole.

6.

I must not be misunderstood, in thus speaking, as if I meant to justify to your Lordship certain consequences which have followed under the circumstances from the attempts of the Tracts for the Times in defence of the Church. I do but wish to show that, even if evil has resulted, it need not have been wanton evil. Nor am I at all insinuating, that our established system is necessarily in fault, because it was exposed to this inconvenience; rather, as I have said, the cause lies in the nature of things, abstract principles being no sufficient measure of matters of fact. There cannot be a clearer proof of this than will be found in a reference to that antagonist system, which it has been the object of the Tracts in so great a measure to oppose. The case of Rome and her defenders is not parallel to that between the Tracts and our own Church, of course; it would be preposterous so to consider it; but it may avail as an *à fortiori* argument, considering how systematic and complete the Roman system is, and what transcendent ability is universally allowed to Bossuet. Yet even Bossuet, so great a controversialist, could not defend Romanism, so perfect a system, without doing a harm while he did a service. At least we may fairly conclude, that what the authorities of the Church of Rome thought to be a disservice to it, really was so at the time, though in the event it might prove a benefit. Dr. Maclaine in a note on his translation of Mosheim, observes of Bossuet's Exposition: "It is remarkable that nine years passed before this book could obtain the Pope's approbation. Clement X. refused it positively. Nay, several Roman Catholic Priests were rigorously treated and severely persecuted for preaching the doctrine contained in the Exposition of Bossuet, which was moreover formally condemned by the University of Louvain in the year 1685, and declared to be scandalous and pernicious. The Sorbonne also disavowed the doctrine contained in that book." (Vol. v. p. 126.)[1]

I am not presuming to draw an illustration from the history of Bossuet, except as regards his intention and its result. No one can accuse him of wantonness. What happened to him in spite of great abilities, may happen to others in defect of them.

---

[1] [These statements of Maclaine's like others which he makes will not bear examination; *vid. supr.* p. 116 note, and also the Catholic Institute's edition of Bossuet's Exposition, in the Introduction to which Maclaine is refuted point by point.]

7.

Several obvious illustrations may be given from the controversies to which the Tracts for the Times have given rise. Much attention, for instance, has of late years been paid by learned men to the question of the origin of our public Services. The Tracts have made use of the results of their investigations with a view of exalting our ideas of the sacredness of our Eucharistic Rite; but in proportion as they have brought to view what may be truly called an awful light resting on its component parts, they have revealed also that those parts have experienced some change in their disposition and circumstances by the hand of time; and accordingly, the higher is the appreciation which those Tracts tend to create in the minds of their readers of the substance of the Service, the greater regret do they also incidentally inspire of necessity, were it ever so far from their aim, that any external causes should have had a part in determining the shape in which we at this day receive it. The effect then has been greatly to raise our reverence towards the whole, yet to fling around that reverence somewhat of a melancholy feeling. I am not defending either process or result, but showing how good and evil have gone together.

Again, as regards the doctrine of Purgatory, that the present Roman doctrine was not Catholically received in the first ages, is as clear as any fact of history. But there is an argument which Roman controversialists use in its favour, founded on a fact of very early Antiquity, the practice of praying for the faithful departed. To meet this objection, the Tracts gave a reprint of Archbishop Ussher's chapter on the subject in his Answer to a Jesuit, in which he shows that the objects of those prayers were very different from those which the Roman doctrine of Purgatory requires. Thus the argument against us is effectually overthrown, but at the expense of incidentally bringing to light a primitive practice confessedly uncongenial to our present views of religion. In other words, if the Churchman is by the result of the discussion confirmed against Romanism, he has also been incidentally, and for the moment, (I cannot deny it,) unsettled in some of his existing opinions.

Or again, the charge brought against the defenders of Baptismal Regeneration has commonly been, that such a doctrine explained away regeneration, and made a mere name and a shadow of that gift of which Scripture speaks so awfully. We answer, "So far from it, every one is in a worse condition for being regenerate, if he is not in a better. If he resist the grace he has received, it is a burden to him, not a blessing. He cannot take it for granted, that all is right with his soul, and think no more about it; for the gift involves responsibilities as well as privileges." And thus, while engaged in maintaining the truth, that all Christians are in a covenant of grace, we incidentally elicit the further truth, that sin after Baptism is a heavier matter than sin before it; or, in maintaining the doctrine of Baptismal Regeneration, we introduce the doctrine of formal Repentance. We fortify our brethren in one direction; and may be charged with unsettling them in another.

Or again, in defending such doctrines and practices of the Church as Infant Baptism or the Episcopal Succession, the Tracts have argued that they rested on substantially the same basis as the Canon of Scripture, viz. the testimony of ancient Christendom. But to those who think this basis weak, the argument becomes a disparagement of the Canon, not a recommendation of the Creed.

My Lord, I have not said a word to imply that this disturbing and unsettling process is indissolubly connected with argumentative efforts in defence of our own system.

I only say that the good naturally runs into the evil; and so, without entering into the question whether or how they might have been kept apart in the Tracts, I am accounting for what looks like wantonness, yet I trust is not.

8.

And perhaps I may be permitted to add, that our difficulties are much increased in a place like this, where there are a number of persons of practised intellects, who with or without unfriendly motives are ever drawing out the ultimate conclusions in which our principles result, and forcing us to affirm or deny what we would fain not consider or not pronounce upon. I am not complaining of this as unfair to us at all, but am showing that we may at times have said extreme things, and yet not from any wanton disregard of the feelings and opinions of others. The appeal is made to reason, and reason has its own laws, and does not depend on our will to take the more or less; and this is not less the case as regards the result, even though it be false reason which we follow, and our conclusions be wrong from our failing to detect the counteracting considerations which would avert the principles we hold from the direction in which we pursue them. And a conscientious feeling sometimes operates to keep men from concealing a conclusion which they think they see involved in their principles, and which others see not; and moreover a dread of appearing disingenuous to others, who are directing their minds to the same subjects.

An instance has occurred in point quite lately as regards a subject introduced into Tract 90, which I am very glad to have an opportunity of mentioning to your Lordship. I have said in the Postscript of a Letter which I have lately addressed to Dr. Jelf, that the "vagueness and deficiency" of some parts of the Tract, in the conclusions drawn from the premisses stated, arose in great measure from the author's being "more bent on laying down his principle than defining its results." In truth I was very unwilling to commit the view of the Articles which I was taking, to any precise statement of the ultimate approaches towards the Roman system allowed by our own. To say *how far* a person may go, is almost to tempt him to go up to the boundary-line. I am far from denying that an evil arose from the vagueness which ensued, but the vagueness arose mainly from this feeling. Accordingly I left, for instance, the portion which treated of the Invocation of Saints without any definite conclusion at all, after bringing together various passages in illustration. However, friends and opponents discovered that my premisses required, what I was very unwilling to state categorically, for various reasons, that the *ora pro nobis* was not on my showing necessarily included in the Invocation of Saints which the Article condemns. And in my Letter to Dr. Jelf, I have been obliged to declare this (viz., that the lawfulness of this invocation was an open question,) under a representation made to me that to pass it over would be considered disingenuous. I avail myself, however, of the opportunity which this Letter to your Lordship affords me, without any suggestion, as your Lordship knows, from yourself, or from any one else, to state as plainly as I can, lest my brethren should mistake me, my great apprehension concerning the use even of such modified invocations.[2] Every feeling which interferes with God's sovereignty in our hearts, is of an idolatrous nature; and, as men are tempted to idolize their rank and substance, or their talent, or their children, or themselves, so may they easily be led to substitute the thought of Saints and Angels for the one

---

[2] [I have said in a private letter of 1845, *Apolog.*, p. 231, "Invocations are not required in the Church of Rome; somehow, I do not like using them except under the sanction of the Church, and this makes me unwilling to admit them in members of our Church."]

supreme idea of their Creator and Redeemer, which should fill them. It is nothing to the purpose to urge the example of such men as St. Bernard in defence of such invocations. The holier the man, the less likely are they to be injurious to him; but it is another matter entirely when ordinary persons do the same. There is much less of awe and severity in the devotion which rests upon created excellence as its object, and worldly minds will gladly have recourse to it, to be saved the necessity of lifting up their eyes to their Sanctifier and Judge. And the multitude of men are incapable of many ideas; one is enough for them, and if the image of a Saint is admitted into their heart, he occupies it, and there is no room for Almighty God. And moreover there is the additional danger of *presumptuousness* in addressing Saints and Angels; by which I mean cases when men do so from a sort of curiosity, as the heathen might feel towards strange and exciting rites of worship, not with a clear conscience and spontaneously, but rather with certain doubts and misgivings about its propriety, and a secret feeling that it does not become them, and a certain forcing of themselves in consequence.

9.

IV. Unless your Lordship had ordered me to speak my mind on these subjects, I should feel that in these reflections I was adopting a tone very unlike that which becomes a private Clergyman addressing his Diocesan; but, encouraged by the notion that I am obeying your wishes, I will proceed in what I feel it very strange to allow myself in, though I do so. And, since I have been naturally led into the subject of Romanism, I will continue it, and explain the misapprehension which has been widely entertained of my views concerning it.

I do not wonder that persons who happen to fall upon certain portions of my writings and them only, and who in consequence do not understand the sense in which I use certain words and phrases, should think that I explain away the differences between the Roman system and our own, which I hope I do not. They find in what I have written, no abuse, at least I trust not, of the individual Roman Catholic, nor of the Church of Rome, viewed abstractedly as a Church. I cannot speak against the Church of Rome, viewed in her formal character as a true Church, since she is "built upon the foundation of the Apostles and Prophets, Jesus Christ Himself being the chief Corner-stone." Nor can I speak against her private members, numbers of whom, I trust, are God's people, in the way to Heaven, and one with us in heart, though not in profession. But what I have spoken, and do strongly speak against is, that energetic system and engrossing influence in the Church, *through which* she acts towards us, and meets our eyes, like a cloud filling her extent, to the eclipse of all that is holy, whether in her ordinances or her members. This system I have called in what I have written, Romanism or Popery, and by Romanists or Papists I mean all her members, so far as they are under the power of these principles; and, while and so far as this system exists, and it does exist now as fully as heretofore, I say that we can have no peace with that Church, however we may secretly love her particular members. I cannot speak against her private members; I should be doing violence to every feeling of my nature if I did, and your Lordship would not require it of me. I wish from my heart we and they were one; but we cannot, without a sin, sacrifice truth to peace; and, in the words of Archbishop Laud, "till Rome be other than it is," we must be estranged from her.

This view which, not inconsistently, I hope, with our

chief divines, I would maintain against the Roman errors, seems to me to allow at once of zeal for the truth, and charity towards individuals and towards the Church of Rome herself. It presents her under a twofold aspect, and while recognizing her as an appointment of God on the one hand, it leads us practically to shun her, as beset with heinous and dangerous influences on the other. It is drawn out in the following extracts, under which I have thought it best to set it before your Lordship, rather than in statements made for the occasion, for the reason I have given above. I think they will serve to show, consistently with those which I made in my Letter to Dr. Jelf, both the real and practical stand I would make against Romanism, yet the natural opening there is for an unfounded suspicion that I feel more favourably towards it than I do.

10.

I have said in my Lectures on the Prophetical Office of the Church,—

"Our controversy with Romanists turns more upon facts than upon first principles; with Protestant sectaries it is more about principles than about facts. This general contrast between the two religions, which I would not seem to extend beyond what the sober truth warrants, for the sake of an antithesis, is paralleled in the common remark of our most learned controversialists, that Romanism *holds the foundation*, or *is the truth overlaid with corruptions*," &c. &c.[3]

Again,—

"I have been speaking of Romanism, not as an existing political sect among us, but considered in itself, in its abstract system, and in a state of quiescence. Viewed indeed in action, and as realized in its present partisans, it is but one out of the many denominations which are the disgrace of our age and country. In temper and conduct it does but resemble that unruly Protestantism which lies on our other side," &c. &c.[4]

---

[3] *Vid.* the passage, *supr.* in vol. i. pp. 40—43.
[4] *Supr.* vol. i. pp. 44, 45.

And again,—

"They profess to appeal to primitive Christianity; we honestly take their ground, as holding it ourselves; but when the controversy grows animated, and descends into details, they suddenly leave it, and desire to finish the dispute on some other field. In like manner in their teaching and acting, they begin as if in the name of all the Fathers at once, but will be found in the sequel to prove, instruct, and enjoin, simply in their own name," &c. &c.[5]

In the following passage the Anglican and Roman systems are contrasted with each other.

"Both we and Romanists hold that the Church Catholic is unerring in its declarations of Faith, or saving doctrine; but we differ from each other as to what is the faith, and what is the Church Catholic. They maintain that faith depends on the Church, we that the Church is built on the faith. By Church Catholic, we mean the Church Universal, as descended from the Apostles; they those branches of it which are in communion with Rome," &c. &c.[6]

And I show, in one of the Tracts, the unfairness of detaching the Canons of Trent from the actual conduct of the Roman Church for any practical purposes, while things are as they are, as follows:—

"An equally important question remains to be discussed; *viz.* What the *sources* are, whence we are to gather our opinions of Popery," &c. &c.[7]

And in the following passage in an Article in the *British Critic* written in the course of last year, the contrariety between the Primitive and Roman systems is pointed out.

"Allowing the Church Catholic ever so much power over the faith, allowing that it may add what it will, so that it does not contradict what has been determined in former times, yet let us come to the plain question, Does the Church, according to Romanists, know more now than the Apostles knew?" &c. &c.[8]

It is commonly urged by Romanists, that the Notes

---

[5] *Supr.* vol. i. pp. 47, 48.
[6] *Supr.* vol. i. pp. 212-3.
[7] *Supr.* p. 105.
[8] *Vid.* Essays, vol. ii. pp. 12—14.

of their Church are sufficiently clear to enable the private Christian to dispense with argument in joining their Communion in preference to any other. Now in the following passage it is observed, that that Communion has Notes of error upon it, serving in practice quite as truly as a guide from it, as the Notes which it brings forward can be made to tell in its favour.

"Our Lord said of false prophets, 'By their fruits shall ye know them;' and, however the mind may be entangled theoretically, yet surely it will fall upon certain marks in Rome which seem intended to convey to the simple and honest enquirer a solemn warning to keep clear of her, while she carries them about her. Such are her denying the Cup to the laity, her idolatrous worship of the Blessed Virgin, her Image-worship, her recklessness in anathematizing, and her schismatical and overbearing spirit," &c. &c.[9]

And in one of the Tracts for the Times, speaking of certain Invocations in the Breviary, I say,—

"These portions of the Breviary carry with them their own plain condemnation, in the judgment of an English Christian. No commendation of the general structure and matter of the Breviary itself will have any tendency to reconcile him to them ; and it has been the strong feeling that this is really the case, that has led the writer of these pages fearlessly and securely to admit the real excellencies, and to dwell upon the antiquity of the Roman Ritual. He has felt that, since the Romanists required an unqualified assent to the *whole* of the Breviary, and that there were passages which no Anglican ever could admit, praise the true Catholic portion of it as much as he might, he did not in the slightest degree approximate to a recommendation of Romanism."—*Tract* 75, pp. 9, 10.

"They" [the Antiphons to the Blessed Virgin] " shall be here given in order to show clearly, as a simple inspection of them will suffice to do, the utter contrariety between the Roman system, as actually existing, and our own ; which, however similar in certain respects, are in others so at variance, as to make any attempt to reconcile them together in their present state, perfectly nugatory. Till Rome moves towards us, it is quite impossible that we should

---

[9] Vol. i. p. 265.

move towards Rome; however closely we may approximate to her in particular doctrines, principles, or views."—*Tract* 75, p. 23.

In the foregoing passages, protests will be found against the Roman worship of St. Mary, Invocation of Saints, Worship of Images, Purgatory, Denial of the Cup, Indulgences, and Infallibility; besides those which are entered against the fundamental theory out of which these errors arise.

11.

v. And now having said, I trust, as much as your Lordship requires on the subject of Romanism, I will add a few words, to complete my explanation, in acknowledgment of the inestimable privilege I feel in being a member of that Church over which your Lordship, with others, presides. Indeed, did I not feel it to be a privilege which I am able to seek nowhere else on earth, why should I be at this moment writing to your Lordship? What motive have I for an unreserved and joyful submission to your authority, but the feeling that the Church which you rule is a divinely-ordained channel of supernatural grace to the souls of her members? Why should I not prefer my own opinion, and my own way of acting, to that of the Bishop's, except that I know full well that in matters indifferent I should be acting lightly towards the Spouse of Christ and the Awful Presence which dwells in her, if I hesitated a moment to put your Lordship's will before my own? I know full well that your kindness to me personally, would be in itself quite enough to win any but the most insensible heart, and, did a clear matter of conscience occur in which I felt bound to act for myself,[1] my personal feelings towards your Lordship would become a most severe trial to me, independently of the higher considerations to which I have referred; but I trust I have

---

[1] [This was intended as a hint that that day *might* come.]

given token of my dutifulness to you apart from the influence of such personal motives, and I have done so because I think that to belong to the Catholic Church is the first of all privileges here below, as involving in it heavenly privileges, and because I consider the Church over which you preside to be the Catholic Church in this country. Surely then I have no need to profess in words, I will not say my attachment, but my deep reverence towards the Mother of Saints, when I am showing it in action; yet that words may not be altogether wanting, I beg to lay before your Lordship the following extract from the Article already mentioned, which I wrote in defence of the English Church against a Roman controversialist in the course of the last year.

"The Church is emphatically a living body, and there can be no greater proof of a particular communion being part of the Church, than the appearance in it of a continued and abiding energy, nor a more melancholy proof of its being a corpse than torpidity. We say an energy continued and abiding, for accident will cause the activity of a moment, and an external principle give the semblance of self-motion. On the other hand, even a living body may for a while be asleep. And here we have an illustration of what we just now urged about the varying cogency of the Notes of the Church according to times and circumstances. No one can deny that at times the Roman Church itself, restless as it is at most times, has been in a state of sleep or disease, so great as to resemble death, &c. &c."[2]

12.

vi. This extract may be sufficient to show my feelings towards my Church, as far as statements on paper can show them. I have already, however, referred to what is much more conclusive, viz. a practical evidence of them; and I think I can show your Lordship besides without difficulty that my present conduct is no solitary instance of such obedience, but that I have in times past observed an habitual submission to things as they are, and have

[2] [*Vid.* Essays, vol. ii. pp. 53—59 for the whole passage.]

avoided in practice, as far as might be, any indulgence of private tastes and opinions, which left to myself perhaps I should have allowed.

And first, as regards my public teaching; though every one has his peculiarities, and I of course in the number, yet I do hope that it has not on the whole transgressed that liberty of opinion which is allowed on all hands to the Anglican Clergyman. Nay, I might perhaps insist upon it, that in the general run of my Sermons, fainter and fewer traces will be found than might have been expected of those characteristics of doctrine, with which my name is commonly associated. I might without offence have introduced what is technically called High-Church doctrine in much greater fulness; since there are many who do not hold it to my own extent, or with my own eagerness, whose public teaching is more prominently coloured by it. My Sermons have been far more practical than doctrinal; and this, from a dislike of introducing a character and tone of preaching very different from that which is generally to be found among us. And I hope this circumstance my serve as my reply to an apprehension which has been felt, as if what I say in Tract 90 concerning a cast of opinions which is not irreconcileable with our Articles, involves an introduction of those opinions into the pulpit. But who indeed will go so far as to maintain, that what merely happens not to be forbidden or denied in the Articles, may at once be made the subject of teaching or observance? There is nothing concerning the Inspiration of Scripture in the Articles; yet would a Bishop allow a Clergyman openly to deny it in the pulpit? May the Scripture Miracles be explained away, because the Articles say nothing about them? Would your Lordship allow me to preach in favour of duelling, gaming, or simony? or to revile persons by name from the pulpit? or be grossly and violently political? Every one will surely appreciate the importance and sacredness of Pulpit instruction; and will allow, that though the holding certain opinions may be compatible with subscription to the Articles, the publishing and teaching them may be inconsistent with ecclesiastical station.

Those who frequent St. Mary's, know that the case is the same as regards the mode in which worship is conducted there. I have altered nothing I found established; when I have increased the number of the Services, and had to determine points connected with the manner of performing them for myself, if there was no danger of offending others, then indeed I have followed my own judgment, but not otherwise. I have left many things, which I did not like, and which most other persons would have altered. And here, with your Lordship's leave, I will make allusion to one mistake concerning me which I believe has reached your Lordship's ears, and which I only care to explain to my Bishop. The explanation, I trust, will be an additional proof of my adherence to the principle of acquiescing in the state of things in which I find myself. It has been said, I believe, that in the Communion Service I am in the practice of mixing water with the wine, and that of course on a religious or ecclesiastical ground. This is not the case. We are in the custom at St. Mary's of celebrating the Holy Communion every Sunday, and most weeks early in the morning. When I began the early celebration, communicants represented to me that the wine was so strong as to distress them at that early hour. Accordingly I mixed it with water in the bottle. However, it did not keep. On this I mixed it at the time. I speak honestly when I say that this has been my only motive. I have not mixed it when the Service has been in the middle of the day.[3]

[3] [When this letter was published, it was at once circulated in reply, that in Littlemore Chapel I had on one occasion in the middle of the day mixed water with the wine in Communion. It was true: writing as I was to the

13.

If I were not writing to my Bishop, I should feel much shame at writing so much about myself; but confession cannot be called egotism. Friend and stranger have from time to time asked for my co-operation in the attempt to gain additional power for the Church. I have been accustomed to answer that it was my duty to acquiesce in the state of things under which I found myself, and to serve God, if so be, in it. New precedents indeed, confirming or aggravating our present Ecclesiastical defects, I have ever desired to oppose; but as regards changes, persons to whom I defer very much, know that, rightly or wrongly, I have discountenanced, for instance, any movement tending to the repeal even of the Statutes of *Præmunire*, which has been frequently agitated, under the notion that such matters were not our business, and that we had better "remain in the calling wherein we were called." Of course I cannot be blind to the fact that "*time* is the great innovator;" and that the course of events may of itself put the Church in possession of greater liberty of action, as in time past it has abridged it. This would be the act of a higher power; and then I should

Bishop about St. Mary's and my doings there, and what had been told him about them there, I forgot what had once accidentally happened at Littlemore several years before; but the pitiless eyes, which during those years were upon me almost from daybreak to nightfall, had noted the occurrence and had taken care to record it. And now the fact was circulated through Oxford to destroy the effect of this Letter. It had taken place at our Anniversary Feast; I had had no intention at all myself of using water, but the clergyman assisting me in the service, at the time I placed the wine on the Table, put into my hand a water-cruet, and I, taken by surprise, knowingly but indeliberately poured some into the cup. As to the disadvantage under which this Letter was written, I will quote my words in a Letter to a friend, as they stand in my Apologia :—"The Bishop sent me word on Sunday to write a Letter to him *instanter*. So I wrote it on Monday, on Tuesday it passed through the Press; on Wednesday it was out; and to-day," Thursday, "it is in London."]

think it a duty to act according to that new state in which the Church found itself. Knowledge and virtue certainly are power. When the Church's gifts were doubled, its influence would be multiplied a hundred-fold; and influence tends to become constituted authority. This is the nature of things, which I do not attempt to oppose; but I have no wish at all to take part in any measures which aim at changes.

And in like manner I have set my face altogether against suggestions which zealous and warm-hearted persons sometimes have made of reviving the project of Archbishop Wake, for considering the differences between ourselves and the foreign Churches with a view to their adjustment. Our business is with ourselves—to make ourselves more holy, more self-denying, more primitive, more worthy our high calling. Let the Church of Rome do the same, and it will come nearer to us, and will cease to be what we one and all mean, when we speak of Rome. To be anxious for a composition of differences, is to begin at the end. Did God visit us with large measures of His grace, and the Roman Catholics also, they would be drawn to us, and would acknowledge our Church as the Catholic Church in this country, and would give up whatever offended and grieved us in their doctrine and worship, and would unite themselves to us. This would be a true union; but political reconciliations are but outward and hollow, and fallacious. And till they on their part renounce political efforts, and manifest in their public measures the light of holiness and truth, perpetual warfare is our only prospect. It was the prophetic announcement concerning the Elijah of the first Advent, that he should "turn the heart of the fathers to the children, and the heart of the children to their fathers." This is the only change which promises good or is worth an effort.

14.

What I have been saying as regards Roman Catholics, I trust I have kept steadily before me in ecclesiastical matters generally. While I have considered that we ought to be content with the outward circumstances in which Providence has placed us, I have tried to feel that the great business of one and all of us is, to endeavour to raise the moral tone of the Church. It is sanctity of heart and conduct which commends us to God. If we be holy, all will go well with us. External things are comparatively nothing; whatever be a religious body's relations to the State—whatever its regimen—whatever its doctrines—whatever its worship—if it has but the life of holiness within it, this inward gift will, if I may so speak, take care of itself. It will turn all accidents into good, it will supply defects, and it will gain for itself from above what is wanting. I desire to look at this first, in all persons and all communities. Where Almighty God stirs the heart, there His other gifts follow in time; sanctity is the great Note of the Church. If the Established Church of Scotland has this Note, I will hope all good things of it; if the Roman Church in Ireland has it not, I can hope no good of it. And in like manner, in our own Church, I will unite with all persons as brethren, who have this Note, without any distinction of party. Persons who know me can testify that I have endeavoured to co-operate with those who did not agree with me, and that again and again I have been put aside by them, not put them aside. I have never concealed my own opinions, nor wished them to conceal theirs; but I have found that I could bear them better than they me. And I have long insisted upon it, that the only way in which the members of our Church, so widely differing in opinion at this time, can be brought together in one, is by a "turning of heart" to one another. Argumentative efforts are most useful for this end under this sacred feeling; but till we try to love each other, and what is holy in each other, and wish to be all one, and mourn that we are not so, and pray that we may be so, I do not see what good can come of argument.

15.

VII. Before concluding, there is one more subject on which I wish briefly to address your Lordship, though it is one which I have neither direct claim nor encouragement to introduce to your Lordship's notice. Yet our Colleges here being situated in your Lordship's diocese, it is natural for me to allude to the lately expressed opinion of the Heads of Houses upon the Tract which has given rise to this Letter. I shall only do so, however, for the purpose of assuring your Lordship of the great sorrow it gives me to have incurred their disapprobation, and of the anxiety I have felt for some time past from the apprehension that I was incurring it. I reverence their position in the country too highly to be indifferent to their good opinion. I never can be indifferent to the opinion of those who hold in their hands the education of the classes on which our national well-being, spiritual and temporal, depends; who preside over the foundations of "famous men" of old, whose "name liveth for evermore;" and from whom are from time to time selected the members of the sacred order to which your Lordship belongs. Considering my own peculiar position in the University, so much have these considerations pressed upon me for a long while, that, as various persons know, I seriously contemplated, some time since, the resignation of my Living, and was only kept from it by the advice of a friend to whom I felt I ought to submit myself. I say this, moreover, in explanation of a Letter I lately addressed to the Vice-Chancellor, lest it should seem dictated either by a mere perception of what was becoming in my situation, or from some sudden softening of feeling under an unexpected event. It expressed my habitual deference to persons in station.

16.

And now, my Lord, suffer me to thank your Lordship for your most abundant and extraordinary kindness towards me, in the midst of the exercise of your authority. I have nothing to be sorry for, except having made your Lordship anxious, and others whom I am bound to revere. I have nothing to be sorry for, but everything to rejoice in and be thankful for. I have never taken pleasure in seeming to be able to move a party, and whatever influence I have had has been found not sought after. I have acted because others did not act, and have sacrificed a quiet which I prized. May God be with me in time to come, as He has been hitherto! and He will be, if I can but keep my hand clean and my heart pure. I think I can bear, or at least will try to bear, any personal humiliation, so that I am preserved from betraying sacred interests, which the Lord of grace and power has given into my charge.

I am, my dear Lord,
Your Lordship's faithful and affectionate Servant,

JOHN HENRY NEWMAN.

ORIEL COLLEGE, *March* 29, 1841.

XI.

RETRACTATION
OF ANTI-CATHOLIC STATEMENTS.

1845.

RETRACTATION

OF ANTI-CATHOLIC STATEMENTS.

LITTLEMORE,

October 6, 1845.[1]

IT is now above eleven years since the writer of the following pages, in one of the early numbers of the Tracts for the Times, expressed himself thus :—

"Considering the high gifts, and the strong claims of the Church of Rome and its dependencies on our admiration, reverence, love, and gratitude, how could we withstand it, as we do; how could we refrain from being melted into tenderness, and rushing into communion with it, but for the words of Truth itself, which bid us prefer it to the whole world? 'He that loveth father or mother more than Me, is not worthy of Me.' How could we learn to be severe, and execute judgment, but for the warning of Moses against even a divinely-gifted teacher who should preach new gods, and the anathema of St. Paul even against Angels and Apostles who should bring in a new doctrine?"[2]

He little thought, when he so wrote, that the time would ever come, when he should feel the obstacle, which he spoke of as lying in the way of communion with the Church of Rome, to be destitute of solid foundation.

---

[1] [This Article is taken from the Advertisement of the "Essay on the Development of Christian Doctrine," published by the Author on his joining the Catholic Church.]

[2] Records of the Church, in the Tracts for the Times, xxiv. p. 7.

Having in former Publications directed attention to the supposed difficulties, he considers himself bound to avow his present belief that they were imaginary.

What he conceived them to be will be seen by referring to his Lectures on the Prophetical Office of the Church,[3] published in the beginning of 1837. In these Lectures there are various statements which he could wish unsaid; but there is one statement in them, about which he has never seen any reason at all for changing his opinion. It is this:—

"In England the Church co-operates with the State in exacting subscription to the Thirty-nine Articles as a test, and that not only of the Clergy, but also of the governing body in our Universities, *a test against Romanism.*"[4]

Such a statement is quite consistent with a wish, on which he has before now acted, to correct popular misapprehensions both of the Roman Catholic doctrines, and of the meaning of the Thirty-nine Articles.

Several years since[5] a Retractation of his appeared in the public prints which he is desirous of formally acknowledging here, and of preserving. It is as follows:—

It is true that I have at various times, in writing against the Roman system, used, not merely arguments, about which I am not here speaking, but what reads like declamation.

1. For instance, in 1833, in the *Lyra Apostolica*, I called it a "lost Church."

2. Also, in 1833, I spoke of "the Papal Apostasy" in a work upon the Arians.

---

[3] [*Vid.* Via Media, vol. i.]
[4] [*Supr.* vol. i. ix. 17, p. 235.]
[5] [In February, 1843.]

3. In the same year, in No. 15 of the series called the "Tracts for the Times," in which Tract the words are often mine, though I cannot claim it as a whole, I say,—

"True, Rome is heretical now—nay, grant she has thereby forfeited her orders; yet, at least, she was not heretical in the primitive ages. If she has apostatized, it was at the time of the Council of Trent. Then, indeed, it is to be feared the whole Roman Communion bound itself, by a perpetual bond and covenant, to the cause of Antichrist."

Of this and other Tracts a friend,[6] with whom I was on very familiar terms, observed, in a letter some time afterwards, though not of this particular part of it—"It is very encouraging about the Tracts—but I wish I could prevail on you when the second edition comes out, to cancel or materially alter several. The other day accidentally put in my way the Tract on the Apostolical Succession in the English Church; and it really does seem so very unfair, that I wonder you could, even in the extremity of οἰκονομία and φενακισμός, have consented to be a party to it."

On the passage above quoted, I observe myself, in a pamphlet published in 1838,[7]—

"I confess I wish this passage were not cast in so declamatory a form; but the substance of it expresses just what I mean."

4. Also, in 1833, I said,—

"Their communion is infected with heresy; we are bound to flee it as a pestilence. They have established a lie in the place of God's truth, and, by their claim of immutability in doctrine, cannot undo the sin they have committed."—*Tract* 20.

5. In 1834, I said, in a Magazine,—

"The spirit of old Rome has risen again in its former place, and has evidenced its identity by its works. It has possessed the Church there planted, as an evil spirit might seize the demoniacs of primitive times, and make her speak words which are not her own. In the corrupt Papal system we have the very cruelty, the craft, and the ambition of the Republic; its cruelty in its unsparing sacrifice of the happiness and virtue of individuals to a phantom of public expediency, in its forced celibacy within, and its persecutions without; its craft in its falsehoods, its deceitful deeds and lying wonders;

---

[6] [The Rev. R. Hurrell Froude, Fellow of Oriel.]
[7] [Letter to the Margaret Professor, *supr*. p. 207.]

and its grasping ambition in the very structure of its polity, in its assumption of universal dominion : old Rome is still alive; nowhere has its eagles lighted, but it still claims the sovereignty under another pretence. The Roman Church I will not blame, but pity—she is, as I have said, spell-bound, as if by an evil spirit; she is in thraldom."

I say, in the same paper,—

"In the Book of Revelations, the sorceress upon the seven hills is not the Church of Rome, as is often taken for granted, but Rome itself, that bad spirit which, in its former shape, was the animating principle of the fourth monarchy. In St. Paul's prophecy, it is not the Temple or Church of God, but the man of sin in the Temple, the old man or evil principle of the flesh which exalteth itself against God. Certainly it *is* a mystery of iniquity, and one which may well excite our dismay and horror, that in the very heart of the Church, in her highest dignity, in the seat of St. Peter, the evil principle has throned itself, and rules. It seems as if that spirit had gained subtlety by years : Popish Rome has succeeded to Rome Pagan : and would that we had no reason to expect still more crafty developments of Antichrist amid the wreck of institutions and establishments which will attend the fall of the Papacy ! . . . . . . I deny that the distinction is unmeaning. Is it nothing to be able to look on our mother, to whom we owe the blessing of Christianity, with affection instead of hatred, with pity indeed, nay and fear, but not with horror ? Is it nothing to rescue her from the hard names which interpreters of prophecy have put on her, as an idolatress and an enemy of God, when she is deceived rather than a deceiver?"

I also say,—

"She virtually substitutes an external ritual for moral obedience; penance for penitence, confession for sorrow, profession for faith, the lips for the heart : such at least is her system as understood by the many."

Also I say, in the same paper,—

"Rome has robbed us of high principles which she has retained herself, though in a corrupt state. When we left her, she suffered us not to go in the beauty of holiness; we left our garments and fled."

Against these and other passages of this paper the same friend, before it was published, made the following protest:—"I only except from this general approbation your second and most superfluous hit at the poor Romanists. You have first set them down as demoniacally possessed by the evil genius of Pagan Rome, but notwithstanding are able to find something to admire in their spirit, particularly because they apply ornament to its proper purposes: and then you talk of their churches: and all that is very well, and one hopes one has heard the end of name-calling, when all at once you relapse into your Protestantism, and deal in what I take leave to call slang."

Then after a remark which is not to the purpose of these extracts, he adds—"I do not believe that any Roman Catholic of education would tell you that he identified penitence and penance. In fact I know that they often preach against this very error as well as you could do."

6. In 1834 I also used, of certain doctrines of the Church of Rome, the epithets "unscriptural," "profane," "impious," "bold," "unwarranted," "blasphemous," "gross," "monstrous," "cruel," "administering deceitful comfort," and "unauthorized," in Tract 38. I do not mean to say that I had not a definite meaning in every one of these epithets, or that I did not weigh them before I used them.

With reference to this passage the same monitor had said—" I must enter another protest against your cursing and swearing at the end of the first *Via Media* as you do. (Tract 38.) What good can it do? I call it uncharitable to an excess. How mistaken we may ourselves be on many points that are only gradually opening to us!"

I withdrew the whole passage several years ago.

7. I said in 1837 of the Church of Rome,—

"In truth she is a Church beside herself; abounding in noble gifts and rightful titles, but unable to use them religiously; crafty, obstinate, wilful, malicious, cruel, unnatural, as madmen are. Or rather, she may be said to resemble a demoniac; possessed with principles, thoughts, and tendencies not her own; in outward form and in natural powers what God has made her, but ruled within by an inexorable spirit, who is sovereign in his management over her, and most subtle and most successful in the use of her gifts. Thus she is her real self only in name; and, till God vouchsafe to restore her, we must treat her as if she were that evil one which governs her. And, in saying this, I must not be supposed to deny that there is any real excellence in Romanism even as it is, or that any really excellent men are its adherents."[8]

---

[8] [As to this extravagant passage, I will but say, 1. That it was not in the writer's mind to use such language of the Catholic Church, but of what he

8. In 1837, I also said in a review,—

"The Second and Third Gregories appealed to the people against the Emperor for a most unjustifiable object, and in, apparently, a most unjustifiable way. They became rebels to establish image worship. However, even in this transaction, we trace the original principle of Church power, though miserably defaced and prevented, whose form—

> 'Had yet not lost
> All her original brightness, nor appeared
> Less than Archangel ruined and the excess
> Of glory obscured.'

Upon the same basis, as is notorious, was built the Ecclesiastical Monarchy. It was not the breath of princes, or the smiles of a court, which fostered the stern and lofty spirit of Hildebrand and Innocent. It was the neglect of self, the renunciation of worldly pomp and ease, the appeal to the people."

I must observe, however, upon this passage, that no reference is made in it to the subject of Milton's lines, who ill answers to the idea expressed in them of purity and virtue merely defaced. An application of them is made to a power which I considered, when I so wrote, to befit such language better, viz. to the Roman Church as viewed in a certain exercise of her pretensions in the person of those two Popes.

Perhaps I have made other statements in a similar tone, and that, again, when the statements themselves were unexceptionable and true. If you ask me how an individual could venture not simply to hold, but to publish such views of a communion so ancient, so wide-spreading, so fruitful in Saints, I answer that I said to myself, "I am not speaking my own words, I am but following

---

considered to be a portion of it, a branch or local church, the Roman branch, as another branch was the widely-spread Anglican communion. 2. That he considered all these branch churches, the Anglican inclusive, inhabited and possessed by spirits of a middle nature, neither good angels nor bad; as he quotes himself in *Apologia*, p. 29, "Daniel speaks as if each nation had its guardian angel. I cannot but think that there are beings with a great deal of good in them, yet with great defects, who are the animating principles of certain institutions, &c. Has not the Christian Church, in its parts, surrendered itself to one or other of these simulations of the Truth?" 3. Though he had very vague ideas of what Catholic divines hold on possession and obsession, he might urge that obsession, and even possession, by evil spirits, may befall the saintly and elect servants of God as well as bad or ordinary men.]

RETRACTATION OF ANTI-CATHOLIC STATEMENTS.

almost a *consensus* of the divines of my Church. They have ever used the strongest language against Rome, even the most able and learned of them. I wish to throw myself into their system. While I say what they say, I am safe. Such views, too, are necessary for our position." Yet I have reason to fear still, that such language is to be ascribed, in no small measure, to an impetuous temper, a hope of approving myself to persons I respect, and a wish to repel the charge of Romanism.

Admissions such as these involve no retractation of what I have written in defence of Anglican doctrine. And as I make it for personal reasons, I make it without consulting others. I am as fully convinced as ever, indeed I doubt not Roman Catholics themselves would confess, that the Anglican doctrine is the strongest, nay the only possible antagonist of their system. If Rome is to be withstood, this can be done in no other way.

Of course the Author now withdraws the arguments referred to, as far as they reflect upon the Church of Rome, as well as the language in which they were conveyed.

[*Oct.* 11, 1883.—Sir William Palmer, in his republication of his "Narrative," &c., in spite of using words of me, of which I feel the kindness, ventures to say that "Newman and Froude had consulted [Dr. Wiseman] at Rome upon the feasibility of being received *as English Churchmen* into the Papal communion, retaining their doctrines." If this means that Hurrell Froude and I thought of being received into the Catholic Church while we still remained outwardly professing the doctrine and the communion of the Church of England, I utterly deny and protest against so calumnious a statement. Such an idea never entered into our heads. I can speak for myself, and, as far as one man can speak for another, I can answer for my dear friend also.]

THE END.

PRINTED BY
KELLY & CO., MIDDLE MILL, KINGSTON-ON-THAMES;
AND GATE STREET, LINCOLN'S INN FIELDS, W.C.

CARDINAL NEWMAN'S WORKS.

PAROCHIAL and PLAIN SERMONS. Edited by the Rev. W. J. COPELAND, B.D. late Rector of Farnham, Essex. 8 vols. Cabinet Edition. Crown 8vo. 5s. each. Popular Edition. 8 vols. Crown 8vo. 3s. 6d. each.

SELECTION, adapted to the SEASONS of the ECCLESIASTICAL YEAR, from the 'Parochial and Plain Sermons.' Edited by the Rev. W. J. COPELAND, B.D. late Rector of Farnham, Essex. Crown 8vo. 5s.

FIFTEEN SERMONS PREACHED before the UNIVERSITY of OXFORD, between A.D. 1826 and 1843. Crown 8vo. 5s.

SERMONS BEARING upon SUBJECTS of the DAY. Edited by the Rev. W. J. COPELAND, B.D. late Rector of Farnham Essex. Crown 8vo. 5s.

DISCOURSES ADDRESSED to MIXED CONGREGATIONS. Crown 8vo. 6s.

SERMONS PREACHED on VARIOUS OCCASIONS. Crown 8vo. 6s.

LECTURES on the DOCTRINE of JUSTIFICATION. Crown 8vo. 5s.

An ESSAY on the DEVELOPMENT of CHRISTIAN DOCTRINE. Cabinet Edition. Crown 8vo. 6s. Cheap Edition. Crown 8vo. 3s. 6d.

The IDEA of a UNIVERSITY DEFINED and ILLUSTRATED. Crown 8vo. 7s.

An ESSAY in AID of a GRAMMAR of ASSENT. Cabinet Edition. Crown 8vo. 7s. 6d. Cheap Edition. Crown 8vo. 3s. 6d.

The VIA MEDIA of the ANGLICAN CHURCH. Illustrated in Lectures, Letters and Tracts written between 1830 and 1841. With Notes. 2 vols. Crown 8vo. 6s. each. Vol. I. Prophetical Office of the Church. Vol. II. Occasional Letters and Tracts.

CERTAIN DIFFICULTIES FELT by ANGLICANS in CATHOLIC TEACHING CONSIDERED. (2 vols.) Vol. I. Twelve Lectures. Crown 8vo. 7s. 6d. Vol. II. Letters to Dr. Pusey concerning the Blessed Virgin, and to the Duke of Norfolk in Defence of the Pope and Council. Crown 8vo. 5s. 6d.

The PRESENT POSITION of CATHOLICS in ENGLAND. Crown 8vo. 7s. 6d.

APOLOGIA PRO VITA SUA. Cabinet Edition. Crown 8vo. 6s. Cheap Edition. Crown 8vo. 3s. 6d.

London: LONGMANS, GREEN, & CO.

ESSAYS on BIBLICAL and on ECCLESIASTICAL MIRACLES.
Cabinet Edition. Crown 8vo. 6s. Cheap Edition. Crown 8vo. 3s. 6d.

DISCUSSIONS and ARGUMENTS on VARIOUS SUBJECTS.
Cabinet Edition. Crown 8vo. 6s. Cheap Edition. Crown 8vo. 3s. 6d.

CONTENTS.—1. How to accomplish it. 2. The Antichrist of the Fathers. 3. Scripture and the Creed. 4. Tamworth Reading Room. 5. Who's to Blame? 6. An Argument for Christianity.

ESSAYS CRITICAL and HISTORICAL. Cabinet Edition. 2 vols Crown 8vo. 12s. Cheap Edition. 2 vols. Crown 8vo. 7s.

CONTENTS.—1. Poetry. 2. Rationalism. 3. Apostolical Tradition. 4. De la Mennais. 5. Palmer on Faith and Unity. 6. St. Ignatius. 7. Prospects of the Anglican Church. 8. The Anglo-American Church. 9. Countess of Huntingdon. 10. Catholicity of the Anglican Church. 11. The Antichrist of Protestants. 12. Milman's Christianity. 13. Reformation of the Eleventh Century. 14. Private Judgment. 15. Davison. 16. Keble.

HISTORICAL SKETCHES. 3 vols. Crown 8vo. 6s. each.

CONTENTS.—1. The Turks. 2. Cicero. 3. Apollonius. 4. Primitive Christianity. 5. Church of the Fathers. 6. St. Chrysostom. 7. Theodoret. 8. St. Benedict. 9. Benedictine Schools. 10. Universities. 11. Northmen and Normans. 12. Mediæval Oxford. 13. Convocation of Canterbury.

The ARIANS of the FOURTH CENTURY. Cabinet Edition. Crown 8vo. 6s. Cheap Edition. Crown 8vo. 3s. 6d.

SELECT TREATISES of ST. ATHANASIUS in CONTROVERSY with the ARIANS. Freely Translated. 2 vols. Crown 8vo. 15s.

THEOLOGICAL TRACTS. Crown 8vo. 8s.

CONTENTS.—1. Dissertatiunculæ. 2. On the Text of the Seven Epistles of St. Ignatius. 3. Doctrinal Causes of Arianism. 4. Apollinarianism. 5. St. Cyril's Formula. 6. Ordo de Tempore. 7. Douay Version of Scripture.

VERSES on VARIOUS OCCASIONS. Cabinet Edition. Crown 8vo. 6s. Cheap Edition. Crown 8vo. 3s. 6d.

LOSS and GAIN: The Story of a Convert. Crown 8vo. 6s.

CALLISTA: a Tale of the Third Century. Cabinet Edition. Crown 8vo. 6s. Cheap Edition. Crown 8vo. 3s. 6d.

The DREAM of GERONTIUS. 16mo. 6d. sewed; 1s. cloth.

London: LONGMANS, GREEN, & CO.

www.ingramcontent.com/pod-product-compliance
Lightning Source LLC
Chambersburg PA
CBHW020536300426
44111CB00008B/688